Mathematics and Society

Mathematics and Society

Numbers and Measures in Early Modern South India

SENTHIL BABU D.

OXFORD
UNIVERSITY PRESS

OXFORD
UNIVERSITY PRESS

Great Clarendon Street, Oxford, OX2 6DP,
United Kingdom

Oxford University Press is a department of the University of Oxford.
It furthers the University's objective of excellence in research, scholarship,
and education by publishing worldwide. Oxford is a registered trade mark of
Oxford University Press in the UK and in certain other countries

Published in India by

Oxford University Press

22 Workspace, 2nd Floor, 1/22 Asaf Ali Road, New Delhi 110 002, India

ISBN–13 (print edition): 978–8–19–483160–0
ISBN–10 (print edition): 8–19–483160–1
ISBN–13 (eBook): 978–0–19–099433–4
ISBN–10 (eBook): 0–19–099433–9
ISBN–13 (OSO):978–0–19–099434–1
ISBN–10(OSO):0–19–099434–7

DOI: 10.1093/oso/9788194831600.001.0001

Typeset in Minion Pro 10.5/14

by Newgen KnowledgeWorks Pvt. Ltd., Chennai, India

Printed in India by Rakmo Press Pvt. Ltd

Dedicated to
all those education workers,
whose endless struggles against injustice nurture new collective practices,
building new knowledge, together!

Contents

Acknowledgments ix
List of Images xiii
List of Tables xv
Note on Transliteration and Conventions xvii
About the Author xix

Introduction: "Fifteen Brahmins and Fifteen Thieves" 1

I. Towards Practice: Mathematics Beyond the Canon 16
- Number Tables 17
- Account Manuscripts and Merchant Practices 20
- Mathematics and Work 25
- Mathematics in the Regions 31
- Mathematical Treatises in Tamil 38
- Introducing *Kaṇakkatikāram* 42
- Introducing *Kaṇita Nūl* 47
- Introducing *Ástāṉa Kōlākalam* 49
- Why These Texts? 51
- Measuring Land 59
- Measuring Gold and Paying Wages 63
  - *Problems Involving Fineness and Weight of Gold* 63
  - *Problems About Mixing Silver and Gold* 64
  - *Method to Compute the Price of Gold* 65
- Measuring Grains 66
- Measuring Stone 68
- Measuring Time 69
- The Not So Practical Problems 71
- Cumulative Addition and Progression Techniques 73
- Residues of Fractions or Parts of Parts Problems 76
- Matching Problems 77
- Exhaustion Problems 78
- Distribution Problems and Magic Squares 79

II. Mathematics of the Practitioner 81
- Orientation: Practical and Beyond 82
- The Accountant as the Practitioner 86
- The Centrality of the *Eṇcuvaṭi* to the *Kaṇakkatikāram* 100
- The Rule of Three in Computing Proportions 108

III. Memory and Mathematics in *Tiṇṇai* Schools 122
What Do We Know About the *Tiṇṇai* Schools? 123
The Local Community as Measuring Public 128
Introducing *Tiṇṇai* Schools 130
The *Tiṇṇai* Teacher 131
The *Tiṇṇai* Student 135
The *Tiṇṇai* Curriculum 137
Mathematics and the *Tiṇṇai* Routine 141
The Learning of Mathematics 142
Mastering the *Eṇcuvaṭi* 152
Knowing Myths and Facts 161
Learning the *Kuḻimāttu* 162
Problem Solving in *Tiṇṇai* Schools 163
Tiṇṇai Curriculum, Pedagogy, and Caste 169

IV. Mathematics Pedagogy for a Public: The Colonial Transition 174
Colonial Transition: The Reshaping of Computation 177
Mathematics for a Public: Early Possibilities, 1800–1840 182
Mathematics for a Public and the Problem of Scrutiny/Assessment, the 1840s Onwards 195
Negotiating Scrutiny and Modes of Memory: Reconciliation with the *Tiṇṇai* Teacher 202

Conclusion: Mathematics and Its Images of the Public 215

Appendix-I: Numbers, Weights, and Measures in the Tamil System 227
Appendix-II: A Brief Note on Tamil Numerical Notation 239
Appendix-III: Poṉṉilakkam, Nellilkkam, Eṇcuvaṭi 243
Appendix-IV: List of Text Books Used for the Study 325
Bibliography 329
Index 341

Acknowledgements

Prof. Sabayasachi Bhattacharya helped shape the study during its early days and has shared the formative concerns of this book, which began as a doctoral dissertation with him. Knowing and working with him has been a very important part of learning and memories of his kindness and support continues to nourish questions in history. I thank him for having sustained his faith in this work. Prof. Indivar Kamtekar's commitment and support have been vital and I heartily thank him for his support and friendship. Prof. K. N. Panikkar's perseverance with movements and his commitment to history have been an abiding inspiration. I would like to thank the Centre for Historical Studies, Jawaharlal Nehru University, New Delhi, for educating us in history and the importance of nurturing convictions in practice. I thank Dhruv Raina and S. Irfan Habib for introducing me to the world of history of science and for teaching me the importance of raising critical questions. R. Ramanujam's abiding interest in issues of mathematics and education as a field of practice has shaped many of the concerns that define the motivation for this study. V. Geetha's convictions and her faith in friendship and the many conversations with her over the years have shaped the concerns of this book. I would like to thank friends and comrades in the field of science and mathematics education, especially in the People's Science Movements across the country, from whom I continue to learn the importance of persevering with struggles to democratise knowledge in classrooms and in the streets.

Prof Francois Gros, Prof. Y. Subbarayalu, and Kannan M. have consistently supported this work at the French Institute of Pondicherry, where I would like to thank all the colleagues and the Librarians, Narenthiran R., Ramanujam K., Saravanan G., and Anurupa Naik for all their support over the years. V. Prakash supported this work in many ways and his insights about the Tamil textual traditions have been a learning experience. Gopinath Sricandane's friendship and support in the preparation of this book were crucial. Pulavar Kannaiyan of Mayilam and K. Venkatachalam of Chengam, Thiruvannamalai District, taught me the basics of the Tamil number system and shared their immense knowledge in this area. I would like to thank the faculty, research scholars, and the Library of the Homi Bhabha Centre for Science Education (Tata Institute of Fundamental Research), Bombay, for hosting me as a visitor and helping me get back to this project. Working with K. Subramanian, Jayasree Subramanian, Aalokha Kanhere, Shweta Shripad Naik, and other friends in the mathematics education community has been an important source of learning. Jurgen Renn, Matthias Schemmel, Sonja Brentjes, and Dagmar Schaffer at the Max Planck Institute for the History of Science, Berlin, and Roy Wagner at ETH, Zurich, have encouraged the formative concerns of the research programme on the social history of mathematical practices in India, and hopefully, this book will help serve this important area of historical studies. Matthias Schemmel and Jens Hoyrup read and commented on the manuscript and I am grateful for their time and support. Conversations with Agathe Keller have always been useful. Pietro Omodeo and Sascha Freyburg have been great companions in the programmatic pursuit of similar histories.

I would like to mention my gratitude to the staff of the Tamil Nadu State Archives and its Library, Chennai; Government Oriental Manuscripts Library, Chennai; Sarasvati Mahal Library, Thanjavur, Tamil Nadu; International Institute of Tamil Studies, Chennai; the Theosophical Society Library, Adyar, Chennai; Ecole Francais de Extreme Orient, Pondicherry; the British Library, London; Bibliotheque National Manuscript Division, Paris; Library of the Ramanujam Institute of Advanced Studies in Mathematics, Madras University; Tamil University, Thanjavur; the Archives and Library of the United Theological College, Bangalore; and the Library of the Jawaharlal Nehru University, New Delhi.

It has been a very long journey and I shall not venture to formally take names of all the friends and comrades who have in their own ways helped along the way and shaped this study, and to each of them, I remain grateful. But I would like to particularly thank Aruna Rathnam for being there, Revathi for keeping faith and standing by me. In Chennai, Karuna, Kalpana, Kamal Lodaya, Shankar, Indu, Balaji, Padma, C. E. Karunakaran, Mohan, and Uma Raman have always cared and provided solidarity. Thomas Mathew and Laurie Vasily's love and support made difficult times bearable. Pratik and Nandini, Sheila Bhalla, Aparna Balachandran and Nagraj Adve, Shanuj, Avinash and Divya, Siddhartha Dasgupta, Kaushik Dasgupta, Aniket and Manjari, Asmita, Amitava Sanyal, Komita Dhanda, Joyoti Roy,

Mala Hashmi, Sudhanva Deshpande, Vijoo Krishnan, Murali and Sujatha, Chirashree Dasgupta, Vidhya Ravindranathan, Roland Wittje, Annapurna Mammidipudi, Minakshi Menon, Benjamin Zachariah, Kavita Philip, Jahnavi Phalkey, Rajshekar, Srividya, Baskar, Udayakumar and family in Kameswaram, Nagapattinam and our Vanavil team have helped me stay on course. Archana Prasad and Dinesh Abrol not only provided a caring home in Delhi but supported me right through. I thank Mara for always being there. I wish to thank Sundar and Sudha, Ravi Bhalla and Anu Pai, Srinivas and Sunitha, Aby and Flavia, Senthil and Bhagy, Theisth, Gaspard, Achraf, Narayana, Parthesarathy, Gopi, Velu, Hema, and Anitha in Pondicherry for being around.

Kishor, Shreya, and Tathagatha's commitment to understanding the relationship between mathematical practice and politics in India to shape resistance to acts of alienation through the privileging of knowledge forms through our fledgling Politically Mathematics Collective continues to be a very important learning process and the questions of this book hence are not mine alone. The cover illustration for this book belongs to our collective and I am glad I could use it for this book.

My family's unwavering care and support have allowed me to pursue this work for a very long time. Balu has stood by and tolerated me during all times. My mother, Manimekalai, along with Egile Tiroutchelvy, Nivanthi, and Niyantha have made this journey possible. My sisters, Shanthi, Agila, and Kamali, and their families, with their care and concerns, have been a source of steady support and warmth. Memories of my father and Chinna stay on and nurture daily life.

Simon Schaffer and Dorothy Ko read the entire manuscript and their critical comments and suggestions for revision have been useful and I thank them both for their kind support. Two anonymous referees of the Oxford University Press provided enthusiastic comments and encouragement to get this book published soon. The editorial staff of OUP, Delhi, have provided useful support and I thank them for the timely publication of this book. I thank Rukma Anil for her time and patience with the proof reading of this book.

Finally, I would like to thank Bhavani Raman, Prachi Deshpande, Vanessa Caru, and Francis Cody for sharing the central concerns of this project and helping me complete it and place it in public. It is their friendship and solidarity which has made this work possible.

List of Images

1.1 A leaf from *Eṇcuvaṭi* manuscript. Courtesy: Manuscript number ENSUVADI-TAMIL-1795-B02307-P-008. From manuscript collections, Department of Manuscriptology, Thanjavur Tamil University, Thanjavur.
1.2 A leaf from a manuscript titled *Periya Veettu Kanakku*, meaning accounts from the household of a notable family. Courtesy: Manuscript number PERIYA VEETTU-K-KANAKKU-TAMIL-1871-B02391-P-131. From manuscript collections, Department of Manuscriptology, Thanjavur Tamil University, Thanjavur.
1.3 Everyday measuring scale of the sculptor, a fresh coconut leaf folded in proportions to make a scale at work. Courtesy: Photograph by the author taken at Swamimalai, 2018.
1.4 Mnemonic measures integral to the sculptor's work. Courtesy: Ganapati Sthapathi and Sri Aurobindo Society, Pondicherry from the book, Ganapathi Sthapathi, Indian Sculpture and Iconography Forms and Measurements, *Sri Aurobindo Society and Mapin Publishing, 2002, Pondicherry, p. 75.*
1.5 A leaf from manuscript *Kaṇita Nūl*. Courtesy: Manuscript number KANITHA NOOL-TAMIL-1243-B01561-P-072. From manuscript collections, Department of Manuscriptology, Thanjavur Tamil University, Thanjavur.
1.6 A leaf from *Kaṇakkatikāram*, EO-541. Courtesy: Manuscript Collections, École française d'Extrême-Orient, Pondicherry.
3.1 Pathshala learning in progress with children writing on sand along with the loud recitation of a student guiding them, monitored by the single teacher. A school in Varanasi in the nineteenth century. Courtesy: https://commons.wikimedia.org/wiki/File:A_private_teacher_in_one_of_the_indigenous_schools_in_Varanasi_(c._1870).jpg, accessed on 20 October 2018.
3.2 A pyal School near Vepery, Madras in the 1860s. Courtesy: https://sites.google.com/site/thumboochetty/EARLY-LIFE, accessed on 20 October 2018. Used under the Creative Commons License from the original source http://dsal.uchicago.edu/
3.3 A manuscript of *Poṉṉilakkam*. Courtesy: Manuscript Collections, French Institute of Pondicherry.
3.4 The working of the *muntiri* series in the *Poṉṉilakkam*. Courtesy: Ganesh Gopal, French Institute of Pondicherry.
4.1 Monitorial system at work in nineteenth century Europe. Courtesy: Wikimedia Commons. Source: https://upload.wikimedia.org/wikipedia/commons/7/75/Monitorial_education_system_Bell-Lancaster_19th_century.png) accessed on 23 October 2018.

List of Tables

3.1 The *muntiri* series
3.2 The *muntiri* series until *mā*
3.3 The memory mode at work in the standard fractions of the *Poṉṉilakkam*
3.4 The *ceviṭu* series in the *Nellilakkam*
3.5 The first table of multiplication in the *Eṇcuvaṭi*
3.6 The multiplication table for *muntiri* in the *Eṇcuvaṭi*
3.7 The multiplication table for *mukkāl in the Eṇcuvaṭi*
3.8 The multiplication table for *ceviṭu in the Eṇcuvaṭi*
3.9 The multiplication table for *nāḻi in the Eṇcuvaṭi*
3.10 The calculation of the square of 11 in the *Kuḻimāttu*
3.11 The calculation of the square of *mūṉṟē mukkāl (3 + 3/4)* in the *Kuḻimāttu*
4.1 Arithmetic curriculum in the Madras Presidency during 1881

Note on Transliteration and Conventions

All terms in italics are Tamil terms in transliteration, for example, '*veṭṭiyāṉ*', '*kaṇakkaṉ*', '*marakkāl*' but with possessives, *Kaṇakkaṉ*'s. The Tamil words have been transliterated according to the conventions of the Madras University Tamil lexicon (see next page for details). Tamil texts and Tamil terms for measuring units appear with diacritics and with italics. Sanskrit-derived Tamil words are generally in their more easily recognisable form. Conventional spelling is used for proper names to the extent possible, 'Satyabama Kamesvaran', 'Rajagopalan', rather than 'catyapama'. But the exception is made to the authors of the primary texts used—*Karuvūr Nañcaiyaṉ, Nāvili Perumaḷ*.

For the sake of readability, proper names, caste names, and place names appear in plain text—for example, 'vellalar' or 'Thanjavur'. English official titles and functional titles are not capitalised except when they become part of a person's name—for example, 'collector', but 'Collector Campbell'. Official departments of Company administration are capitalised—for example, 'Board of Revenue'. Depending on context, 'Madras' denotes the city of Madras (now Chennai) or Madras Presidency, the territorial administrative region directly ruled by the English East India Company in the early nineteenth century in south India. In footnote references to Company documents from the Tamil Nadu State Archives, Madras (now Chennai), I have referenced the location of the collection as Chennai.

References to archival sources from Company collections appear in a form for ready reference by series, location, date, volume number, and page. Private papers and missionary sources appear in the convention used by the catalogues of the collection. I have used abbreviations for archival series and for journal names.

About the Author

Senthil Babu D. is a historian in the Department of Social Sciences, French Institute of Pondicherry, India. He did his PhD from the Centre for Historical Studies, Jawaharlal Nehru University, New Delhi, and is currently involved in shaping a research programme in the social history of mathematical practices in India. His other interests include the historical study of the changing relationship between nature, knowledge, and labour in the history of sciences in India. He is also a member of the Politically Mathematics Collective, www.politicallymath.in. He is part of the Editorial Board of Verum Factum: Studies and Sources on Political Epistemology, https://verumfactum.it/.

Introduction:
"Fifteen Brahmins and Fifteen Thieves"

> Fifteen Brahmins and fifteen thieves had to spend a dark night in an isolated temple of Durga. The goddess appeared in person at midnight and wanted to devour exactly fifteen persons, since she was hungry. The thieves naturally suggested that she should consume the fifteen plump Brahmins. But the clever Brahmins proposed that all the thirty would stand in a circle and that Durga should eat each ninth person. The proposal was accepted by Durga and the thieves. So the Brahmins arranged themselves and the thieves in a circle, telling each one where to stand. Durga then counted out each ninth person and devoured him. When the fifteen were eaten, she was satiated and disappeared, and only Brahmins remained in the circle. The problem is, how did the Brahmins arrange themselves and the thieves in a circle?[1]

The historian of mathematics, S. R. Sarma found this problem invoking the cunning of Brahmins in a village accountant's or a *karaṇam's* copybook in Andhra Pradesh. The problem was recorded in a classical metre of Telugu. The copybook could belong to the precolonial period, but a farmer from the region also knew it and could pose the problem orally.[2] The same problem

[1] S. R. Sarma, the historian of mathematics found this problem in a copybook of a *karaṇam* in Andhra which is cited in his work, S. R. Sarma, 'Mathematical Literature in the Regional Languages of India', *Ancient Indian Leaps into Mathematics*, eds. B. S. Yadav and Man Mohan (Boston: Birkhaüser, 2011), 210–211.

[2] Ibid. The copybook, says Sarma, had another variant where the problem was posed using 30 Brahmins and 30 thieves in a circle. But it is not sure when both problems were exactly recorded in the books. Both a 'Christian-Jew' version and the Japanese step-mother and a clever son version are given by Sarma, who says these problems were called as Josephus problems named after a Jewish historian, Flavius Josephus (37–100 CE).

Mathematics and Society. Senthil Babu D., Oxford University Press. © Oxford University Press India 2022.
DOI: 10.1093/oso/9788194831600.003.0001

was known in tenth-century Europe with different actors. The European problem involves fifteen Jews and fifteen Christians in a leaking boat when the boatman, who happened to be a Christian, throws out the Jews just like the thieves. In Japan, in the twelfth-century, the same problem appeared in the form of a conniving stepmother, her sons and step-sons, when one clever step son figures out the trick and saves himself.

Mathematical problems like this circulated in regions as different as early modern Andhra, twelfth-century Japan, and tenth-century Europe. They traversed the realm of the oral and the written.

The example of the problem involving the cunning Brahmins demonstrates with great clarity how mathematics acquires meaning when viewed through social relations. The social life of mathematics in South India was enmeshed in caste, language and place. It acquired meaning through historical processes that shaped its circulation and localization. This is one of the reasons why, rather than plot the diffusion of mathematics, this book investigates mathematical practices in the social world that generated such problems.

What, then constituted mathematics in pre-modern Indian society? What kind of practices could be understood as 'mathematical' well before what we know as mathematics today came into being? How was mathematics experienced by different social groups at particular times? How do we write a history of mathematics in India that is sensitive to the dictum that the 'past of mathematics should not be confused with that of mathematics in its past'?[3] In other words, how do we reconstruct the past of mathematics through its various practices than its present may lead us to suppose.

In recent times, historians of mathematics have been increasingly working on situating mathematical practice in historically specific conditions. This interest is perhaps an outcome of the cross-pollination of ideas between historians of science and historians of mathematics. While there has been a call for a 'reunification' of these two disciplines, the task is particularly difficult for the historian of mathematics because the challenge

[3] Fumikazu Saito, 'History of Mathematics and History of Science: Some Remarks Concerning Contextual Framework', *Educacao Matematica Pesquita* 4, no. 3 (2012): 363–385. Saito draws upon Canguilheim's caution in the 1970s addressed to the historians of science at that time, but the fact that it is being noticed by historians of mathematics only now is reflective of the shifting interests in this field of study and how it is opening itself up to concerns that have become central to the practice of history of science in recent times.

facing historians of mathematics is that of writing 'a historical account of a field that appears to reside beyond the bounds of history'.[4] Historians of mathematics have traditionally focused on the technical content of mathematical reasoning, thereby primarily addressing the working mathematicians rather than a broader public.[5] This narrow approach to history has limited our understanding of mathematization or mathematics as social practice.

As Sophie Roux[6] suggests, 'the grand narrative about mathematization has to be replaced with a dense spectrum of various mathematical practices: real practices like manipulating numbers, extracting roots, representing perspective in pictures, compounding proportions, arranging numbers in tables, following rules and algorithmic procedures, knitting propositions together, visualizing magnitudes in geometric diagrams, solving problems, measuring fields with specific instruments, drawing curves, making deductions and plotting the routes of ships'. Roux suggests that practice, one might think, is 'indefinitely extendable' and therefore ambiguous. But she says that this ambiguity has 'intellectual benefits' for it compels us to reflect on what our histories commit to, and it helps us 'ask ourselves what speaking of practices commits us to'.[7]

How were such knowledge practices transmitted by different agents, in particular settings and with distinct orientations. In the Indian or South Asian context, the problem of transmission is particularly complex because of its diverse regions, communities, languages and landscapes. Yet, studies that foreground the region or sources in spoken languages are very few. As a result, a single regional or linguistic history is artificially projected to represent an imagined subcontinental or civilizational space. For example, studies of Sanskrit or Bengal are made to stand for India.

Mathematics and Society studies a regional tradition of mathematics in the Tamil-speaking areas of Southern India. It questions a received picture of the Indian history of mathematics. It reflects on how specific, historically situated mathematical practices reveal the limitations of nationalist frameworks of narrating histories of science. But it shall also

[4] A. R. Alexander, 'Introduction, Special Issue on "Mathematical Stories"', *Isis* 97 (2006): 680. Also cited in Saito, 'History of Mathematics and History of Science', 365.

[5] Jeremy Gray, 'History of Science and History of Mathematics Reunited?', *Isis* Special Issue 102 (2012): 511–517.

[6] Sophie Roux, 'Forms of Mathematization', *Early Science and Medicine* 15 (2010): 319–337.

[7] Ibid.

not endorse a Tamil nationalist reading of this tradition either. On the contrary, this book explores the history of mathematics in South India in terms of its varied public circulation. It tries to understand what sorts of audiences were imagined for various experiments and investigates modes of mathematical practice, teaching and learning. It attempts to engage with historical sources as records of practice and seeks to bring the world of the practitioners as central to a social history of mathematics in India. It demonstrates how such an approach would help us depart from the preoccupation of dualisms of theory and practice, nation and region, Sanskrit and the vernacular, pure and applied that has remained the preoccupation of scholarly literature. Rather, it situates practices and pathways of mathematization in early modern South India within the political economy of resource distribution to interrogate the character of abstraction in and from practices. It asks how do we understand and contend with the quest for universalism in knowledge amidst social segregation and fragmentation, and caste bound occupational hierarchies. How could such an inquiry help us to contend with the task of annihilation of hierarchies in knowledge, work and in society to re-imagine modes of democratization and freedom in our own pedagogic practices.

The history of mathematics in India has thus far primarily been an engagement with a corpus of texts recorded in Sanskrit.[8] The dominant view of precolonial science in India has foregrounded Sanskrit texts as canonical, effectively making Sanskrit the core of such knowledge creation and transmission.[9] It is important to emphasize here that the canonization of what came to be known as 'Indian mathematics' was itself a product of a global circulation of knowledge in the eighteenth and nineteenth

[8] B. B. Datta and A. N. Singh, *History of Hindu Mathematics: A Source Book*, 2 vols (Bombay: Asia Publishing House, 1962) has been a standard source book for historians of mathematics and their students. A very useful and lucid summary is David Pingree, *Jyotihsastra Astral and Mathematical Literature, A History of Indian Literature*, Vol. VI, ed. Jane Gonda (Wiesbaden: Harrassowitz 1981). Kim Plofker, *Mathematics in India* (Princeton: Princeton University Press, 2009), a recent comprehensive survey of the Sanskrit mathematical tradition in India, which is sensitive to problems of limitations that the sources present to the historian in attempting a reconstruction of mathematical thought from the Indian past.

[9] M. D. Srinivas, writing in 1992, said that out of about 285 texts edited and published on the subject of Indian astronomy, there were about fifty which belonged prior to the twelfth century; seventy-five between the twelfth and the fifteenth centuries and one hundred and sixty-five from the sixteenth to the nineteenth centuries. Despite such a high number of texts considered, he did not even begin to consider why there were no non-Sanskrit texts. M. D. Srinivas, 'The Methodology of Indian Mathematics and its Contemporary Relevance', *PPST Bulletin* no. 23 (June 1992).

centuries when Sanskrit mathematical works were translated and edited by European scholars during the colonial encounter. This historical process was marked by contending ideologies within the European Indological efforts, themselves shaped by a wider history of the Empire, which marked Indology in the first place.[10]

Indology recognized and canonized only the dignified Sanskritic tradition. The knowledge of many practitioners of mathematics was rendered invisible. Indian nationalist scholarship, for its own ideological purposes, largely reinforced this canonization.[11] The historians of the exact sciences, on the other hand, who looked for traces and pathways of mathematical ideas in different culture areas across the world, with their conviction to the study of techniques in texts have created a very useful archive, but have once again stuck to the Sanskrit base.[12] Such scholars have also studied interactions between the Sanskrit tradition and the Jain and the Islamic traditions within India.[13]

The quest for non-western mathematical traditions rightly desires to correct the injustice of sustained Eurocentrism, but once again recognizes only the Sanskritic tradition as 'Indian'.[14] Of course, the modern working mathematician in search of history for his own practice has only taken one particular tradition as the national tradition.[15] Critical scholarship

[10] Dhruv Raina, 'Jean-Baptiste Biot on the History of Indian Astronomy (1830–1860): the Nation in the Post-Enlightenment Historiography of Science', *Indian Journal of History of Science* 35, no. 4 (2000): 319–346; Dhruv Raina, 'French Jesuit Scientists in India: Historical Astronomy in the Discourse on India, 1670–1770', *Economic and Political Weekly* 34, no. 5 (1999): 30–38; Dhruv Raina, 'Contextualizing Playfair and Colebrooke on Proof and Demonstration in the Indian Mathematical Tradition', *The History of Mathematical Proof in Ancient Traditions*, ed. Karine Chemla (Cambridge: Cambridge University Press, 2012); Dhruv Raina, 'Situating the History of Indian Arithmetical Knowledge in George Peacock's Arithmetic', *Indian Journal of History of Science* 46, no. 2 (2011): 235–250; Agathe Keller, '"Is 'Hindu mathematics' a European idea?"/ Son las "matematicas hindues" une aidea europea? Aportaciones sobre la politica en la historia de la aritmética', Publicacions de la residència d'investigadors, 38, p. 332, 2013; Agathe Keller, 'George Peacock's Arithmetic in the Changing Landscape of the History of Mathematics in India', *Indian Journal of History of Science* 46, no. 2 (2011): 205–233.

[11] Dhruv Raina, 'Historiographic Concerns Underlying Indian Journal of the History of Science: A Bibliometric Inference', *Economic and Political Weekly* 33, no. 8 (1998): 407–414.

[12] David Pingree, *Census of Exact Sciences in Sanskrit*, series A, vols. 1–5 (Philadelphia: American Philosophical Society, 1970–1994).

[13] Kim Plofker, 'Links Between Sanskrit and Muslim Science in Jaina Astronomical Works', *International Journal of Jaina Studies* (Online) 6, no. 5 (2010): 1–13.

[14] George Joseph Gheverghese, *The Crest of the Peacock; Non European Roots of Mathematics* (Princeton: Princeton University Press, 2011).

[15] S. G. Dani, 'Ancient Indian Mathematics: A Conspectus', *Resonance* (March 2012): 236–246. See also the Special Section on 'Mathematics in India', *Current Science* 99, no. 3 (2010).

on the Sanskritic mathematical tradition has restricted itself to the study of distinct features that could be used to characterize that tradition.[16] We can see in this a tendency to favour the identification of canonical texts over an investigation of mathematical practice. It is almost as if there is a canonical imperative written into the histories of hegemonic languages such as Sanskrit. This canonicity attributed to Sanskrit works has shaped the analysis of mathematical and other scientific materials in various other subcontinental languages as one of translation and adaptation. Historians of mathematics have looked mainly for *translations* of these canonical texts in different regions and languages. It was held that the canonical works could exist only in Sanskrit; other languages could only contain translations and adaptations. They have not explored the possibility of different and unique types of regional mathematical knowledge located among various kinds of practitioners.

The 'translation' of a canonical 'Bhata-Bhaskara' tradition, the tradition of the *great books*, does not encompass the history of all mathematical knowledge and its transmission. This book raises the question whether the canon might have abstracted and theorized from the work of real-world practitioners and presented itself as more dignified and distinctive? The question sounds polemical. But it is demonstrable that there was in early modern India, the mathematical worlds of theoreticians and practitioners were entangled, and these mathematical worlds were experienced and localized quite differently by different social groups. Artisans, accountants, scribes, teachers and students were some such practitioners.

To examine the ways in which actual practitioners engaged with and transmitted knowledge is, therefore, to write a social history of mathematics in India. It is to retrieve the worlds in which the practitioners were located. It is an effort to unpack the social context within which such knowledge was embedded and to address its spatial content critically. This approach addresses the social and power relations through which canonical theoretical texts were produced by distinguishing them from actual practices and deemed 'dignified'. It makes us sensitive to the power-laden way in which knowledge is made and legitimated. It

[16] Roddam Narasimha, 'Epistemology and Language in Indian Astronomy and Mathematics', *Journal of Indian Philosophy* 35, nos. 5–6 (2007): 521–541.

attempts a history of mathematics where 'clerks and craftsmen',[17] teachers and students are the central figures. Mathematical treatises, elementary number primers, table books, colonial educational records, and modern textbooks become records of pedagogic practices. This book tries to develop such an approach for the period between the seventeenth and the nineteenth centuries.

The argument here is that we move from texts to practice. Texts might act as vehicles of social power, reproducing hierarchies of knowledge. But practice becomes a realm of exercising that power. We have to be aware that texts may not represent actual practices of knowledge, or at least adequately so.[18] This allows us to situate the social contexts of specific corpuses of texts, over and beyond their own ideological claims of universality. As Jim Bennett shows, texts can also be treated as 'evidence of action, regardless of their role as pointers to disembodied ideas, this invites a more disinterested appraisal of books as evidence rather than one motivated by a search for conceptual originality, and so may furnish a better grounded appreciation of the priorities of the time'.[19] Such an approach involves retrieving the practitioners and their specific modes of transmission of mathematical knowledge.

What were the types of mathematical knowledge in circulation within different kinds of socio-cultural practices, and who were the practitioners? How did these, in turn, shape institutions that sustained their practices?

[17] Jospeh Needham's quest to study the relationship between knowledge and practice through the historical relationship between 'clerks and craftsmen' has inspired many historians. For a brief discussion on various stances among Marxist historians of science on the relationship between knowledge and practice, including Needham, see Jens Høyrup, 'Practitioners – school teachers – "mathematicians": The divisions of pre-Modern mathematics and its actors', *Contribution to the conference Writing and Rewriting the History of Science 1900–2000* (5–11 September 2003): 4–8. For the life story of the Needhamian problem in India, see Dhruv Raina, *Needham's India Network The Search for a Home for the History of Science in India (1950–1970)* (Delhi: Yoda Press, 2015). Also, Dhruv Raina and S. Irfan Habib, 'The Missing Picture: The Non-emergence of Needhamian History of Sciences in India', *Situating the History of Science Dialogues with Joseph Needham*, eds. S. Irfan Habib and Dhruv Raina (New Delhi: Oxford University Press, 1999), 279–302.

[18] As Saito suggests, certain documents can also be read as processes, and not results, like in the case of mathematical instruments, like the quadrant used for navigation, the cross-staff used for mensuration tasks. Various manuals about the instruments and their use show how instrumentation as an ongoing issue of the time was embedded in practical aspects of mathematics. Practical aspects themselves are not in the sense of application of theoretical mathematics but as 'manipulative knowledge which may or may not encourage new theoretical ideas that may or may not answer a practical need', Fumikazu Saito, 'History of Mathematics and History of Science', 377.

[19] Jim Bennett, 'Practical Geometry and Operative Knowledge', *Configurations* 6 (1998): 198.

I draw upon Jens Hoyrup's useful categorization in response to these questions, as a starting point to navigate the worlds of early modern and modern mathematics in India.[20] Hoyrup categorizes mathematics practice into different orders. His first category of craft-centred apprenticeship serves as an axis of knowledge transmission. Various craftsmen, like sculptors, for example, or masons, or boat-makers, needed and used mathematical knowledge as part of their craft. Regular calculations, discrete insights and experiences or formulae, were fused within the overall work and skill required for the craft. When a particular practitioner domesticated new knowledge and made it part of his articulated skill to craft/compute better, it still remained within the community of practitioners. As we know, in the Indian context, these were most often organized through caste.

Hoyrup's second category consists of non-practising teachers who also served as transmitters. In this vision, an ideal teacher's job in a local school in South India would be to teach the rudimentary basis of the practitioner's knowledge (like that of the scribal communities of *kayasthas* in the North and the *kanakkuppiḷḷais* of the South) but not necessarily teach the uses of that knowledge in practice. Everyone could learn the computational skills of the professional accountant in such a mode of transmission without necessarily having to become an accountant. Like in the case of the arithmetic learning in the Tamil *tiṇṇai* schools, where arithmetic learning ideally enabled everyone in the basics skills required for account keeping but was not meant to make everyone an accountant. Hoyrup's final category is scientific, theory-centred knowledge which in South India was taught to Brahmins. This mathematical knowledge, developed through a long and sustained engagement with astronomy, emerged as a distinct mode of transmission because it was necessarily delinked from actual sites of craft and practice and their caste contexts.

Given its high theoretical abstraction, and ritual status within which this knowledge was circulated and transmitted, this kind of mathematical knowledge also emerged as more dignified than those embedded in practising contexts. In this context, caste is not merely a social identity

[20] Jens Høyrup, 'Practitioners – school teachers – "mathematicians": The divisions of pre-Modern mathematics and its actors', *Contribution to the Conference on Writing and Rewriting the History of Science 1900–2000*, Les Treilles (September 2003): 5–11.

that would make this apparent division of labour natural to its logic. But I want to explore how caste worked as a knowledge-making category within regions.

Following Hoyrup's suggestion, this book elaborates the *Kaṇakkatikāram* tradition in Tamil by plotting its history around two sites of transmission, that of the craft and work traditions of numeracy and teaching of mathematics by teachers. Mathematics and Society, then concludes by reconstructing how these practices were reorganized under colonial rule.

The *Kaṇakkatikāram* tradition in the Tamil region, examined at length in this book, assumes significance in this context. This involves going beyond the vexed issue of temporal priority that defines the hunt for translations of canonical texts from Sanskrit into regional languages. I shall not end up concluding, as Sheldon Pollock has done, that Sanskrit was the language of science in precolonial India and thereby treat the regional texts as vulgar forms of Sanskritic knowledge.[21]

Historical and material conditions of knowledge transmission demand that we reconstruct socially embedded mathematical practices. These constituted the base upon which a different kind of mathematization proceeded. In the *Kaṇakkatikāram* texts, the producers, workers

[21] Sheldon Pollock, 'The Languages of Science in Early Modern India', *Forms of Knowledge in Early Modern Asia Explorations in the Intellectual History of India and Tibet, 1500–1800*, ed. Sheldon Pollock (Durham: Duke University Press, 2011). He says, as a general rule, 'The language of science and its broader norms that, with the Hinduization of Sanskrit in the present age, we are apt to forget: the vehicle of organized, systematic *laukika*, or this-worldly, knowledge before colonialism was Sanskrit, while the regional languages, at least in their incarnation as literary idioms, were in the first instance the voice of *alaukika*, or other-worldly, wisdom', p. 25. It should be noted that the only exception that he would give to the 'vernacular' as anomalies would be from their histories of grammar and related disciplines of poetics, and lexicography, especially presenting a 'significant, and puzzling, unevenness between North and South India'. p. 24. Recent studies have brought out a significant realm of practices recorded in Persian, which show a world of Iranian *siyaq* mode of writing and account keeping adapted to the Indian context during the Mughal Empire, which was taken up by Indian scribes. These texts point to a systematic engagement with counting, measuring, weighing, keeping time and record keeping, and most importantly accompanied by system codes reflecting professional virtuosity and good conduct. See Najaf Haider, 'Norms of Professional Excellence and Good Conduct in Accountancy Manuals of the Mughal Empire', *International Review of Social History* Special Issue, 56 (2011): 263–274. We also know of a realm of literary practice in Sanskrit that addressed local audiences and remained very vital and organic to the regional world, made possible by the knowledge of two languages. If this is true for literary practice, the real messy world of engagement with measuring and weighing would also have had such encounters around the time, when the 'death of Sanskrit' is foretold. See Yigal Bronner and David Shulman, ' "A Cloud turned Goose" Sanskrit in the Vernacular Millennium', *Indian Economic and Social History Review* 43, no. 1 (2006): 1–30.

and administrative professionals represented themselves through their work and skills. Their work might have seemed laborious, practical, physical and therefore unworthy of critical examination to historians. In my approach, they reveal properties of counting, measuring, weighing, assessing, estimating, etc., which are manifestations of the abstract in the everyday. These were processes by which a generalized system of knowledge got encoded in practice and vice versa. Further, the practice did not merely mean application. For example, they did not study theoretical geometry first and then applied it in their work, which involved practical mensuration. Application is usually taken to be a mechanical act, devoid of subjectivity and ignores the social conditions in which specialized knowledge forms circulated. Therefore a distinction between pure and applied knowledge is thus rendered irrelevant in this framework. Indeed to consider practitioner's mathematics as exemplars of applied knowledge alone would be to accept the very canonicity, dignifying only one kind of traditions, which I seek to depart from.

The *Kaṇakkatikāram* tradition shared some features of arithmetic knowledge with canonical Sanskrit texts. These included, for instance, methods of problem solving and problem posing, rules and procedures of computations involving practical situations, fundamental arithmetic operations, summations of series, methods to solve proportionality problems like the rule of three and so on. Yet, these texts are distinct from Sanskrit in that they significantly foreground the work of the working accountant, teacher and the student engaged in measuring and counting in the realm of land, labour and wages. The work of the accountant is an all-pervasive presence in the texts. The texts also reveal distinct elements of environment of teaching and learning defined by the mode of recollective memory. As I discuss later in this book, they consistently avoid the algebraic mode explicitly, which might explain why these practitioners remained outside the purview of the historian's quest for a mathematical universe. Throughout this book, we use terms such as mathematization, computational knowledge, numerical practice interchangeably to underline the ambivalent task of characterizing the mathematical nature of practices in precolonial south Indian society. Such ambivalence is integral to reconstruct practices in their context. Moreover, it shows how we could understand their pursuits not to anticipate the disciplinary idioms of mathematics as a system of abstracted principles that are objective and transhistorical but as a product of nexus of localized and situated principles rooted in problem solving, where the quest for imaginable solutions remained key to such a practice. The first three chapters might require an understanding of the Tamil number system, the place of weights and measures in relation to the number system and its notations. Appendices I and II provide a brief introduction to these aspects, whereas Appendix III provides a complete translation of the Tamil number primers, which were central to the practices of this tradition. I request the interested reader to use them as a guide in order to follow some of the descriptions and arguments.

The first chapter, Mathematics Beyond the Canon, on the *Kaṇakkatikāram* corpus of texts, examines their socially embedded practice of computations, whereas pointing to their quest for generalization. The problem solving methods in these texts were not 'inventions' or 'discoveries' in the commonly assumed sense but point to how mathematics as a social activity made numeracy distinctively public. The mathematical content in these texts points to different kinds of mathematization and different experiences of mathematical practice in a caste society. They demonstrate the elastic and flexible nature of the boundaries between concrete and abstract engagements. Grasping this flexibility enables us to critically look at the continuous quest for a context-free abstraction that has come to define mathematical activity of our present. This might even help actually humanize and concretize mathematics education.

The second chapter on the Mathematics of the Practitioners attempts to show how mathematical knowledge circulated through the realm of practice, primarily in activities of measurement. Memory techniques were central to the circulation and transmission of such practices, helping them transmit beyond the practitioner to non-practitioners. This chapter argues that the mathematical practice of the practitioners in this tradition was grounded in the political economy of resource distribution and remained central to that social order. It also points out how the canonical tradition's practices were distant from these transactions, and hence raises the question about the character of abstraction in mathematization in precolonial Tamil country by situating it in social segregation and fragmentation, without losing sight of how the exercising of ritual and political authority conditioned modes of abstraction and generalization, through the particular occupational and social location of the different practitioners, be it the village accountant or the Brahmin astronomer. Moreover, it suggests that the pedagogic transactions between the school, the household and the workplace could bring us closer to the world of the practitioners.

Several studies of scribal schools elsewhere in the world, for example, the Islamic[22] or Italian merchant schools[23] have underlined the function of schools in the development of mathematics education and mathematics itself. They have shown that 'a seemingly simple category could cover phenomena of widely different character'.[24] The third chapter on Memory and Mathematics in the elementary *tiṇṇai* schools demonstrates a certain similar pedagogical environment in South India. This was, of course, a school environment where institutionalized education was plagued by caste-based physical segregation and social control. Despite the social exclusivity of teaching and learning, the activities of production and measurement enabled familiarity with numbers, at least to those who participated in such activities. This chapter uses nineteenth century colonial records to study these elementary institutions of learning, where arithmetic pedagogy was central. The elementary manuals like the *Eṇcuvaṭi* tables also provide a complex and detailed picture of the nature of pedagogic practices in these institutions, whose orientation was not simply to impart arithmetic ability, but to also provide functional training in the arts of recollective memory[25] as a crucial resource to cultivate ways with numbers.

The final chapter on Mathematics Pedagogy for a Public examines the onset of the colonial encounter in the world of mathematical knowledge. At the same time that Indology began canonizing Sanskrit texts as Indian,

[22] Dale F Eickelman, 'The Art of Memory: Islamic Education and Its Social Reproduction', *Comparative Studies in Society and History* 20, no. 04 (1978): 485–516. For a history of the ciphering schools in North America, see Ken Nerida Ellerton and M.A. Clements, *Rewriting the History of School Mathematics in North America 1607–1861 The Central Role of Cyphering Books* (London: Springer, 2014).

[23] Frank Swetz, *Capitalism &Arithmetic The New Math of the 15th Century* (Illinois: Open Court Publishing, 1987); Jens Høyrup, 'Jacopo da Firenze's Tractatus Algorismi and Early Italian Abbacus Culture', *Science Networks Historical Studies* 34 (Springer Science & Business Media, 2007).

[24] Jens Høyrup, *Practitioners – School Teachers – 'Mathematicians': The Divisions of Pre-Modern Mathematics and Its Actors* (September 2003): 5–11.

[25] Recollective memory was a mode of learning where to memorize was not to build storage of various facts like numbers, but to recall in specific contexts. Memorization here will not be merely an aid in learning, but it constituted learning itself. We will see how this was the case in the learning of arithmetic in the Tamil schools of the eighteenth century.

both partakers of the 'dignified' abstract tradition within mathematics as well as practitioners were faced with a new system of rules and a new way of doing mathematics. This encounter took place through their participation in the making of the new colonial revenue administration. This administration sought to appropriate local professionals, both learned pandits and village accountants, for their 'familiar' knowledge.

But this colonial encounter was explosively played out elsewhere, in the new schools. This encounter in the elementary institutions of arithmetic learning throughout the nineteenth century are to be found in the continuous processes that marked the appropriation, negotiation and at times coercion of the *tiṇṇai* schools into becoming the vehicles of transmission of the new way of doing mathematics. Through a careful elaboration of the changes in policy and practice over the course of the nineteenth century, the chapter shows how the single most liability for the colonial masters—rote memory in education—actually ended up getting institutionalized in the teaching and learning of arithmetic. This constituted a very different public for mathematics. It meant distinct notions about competence. We will then see how the conditions of encounter with modern mathematics for this public effectively constrained any possibility of making maths their own.

In the same period, we do come across fascinating cases (the Madras System of Tuition, for example) that have attracted recent scholarship in the history of science and education invested in writing 'interconnected' and 'global histories'. Indeed we can plot interdisciplinary conversations, as we will see, between different forms of pedagogy, philology and numeracy, and dense traffic between European systems of knowledge and South Asian traditions.[26] The circulation, historians of science have argued, was made through intermediation and brokering.[27] But interestingly, many of these histories desire some recuperation of a universalist/shared knowledge in the making, even if they were mired in relationships of asymmetry in power.[28] In recent years, a growing body of scholarship

[26] Simon Schaffer, 'How Disciplines Look', *Interdisciplinarity: Reconfigurations of the Social and Natural Sciences*, eds. Andrew Barry and Georgina Born (London: Routledge, 2013), 57–81.

[27] Lissa Roberts, Kapil Raj and James Delbourgo, *The Brokered World: Go-Betweens and Global Intelligence, 1770–1820* (Sagamore Beach, MA: Science History Publications, 2009). Also, Lissa Roberts, 'Situating Science in Global History Local Exchanges and Networks of Circulation', *Itinerario* 33, no. 1 (2009): 9–30.

[28] Kapil Raj, 'Beyond Postcolonialism … and Postpositivism: Circulation and the Global History of Science', *Isis* 104, no. 2 (2013): 337–347.

has sought to critique the assumption of domination and inequality in the production of colonial knowledge about colonial subjects. In the case of science,[29] one distinct stream has taken on the study of domestication or localization or naturalization of scientific knowledge.[30] While acknowledging how such processes stayed very much part of a transnational flow contributing to a process of globalization, it nevertheless stresses the necessity of a 'situated universalism', not to retain a sense of difference but to remain sensitive to conditions of participation in the making of knowledge.[31] Another scholarly tradition has preferred the idiom of circulation as a way to relocate modern science.[32] It has preferred to highlight a more interactive, fragmented and multi-directional flow of information and making of knowledge between colonial and indigenous peoples.

This book will not highlight such feel-good global histories. Instead, my goal here is to tell a different story about alienation and power. The story of the changing modes of pedagogic practices in arithmetic in the nineteenth century Madras detailed in this book shows how the effort to nullify functionality (as an orientation toward local transactions in letters and numbers as the primary objective of teaching and learning) from within the *tiṇṇai* school arithmetic was also a story of alienation from practice for the elementary student and the teacher, if not for its local

[29] For what have now become standard sources for the study of history of science and colonialism, see Deepak Kumar, *Science and the Raj* (Delhi: Oxford University Press, 1995); Zaheer Baber, *The Science of Empire: Scientific Knowledge, Civilization, and Colonial Rule in India* (Delhi: Oxford University Press, 1998); Pratik Chakrabarti, *Western Science in Modern India: Metropolitan Methods Colonial Practices* (Delhi: Permanent Black, 2004); David Arnold, *Science, Technology and Medicine in Colonial India, Vol. III. 5 of The New Cambridge History of India* (Cambridge: Cambridge University Press, 2000).Also see Abha Sur, *Dispersed radiance: Caste, Gender, and Modern Science in India* (Delhi: Navayana, 2011).

[30] Dhruv Raina and S. Irfan Habib, *Domesticating Modern Science: A Social History of Science and Culture in Colonial India* (New Delhi: Tulika Books, 2004).

[31] Dhruv Raina and S. Irfan Habib, 'Ramchandra's Treatise through the Haze of the Golden Sunset: An Aborted Pedagogy', *Social Studies of Science* 20, no. 3 (1990): 455–472; Dhruv Raina, 'Mathematical Foundations of a Cultural Project or Ramchandra's Treatise "Through the Unsentimentalised Light of Mathematics"', *Historia Mathematica* 19, no. 4 (1992): 371–384. These two articles examine a unique, albeit aborted pedagogical attempt in mathematics at Delhi College during the early nineteenth century. For a broad historical overview, see Dhruv Raina, 'The Naturalization of Modern Science in South Asia: A Historical Overview of the Processes of Domestication and Globalization', *The Globalization of Knowledge in History, Max Planck Research Library for the History and Development of Knowledge*, eds. Jurgen Renn, et al., http://www.edition-open-access.de

[32] Kapil Raj, *Relocating Modern Science Circulation and the Construction of Scientific Knowledge in South Asia and Europe Seventeenth to Nineteenth Centuries* (Delhi: Permanent Black, 2006).

public. Such elementary students' relationship with the colonial powers was not merely 'asymmetrical'. Their entire experience with mathematics was fundamentally constituted by 'asymmetry'. The story of the nineteenth century arithmetic textbooks in Madras brings to the fore a new mode of evidence in the history of mathematics. This story about the context of production and marketing of textbooks shows how processes of domestication of knowledge in circulation could have contained the possibility of making arithmetic knowledge one's own. In practice, however, the institutionalization of a textbook and examination centred pedagogic practice made it difficult for young learners to actually participate in the transmission of that knowledge. This, as I argue, is not merely a problem of translation of scientific knowledge, but one of power and social inequality in knowledge.

The critics of universalist knowledge making have argued how the production of cultural difference was inherent to the project of universal knowledge precluding its realization and making it in many ways, a mode of exercising power.[33] My own interest is not to emphasize the difference between the Western and Indian knowledge systems. Rather, I wish to consider more closely how social fragmentation sustained by caste and reinforced by colonial rule precluded the creation of universal knowledge. This process shaped how knowledge was translated, transmitted, theorized and remembered. I write this analysis not to romanticize indigenous knowledge, but to ask what sorts of publics were imagined for mathematics and how these were articulated.

[33] Sanjay Seth, *Subject Lessons: The Western Education of Colonial India* (Durham: Duke University Press, 2007).

I

Towards Practice: Mathematics Beyond the Canon

Can we reconstruct how mathematical knowledge and texts circulated in precolonial societies in the subcontinent beyond the Sanskrit canonical tradition? The study of great books of mathematics in Sanskrit, comprising the *Bhata-Bhaskara* tradition, is well known in the Indian history of mathematics.[1] Another less-trodden path guides us to consider mathematics in distinct spatial, institutional, and social-cultural locations and directs us towards the world of practitioners and their mathematical engagements. Who were such practitioners, what were their modes of transmission, and what vectors did they choose? If we assume logically that the practice entailed in Sanskrit texts was only one variant of what constituted mathematical practice in precolonial India, then what sources could we draw upon? Taking the classification laid out in the Introduction as a working guide, I venture to explore this typology in the precolonial Indian context.

This chapter surveys pedagogical tables, accounting books and manuals, and regional treatises in various Indian languages, as well as the material domains of craft and agricultural work, as critical textual and

[1] I draw upon the typical lineage of Indian mathematics that is commonly acknowledged, Aryabhata (5th century), Bhaskara I (7th century), Brahmagupta (7th century), the Bakshali Manuscript (c. 8th century), Mahavira (9th century), Bhaskara II (12th century), and followed by what has come to be known as the Kerala School led by Madhava (14th century). The phrase Bhata-Bhaskara tradition is not in anyway to simplify the tradition itself but to denote the dominant image of Indian mathematics and how a canonical tradition came into being. For a cogent and useful discussion on the emergence of the canonical tradition, including discussions about the mathematics of all the above figures mentioned above, see Kim Plofker, *Mathematics in India* (Princeton: Princeton University Press, 2011). For a discussion of similar tendency in European historiography, see Jens Høyrup, 'Practitioners – School Teachers – "Mathematicians": The Divisions of Pre-modern Mathematics and Its Actors', *Contribution to the Conference on Writing and Rewriting the History of Science 1900–2000*, Les Treilles, 5–11 (September 2003). I borrow the phrase, the great book syndrome from Høyrup's corpus of work, where the equivalent there would be Fibonacci's Liber Abbaci.

Mathematics and Society. Senthil Babu D., Oxford University Press. © Oxford University Press India 2022.
DOI: 10.1093/oso/9788194831600.003.0002

material sites for a social history of precolonial Indian mathematics. Tables and accounting manuals provide an important glimpse into mathematical learning, representation and regional variations and standards of numerical practices. The domains of craft and agricultural work, on the other hand, allow us to glimpse the centrality and materiality of measuring, proportions and counting practices. My overall goal in this chapter is less to underline how little we know about the precolonial history of mathematics in the subcontinent (although that is indeed the case). Instead, it is to discuss the many different kinds of sources for a social-historical exploration and the methodological possibilities for accessing, retrieving, and reconstructing diverse mathematical practices. The nature of computational work recorded in these materials allows us to discern particular orientations and their contingent modes of practice among different practitioners, like school teachers, accountants in the palace or at the merchant house or at the revenue office and in the workshop of the sculptor and other artisans. The discussion about the variety of such sources is to draw our attention to the possibilities to raise important questions about pathways of mathematization.

Number Tables

Number tables or number primers remain in some ways the foundation of mathematical knowledge and have a very long history that extends into precolonial times. They were used in some form or the other in the *pathshalas* (elementary schools) all over the country. For long considered artefacts of a computational past, historians of mathematics have only recently acknowledged the historical significance of tables as important vehicles for making mathematical learning and representation possible.[2] Our knowledge about the ubiquity of arithmetic tables comes from British colonial surveys in the Indian subcontinent. British surveys on indigenous education undertaken in the first half of the nineteenth century in the different provinces show that these tables

[2] M. Campbell-Kelly et al., eds., *The History of Mathematical Tables From Sumer to Spreadsheets* (Oxford: Oxford University Press, 2003)

were central to the curriculum and manuals of *pathshalas*.[3] S. R. Sarma has suggested that number tables might have been 'too trivial' for the Sanskrit mathematical texts or their commentaries to mention, even though they may have a very long history. There are occasional references to these tables in Telugu texts suggesting their use in the early centuries of the second millennium in the Andhra–Karnataka region. Sarma found 'specimens of some Middle Indo-Aryan or Prakrit arithmetic tables' from a commentary to the Telugu text *Pavuluriganitammu* by Mallana, which occasionally cites from the Prakrit arithmetic tables.[4] This, along with the Kannada name *maggi* for tables, hints at their use in the early medieval Andhra–Karnataka region. D. D. Kosambi, the historian-mathematician, mentions the use of such tables in the Marathi speaking region after the name of Hemadri, who was the Chancellor of the Exchequer under the last Yadavas of Devagiri in the thirteenth century. Even in the Hindi/Hindawi-speaking areas of the country, it was a common practice to learn multiplication tables. Sudhakara Dwivedi traces the Hindi word '*pahara*', which denotes multiplication tables, to the famous sixteenth-century poet Tulsidas, who coined a profound metaphor using tables for the number nine. Tulsidas said that the sum of digits in each multiple of nine is always nine; just as nine is inherent in all its multiples, so is the Lord Rama ever-present.[5] As we shall see later in this chapter, the *Subhankari* tradition in Bengal had its own version of tables. Sarma cites instances of observations of several European accounts about the learning of arithmetic tables in present day Maharashtra and Gujarat.

My research led me to a vast collection of Tamil table books called the *Eṇcuvaṭis*, variations of which are found in different manuscript collections.[6] The *Eṇcuvaṭi* manuscripts contain elementary arithmetical tables in the Tamil system (See Image 1.1). They consist of number tables, tables of land measures, volumetric measures, weighing

[3] For these surveys, see Dharampal, *The Beautiful Tree: Indigenous Indian Education in the Eighteenth Century* (Delhi: Biblia Impex, 1983).

[4] S. R. Sarma, 'Some Medieval Arithmetical Tables', *Indian Journal of History of Science* 32, no. 3 (1997): 191–198.

[5] Ibid.

[6] These manuscripts could be found in the Government Oriental Manuscripts Library, Chennai and several other repositories in Tamil Nadu and even abroad, like in the Bibliotheque National, Paris. I have listed the collections that I have consulted in the Bibliography.

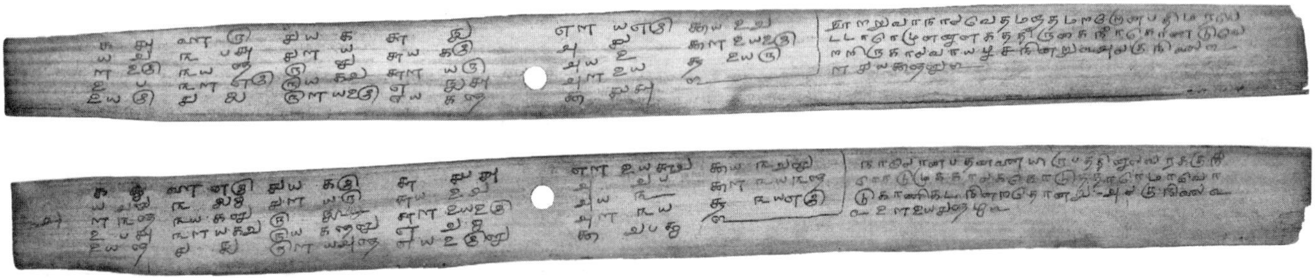

Image 1.1 A leaf from *Eṇcuvaṭi* manuscript. Courtesy: Manuscript number ENSUVADI-TAMIL-1795-B02307-P-008. From manuscript collections, Department of Manuscriptology, Thanjavur Tamil University, Thanjavur.

measures, and tables to calculate time. There is a strong pedagogic basis to their very organization. They are not textbooks in the modern sense but products of learning generated by the arithmetic practices of a specific location, the elementary *pathshala,* or *tiṇṇai* school. Every *tiṇṇai* student during the process of memorizing the various arithmetic tables wrote their own *Eṇcuvaṭi*s,[7] almost as an end product of their training. We will repeatedly return to the significance of these tables for a social history of mathematical practice and how crucial they were to different kinds of practitioners. Such table books are still widely available even today. Historians need to urgently preserve them and study them systematically in different languages so that they are no longer relegated to the realm of the 'trivial' merely because Sanskrit texts do not mention them. These historical materials are compelling evidence of the fact that the practices captured in Sanskrit texts were themselves only one variant of what constituted mathematical practice in precolonial India.

Account Manuscripts and Merchant Practices

Manuscripts of accounts and records of merchant practices constitute a very significant portion of different archival collections, both private and public. The contents of these manuscripts are diverse. State-related revenue accounts, land revenue details, temple accounts, private income-expenditure accounts, and several kinds of registers of the public offices are the commonly known types. The *mahajani* account-keeping practices, their manuals, and various other forms of training in bookkeeping methods in parts of North India and Gujarat await serious historical attention.[8] Similarly, the accounting practices and training in computational arts of merchant castes like the *Nakarattārs*

[7] In the Tamil schools during the precolonial period, the students would begin their learning of arithmetic with the number tables with a practice of reciting aloud and writing simultaneously on sand. The writing of the entire table book called the *Eṇcuvaṭi*s on palm-leaves by each student by himself will mark the culmination of learning arithmetic. This process is discussed in detail in Chapter 3. For the entire translation of these number tables, see Annexure III.

[8] See Nita Kumar, *Lessons From Schools: The History of Education in Banaras* (New Delhi: Sage Publications, 2000) for glimpses into the world of *mahajani* schools.

in the Tamil-speaking region are yet to be seriously studied.[9] In the case of South India, significant collections of other accounts manuscripts are found in the Kerala State Archives, the Mackenzie Collection, the Chingleput Revenue Accounts and another corpus called the *Mutaliyār* manuscripts from *Aḻakiyapāṇṭipuram* of the southernmost part of present-day Tamil Nadu, called *Nāñcilnāṭu*. The Kerala collection houses the various account registers of the Travancore state, mostly from the period 1742–1873, numbering about 13,000. They also house the accounts of the Padmanabaswamy Temple of Trivandrum for the period 1304–1936, numbering about 3,500 registers. The well-known Mackenzie collection has many manuscripts of this kind. These manuscripts are preserved in the Government Oriental Manuscripts Library (GOML) in Chennai. The Descriptive Catalogue of the Library shows that some of the manuscripts in the collection have details of revenue or simple income-expenditure accounts, which were mostly collected from the village accountants or the *kaṇakkuppiḷḷais*. However, as yet, we have little idea of the standards and variations of numerical practices that formed part of the system of accounting in different parts of the region.[10] The *Mutaliyār* manuscripts belong to the eighteenth century. They are mostly land revenue accounts of the *Mutaliyār* community of the *Nāñcilnāṭu* area. They provide information about the land and social structure of the time (see Image 1.2 for a manuscript showing household accounts of a landed family).[11] The other corpus that remains unstudied to date is that of the Modi manuscripts housed in the Sarasvati Mahal Library and at the Thanjavur Tamil University, both in Thanjavur. The Thanjavur Maratha rulers maintained these

[9] For a brief account of how this caste trained its kin to equip them for their unique business practices and training in the computational arts, see P. Annamalai, *Nakarattār Kaṇakkiyal Muṟai* (Chennai: Manivasakar Pathippagam, 1988).

[10] Pulavar Kannaiyan, who was a traditionally trained pandit with practical knowledge about Tamil accounting practices as well as mathematical texts prevalent in the region, worked briefly with the Thanjavur Tamil University collections of manuscripts, and has detailed notes of the nature of computational practices that went into such record keeping. I am grateful to him for teaching me the basics of the Tamil computing system (as I have given in Appendices II and III) and sharing his valuable knowledge, including pointing out to me that this vast corpus of records have in them a world of computation to be discovered. He has also recorded the presence of the Ramnad village accounts in the Sivagangai Collectorate office, the Vandavasi Block's Ponnur village accounts in the Institute for Asian Studies in Chennai and the interesting records spanning several centuries of accountants working for the Tiruvatuturai Saivite monastery.

[11] See A. K. Perumal, *Nāñcilnāṭṭu Mutaliyār ōlaiccuvaṭikaḷ Kāṭṭum Camūkam* (Chennai: Makkal Veliyitu, 1999) for a detailed account of this corpus of manuscripts.

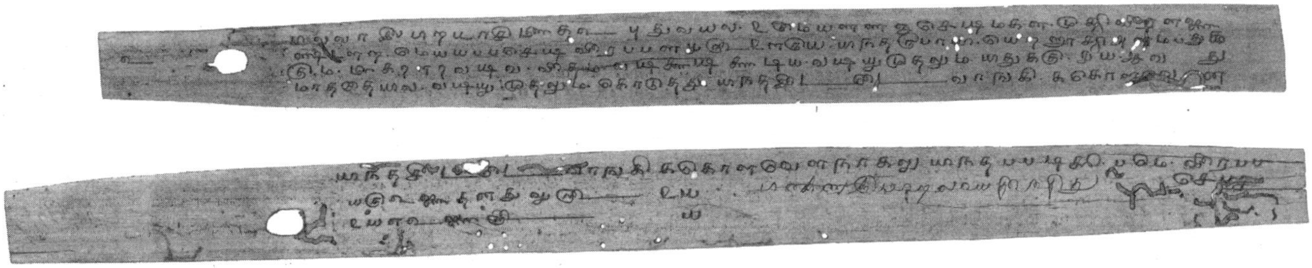

Image 1.2 A leaf from a manuscript titled *Periya Veettu Kanakku*, meaning accounts from the household of a notable family. Courtesy: Manuscript number PERIYA VEETTU-K-KANAKKU-TAMIL-1871-B02391-P-131. From manuscript collections, Department of Manuscriptology, Thanjavur Tamil University, Thanjavur.

accounts. The Chingleput district revenue accounts have shown that notation practices for Tamil numerals and for weights and measures found in many medieval inscriptions continued well into the eighteenth century.[12]

A detailed study of the Tamil materials may provide us with an understanding of the numerical practices—used for counting and measuring, both in everyday life and in schools—over several centuries in the region. They can also allow us to explore the similarity of notations across regions and eras, as well as their relationship to different standards of weights and measures. It is particularly important for a social historian of mathematics to study the emergence of computational notation in regional languages and the huge variations in their standards. Such a spread of notational forms with varying standards is understandable when seen against a palaeographic account of the development of the Tamil script, but it still does not shed light on the nature of innovation, or its absence, in numerical notation over a long period of time.[13]

Also, from the point of view of the history of mathematics, it is important to ask what conditions prompt change or stability in notations.[14] Does it depend on the carriers of computational knowledge operating in occupational and caste environments, where communication remained highly restricted in the course of training? It is difficult to imagine a context for innovation if we look at the restricted spheres such as family enterprises because the transmission of the skills would be closely guarded. On the other hand, we can get an understanding of the innovations from the teaching of numeracy to upper

[12] These accounts have recently been published in both English and Tamil, and will be very useful to historians of eighteenth century Tamil society, as well as to social historians of mathematics. See M. D. Srinivas, T. G. Paramasivam, and T. Pushkala, eds., *Thirupporur and Vadakkuppattu: Eighteenth Century Locality Accounts* (Chennai: Centre for Policy Studies, 2001). Thirupporur and Vadakkuppattu in the title are the names of the villages where the survey was conducted.

[13] For a recent discussion on mathematical notations in history, see Stephen Chrisomalis, *Reckonings: Numerals, Cognition, and History* (MIT Press, 2020).

[14] In the Tamil system, there were distinct notations for whole numbers, fractions and units of measurement. But for all other forms of arithmetic operations—used in account registers, school manuals and in mathematical treatises—were distinguished by a mere hyphen. The actual arithmetic operation was conveyed linguistically, through the various words for the numbers. For a brief note on the historical development of the Tamil numerical notation, see Annexure II.

caste communities in the *tiṇṇai* schools. (These schools are discussed in detail in Chapter 3.) Given the fact that these schools were widespread and that the teaching of numeracy through the *Eṇcuvaṭis* was definitely predominant, how does one understand the relationship between the standardization of measures and the development of computational notation? This is significant because notations for various fractional values for different weights and measures are in symbolic forms, which surely underwent some innovation and were sharpened for pedagogic purposes. Only further research of this wide variety of manuscripts in relation to actual practitioners can yield some awareness about the nature of Tamil numerical notation. Such an approach of inquiry rests on two crucial assumptions. The first is that there is a direct correlation between change in notations and the development of mathematical knowledge. The second is that such a development of mathematical knowledge would have found its way into different layers of numerical practices prevalent across spheres of activity. In other words, the relationship between different numerical practices and their pedagogic backgrounds will have to be ascertained on a historical basis before any satisfactory explanation can be provided for the prevalence of common notational systems over a few centuries.[15] To summarize my argument here, this corpus of sources suggests the possibility of a regional historical epistemology of numerical practice.[16] Finally, this study of mathematical notation is significant not merely from the point of view of the history of mathematics but also to meaningfully intervene in the often

[15] For a detailed and fascinating world of this dimension of the history of mathematics, see Georges Ifrah, *The Universal History of Numbers*, 4 Volumes (New Delhi: Penguin Books, 2005). Especially Vol. II for a detailed discussion on Indian numerals.

[16] For an outline of what historical epistemology is in the study of numerical practice and thought, and how it helps us situate the development of mathematical thought itself in material and cognitive worlds of practitioners, see Peter Damerow, 'The Material Culture of Calculation: A Conceptual Framework for an Historical Epistemology of the Concept of Number', Vol. 117 (Berlin: *Max-Planck-Inst. für Wissenschaftsgeschichte,* 1999). Also see Peter Damerow, *Abstraction and Representation: Essays on the Cultural Evolution of Thinking* (Boston: Boston Studies in the Philosophy and the History of Science Series, Vol. 175, 1996), especially Chapter 10. Also, it would be useful to bring in the lessons drawn from Lave's work on culture and cognition in interaction with each other in material settings as constitutive of mathematical thinking as a historical process. See Jean Lave, *Cognition in Practice: Mind, Mathematics and Culture in Everyday Life* (New York: Cambridge University Press, 1988). I thank Simon Schaffer for drawing my attention to this work and suggesting possibilities for a historical inquiry along such lines.

parochial claims made about regional contributions to the historical development of notation.

Mathematics and Work

Another realm that testifies to forms of transmission among the practitioners is the domain of work involving artisanal communities and craftsmen, such as carpenters, sculptors, goldsmiths, etc. Although the practice of apprenticeship in various crafts and artisanal work varies with the nature of the profession and the community, the nature of mathematical engagement across such crafts involves learning on the job. There are several manual-like texts for certain crafts such as sculpture, both in regional languages (e.g. *ciṟpa cennūl*) and in Sanskrit (e.g. *Māyamata*). At any given time, very few individuals could likely situate and understand the content of these texts. Instead, the fact that forms of these crafts and arts have continued to thrive points to the centrality of learning and knowledge transmission at work. Traditional stone and wood sculptors in South India, the bronze sculptors of *Swamimalai* in Thanjavur, artisanal groups like carpenters and blacksmiths continue to operate and transmit specialized knowledge through work.[17] There have been recent attempts to initiate such studies on boat makers in West Bengal. These boat makers employ traditional techniques to build large deep-sea fishing boats up to fifty or sixty feet in length. Most of them have had very little formal schooling and cannot read or write. They work without a blueprint but ensure that the planks are constructed in strict proportions to the measurements of the hull.[18] Detailed anthropological studies on these and other communities,

[17] One of the earlier studies to look at the artisan's workshop was Jan Brouwer's study which analyzed the material culture of the artisan's workshop as expressions of thought, and oral traditions as a continuing source for transmitting ideals and perceptions of work. He conceptualizes a world wherein craft, tools, the workshop and its products together constitute a system of communication, endowing the smith's furnace with meanings. See Jan Brouwer, *The Makers of the Modern World: Caste, Craft and Mind of South Indian Artisans* (Delhi: Oxford University Press, 1995).

[18] Swapna Mukhopadhyay, 'Making Visible: Mathematics of Cultural Practices', Presentation at the National Seminar on Historical and Cultural Aspects of Mathematics Education, Indira Gandhi National Open University, New Delhi, December 2–3, 2011.

and their way of work and learning as a continuous process, are yet to be undertaken in the country.[19] Computing remains central not just to the world of artisans but also to the world of agricultural work.[20] The integration of the world of measuring and its embeddedness at work in the paddy fields of the Kaveri Delta area in South India reveals how certain histories of labour remain enmeshed in the histories of counting practices.[21]

The world of craftwork is steeped in the world of measuring and proportions, creating new material forms through the acts of constant measuring and materially inscribing proportions. An interesting contradiction about this material practice is that though the work happens in the workshop without any written measurements, certain foundational texts are repeatedly invoked as testimonies of continuous systems of practice, especially in the cases of the sculptor and the architect. The great architect and sculptor, V. Ganapati Sthapathi (1927–2011), draws a scientific lineage to his practice from the genius of Mayan, who authored several texts, including the *Māyamata*. He invokes Mayan as one who has taught the world that

> for every bit of vibration there is a material space produced and conversely for every unit of material space generated, there is a corresponding unit of time-measure. As every time-unit produces equal sized space, it can be logically stated that Time and Space are equal in measure . . . such an extraordinary and indigenous science is still kept in the dark, thanks to the apathy on the part of the scientific community and the ruling class of our country.[22]

[19] There is also a growing interest in the history of science towards artisanal and artist practices in the making of early modern European scientific culture. See Pamela Smith and Paula Findlen, eds., *Merchants and Marvels: Commerce, Science and Art in Early Modern Europe* (London: Routledge, 2013).

[20] For an interesting discussion about this in the context of agricultural and plantation work, see Akhil Gupta, *Postcolonial Developments: Agriculture in the Making of Modern India* (Durham: Duke University Press, 1998), and Valentine E. Daniel, *Charred Lullabies: Chapters in an Anthropology of Violence* (Princeton: Princeton University Press, 1996).

[21] For a very interesting work that studies both Tamil mathematical texts from the early modern period and takes them to the field in the villages of the Kaveri delta area, see K. Vijayalakshmi, *Tamiḻar Paṇpāṭṭil Aḷavaikaḷ* (Thanjavur: Annam, 2006).

[22] V. Ganapati Sthapathi, *Contributions of Viswakarmas to the Science, Technology and Culture of Indian Origin* (Chennai: Dakshinaa Publishing House, 2000), 39.

Sthapathi goes on to invoke Mayan when he discusses the central place of the number eight in the act of creation and in the universe. This 'mathematical order of eight' applies to the human form, too: 'the length of the face is taken as a single unit, that is, 1 *tāḷam* (a unit of time as well as space). Face Length—1 *tāḷam*; Neck Bottom to Chest line—1 *tāḷam*; Chest line to navel—1 *tāḷam*; Navel to Lower abdomen—1 *tāḷam*; Length of thigh—2 *tāḷams*; Length of leg—2 *tāḷams*; Total 8 *tāḷams*'.[23] Please see Image 1.3 for a grammar of measures at work of a Sculptor.

This is how Sthapathi integrates the world of numbers with his craft.[24] It is notable that he felt it necessary to draw up a historical lineage and a theory of practice for the sculptor. Sthapathi argues that Mayan must have walked the earth during the 'caṅkam days', probably in Southern Tamil country. He claims Mayan wrote twelve technical works, equating each of these to the twelve vowels in the Tamil language: 1. *Ōvia Chennool*—Treatise on drafting and painting, 2. *Cirpama Chennool*—Treatise on Iconometry, 3. *Kattita Chennool*—Treatise on Architecture, 4. *Nilamanai Chennool*—Treatise on House Building Suited to the Quality of Land, 5. *Manainila Chennool*—Treatise on Land for House Building, 6. *Vaniyal Chennool*—Treatise on Astrophysics, 7. *Perunatana Chennool*—Treatise on the Divine Dance, 8. *Mulikai Chennool*—Treatise on Herbs, 9. *Kanitama Chennool*—Treatise on Mathematics, 10. *Marakkala Chennool*—Treatise on Ship Building, 11. *Vinkala Chennool*—Treatise on Space Ship, 12. *Elisai Chennool*—Treatise on the Science of Music ... in short, what is missing in Sanskrit texts, that is the aspect of science, is found in full measure in the Tamil texts.[25] Although the other eleven are no longer to be found, what remains in use is the *Ciṟpa Cennūl*, which Sthapathi uses for his own practice.

We see here the felt need to relate to both the Sanskrit tradition of the *Mayamata* and the Tamil 'caṅkam tradition' at the same time on the part of this modern Tamil/Indian sculptor. Doing so provides for him and his

[23] Ibid.

[24] Even though he has left behind a huge array of works as a sculptor, Sthapathi is best known for creating the statue of Thiruvalluvar in Kanyakumari. More importantly, he not only had a graduate degree in mathematics, but also trained several generations of young sculptors and was the Principal of the Government College for Sculpture at Mahabalipuram during 1957–1960.

[25] Sthapathi, *Contributions of Viswakarmas*, Annexure V, pp. xii–xiii.

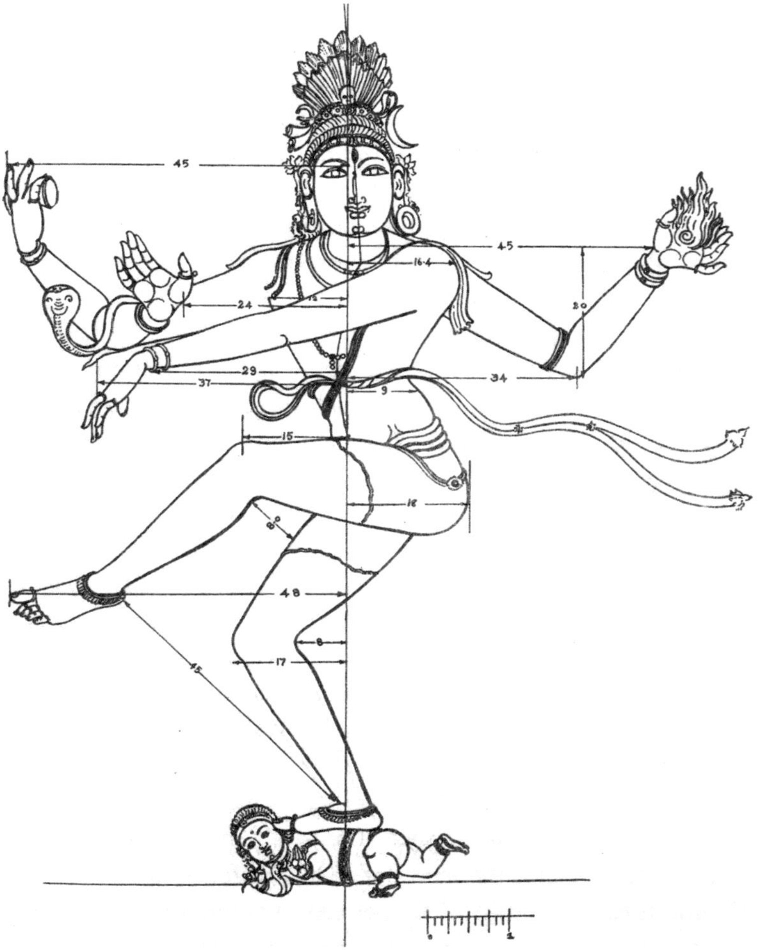

Image 1.3 Mnemonic measures integral to the sculptor's work. Courtesy: Ganapati Sthapathi and Sri Aurobindo Society, Pondicherry from the book, Ganapathi Sthapathi, Indian Sculpture and Iconography Forms and Measurements, *Sri Aurobindo Society and Mapin Publishing, 2002, Pondicherry, p. 75.*

craft both an Indian-ness and a Tamil-ness, enabling the community of 'Viswakarmas' (sculptors) to seek an ancient heritage while they address a global market for their products. But the yearning for a 'sacred geometry' to the sculptor's practice had to be framed in theory, within which the Tamil and Sanskrit pasts might not coexist. This claim to a glorious legacy and expression of historical virtuosity for the practitioner had to necessarily take place through a language of distinction and the imagining of a theory of sacred geometry. In the actual practice of the sculptors of *Swamimalai* even today, this theory of geometry is embodied in something as everyday as the coconut leaf. The leaf, folded into eight parts, and then further folded into subdivisions, still continues to guide the sculptor to make proportions come alive in stone, bronze, and wood. The sculptors use a fresh coconut leaf and fold them to make the marks of division visible and fix proportions into the clay form. There is little else that aids the sculptor's measurement at work. Though the material for encasing the wax mould has changed from the sand from the Kaveri riverbank to plaster of paris, the 'sacred geometry' is still ruled by the fresh coconut leaf, as captured in the Image 1.4 from a sculptor's workshop in present day Swamimalai.

But an interesting attempt to study Indian sculpture through the prism of measure and proportions is that of Mosteller's study of north Indian sculptures who wanted to develop analyses modelled upon the artist's own understanding and approach to his forms, that

Image 1.4 Everyday measuring scale of the sculptor, a fresh coconut leaf folded in proportions to make a scale at work. Courtesy: Photograph by the author taken at Swamimalai, 2018.

is 'to understand the stylistic significance of form in Indian sculpture through its measure'. He suggested that in the approach of the traditional 'Indian sculptor', measure and proportion function as integral parts of a mnemonically coded system for transmitting artistic forms over time. To him, this system was also a 'constructive' one relying on the use of visual devices consisting of drawn lines and points. The initial delineation of such devices is the first step of a learned procedure or technique of execution which translated the two-dimensional drawing to a three-dimensional sculpture. The complex process of this translation was guided by a mnemonic process where in the artist memorizes the volumes of his forms and their dynamic relationships to one another in conjunction with a working technique that facilitates their realization. He proposed through this study that the Indian tradition linked measure and form—proportion and morphology—by the use of this system. He also uses texts such as the *Pratimalaksanam* and the *Visnudharmottara* to study their prescriptive elements in ascribing proportions to particular segments of an image and points to 'silences' in the texts and ambiguities that point to how certain relationships of proportions within the carving of the same image show that they were only transmitted and preserved in the 'minds of the artists'.[26]

It is precisely these silences and ambiguities which points to the centrality of practice at the workshop of the sculptors, where the mind and the hand simultaneously measures and chisels, bringing the linear measures of bodily embedded units like cubits, and proportional units like *tāḷams* in alignment with volumes or depth to be carved. Thus measures in practice become generative and creative at the same instance, when counting and estimation, as computational activities assume concrete qualities, embedded in the work of the sculptor. This brings into question the often assumed distinction between the abstract and the concrete in the history of mathematical practices. We then have to study the real on-site processes of transmission of practices in the chain of production

[26] In this study, he did a proportional analyses of 110 standing images dating from circa second century BC to 500 AD in North India, to identify a set of specific measurements which would then define the proportional system used for a particular image. See John F. Mosteller, *The Measure of Form A New Approach for the Study of Indian Sculpture* (New Delhi: Abhinav Publications, 1991).

of images in the sculptor's workshop. This also requires that the actual use of prescriptive elements of texts be tested in the context of the practices in the workshop in order to draw our attention towards the reflexive apparatus of the practitioners in relation to the codes prescribed in the texts.

Mathematics in the Regions

A great deal of disciplinary labour is required to document the regional mathematical tradition rigorously, and this rigour can only be developed by understanding the historiographical and political processes for their occlusion from the critical scholarship. S. R. Sarma's valuable work recently documented the presence of various such 'regional literature' of mathematics.[27] He pointed to the close association between the professional scribal communities like the *kayasthas* in the North, the *karaṇams* in the South, and the merchant communities of Western India. The *kayasthas* had their 'professional variety of arithmetic' called *kaitheli amka* in verse form, which was published as *Kautuk Aru Kaitheli Amka* in Assam by Dandiram Dutta. In the East, Odisha seems to have had a rich heritage of mathematical treatises, like the *Lilavatisutra*, which was a very popular text for all age groups to study maths. A recent initiative has shown how there are at least four different genres of mathematical texts in Odisha, which include number primers used in elementary schools, accountant manuals, compilations of problems that were composed in musical 'ragas' and translations of generic texts like the Lilavatisutra.[28]

[27] S. R. Sarma, 'Mathematical Literature in the Regional Languages of India', *Ancient Indian Leaps Into Mathematics*, eds. B. S. Yadav and Manmohan (Boston: Birkhaüser, 2011), 201–211. In many ways, this work by Sarma has been inspiring for us, who have now come together to systematically document and create an archive of regional mathematical literature in all Indian languages. Such an online archive is in its making and will soon be placed in the public domain, with links available via the website of the French Institute of Pondicherry, https://www.ifpindia.org/. His encouragement to this initiative has been valuable.

[28] About 300 manuscripts in the collection of the Orissa State Museum are being catalogued currently by Prof Gauranga Dash, a distinguished Odisha scholar and will be published soon online in the online archive that was mentioned in the previous note. He is also preparing a bilingual edition of the Lilavatisutra, representative of the genre of texts found in the Odiya collection.

The *Śubhaṅkarī* tradition has received much more attention within Bengal. Santanu Chacraverti has collated various sources of information on *Śubhaṅkarī*, its surviving texts, its mathematical content recorded in *arjya* verses that deal with computations in activities related to agriculture and commerce. He grounds them in the *pathshala* tradition of the precolonial times. These texts primarily involved the learning of the *arjyas*, with verses of two kinds—first, those who once memorized and understood facilitated computation when working with localized units of measure and currency, and second, verses that posed simple mathematical problems. They also contained multiplication tables. The teaching of the *Śubhaṅkarī* continued well into the nineteenth century in Bengal but has been largely ignored by the Indian historians of mathematics since 'they did not care to deal with subjects as elementary as counting skills and popular negotiations with weights and measures or how children were taught elementary numerical skills. Moreover, the *Śubhaṅkarī* belonged to the immediate precolonial past, and for a long time, the immediate precolonial past tended to be viewed as deeply lacking in most respects, and even the most charitable of Hindu nationalist opinions saw this period as quite inferior to the resplendent epoch of ancient Indian history'.[29] Chacraverti then goes on to illustrate certain chosen problems involving units of measures in land, money and weights. He also illustrates a set of problems that are less practical, like the one below:

A Pir has his estate in a Mecca city
His estate measures a hundred crore Bigha
Hundred blades make a bundle
Each blade has a hundred grains,
The Pir's blessing ensures uniform yield
Seven Kahan bundles are there in a Bigha
'How many grains of rice are there'
asks the Pir to his Kayastha[30]

[29] Santanu Chacraverti, *Śubhaṅkarī*, The Asiatic Society Monograph Series No. XLIII (Kolkata: The Asiatic Society, 2007), 3.
[30] Ibid., p. 109.

Chacraverti surmises that the *Śubhaṅkarī* 'incorporates rules that were prepared by people who were in no position to transform the units that prevailed; they only sought to formulate rules that would make negotiating with these units somewhat less difficult'.[31] But this also 'represented a tradition of democratic knowledge—a body of learning and skill not confined to the upper classes or castes'.[32]More recently, Najaf Haider has unearthed a set of texts from the seventeenth century known as *Dastur-u-Amal,* written in Persian, the language of administration of the Mughal empire. These texts were written by accountants and record keepers and aimed at those who wished to be trained in professional record keeping and accounting. The technical parts of these texts usually contain six themes: 'numbers, notions of time and calendars, accountancy, record keeping, the duties of government officials'. The first section on arithmetic and computation includes 'multiplication tables, calculation of crop yields, salaries, wages, rates of interest, surface areas, surface areas suitable for land, cloth, stone, wood and so on, and tables to calculate agricultural land, units of weights and measures such as those for jewellers, goldsmiths, and grocers, currency exchange rates, and tables for calculating fractions of money'.[33] The subsequent sections deal with calendrical time-measures, and principles of accountancy, denoting a transition from the Indian style of accountancy into an adaptation of the Iranian style, which used a special technique of writing known as *siyaq*. These manuals also contain actual or illustrative records of the Mughal state, while a few do have a prescriptive list of virtues of good conduct that would suit an ideal accountant-professional in the seventeenth century.

The diversity in regional mathematical traditions, contends Sarma, reflects the spatially diverse systems of metrological practices in various regions, and also within the same language region. Sarma states that some of such regional texts could be translations from prevalent Sanskrit texts. The *Gaṇitasārakaumudī* was composed by Thakkura Pheru, in

[31] Ibid., pp. 123–124. [emphasis in the original]

[32] Ibid., p. 163. Somewhat perplexingly, S. R. Sarma in an addendum to his article 'Regional Literature in Mathematics' takes note of the *Śubhaṅkarī* tradition and the work of Santanu Chacraverti, but calls it a work filled with 'post-modernist jargon'. This possibly reflects a difference between two contending worlds of historians, rather than mere vocabulary.

[33] Najaf Haider, 'Norms of Professional Excellence and Good Conduct in Accountancy Manuals of the Mughal Empire', *International Review of Social History* 56, Special Issue (2011): 265.

Apabrahmsa, during the early years of the fourteenth century (before 1318). A learned Jain assay master at the court of Khalji Sultans, Pheru's text was almost a phonetic translation of Sridara's Sanskrit texts *Trisatika* and *Patiganita*. But several examples used in the regional literature were drawn from the different localized professions involving traders, carpenters, masons; sections on solid geometry which contain rules for calculating volumes of bridges, crop yields, and magic squares. In a critical introduction and translation of the *Gaṇitasārakaumudī*, S. R. Sarma and other scholars have painstakingly established the influence of Sanskrit works like that of Sridara's *Trisatika* and *Patiganita* and Mahavira's *Ganitasarasangraha*, by drawing elements of resemblance as well as variations between these texts. As they note, Thakkura Pheru, a Srimala Jain, who was from a community known for their expertise in banking and minting, also wrote several other scientific works and was an important 'mediator between Sanskrit and Islamic traditions of learning; mediator between the elite Sanskrit and popular Apabrahmsa, and also a mediator between *sastra* and commerce'.[34] This text,

> 'extends the range of mathematics beyond the traditional framework of the earlier Sanskrit texts, and includes diverse topics from the daily life where numbers play a role ... Pheru's aim is not to merely compose just one more neutral text on mathematics, but to produce a practical manual which is useful for all numerate professionals[35] like bankers, traders, accountants and masons. The value of the *Gaṇitasārakaumudī* lies, to a large extent, in this supplementary material, which offers us a

[34] *Gaṇitasārakaumudī The Moonlight of the Essence of Mathematics by Thakkura Pheru*, Edited with Introduction, Translation and Mathematical Commentary by Sreeramula Rajeswara Sarma, Takanori Kusuba, Takao Hayashi, Michio Yano (SaKHYa) (Delhi: Manohar, 2009), xiv.

[35] This term, 'numerate professionals' is a very interesting category, particularly for the practitioners in the agrarian mercantile world, like it has been useful for most premodern mathematical practices. Eleanor Robson, in particular has brought to us the world of 'professional numeracy' of old Babylonian scribes where the issues of 'numerate justice' was central to their practice. See Eleanor Robson, 'Mathematics, Metrology, and Professional Numeracy', *The Babylonian World* (2012). doi:10.4324/9780203946237.CH29. Also, see her Eleanor Robson, 'More Than Metrology: Mathematics Education in an Old Babylonian Scribal School', In *Under One Sky: Mathematics and Astronomy in the Ancient NEAR (Alter Orient und Altes Testament, 297)*, eds. J. M. Steele and A. Imhausen (Ugarit-Verlag, 2002), 325–365. However, in the Tamil context, the use of the term professional needs to follow caution because of the caste bound nature of occupations and the strictures that it brought in to questions of transmission of knowledge within and beyond occupational and social hierarchies and place.

glimpse into the life of the Delhi-Haryana-Rajasthan region in the early fourteenth century as no other mathematical work does'.[36]

Sarma and his co-editors argue that such 'supplementary material' displays a 'looseness of structure', in that it contains 'mechanical shortcuts in commercial arithmetic, mathematical riddles, rules for converting dates and magic squares'. It also includes another section that enumerates the average yield per *bigha* of several kinds of grains and pulses, proportions of different products derived from sugarcane and the amount of ghee that can be obtained from milk. But importantly, the editors also conclude that the material in these supplementary sections are unique, 'in the sense that such material occurs for the first time in a mathematical work and consequently no parallel exists in Sanskrit mathematical texts'.[37]

Even in the case of texts of a non-professional genre like the *Pavuluriganitamu* in Telugu, which seems to have been a translation by Mallana of Mahavira's *Ganitasarasangraha* in the eleventh century, there are interesting variations, as reported by S. R. Sarma. If *Ganitasara* had five methods of squaring and seven methods of cubing, Mallana had only one each and avoided the algebraic route. In case of examples, more interestingly, there are forty-five additional examples under multiplication and twenty-one in case of divisions that are not found in the Sanskrit source.[38] Sarma and his team have brought Thakkura Pheru's computational practice to light in great detail and with rigour. Their effort doubtless needs to be emulated, if one has to enter the world of the practitioner's mathematical pursuit in India. But it seems to me that the ease with which such research distinguishes between a Sanskrit great tradition and a regional little tradition should give us pause. By drawing this distinction, Sarma suggests that 'while mathematical ideas and processes were systematized in Sanskrit manuals, the broader dissemination of these ideas took place in the regional languages. Conversely, Sanskrit has also absorbed much from the local traditions'.[39] Although the give and take between the Sanskrit and regional texts seems reasonable, is the binary

[36] Ibid., p xvii.
[37] Ibid., p. xviii.
[38] S. R. Sarma, The 'Pāvulūrigaṇitamu: The First Telugu Work on Mathematics', *Studien Zur Indologie Und Iranistik*, eds. George Buddruss et al. (Reinbek: 1987).
[39] Sarma, *Mathematical Literature in the Regional Languages*, 201–202.

characterization of this exchange—with one as producer and the other as transmitter—a bit too easy and quick to conclude that the 'theoreticians of mathematics wrote in Sanskrit, the practitioners of mathematics wrote in the regional languages'. Was the practitioners' mathematics always about formulating 'short cuts'? Were they merely 'mechanical'? Even when they decided not to be so practical, were they merely posing 'riddles' under the village tree?

This repeated framing of the diversity of mathematical knowledge in these tight binaries begs several historical and conceptual questions. What constituted theory in mathematics over several centuries and what constituted the practical? When do we discern, historically, such a division of labour in knowledge within the pursuit of mathematics? What makes the Sanskrit mathematical manuals theoretical and, therefore, all subsequent acts of translation to be mundane and practical? Did the team select a schema for their Sanskrit canonicity—even though we know that Sanskrit textual traditions include several practical texts? This framing of the texts does not explain why regional language commentators selected and chose what they did, and ignored a whole lot from within the Sanskrit manuals. As a corollary, this formulation also does not explain why the theoretical treatises of Sanskrit mathematics like *Lilavati* felt the need to 'dirty their hands', as it were, with the practical world of commerce (and, notably, not the agrarian) if indeed theory was their primary interest and intent. Pheru's text clearly demonstrates an interest in agrarian production and taxation, yet it is curious that the great tradition did not consider it important to 'absorb' the mathematics of this realm of production and taxation, in effect, of the practitioner, despite the fact that the Sanskritic mathematical tradition remained alive with texts getting copied and commentated well into the nineteenth century. Did the theoretician never translate the practitioner's preoccupation?

We also understand precious little about the concrete reasons that compelled individual commentators or authors of regional-language texts. Why did Pavuluri Mallana, the *karaṇam* from the Telugu-speaking region, get interested in formations such as the 'necklace numbers', which form an array resembling a necklace? Was it for aesthetic pursuit, attracted by their simple elegance, or was it just to make innocent recreation possible for the simple villagers under a tree? Why was the *Subhankari* interested in prime numbers of a particular kind? Would such a pursuit with numbers continue to make him 'practical'? It is a truism, and a completely unsubstantiated assumption in the scholarship on the history of mathematics, that every time a practitioner of mathematics moves beyond the 'practical', it is deemed to be for a recreational purpose. Similarly, the practitioner is eternally glossed as a layman, or, indeed, speaking only to the layman. To be more specific, when the practitioner uses the rule of three in such diverse problem types, including proportionate division, it is deemed only 'mechanical'. The memorizing of multiplication tables in Avadhi by the people in Uttar Pradesh is glossed as a 'cultural' pursuit and not mathematical. Thakkura Pheru, Pavuluri Mallana and the *Subhankari* actively elude the algebraic mode but are nevertheless only seen as having 'translated' Mahavira and Sridara. Why did the regional practitioner not engage with the canonical algebraic text, *Bijaganita* of Bhaskara? As a result of this overall formulation of the translation trajectory from Sanskrit to regional languages, the scholarship is unable to explain how the famous 'Jospehus problem', unknown to Europe till the tenth century and in Japan till about the twelfth century, was articulated in Andhra as a riddle, posed as verse in classical Telugu metre and was still known to Sarma's farmer friend, who gave a solution in free verse.[40]These are not merely rhetorical questions, but concrete problems to be pursued for the history of mathematics in India. Here, the four themes suggested by Jens Høyrup to escape the 'internalist–externalist' predicament in the history of mathematics are of relevance to us.[41]

[40] The Jospephus problem is as follows: 'Fifteen Jews and fifteen Christians were traveling in a boat when the boat developed a leak. So the Christian captain arranged all the thirty persons in a circle and kicked out each ninth person and thus got rid of all the Jews'. Sarma, *Mathematical Literature in the Regional Languages*, 210.

[41] Høyrup's guide include, (1) 'desacralization without denigration', where alternatives to viewing mathematics as a timeless truth towards which mathematicians everywhere, throughout time, work undisturbed, need not be relativist; (2) 'actors participate in institutions', where both actors and institutions mutually influence each other; (3) 'the dialectic between tradition and actual situation', as in successive generations presuppose the work of previous ones, but importantly, 'in the forms that it is actually known and understood'; and (4) 'the relation between "high" and "low" knowledge. Measuring, counting and weighing' are indeed the (most practical and hence low) starting points in mathematics ... This transformation of low into high knowledge is a constant characteristic of premodern mathematics, whereas the reverse process ... became the cardinal ideology of utilitarian mathematicians from the late sixteenth century onward while remaining in actual reality only one facet of a twin movement. See Jens Høyrup, *In Measure, Number and Weight: Studies in Mathematics and Culture* (Albany: SUNY Press, 1994), xv–xvi.

I ask these questions, therefore, to craft a method for the history of mathematics that situates knowledge forms and the ways of their pursuit, in time, locality, language and caste, before we enter the iron cage of knowledge classification and subject our material to the binary labels of theory-practice, pure-applied, great-little, or the nation-region. Allowing the practitioner his place in the writing of social history also would mean that his place in the social and occupational context of a caste society where professional training was bound to caste-bound kinship, rendered hierarchies of privilege to knowledge practices in society. The village accountant could be lower than the ritually sanctified practice of the Brahmin astronomer, but the fact that he stayed above the actual measurers and practical surveyors and tank irrigators in the caste and occupational hierarchy conditioned the nature of difference in pedagogic know-how and know-why in knowledge practices. This begs a research programme in its own right, a programme which will remain sensitive to the manners, methods and orientation of the history of mathematics so that no actor, no realm of practice gets privileged once again.

Mathematical Treatises in Tamil

I would like to examine arithmetic tables and mathematical treatises from the Tamil-speaking region of South India. In the rest of this chapter, I describe in detail these Tamil treatises in mathematics and the nature of computational practices recorded in them. In the process, I also examine how these texts have been received thus far through the prism of cataloguing, editing and publishing practices in the Tamil-speaking area. These serve as a stark reminder to the historian of the pitfalls of the uncritical reception of the past within nationalist frameworks.

These manuscripts reflect a detailed engagement with mathematical practice. Enumeration of problems and methods of their solution in computation are general characteristics in them. I call them *Kaṇakkatikāram* texts, to generically name several texts of the same type. There are several variations of the same text called the *Kaṇakkatikāram* too. In the various versions of *Kaṇakkatikāram*, there are references to other such treatises namely, *Ērampam*,[42] *Aticākaram*, *Kaḷampakam*, *Tiripuvaṉatilakam*,

[42] Mu. Arunachalam refers to the mention of *ērampam* as a text in mathematics in Parimēlaḻakar's verse 302 of the *Thirukkural*. see Mu. Arunachalam, *History of Tamil Literature Through the Centuries, XV Century* (Thiruchitrambalam: Gandhi Vidyalayam, 1969), 345.

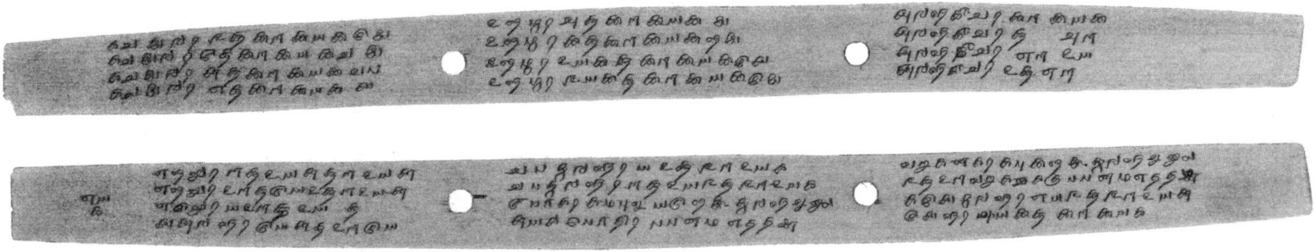

Image 1.5 A leaf from manuscript *Kaṇita Nūl*. Courtesy: Manuscript number KANITHA NOOL-TAMIL-1243-B01561-P-072. From manuscript collections, Department of Manuscriptology, Thanjavur Tamil University, Thanjavur.

Kiḷarālayam, Kaṇitarattiṉam, Ciṟu Kaṇakku, Kuḻi Varukkam, Peruṅkuḻi Māṟal, etc. Most of the above are not available. Examination of the catalogue of the GOML, Chennai, shows that some manuscripts like the *Kaṇitāmirtam*[43] are classified under mathematics, but these deal with astrological computations. There is another incomplete manuscript called *Kaṇakku Nūl,*[44] meaning a Book of Mathematics, but this one is too damaged to be studied. There is another complete manuscript called *Perukuḻi*[45] that is classified as an elementary treatise on arithmetic with tables giving the squares of certain numbers for finding area. There are also other manuscripts like *Titikaṇitam* and *Kirakaṇakaṇitam*, which are yet to be examined in detail, even though their names point to a priority towards astronomical engagement.[46] Other similar manuscripts of interest to us, awaiting study are *Tamil Kaṇakku,*[47] *Kaṇita Cāttiram,*[48] *Kuḻi Varukkam,*[49] *Nel Kaṇakku,*[50] *Pala Kaṇakku,*[51] *Muttu Kaṇakku,*[52] *Viṭukatai Kaṇakku,*[53] *Kaṇita Curukkam,*[54] *Kaṇita Tivākaram,*[55] *Kaṇita Vākkiyam,*[56] *Kaṇitākamam,*[57] *Kaṇitamaṉiyam,*[58] *Bālaciṭcai Kaṇitam,*[59]

[43] R. No. 468 and R. No. 557, GOML, Chennai.

[44] R. No. 497, GOML, Chennai.

[45] R. No. 204, GOML, Chennai.

[46] R. No. 894 and R. No. 245, respectively, of the GOML, Chennai. While the former deals with calculation of time, the latter deals with computation of eclipses, mostly in terms of the consequences of eclipses on humans.

[47] *Tamil Kaṇakku*, R. No. 2403, GOML, Trivandrum. It means, 'Tamil Mathematics'.

[48] *Kaṇita Cāttiram*, R. No. 3920, GOML, Trivandrum and also in Mss. 9675, Sri Venkateswara University, Tirupati.

[49] *Kuḻi Varukkam*, R. No. 2451, GOML, Chennai. This is a table of area measures.

[50] *Nel Kaṇakku*, Mss. 1407, Saraswati Mahal Library, Thanjavur. This means, Mathematics of grains.

[51] *Pala Kaṇakku*, R. No. 2201, GOML, Chennai. The title means Different kinds of Computations.

[52] *Muttu Kaṇakku*, R. No. 8086(b), GOML, Trivandrum. This means Computations of Pearls. Names such as these appear in catalogues of publishers in the nineteenth century mentioning that it pertains to the computations of merchants on the East coast of Tamil region, in particular by the Islamic traders along that coast.

[53] *Viṭukatai Kaṇakku*, Mss. 1110, Thanjavur Tamil University Manuscript Collection, Thanjavur. This means Riddle Mathematics.

[54] *Kaṇita Curukkam*, R. No. 1148, R. No. 437, R. No. 6673, all in GOML, Chennai.

[55] *Kaṇita Tivākaram*, Mss. 296, International Institute of Tamil Studies, Chennai. This is probably a collection of verses that are part of the *Eṇcuvaṭi*, the Tamil table book, which point to the sum of the products of each table.

[56] *Kaṇita Vākkiyam*, R. No. 5445 and R. No. 5446, GoML, Chennai.

[57] *Kaṇitākamam*, R. No. 2166, GoML, Chennai.

[58] *Kaṇitamaṉiyam*, R. No. 6364d, GoML, Trivandrum.

[59] *Bālaciṭcai Kaṇitam*, R. No. 8894, GoML, Trivandrum.

Keṭṭi Eṇcuvaṭi,[60] and *Kaṇitāmirta veṇpā*.[61]Edited versions of some of these texts are available. *Kaṇakkatikāram* seems to have been widely known and was first printed in the year 1862.[62] It was printed thrice since then, from different locations till 1958, when the South Indian Saiva Siddhanta Publishing House brought out an edition. Satyabama Kamesvaran of the Sarasvati Mahal Library, Thanjavur, undertook the formidable task of collating different versions of *Kaṇakkatikāram*, both in palm leaf and paper from different libraries, and has critically edited and published many of them. The first was a collected edition of *Kaṇakkatikāram (1998)*,[63] followed by a critical edition of a 1783 version, in collaboration with the Tamil scholar P. Subramanyam (2007),[64] and another version of *Kaṇakkatikāram*, authored by one Suriyabooban, titled *Kaṇakkatikāram Part II* (2007).[65] The 1783 text is the only version that could be dated.

In addition to the *Kaṇakkatikāram*, the *Kaṇita Nūl*, written in 1693, was also critically edited and published recently by the Institute of Asian Studies, Chennai. This manuscript was part of the GOML collection but versions of the same were also found in the collection of the Tamil University, Thanjavur (see Image 1.5). P. Subramaniam and K. Satyabama have critically edited this text and published it in two parts. The Tamil version has also been translated into English in this edition.[66]A third text called the *Āstāṉa Kōlākalam*, of the GOML collection was published by the GOML itself in 1951, critically edited by

[60] *Keṭṭi Eṇcuvaṭi*, R. No. 6754, GoML, Chennai.

[61] *Kaṇitāmirta Veṇpā*, R. No. 7976, GoML, Chennai.

[62] A survey of printed versions of *Kaṇakkatikāram* shows there are at least thirty printed books, published in different places, almost once every year, with the earliest we could find in the year 1856 in Madurai, then continuously till the 1920s. The Roja Muthiah Research Library in Chennai alone has about thirty printed versions of *Kaṇakkatikāram*, all published during this period of fifty years. Apart from questions pertinent to the nature of print culture and the place for a book like *Kaṇakkatikāram in it, the persistent use value for the book to have such a constant circulation through these years is to be studied.*

[63] *Kaṇakkatikāram—Tokuppu Nūl*, ed. K. Satyabama Kamesvaran (Thanjavur: Sarasvathi Mahal Library, 1998). All subsequent references to *Kaṇakkatikāram* in the book would only refer to this particular edition, as *Kaṇakkatikāram* (1998), unless otherwise mentioned.

[64] *Kaṇakkatikāram*, eds. P. Subramaniam and K. Satyabama, Chennai, 2007.

[65] Suriyabooban *Kaṇakkatikāram* (*Pakuti* II), ed. K. Satyabama, Thanjavur, 2007.

[66] *Kaṇita Nūl: A Treatise on Mathematics*, Part I, eds. P. Subramaniam and K. Satyabama (Chennai: Institute of Asian Studies, 1999). All subsequent references to *Kaṇita Nūl* would only

Thirumalai Saila Sarma.[67] We do not know the exact date of this text but it could belong to the eighteenth century. Since then, Satyabama herself has brought out another collected edition of *Āstāṉa Kōlākalam* by studying three different manuscripts in the Sarasvati Mahal Library's collection.[68] Let us now look at these texts in turn.

Introducing *Kaṇakkatikāram*

The editor of the collected edition of *Kaṇakkatikāram*, Satyabama, used twenty-three different versions of manuscripts preserved in the GOML, Chennai, Sarasvati Mahal Library, Thanjavur, the library of the International Institute of Tamil Studies, Chennai, the library of the *Madurai Tamil Caṅkam* and in the Thanjavur Tamil University Library. Along with the original manuscripts, she has also made use of several printed editions of *Kaṇakkatikāram*. They were published in 1862, 1899, 1938, and 1958, respectively.

The mathematics in these texts is presented in Tamil prosody, following different metrical patterns. Usually, the verses are followed by a commentary in prose. The problems are posed in prose style, but a few problems are presented in verse, and sometimes in both prose and verse. Most of the manuscripts are similar in structure and broadly correspond to each other in terms of the division of the contents into distinct units, and in the metrical structure of the verses used. However, some of the problems vary, in terms of the magnitudes and objects used in them. The author of *Kaṇakkatikāram* is mentioned as *Kāri Nāyaṉār*, of a place called *Koṟukkaiyūr*. The present-day location

mean this particular edition. Also, *Kaṇita Nūl* Part II, eds. P. Subramaniam and K. Satyabama (Chennai: Institute of Asian Studies, 2005).

[67] Thirumalai Sree Saila Sarma, ed. *Āstāṉa Kōlākalam*, Madras Government Oriental Series No. III (Madras: Government Oriental Manuscripts Library, 1951). All subsequent references to this will be *Āstāṉa Kōlākalam* (1951).

[68] K. Satyabama, ed. *Āstāṉa Kōlākalam*, Thanjavur Sarasvati Mahal Publication Series No. 464 (Thanjavur: Sarasvati Mahal Library, 2004). All subsequent references to this will be *Āstāṉa Kōlākalam* (Guntur).

of this place cannot be ascertained, nor can the age of the manuscript. It is generally believed to be from the seventeenth century, but Mu. Arunachalam, whose word commands much respect in Tamil scholarship, dates *Kaṇakkatikāram* to the fifteenth century. His reasoning is that this kind of work and style is not found in the literary boom of the sixteenth to the eighteenth centuries. While a general belief assigns Kāri to the fourteenth century without any rationale, we definitely know that he did not live in the nineteenth century. The reasonable conclusion, therefore, is that he could have lived in the fifteenth century, probably in a place called *Kuṟukkai*, near *Māyūram*, presently in the Nagapattinam district of Tamil Nadu.[69] He also infers that both the verses and the prose commentary were written by the same author, *Kāri Nāyaṉār*. The verses are addressed to a feminine gender, technically known as *makaṭū muṉṉilai* in Tamil grammatical treatises.[70] Exposition of mathematics to the world is the stated objective in the text. In some manuscripts, there are also other names found like *Purāri Nāyaṉār*, or *Poṟkaṇava Nāyaṉār* but the name of *Kāri Nāyaṉār* occurs most often. Given that the copies of the manuscripts were procured from different regions of present-day Tamil Nadu, we can surmise that the text enjoyed wide circulation. Since most of the original versions in palm leaves did not contain a proper colophon, there is no proper information about the people who owned these manuscripts. One manuscript, which did have a colophon, says that the person who copied the text was a son of a *mirasidar* of *Āraṇipāḷaiyam*. Some hints of the provenance of the manuscripts in the GOML emerged from curatorial data. The people who donated or sold these manuscripts to the GOML were from different places, ranging from one Sankaravenkataramana Ayyar of *Periyakuḷam* in southern Tamil Nadu to one Kader Baig Sahib of Triplicane, in Chennai to Vatamalai Nampi Cettiar of Putunakaram,

[69] Arunachalam, *History of Tamil Literature*, 344–346.

[70] According to Tamil grammatical conventions, the literary authors imagine a male or a female reader and compose verses. This is standardized literary practice. When addressed to the male, the rule is called *āṭū muṉṉilai* and when addressed to the female, it is called *makaṭū munnilai*.

Malabar. Such details definitely point to a broad spectrum of circulation of the text. The *Kaṇakkatikāram* 1783 text also clearly says that it was used by four students and belonged to Subramaniam and Muthukkaruppan.[71]

We can plausibly argue that the title of the text, *Kaṇakkatikāram* does not denote the name of a particular book but could be a generic name given to all texts, just as most of the medical and *siddha* manuscripts in Tamil are often called *Akattiya Nūl,* a practice common in Tamil textual traditions. Also, it is also possible to surmise that the age of the original text might be older than the ones available today, which would explain the generic name attached to all subsequent works that followed the same patterns of classification and presentation. This uncertainty makes it difficult to ascertain a historical evolution or development of mathematical knowledge by dating alone. This is not to argue for a general mode of derivativeness, and ascribe the common features of all available texts to one particular original and render these available texts derivative. In this particular case, the variations found in the available texts are largely confined to objects and examples, except for some variations in exposition of techniques and rules for computation. Another text studied here, called *Āstāṉa Kōlākalam,* mentions *Kaṇakkatikāram* as one kind of master treatise on mathematics and talks about the familiarity of the work across boundaries.[72] The acknowledgement of the presence of each text, along with others, does point to the existence of a corpus of a definite system of mathematical knowledge that was in active circulation and production during the seventeenth and the eighteenth centuries. They continued their life in nineteenth century print and palm-leaf media, indicating a cross-pollination of manuscript and print culture well after the introduction of print culture in the region.[73] See Image 1.6 for a leaf from a manuscript of *Kaṇakkatikāram.* The *Kaṇakkatikāram* has six distinct

[71] *Kaṇakkatikāram* (1783), 12.
[72] *Āstāṉa Kōlākalam* (1951), 68.
[73] Interestingly, there is also case of one printed version of *Kaṇakkatikāram* getting copied into palm-leaf manuscript in 1868 by Arumuga Mudaliar, son of Vedagiri Mudaliar, who was known as one of the teachers par excellence in Tamil literature and grammar.

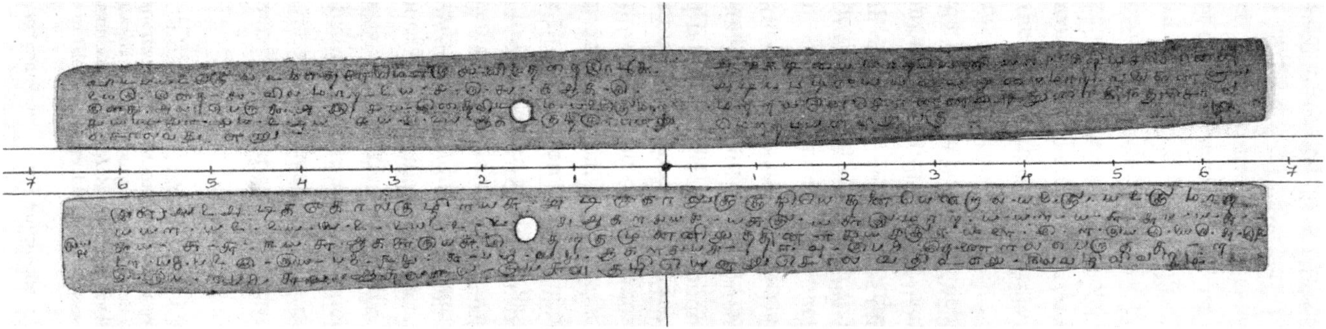

Image 1.6 A leaf from *Kaṇakkatikāram*, EO-541. Courtesy: Manuscript Collections, École française d'Extrême-Orient, Pondicherry.

sections, classified according to the objects of computation rather than the techniques adopted. They are:

1. Land
2. Gold
3. Grain or Paddy
4. Rice
5. Stone
6. *Kāl* or measuring vessel.

It has sixty *inam* (meaning types, variations in kind), of which twenty-three deal with land, twenty with gold, six have to do with grain or paddy, two with rice, three with solid stones, one has to do with volume measures, and five general verses.[74] Some *Kaṇakkatikāram* texts also talk about sixty-four verses.

The section on land deals with various ways to measure the area of lands of different dimensions in both whole and fractional magnitudes, along with computations related to total produce from an estimated area, the estimation of profit, and so on. The section on gold deals with various computations related to the estimation of the quality of gold, its price, and computations related to various mixtures in the making of gold, etc. Gold also was used for units of money, and this section also deals with computations related to transactions in money in varied situations. The sections on grains or paddy, rice, and volume measures deal with a score of techniques to compute volumes of grains using different units, conversion techniques, profit and loss calculations, etc. The section on solid stones deals with various rules and problems related to measures of solid squares, rectangles, or even sometimes of irregular solid bodies. There is also a section on water that almost exclusively deals with the distribution of irrigation water involving tanks and canals. In the last unit called the general section are found problems that use different rules and techniques that are enumerated in some of the above sections. But the tone of the problems is not oriented necessarily to the practical, and hence these

[74] *Kaṇakkatikāram*, 112–113.

are classified as *potukkaṇakku* or 'general problems.' Each of the above sections will be examined in detail during the course of this chapter.

Introducing *Kaṇita Nūl*

As noted above, the *Kaṇita Nūl* is a manuscript[75] in the collection of the GOML, Chennai, which the editors have critically edited in modern Tamil, along with an English translation. Using standardized editorial conventions with respect to palm-leaf manuscripts, the editors have presented the contents of the manuscripts in modern Tamil notation, without discarding the original version.

The author of this text, Karuvai Nañcaiyaṉ, mentioned in the initial verses, adopts literary conventions in Tamil, and the mathematics is presented in verse, using different forms of Tamil prosody. Like in *Kaṇakkatikāram*, the standard form of presentation is that the verses are followed by commentary in prose, an example and a problem based on the verse. Some of the problems are also composed in verse. The author has used ten kinds of verse patterns in this treatise. The editors argue that his knowledge of Tamil grammatical traditions and their application in the composition of the text points to a sophisticated literary skill. These verses are composed according to the rules laid down in the Tamil grammatical treatise called *Naṉṉūl*, while introducing the author, the purpose of the text, the name given to the text and the age of the text. The town *Karuvai* was part of the *Koṅku* region of the Tamil landscape and is now called *Karūr* in Tamil Nadu. The year in which the text was composed is also mentioned in a special verse, and the date is calculated as 1693 AD.

The author is also explicit in stating that the work is not original but adaptive, based on other mathematical works: 'As I went through the mathematical treatises composed by our forefathers, I wondered how they were able to create such good models. Today I make bold to write a treatise myself. This is like an ornamental doll in a tower thinking that it supports the tower itself'.[76] This text also adopts the technique of addressing a feminine

[75] R. No. 8641, GOML Chennai; *Kaṇita Nūl* recorded in the first 78 of 110 leaves.
[76] *Kaṇita Nūl*, 27.

reader, namely *makaṭū munnilai*, in Tamil, as *Kaṇakkatikāram* does. The ownership of the copies of this manuscript is not known and hence, we do not know much about the spread and the nature of the circulation of this work in the region. This work is also not acknowledged or referred to either in *Kaṇakkatikāram* or *Āstāṉa Kōlākalam*. Given these and the sophistication in terms of classification and structure of mathematics in the text, it is probable that this could have been composed after *Kaṇakkatikāram* or the *Kōlākalam*. The work is divided into six different sections: Number, Land, Grain, Gold, Stone and Time. *Eṇvaḻi carukkam* or Section on Numerals in 14 *vikaṟpams*, 18 verses, and 18 problems:

1. *Kōl aḷavu carukkam* or section on Land dealing with linear measures in 29 *vikaṟpams*, 20 verses, and 30 problems.
2. *Kāl aḷavu carukkam* or the section on Grain, dealing with cubic or measures of capacity in 9 *vikaṟpams*, 5 verses, and 12 problems.
3. *Tulā aḷavu carukkam* or the section on Gold, dealing with measures of weight in 12 *vikaṟpams*, 18 verses, and 9 problems.
4. *Nāl aḷavu carukkam* or the section on Time, dealing with measures of time in 6 *vikaṟpams* and 9 verses alone.

These are, therefore, 70 *vikaṟpams* in total. There is a section classified as *Teiva atikāra carukkam* where certain kind of problems is posed in the name of Gods. This section contains seven verses and seven problems. This is synonymous to the general section in *Kaṇakkatikāram*, where the various rules of computation enumerated in the different sections are posed as different types of problems. There are 89 verses and 76 problems in total.

A unique feature of this text, when compared to both *Atikāram* and the *Nūl*, is the explicit cosmological significance attached to numbers

eḻuttiṉ iyalpē ceṟṟiṉir kampam
ilakkattiṉ iyalpē mēruviṉ nilaiyē[77]

The author says, in the verses above, that although letters and numbers are considered the two eyes in the Tamil tradition, the study of letters is

[77] *Kaṇita Nūl*, 66.

like a shaky pole in a muddy field. The study of numbers, on the other hand, is an exercise as stable as the mountain *Mēru,* and the world stands merged with the science of numerals. The concept of one is significant because both its higher denominations and the lower ones are infinite, just like the *Para-pirammam,* which transcends all realms of the universe. Interestingly, the concept of infinity, which is usually attached cosmological significance in many cases, is given an interesting twist here, by posing the number One as the most significant conception, where in it stands in the middle of the higher and the lower, just like God, who can traverse and transcend the higher and the lower realms. It is also worth noting here that in the absence of zero, in Tamil, the number one takes a similar role.[78]

Introducing *Āstāṉa Kōlākalam*

This work is an edited version of a palm-leaf manuscript, acquired by the GOML in 1921–22, by one Sankara Vēṅkaṭa Rāmayyaṅkār of Periyakulam in southern Tamil Nadu.[79] This manuscript was edited and published in 1951 as part of the Madras Government Oriental Series when the Library began publishing original manuscripts in print. But from the text, it is not clear when this was written originally, but we could discern from various factors explained below that it could have been written after the *Kaṇakkatikāram* and therefore could belong to the seventeenth or the eighteenth centuries. The editor was Thirumalai Saila Sarma, of whom nothing is known. The General Editor of the Series and the then Curator of the GOML in his preface regrets that the editor could not write an introduction 'due to various causes', even as most of the explanations given in the body of the text keep referring back to the non-existent introduction!

[78] I would urge the reader to refer to Appendices II and III to understand the Tamil number system, where one could understand its uniqueness in terms of arranging numbers in three layers as large, middle and small numbers with a detailed system of notations.

[79] The original is of the size 16½' × 1⅝', in eighty-four leaves with six lines per page. It is classified as a 'Treatise on Arithmetic' in the Descriptive Catalogue of the Library.

The editorial conventions adopted do not help in any way to understand the work, and there is no way to distinguish between what originally is there in the manuscript to what was added on by the editor himself. We know less about the text because of such reasons. However, the author of the work has been identified as *Kūṭal Nāvili Perumāḷ*. *Kūṭal* could be modern day *Madurai*. This work has 57 verses, and runs as a continuous text with no clear classificatory schema. However, the methods and objects that are dealt with are very similar to both *Kaṇakkatikāram* and *Kaṇita Nūl*. The author, in the initial verses, acknowledges a corpus of mathematical texts called *Kaṇakkatikārams* as the '*guru*' and says that his work is derived from them and intended to 'briefly state'[80] several techniques of computations involving counting, measuring, commercial calculations, etc. The verses are composed following different metric patterns. There are also commentaries in prose as part of the text and some problems towards the end of the manuscript that are presented in prose style. The notation used in the original is of old Tamil notation. This text also follows the same system of classification based on objects of computation, which are Land, Grain, Gold, and Stone.

The initial verses also record that the text was written to aid the practice of mathematics. The author writes that there are people who, the moment they leave school, forget all about *Eṇcuvaṭi* (the mathematical tables) and cannot solve a single problem when they are asked to write accounts. But there are also others who, without the slightest hesitation, can offer solutions to anything asked. This summary (*Kōlākalam*) will help the 'intelligent' (*yuktikāraṉ*) sharpen his skill so much that he can be comfortable even when confronted by four *kaṇakkuppiḷḷais* (accountants), thus making him one such person among a thousand. At the same time, it is also meant for the 'numerically weak, but the only difference is that the numerically stronger will be like the fragrance of a golden flower'.[81]

80 *Āstāṉa Kōlākalam*, verse no. 3, 1.
81 *Āstāṉa Kōlākalam*, 1–2.

Why These Texts?

In these texts, we can find how measuring practices using the rod and the capacity vessel and the weighing stones are brought into the realm of mathematical pedagogy in the school and in the work place. This important transformation in the processes of mathematization of practical measuring is embodied in the rules, procedures, and problems found in these texts. This was aided by the processes of abstraction of the material and embodied acts of measurement into a system of numerical order, when quantities and their units became numbers with distinct notations found in the elementary number primers, as Appendix I and II discuss. We will have the occasion to discuss this traffic between training in school and the work place, further in Chapters 2 and 3.

To begin with, it must be admitted that these three texts cannot be clearly chronologically fixed except for *Kaṇita Nūl*, which is dated to 1693 AD and one *Kaṇakkatikāram* version to 1783. Nevertheless, they form a coherent set of sources for our purposes here. They might have been in circulation in the seventeenth century and later, with the increase in the use of palm-leaves as a stationary medium to write. Secondly, with multiple versions of *Kaṇakkatikāram* we know that it is not one particular text, but a generic name given to such texts, which are more or less similar in terms of the structure of mathematics presented in them. Given the fact that it had a widespread circulation across territorial and political boundaries in the Tamil-speaking areas, the acknowledgement in *Āstāṉa Kōlākalam* of *Kaṇakkatikāram* as its 'guru', and the humble intention stated in *Kaṇita Nūl* as an adaptive work 'based on the work of ancestors', we may reasonably argue that these three texts can be taken together to constitute a system of mathematics that was in use and in active circulation. The scheme of classification of rules and problems adapted in all the three texts are similar in terms of the objects of computation, namely, number, land, grain, gold and weight, thus lending weight to this argument.

The techniques and verse patterns used in the composition of the texts also are similar, though there are some important differences among a shared ethos. In fact, both *Kaṇita Nūl* and *Āstāṉa Kōlākalam* contain in them elements of textual organization and styles of language employed, which helps us to conjecture that these were both efforts to improve upon *Kaṇakkatikāram* and to situate its use for particular needs. Karuvūr Nañcaiyaṉ, writing in 1693, thought it necessary to compose his own verses, using ten different styles of classical metre, without deviating much from the problem types and methods of *Kaṇakkatikāram*. While the majority of *Kaṇakkatikāram* verses are in the classical *veṇpā* metre, a widely used form that aids recollective memory much more than any other form, Nañcaiyaṉ thought it important to employ not the *veṇpā*, but other metres.[82] Also he consciously follows the literary conventions of writing as prescribed in the *Naṉṉūl*[83] in setting out the objective of his project, right through the exposition of computational problems and methods of their solution. Its accompanying style of prose commentary also remains uniform throughout the text, making it a unique, one-off text composed in line with the *Kaṇakkatikāram* genre. The other important distinction in this text is the classification of the methods. Nañcaiyan introduces a completely new section devoted to numbers, which is not the case in any of the *Kaṇakkatikāram* texts. This is not to say that the latter does not deal with the issues that Nañcaiyan does, but to emphasize that he clearly separates the realm of numbers independent of their association with weights and measures, and indulges in certain methods like arithmetic and geometric progression of both integers and fractions.

Āstāṉa Kōlākalam is a text in contrast to *Kaṇita Nūl*. It does not aspire to literary elegance. Instead, it employs a highly lucid and spoken Tamil, as if the author narrated the entire content to a committed student in just one go, and uses verses (mostly from *Kaṇakkatikāram* texts) selectively. It is more like a prose text interspersed with verses, particularly the Guntur version of this text. Its author pays tribute to *Kaṇakkatikāram* but also states clearly how he sees it important to delineate the problems and the methods of *Kaṇakkatikāram* more clearly:

[82] The majority of the verses follow the *kalitturai* (56) and the rest are *kaliviruttam*, *eṇcīr āciriya viruttam*, *eḻucīr viruttam*, *aṟucīr viruttam*, *kuṟaḷ veṇcenturai*, *pakṟoṭai veṇpā*, *kaliveṇpā*, *āciriyappā* and the classical *veṇpā* used just in five instances in the text.

[83] *Naṉṉūl* is a classical Tamil text that resonates with the form of the modern notion of a manual of writing in Tamil, where the objective is not so much to guide the production of great literature but to make the author write correctly. It is also known as a text in the Jain tradition in the Tamil country. See U. Ve. Swaminatha Ayer, ed. *Naṉṉūl Mūlamum Caṅkara Namaccivāyar Uraiyum* (Chennai: U.V. Swaminatha Aiyar Library, 1953).

> This *Kaṇakkatikāram* was composed by the scholar Porkanavan for the use of the young and adults. This *atikāram* will address problems related to all kinds. Problems of the quantities of three, five, seven, nine and other types that follow can be seen. Since *Kaṇakkatikāram* is vast in substance, children will have to learn this just like the way they learn *Tivākaram, Eṇcuvaṭi* and the *Nikaṇṭu Uriccol.* So, after cleaning the floor and worshiping *Piḷḷaiyār* with flowers, a full measure of grains, along with betel leaf and nuts and fees, breaking a coconut, lighting lamp, if the student recites a problem, after the teacher, if the child is a gifted one, then he will follow what is taught to him like a river, but if he is not so bright he will go step by step.[84]

The clear pedagogic purpose that the author describes will be discussed further in the next chapter. What I want to emphasize here is how the author places his endeavour and orients his reader. He notes that

> mathematical works with names like *peruṅkaṇakku, ciṟukaṇakku, malaiyān kaṇakku* appear in different places and letters, and jump into the ocean of computational methods unaware of its depth, and decide to give up even when the water is just neck-deep, while often they do not even realize how deep the ocean is.[85]

Therefore he takes it upon himself to discern that missing sense of awareness, despite their depth, and yearns to bring in the sense of clarity by providing a typology of problems and methods and a new terminology for each type of problems.[86] These different kinds of engagement constitute what I would designate as the *Kaṇakkatikāram* tradition of computation. Given how little we know of the tradition, can we surmise that the continuous reproduction of these texts indicates continuity in practices

[84] *Āstāṉa Kōlākalam* (Guntur) , 25–26.
[85] Ibid., p. 26.
[86] Also throughout this text, we find new terms that are not found in the *Kaṇakkatikāram* for number types and procedures associated with numbers: like *cilvānam* (for fractions), *vittēru ilakkam* (similar numbers but with unique relationship between them like 4, 40, 400), *māṟupākam* (numbers that are different but involved in the same arithmetic operation say 3¼ and 15/16 and several others). Also, another interesting aspect to this text is that while *Kaṇakkatikāram* and *Kaṇita Nūl* have certain Sanskrit terms for whole numbers and fractions, this text has only Tamil names for each of the same numbers. See *Āstāṉa Kōlākalam* (Guntur).

and its relevance? I will try and answer this through the actual content of mathematics in these texts. But before that, I will briefly dwell on the manner in which these texts were received within the Tamil-speaking region to underline how the entry of these texts into print culture delinked them from their actual orientation of practice, towards an ideological reconstruction of that practice in the 1950s. The texts were printed, and they have been largely circulated among Tamil scholars rather than among scholars of Indology.[87]

As we have emphasized earlier in the chapter, an ideological privileging of Sanskrit texts within the history of mathematics kept such regional language materials as the *Kaṇakkatikāram* texts in historiographical shadow. We must, however, take note of the alternative discourse within which the *Kaṇakkatikāram* came to the forefront in the 1950s in Tamil Nadu, the heyday of Tamil nationalism. The Saiva Siddhantha Publishing house published an edition of *Kaṇakkatikāram*, with the publisher's lament that they could not find a single mathematician interested in helping to edit the text. It was reportedly only the conviction of the Director of the publishing house, Subbiah Pillai, who finally completed the task with the help of another Tamil pandit, Su. A. Ramasamy Pulavar, in matters of verse and prose. It was a pandit who edited the text and not a mathematician. Pillai ridiculed the author, Kāri Nāyaṉār, for the verse with which almost all *Kaṇakkatikāram* texts begin: 'I have taken up the task of saying in Tamil, what Brahmins wrote in Sanskrit' and ascribed it to a larger Brahmin-Sanskrit conspiracy[88]:

[87] David Pingree's *Census of the Exact Sciences* Project records the existence of *Kaṇakkatikāram*, but what clearly requires further investigation is the fact in the Census we hardly see any direct reference to translations of Sanskrit *ganita* texts into Tamil, but only texts related to *vaastusastra*, *cilpasastra*, and astrological texts. For the *Kaṇakkatikāram* in the Census Project, see David Pingree, *Census of Exact Sciences in Sanskrit*, Series A, Volume 2 (Philadelphia: American Philosophical Society, 1971), 31.

[88] *āriya moḻiyāl antaṇar eṭuttu uraitta cīṟiya kaṇita nūlai … tamilāṟ colluvēṉ ciṟantavar ikaḻārammā*. See *Kaṇakkatikāram*, Chennai, 1958, p. 8. Different versions have different verses to begin with, but this reference to the language of Sanskrit is constant and they also list the name of Sanskrit texts: *Ancanam*, *Ceitavam*, *Govindanārpatikam*, *Bhuvanatipam*, and *Ganitaratnam*. While this verse connotes direct translation there are other verses that connote how *Kāri Nāyaṉar* could have drawn up on both Sanskrit and Tamil, like the one in the 1783 version which suggest drawing upon both traditions: *āriyan taṉṉiṉālum aruntamiḻ taṉṉiṉālum* (verse 7); and in the next verse mentions Tamil ancestry *eṉ karuti vaṇ tamiḻōr eṇṇi eṭuttu uraittum* (verse 8)—meaning, all the knowledge of Tamils about numbers is presented here.

Aryans invaded our country and preached their language as the divine language, that Aryans were men from heavens living on this earth, that we should celebrate only their books and worship only them, and to align with this theory, composed several books and probably this author (*Kāri Nāyaṉār*) belonged to such times when that conspiracy was being enacted ... he was not the first person to yield to this conspiracy as there are several scholars in Tamil who have this false assumption that claiming a part in the Aryan language will make them famous and there are still people who think so.[89]

He argued his case further by saying that the units that Kāri Nāyaṉār uses—the notation for units like *oru mā, iru mā* and fractions like *muntiri* and number symbols had been in use in the Tamil country for several centuries as testified by history, literature, and countless inscriptions. Therefore, '*Kaṇakkatikāram* is a Tamil text and not derived from Sanskrit'. However, he also commended the mathematical brilliance of the author, insisting that the significance of the work would be clear only to the mathematical expert.

Claiming a cultural and hence civilizational autonomy for Tamil, we know, was a constitutive feature of Tamil nationalism; such an analysis was, therefore, not surprising, coming as it did from a publisher known for patronizing the editing and publication of classical Tamil texts. As early as 1902, *Centamiḻ*, the journal published by the renewed Madurai Tamil Sangam carried an article which argued that it was the Tamil number system that gave rise to the modern number system itself; it did so by reconstructing an orthographic history of Tamil numerical notation in a way that each symbol ended up becoming the modern Indo-Arabic numerals.[90] But let us also acknowledge that although these narratives of cultural pride were a product of certain historical and critical process, the Tamil nationalist argument for a place in the history of mathematical thought did not critically engage with mathematical practice or its practitioners. Their historical burdens, in some ways, overdetermined their contestation of Sanskrit Indology. Questions regarding practitioners and practice have to be raised within their framework of establishing the antiquity of the Tamil cultural innovation too.

[89] Ibid., p. 8.

[90] *Tamiḻarē Ulakiṟku Eṇkaḷai Koṭuttatu*, Centamil, 1902.

The lives of printed books are unpredictable. And so it was with the Saiva Siddhantha's *Kaṇakkatikāram*. Somewhat unusually, the text made its way into one survey of South Indian mathematics. K. R. Rajagopal's interesting survey of mathematics in the regions of South India in 1958–59 critically acknowledged the effort without any reference to regional or linguistic nationalism.[91] Rajagopal argued that the Tamil number system was unique and had been in continuous use since the twelfth century, even though to him, the *Kaṇakkatikāram* work itself was rather 'elementary in nature' due to its lack of Algebra, and unlike many Sanskrit texts, it was not systematically classified. *Kaṇakkatikāram* was less appealing for one more reason: its approximation of the ratio of the circumference to the diameter of the circle, the value of the famously modern pi was only 3.2 and not 3.1416, 'which is not a good approximation at all. Even the earlier value of square root of 10 was better than this'.[92] Ultimately, despite his sensitivity to historical detail, Rajagopal's final judgement was still delivered in terms of the Sanskrit model and its achievements.

What is remarkable is that both these contending assessments of the *Kaṇakkatikāram* tradition, for distinct reasons, converged towards the historical context of the 1950s. These assessments were unable to see the possibility of contending mathematical practices in history. During this decade, there was a concerted effort to publish printed editions of texts available with the GOML, Chennai. As part of this effort, several interesting regional language texts also got published, particularly those that were classified as technical treatises. *Kaṇakkusāram* in Malayalam and *Āstāṉa Kōlākalam* in Tamil were two mathematical texts that got published as part of this initiative. The editor chosen for the *Āstāṉa Kōlākalam* project was Thirumalai Saila Sarma. Sree Saila Sarma was in many ways an ideal choice for this task, as he could have been proficient in three different traditions of mathematical practice—he understood the mathematics as well as the Tamil in

91 K. R. Rajagopalan, 'Mathematics in Tamil Nadu', *Bhavan's Journal* 5, no. 20 (May 3, 1959): 41–44.

92 Ibid., p. 43. For his survey in the other three languages, see the following issues of the journal: for Karnataka, Vol. 5, no. 6, October 1958; for Andhra, Vol. 6, no. 8, November 1959, for Kerala, Vol. 6, no. 10, December 1959.

Āstāṉa Kōlākalam, he definitely knew the Sanskrit Bhata-Bhaskara tradition quite well, and thirdly, he knew modern mathematics and might have been formally trained in a university.[93] Yet, we can see that Saila Sarma echoed the assumptions and sentiments of his times in his editorial practice.

Saila Sarma was quite faithful to the original text of *Āstāṉa Kōlākalam,*[94] until he came to verse no. 45, which prescribes the algorithm to find the area of a circular land. Here, the original says, that given the circumference, in order to arrive at the diameter, one must follow a series of steps involving multiplying by 5/16, square the product, multiply again by 1/16, and then by 1/320 again and so on. However, in the last line of the verse, the original verse says that the ratio of the circumference to the diameter can be given by *mūṉṟoru nālu mā,* which is 3 + (4 × 1 mā) = 3 + (4 × 1/20) = 3 (1/5) = 16/5 = 3.2. From this point onwards, for the next eighty-odd pages, the editor takes an entire detour, shifting gears from Aryabhata, to modern spherical trigonometry, to Nilakantha Somasutva's commentary of the *Aryabhatiyam* to Madhava and Sridara[95]—on the mere connection provided by the value of pi. He argues that the value of the pi was different for all these different authors, and accounts for them in the way each author computed it. He then asserts that he was able to find a difference in the value of pi using modern algorithms, which he terms the 'MACHIN' method, where the difference is seen only after seven decimal places. (He argues that he himself was the first one to arrive at this in the year 1940).[96] The point of Saila Sarma's laborious detour, in his own quaint admission, was ultimately to establish the fact that 'the sources for any kind of modern mathematical production are the mathematical sutras from the age of the *maharishis*'.[97] What his detour definitely achieved, was to connect Aryabhata to *Āstāṉa*

[93] As noted above, we do not know anything about Saila Sarma, the editor from this publication. The publisher's note mentions that for various reasons, the introduction written by Sarma to the book could not be printed, even though at several instances within the book, we are compelled to refer to the non-existent introduction.

[94] Editorial conventions for editing Tamil palm-leaf manuscripts had definitely matured by 1951, with the tradition initiated by doyens like U. Ve. Swaminata Ayyar.

[95] The detour starts from p. 52 and continues to p. 140 of this edition of *Āstāṉa Kōlākalam (1951).*

[96] See *Āstāṉa Kōlākalam (1951),* 57.

[97] Translation mine, *Āstāṉa Kōlākalam (1951),* 140.

Kōlākalam and then to modern spherical trigonometry[98]—*mūnṟoru nālu mā* to *pariti/vyasa* to tangents and sine ratios marked this relationship,[99] through the reconstruction of the different pasts of one particular form of a mathematical ratio. The above three contrasting cases of reception of the *Kaṇakkatikāram* texts, all in the 1950s tell us about the production of a particular image of what constituted not just mathematical practice but also the specific contours of what constituted 'Indian mathematics'. Given that all these projects were in some way or other projects of commensuration, placing texts in some nationalist or sub-nationalist framework, can we seek a sense of methodological pluralism from these efforts? Revisiting the context in which such perceptions and histories were written is as important for us in order to remain conscious of the formative elements of such ideological practices that occluded the social, the local, and the practitioner a place in their history.

So what exactly was the mathematics in these texts? Were there anything more than the value of pi in them? Was there anything Tamil about the mathematics of the *Kaṇakkatikāram*? Or, did *Kaṇakkatikāram* have within it a possibility of a movement towards spherical trigonometry from its preoccupation with practical mensuration? Did the seventeenth century practitioner anticipate Tamil-ness and the significance of the value of the pi?

Let us turn our attention to the actual content of mathematics in the *Kaṇakkatikāram* corpus. In the following pages, I try and present the objectives of the problems and their methods of solutions, following the classification that is laid out in the texts themselves. The presentation is not representative of all the problems in these three texts, but is meant to offer only a glimpse into their world of computations. A substantial portion of the *Kaṇakkatikāram* texts are about tabulating the various standard measures and their sub-units in relation to each other, which

[98] In another interesting passage, the editor says that such 'circle related problems were always very cleverly computed by our ancestors from time immemorial like Aryabhata, Varakamikira, Surya, Vyasa, Vasisht, Parasarar and so on'. See *Āstāṉa Kōlākalam* (1951), 53.

[99] Now, these 88 pages of the editor's detour would provide ample material for a separate project, especially when taken along with the Krishanaswamy Ayyangar, the *Centamiḻ* and the Saiva Siddhanta Kalakam's preface to *Kaṇakkatikāram*. But, here, I feel it is important to just to record the details as a way to raise the issue of different way in which regional language texts were evaluated both within the region and in the nation.

will be presented in the Appendix. The reader can also refer to the translation of the *Eṇcuvaṭi* in the Appendix III. For now, I will confine myself to the main categories of land, gold, grain, stone and time.[100] I would like to point out that all the standard units of measures that are used in the following sections are tabulated in Annexure I.

Measuring Land

Most of the types of problems and the associated methods of solution, along with a few rules in this section, are concerned with the measurement of an area of land of different dimensions. The main variable in these cases is the different standards of the measuring rod, the *aṭikōl*, which I will call the foot-pole. This foot-pole differed according to geographical region as well as social hierarchy. For instance, in the area called as *Cōḻamaṇṭalam* (the Chola territory), the standard foot-pole will be 12 *kōl*. So, with a standard 12 *kōl* measure, 100 *kuḻi* will be equal to one *mā*; 20 *mā* = 1 *vēli*; 256 *kuḻi* = 1 *patākam*; 522 *kuḻi* = 1 *urakam*. But in the case of *Toṇṭaimaṇṭalam*, the area of 1000 *kuḻi* was taken as the *patākam*. There were also systematic classifications of various types of land with specific names assigned to them. But let us return to our focus on problems and methods.

For a square shaped land, the area was measured by multiplying the two sides. The sides were usually termed *teṉkai-vaṭakai kōl* (south-north *kōl*) and *mēlkai-kīḻkai kōl* (Up-Down *kōl* or could also mean East-West *kōl*). Let me illustrate this problem with a verse and the commentary to it from the text:

kaiyōṭu kaiyai tākki kalantiru piḷavu ceitu
noyyatōr kaiyai vaittu peiyatōr kaiyāl māṟil
vaiyamuṇṭāka coṉṉa nilaṅkaḷ āṉavaikaḷ ellām
veyyavaṉ tiralkaḷ pōla viḷaṅkumāl taraṇi mītē

[100] For the sake of uniformity and ease, I will take examples from only one text. In this case, the *Kaṇakkatikāram* version written in 1783, throughout this section, unless otherwise stated, the verse numbers will correspond to this edition of the *Kaṇakkatikāram*.

teṉkaikōl 13. *vaṭakaikōl* 11. *Āka kōl* 24. *iṭai pātiyākka* 12. *kīḻkaikōl* 9. *mēlkaikōl* 19. *Āka kōl* 28. *itaipātiyākka* 14. *itu māṟumpaṭi* $10 \times 10 = 100$, $4 \times 10 = 40$, $2 \times 10 = 20$, $2 \times 4 = 8$, *āka* 168. *ātalāl kuḻi* 168 *eṉṟu colvatu.*[101]

The verse states, that if you add the sides, divide each by 2, and multiply with each other, then you will get all the land (area) in the world like the rays of the Sun on Earth.[102] There is no prose commentary to this verse, but is immediately followed by a problem to demonstrate the rule, in this case. The solution is obvious. Likewise, for each type of land there are verse-rules and problems to demonstrate them. These include the area of rectangular land, land pointed at one end, triangular land, circular land, land in the shapes of a bow, fan and so on. In the case of measures involving fractions, which were very common, the rule was to convert the fractions in terms of certain standard units like the *mā kāṇi* (1/20 + 1/80 or 1/16) and then multiply the product twice over by *mā kāṇi* to get the area. Area of a triangular land would bring in the *neṭuṅkai kōl* or the long side *kōl*, the perpendicular dimension and to proceed with the multiplication of this with the other side. It then identifies other types of land—*tuṭi, tōrai, muḻavu, cuḷaku, eṟumpu, cūlam*[103]—the area for all these types will involve the computation of the mean measures and multiply it with the perpendicular measure.[104] Another interesting problem is to measure the area of a bow shaped land: the half of the length of the bow-string is to be multiplied with the length of the arrow to give the area.[105] In the case

[101] *Kaṇakkatikāram* (1783), verse 81, p. 125.

[102] This is the classic example of what is known as the surveyors' formula in the history of mathematics, which is simply 'average length times average width'. For an interesting discussion on the transmission questions related to this formula, particularly in some neopythagorean sources to the recorded practices of the agrimensores in the Greco-Roman world to Mahavira's ninth century Jain text Ganitasarasangraha and to the Chinese Nine Chapters, see Jens Høyrup, 'Seleucid Innovations in the Babylonian "Algebraic" Tradition and Their Kin Abroad', *From China to Paris: 2000 Years Transmission of Mathematical Ideas*, eds. Yvonne Dold-Samplonius et al. (Stuttgart: Franz Steiner Verlag, 2002), 9–30. Also see O. A. W. Dilke, *The Roman Land Surveyors: An Introduction to the Agrimensores* (Newton Abbot: David and Charles, 1971).

[103] These are conventional terms that were in use. *Tuṭi* is the land with two large ends with a narrow middle; the land with two circular heads with a long middle is called *muḻavu*; land in the shape of a ring with a squared top is called *tōrai*; land with one head resembling a square and the other head like a circle is called *cuḷaku*; land in the shape of a *cūlam* meant land like the *trishul*.

[104] Ibid., verse 83, 129.

[105] Ibid., verse 85, 131

of circular land, half of the measured circumference is added with *araiyē orumā* (½ + 1/20) and multiplied with the measured diameter to get the area. This is stated in the form of a verse-rule:

vaṭṭattu araiyum araiyē orumāvum
viṭṭattai koṇṭu virittu kōl – maṭṭam
vaṇaṅkāmal viṭṭat tālē matikka veṉṟu
aṇaṅkē orumā varai

To find the measure of the diameter of a circular land, the verse is given as

vaṭṭattai piṭṭaraikkāl vāṭṭiataṅ cālēṟṟa
viṭṭat taḷavāku meṉ

Which is to say, halve the circumference and multiply it with *araikkāl* (1/8) and by five: If the circumference = 40, its half will be 20. On multiplying by 1/8, we get 2 ½; multiplying by 5, we get 12½.

To find the circumference, given the diameter, the rule is

viṭṭam iraṭṭittu nāṉmāvil vāṭṭiya teṭṭāyōṟṟa
vaṭṭat taḷavāku meṉ

Which is to say double the diameter and multiply by 1/5 and 8.[106] Likewise, we find rules for calculating the cubic area of a pond followed by a series of problem types that pertain to the measuring pole used and area. The variations are, 'given one measure of the pole used and its area, find the area for a different pole that is given.' For example, 'if a 16 foot-pole is used the area is 256 *kuḻi*, what will be the area if a 24 foot-pole is used?' There is also a problem that demonstrates if the measure of the used pole is doubled, then the area increases four times.[107] There are problems to convert area measure in terms of other units like mā and *vēli*. To deduce the area occupied by trees in a given piece of land in order to compute the effective area as a problem type is also stated. Just to give an interesting problem from the text: 'By a 16 foot-pole, one *mā* of land had

[106] All three rules for circles are in verses 87, 88, 89 in Ibid., pp. 133–135.
[107] Ibid., p. 147.

100 *kuḻis*. In this one *mā* of land, 1000 handlooms of one *square cāṇ* each could be obtained, then what is the land required to make 5000 looms and how much land would remain vacant?' Another problem is to find the extent of cultivated and used land in a village: 'if the total *vēli* is 1000, and if 1/10th has been sown; 1/8th has been transplanted; ¼th has nurseries and ½ has matured paddy, how much was the wasteland and how much was the cultivated area?'[108] This more or less covers the kind of problem types concerning geometrical mensuration and associated methods of computation that involve land.

In a different section, but one that still concerns land, the *Kaṇakkatikāram* (1783) lists an entire set of problems to compute the value of land. These are primarily proportionality problems that involve the rule of three, and will be discussed in the next chapter. For now I will present a few problem types to provide an understanding of the context in which this computational method was employed. There are two variations involved: given the area, find the value or vice-versa. Problems of sharing the value in joint holdings appear as a third type, where the method would be to multiply each share by the gain and divide the product, with the total area. There are also a set of problems that compute the payment of wages in kind and in money for tilling the land, to labour, where usually one has to recognize the order in which the quantities are given and then use the direct or the reverse rule of three.[109] There is also one particular variety of problem, which is to compute the quantity of water from a tank to irrigate a given extent of land. The generic problem asks: 'If a lake's sluice measuring one *cāṇ* height and one *cāṇ* width is open, it will let water in one *nāḻikai;* what if the measure of the sluice is two *cāṇ* on each side?' The other problem is to use multiple sluices and the rate of water flow to ask time taken to irrigate land if all sluices are opened at the same time. Finally, there are problems that deal with paying taxes on land and the yield of single as well as multiple holdings. Interestingly, the tax is assigned for the entire settlement's total land, and figuring out the share of each landholder in the payment of the tax is a typical problem in this genre.[110]

[108] Ibid., p. 160.

[109] For a whole set of problems in relation to value of land, payment of wages and several variations, please see *Kaṇakkatikāram* (1783), 271–290.

[110] Ibid., pp. 197–198.

Measuring Gold and Paying Wages

The problems presented in the section deal with the measurement of gold as well as grains, even though it is classified as *poṉ vaḻi carukkam*, meaning 'in the order of gold,' thereby marking it as a generic type for all methods of weighing things. While most problems deal with gold as a metal and its mixtures, there are equal measure of problems that deal with gold as a unit of money and thus, problems dealing with payment of wages and sharing profits. This would mean that this section of problems in all the three texts uses the problem type of proportions—simple or direct proportions, inverse proportions as well as problems that involved multiple quantities. I shall present examples from each to provide a sense of the problem types, from the text *Kaṇita Nūl* (1693). For the various standards of the units of weights used in these texts, please refer to Appendix I. The term *māttu*[111] used here mostly is a unit of fineness of gold, which is often translated in the Sanskrit corpus as 'touch,' related to the touchstone.

As in the previous section on land, I will begin this section too by presenting a typical verse with its commentary and then go on to list the other problem types, because the purpose is here to make the reader aware of the problem types and suggested methods of solutions. In this particular case, I will present one verse each from *Kaṇakkatikāram* (1783) and *Kaṇita Nūl*, that deal with the same problem, just to show how they are composed in each:

Problems Involving Fineness and Weight of Gold

eṭṭu māttil paṇaveṭai reṇṭaiyum
ēḻu māttilē reṇṭu paṇaveṭaiyum
tiṭṭamāka urukkiṉāl mātteṉṉa
tēru meṉṟaṉar tiṇpuvi mītuḷōr
iṭṭa mākavum māttiṉil paṇaveṭai

[111] The Tamil Lexicon surprisingly does not have an entry for *māttu*, but the *Dictionary of Contemporary Tamil* says that *māttu* is a degree of fineness of gold. The English Karat which is a unit of weight derived from Arabic is equal to 400 mg.

yokkavē perukkit tokai ceitatai
tiṭṭamāka paṇaveṭai nālukku
īyntu colvatu tokai tāṉākumē[112]

This is a problem in verse. When a 8 *māttu* gold weighing 2 *paṇaveṭai* (unit of weight) and another 7 *māttu* gold weighing 2 *paṇaveṭai* are melted, what would be the resulting *māttu*? The method is to multiply the *māttu* and *paṇaveṭai* of each gold and add them. That is (8 × 2) + (7 × 2) = 16 + 14 = 30. Add the weights, 2 *paṇaveṭai* + 2 *paṇaveṭai* = 4 *paṇaveṭai*. Now divide the previous 30 by this 4, to get 7½. Therefore, the resultant *māttu* gold will have a *māttu* of 7½.

But for the same problem type, the *Kaṇakkatikāram* (1783) states a rule:

okkum poṉṉākum oṉṟiraṇṭu tāḻntavaṟṟai
mikka vakaiyāl viḷampeṉṟāl – akkaṇamē
coṉṉa poṉṉāl tokai ceitu cevvaik kīyntu
iṉṉataṉai poṉṉeṉṟu iyampu[113]

This is to say, if you treat a gold of 8 *māttu* weighing 2 *paṇaveṭai* and get a gold of 10 *māttu*, what will be the *paṇaveṭai*?

Then the rule is to multiply the *māttu* and the *paṇaveṭai* of the first gold and divide it with the second *māttu*. Likewise there are several combinations dealing with purity and weight.

Problems About Mixing Silver and Gold

One set of problems deal with finding the added weight of silver in a given *māttu* of gold. For example, 'when 4 *paṇaveṭai* of gold with 7 ½ *māttu* is mixed with one *paṇaveṭai* of silver, what will be *māttu* of the resulting gold? The original *māttu* has to be multiplied by its weight to be divided by the total weight, to yield the final refinement: *māttu* 7½ × 4

[112] *Kaṇita Nūl* (1693), verse 58, 212.
[113] Verse 110, *Kaṇakkatikāram* (1783), 165.

paṇaveṭai = 30; weight of gold 4 and silver 1-5; the new *māttu* is 30/5 = 6 *māttu*.' The other variation would be to find the weight of silver added when the other quantities are given.[114]

Method to Compute the Price of Gold

The problem of this type is to find the cost (in units of *paṇam*) of gold, when the *māttu* is given. Like the simple proportion problem: 'if the cost of 1 *kaḻañcu* of gold with 10 *māttu* is 14 *paṇam*, what would be the cost of a 8 *māttu* gold? Then you divide the *māttu* and *paṇam* of the given gold and multiply it by the other given *māttu*.'

The same principle works in problems related to payment of wages, which are called as *cevittan kaṇakku*. That is, the method of finding the gold in 6 *māttu* for one who worked for five days, when one worked for fifteen days and gets 4 *paṇaveṭai* gold in 9 *māttu*. The last quantity of 9 *māttu* gold and its weight 4 is multiplied which is 36. This has to be multiplied with the number of days of the first, which is 5 = 180. Now, divide this by the last given number of days, which is 180/15 = 12. Now divide this by the first *māttu* 6, which is 2 *paṇaveṭai*.[115] There are several variations which are meant to familiarize the ordering of the given quantities so that the right solution to find the result is by using the rule of multiple proportions. The exercises seem to orient the learner towards an identification of the problem in such a way that one could first find the right ordering, and then proceed with a known method to find the solution.

The other multiple proportion problems also deal with proportional division of wages. For example, the problem of sharing wages among a group of palanquin bearers. 'Five palanquin bearers get their annual wages in proportions of 10, 9, 8, 7, 6 each, in terms of *kaḻañcu* gold. If all of them receive 1000 *kaḻañcu* of gold, how would they share it?' Then, the total share is found by addition, 10 + 9 + 8 + 7 + 6 = 40. The first bearer's share is 10 *kaḻañcu*. To get his share, 10 is multiplied with the total wage, 1000 *kaḻañcu*, and divided by the sum of shares, which is 40; which is,

114 Verses 68, 69, Ibid., pp. 224–226.

115 For this problem types, see *Kaṇita Nūl* (1693), verses 70–73, 226–229.

10000 divided by 40, which is 250. Likewise for the second bearer's 9, his share will be 225. The third bearer's 8 will get 200, the fourth 175 and the fifth, 150.[116] There are, similarly, income and profit sharing problems. The *Kaṇakkatikāram* and the other texts classify these problems in to two types, *uḷmaṇam* and *puṟamaṇam*—*uḷmaṇam* is a situation where the total income is greater than the total shares of each person; *puṟamaṇam* is one where the total income is lower in relation to the total shares.[117] So, here we can see how every technique in a procedure seems to presuppose the knowledge of previously learned techniques, but all of them cover all the standard units and sub-units of gold's purity, its weight and its use as money to pay wages.

Measuring Grains

This section is classified as *kāl*, where the *kāl* comes from *marakkāl*, the unit of measuring grains. They are also called as *mukattal aḷavai* in Tamil, which means capacity measures. For the standard units of capacity, in relation to each other and also the various units for different commodities, please refer to the Appendix I. These conversion tables are vital to solve the problems given in these texts. I would like to alert the reader to our initial discussion on how practical measuring activities were abstracted into the order of numbers here, because the elementary number primer in Tamil, called the *Nellilakkam* actually treats units of grain like numbers and iterates an entire table to be memorized. This table is translated in full in Appendix III, and a detailed discussion will follow in Chapter 3 on the nature of arithmetic training in the *tiṇṇai* schools.

Here I will very briefly illustrate a few problem types about grain. The first set, which involves unit conversions, is fairly elementary. For example, it has problems that deal with finding the *kalam* units of paddy when measured by a different unit, *naḻi kāl*. Then, there is another variation: 'Given the total *Kalam* of paddy, find the used measure in terms of

116 *Kaṇakkatikāram* (1998), 226.

117 For a whole range of problems of this type, and two specific rules for both situations, which are in a generic sense using the ordering of the known quantities and then using the rule of multiplication and division of these quantities in a particular order, like the proportion problems. See *Kaṇakkatikāram* (1783), 201–215. This also has a one off problem that is about distribution of pearls according to given proportions with an interesting setting.

naḻi kāl.' There are also barter problems, to barter rice for gold. 'When a 7 *paṇaveṭai* gold with 8 *māttu* will get 10 *kalams* of paddy, how much *kalam* will be obtained when 2 *paṇaveṭai* gold with 7 *māttu* measured with 7 *naḻi kāl*?' These are typical multiple proportion problems that bring in the rule of five, seven, nine and so on. The techniques described in these problems, again, like in the previous cases of proportion problems, seem to be orienting the learner to identify the nature of the quantities in a given order and then subsequently proceed with the solution which is then a familiar terrain. For example, let me illustrate a problem involving the rule of seven.

aṭiyuṭaṉ āṟumāṟi amarntataṟku
nītikkum ēḻali nimirntapiṉ - mātē
iraṇṭu mutal aintaḷavu ēṟratai tāṉ māṟi
tiṟantaṉai īntu peyar ceppu.[118]

This is best illustrated in the text by a problem: 'On multiplying the first 5 *nāḻi* with the sixth value of rice and the seventh value of 6 *nāḻi*, we get 30. Keep that apart. On multiplying the third value of 8 *nāḻi* by the fourth value of 25, we get 200. Multiply this by the fifth value of 3 *nāḻi*, to get 600. Multiply this by the second value of 3 *nāḻi* to get 1800. Now, at the end, divide this by the first computed 30, to get 60 *kalams* of paddy.'

By similar problem types, then, the conversion of paddy grains to rice are also dealt with, which in certain *Kaṇakkatikāram* texts are given their own special sub-section, called the *arici vaḻi carukkam* or the rice section. They also proceed as the conversion of units of paddy, to yield units of rice in terms of a different unit. But multiple proportion problems also have many interesting examples, all of which actually point to concrete instances in practical life, wherever capacity measures and their conversions are dealt with in daily working lives. Take this one: 'How many times a person will have to pound with how many breaths he has taken to get how many units of rice from the given paddy?'[119]I shall not dwell further into the nature of problems in this section, because mathematically they all deal with the same techniques but applied to all imaginable

[118] *Kaṇakkatikāram* (1783), verse 146, 229.
[119] Verse 154, Ibid., p. 246.

situations when capacity measures come up, that is to keep accumulating a stock of methods so that any situation could be handled, readily.

Measuring Stone

The *Kaṇakkatikāram* has a section called *kal*, meaning stone. Here, problems of solid bodies are handled, say, dividing one solid into several units of given dimensions. The *Kaṇita Nūl* however has only one problem in this type, which is to quarry a hill of a given dimension into pillars of uniform units. The first problem would be to compute the stone measure, and the rule is:

> *kallukku aḷavutāṉ nāṟcāṇ muḻavakalam*
> *collil kaṇañcāṇ ēṟṟi – nalla*
> *viṟalai melliyalāy cāṇukku cāṇmāṟi*
> *mākāṇi araikkālil kaḻi*[120]

> Multiply the width and length with the thickness in terms of the unit *viṟal* (a sub-unit of *cāṇ*), multiply it by *mā kāṇi* (1/16) and then by *araikkāl* (1/8) to get the stone measure. To show this with a problem:
>
> If the length is 4 *cāṇ*, width is 2 *cāṇ* and thickness is 12 *viṟal*, product of all three is 96. Now, multiply it by *mākāṇi*, 1/16 will give 6. Again multiply this by 1/8, which is ¾ .

So, the common method prescribed seems to be: while the length and the breadth will be in terms of the unit *cāṇ* the thickness will have to be in terms of the unit *viṟal*, and then, to raise their product with 1/16, and then by 1/8 to get the stone measure. The same method is then extended to excavate solid bodies out of a given stone, or what could be called the quarrying problems, getting pillars out of a hill or even getting grinding stones of a given stone measure. Here, there will simply be one more

120 *Kaṇakkatikāram* (1783), verse 156, 253.

addition operation of division, where the required measure of the stone has to be divided with the source stone measure.

Measuring Time

Most *Kaṇakkatikāram* texts are concerned with time only to the extent of delineating time units and their relation to each other. In case of problems, typically, we will have problems of irrigation as seen earlier in the example of the lake's sluice gates: the area of land irrigated and the number of sluice gates of a tank are given, and time becomes a factor in such problems. But there are also versions where the idea of time is related to the computation of years in an era. One particular text, Suryabooban's *Kaṇakkatikāram* has an entire section on time, but that is mostly related to calendric time computation. It is in *Kaṇita Nūl* that we get a full section devoted to time, fundamental units of time, units of a year, *cakāptam*, computing the current year in *kali yukam*, to calculate the birth of a new year, month and finally, the measures to make an instrument to measure time. In the verse that gives the method to find the number of years in a *cakāptam:*

muṉṉāka vaiṅkaraṉ tāḷ toḻutupiṉ mūvirupāṉ
taṉṉō ṭirupat tēḻai māṟi piṉ tāṉ tokai cey
taṉṉāḷ varaimaṭṭum ceṉṟāṇṭu kūṭṭiya tāntokaiyil
piṉṉām patiṉoṉṟu nīkkac cakārttattiṉ pēr varumē[121]

The rule is to take 60, since this is the number of years in a cycle. Multiply this by 27, one gets 1620. This again is to be multiplied by 27 + 1, that is 1620 × (27 + 1) = 45360. This will be the unit of one *cakāptam.*

To compute the current year in *Kali yukam*, the rule is as follows:

matiyāka vāṇṭa ṟupatiṉai mēṟpaṭi vaittuṭaṉē
etirākavē eṇpatutāṉ māṟi ēṟiya tintokaiyō

[121] *Kaṇita Nūl*, verse 77, 234.

ṭatiṉār ṟuṟaimaṭṭuñ ceṉṟāṇṭu kūṭṭiya tantokaiyiṟ
pativākavē paṉṉi raṇṭāṇṭu tāṉ taḷḷi pār kaliyē[122]

One complete cycle of years is 60, beginning from the first year called the *pirapāva*. This is to be multiplied by 80. After this, the number of years past in that cycle till the current year is to be added. When 12 is deducted from this sum, the current year will be obtained. Similarly, the method to calculate the time of the birth of every month according to the Tamil calendar year is also given. For this the first month, *cittirai* is to be taken as the base. Beginning Friday, the number of *nāḻikai* past have to be taken as a unit. When 2 days and 55 *nāḻikai* are added, the time of the birth of the month of *vaikāci* is obtained.

When 6 ½ days and 20 *Nāḻikai* are added, the time of the month of *Puraṭṭāci* is obtained.

When 4 days and 56 *Nāḻikai* are added, the time of *Āṭi* and *Aippaci* months are obtained.

When 6 days and 46 *Nāḻikai* are added, it gives the birth of the month of *Kārttikai.*

When 1 day and 20 *Nāḻikai* are added, the month of *Mārkaḻi* is obtained.

When 1 day and 54 *Nāḻikai* are added, we get the month of *Tai.*

When 4 days and 7 *Nāḻikai* are added, we get the month of *Māci.*

When 5 days and 55 *Nāḻikai* are added, the final month of *Paṅkuni* is obtained.

In this list of months, *Āṉi*, *Āṭi* and *Āvaṇi* are not given as per the Tamil calendar.

The final verse of the *Kaṇita Nūl* describes the characteristics of an instrument that is used to measure one standard *nāḻikai*. One of the manuscripts in the *Kaṇakkatikāram* corpus also exactly repeats the measures of the instrument. The details of the instrument are given below: 'A vessel weighing 12 *palam* is taken. It should then be reduced to 10 *palam*, with a height of 6 *viral* and diameter of 12 *viral*. A golden needle weighing 32 *mā*

[122] *Kaṇita Nūl*, verse 78, 234.

with a length of 4 *viṟal* is then taken to make a hole in the base. The time taken for water in the vessel to pass through the hole is a *nāḻikai*.'[123]

The Not So Practical Problems

Let us now turn our attention to a particular set of problems that are not classified under any distinct section like land, gold, grain but are called general problems. These are generally assumed as recreational problems in the history of mathematics literature. But I would like to argue otherwise, and say the very idea of an innocent recreation in the context of problem solving in premodern mathematical cultures requires fundamental reorientation. In the context of premodern Tamil country, it requires an understanding of the historical and social context in which computational knowledge was in circulation. This is the objective of the next chapter; I will list the representative problems in this genre here, and discuss this issue briefly. This is because, understanding the historical context is important before we characterize these problems as recreational or expert problems: they beg the questions about who counted as an expert, why would they come up with these problems, and what the social nature of circulation of these problems was. In Chapter 3, we will have occasion to discuss the social context of the circulation of these problems involving the problems solving session in the schools and that of the household and the community in the village. But it is possible to argue that a common pool of such problems were created and came in circulation through this pedagogic traffic. Suffice here to mention that it is critical to question the historiographical characterization of a social and institutional culture of problem solving, where in the school seemed to have centrally anchored and sustained the culture, notwithstanding the idiom of the recreational in the tone and tenor of such problems.[124] The first set in the

[123] Prof. S. R. Sarma pointed me to the extensive presence of the time measuring vessels in the Sanskrit tradition and to certain physical collections of such clocks, documented in his Descriptive Catalogue of Astronomical Instruments, available at https://srsarma.in/catalogue.php. For his work on the subject, see S. R. Sarma, 'Setting up the Water Clock for Telling the Time of Marriage', In *Studies in the History of the Exact Sciences in Honour of David Pingree*, eds. Charles Burnett et al. (Leiden-Boston: Brill, 2004), 302–330.

[124] It would be appropriate here to mention that one of the reasons for my argument was substantiated during my field work in the villages of the Kaveri Delta area in Southeast Tamil

Kaṇakkatikāram which is of interest to us are those that involve familiar objects like fruits and animals, often accompanied by verses that sometimes state facts like the age of different animals. But other verses state techniques to count seeds inside fruits, like say in a jack fruit or a wood apple, which involved familiarity with a fact. For instance, in order to find the number of slices of fruit inside a jack fruit, one is supposed to count the number of spikes around the base stalk in the fruit. Once you know this fact, then the rest is computation. The verse says, 'count the number of spikes and multiply by eight, again by half.'[125] Certain other types involve computation of units of measures, but are oriented to test the memory skills of the student in the context of reduction of measures involving large numbers. Consider the problem where a farmer in the rich Cōla country sun-dried his precious paddy seeds, which a few sparrows polished off, without a single grain left. The farmer, who returned to see this, threw down his spade at them killing one of the birds. When he sliced the bird open, he found there were three paddy grains. How many birds would have eaten one *kalam* of paddy? The solution is straightforward wherein you convert *kalam* into *nāḻi* (96), reduce *nāḻi* to 14,400 individual grains, multiply it by 96 to give 13,82,400 which is to be divided by 3, the number of grains found in the bird, the quotient is 4,60,800 which will be the number of birds. Within the same type are the numerous horse problems that involve the multiple rule of three, again oriented to show skilful use of methods learnt. 'If the price of a horse which runs forward by ten feet, backward by 8 feet, 12 *poṉ*. Then what is the price of a horse which runs forward by six feet and runs backward by

Nadu as part of a project on Anthropology of Mathematics, where the few elders I met, who could recite some of the problems mentioned here happen to be also those who had gone to the traditional tinnai schools that survived well into the 1950s in this region. However, none of them could recite the procedure to solve such problems while they would mention just the final answer. But then again, during the emergent print culture in the late nineteenth century in the Tamil speaking region, several popular books in circulation also printed some of these problems along with assorted recipes for medicine, magic and longitude in life. Such a culture continued well into modern day Tamil speaking region, as a recent publication of collection of such problems testifies. See the popular publications authored by Dharmaraj Joseph who has compiled and modified such problems to the modern context. Some of his books are, Dharmaraj Joseph, *tāttā coṉṉā kaṇakkukaḷ* (Grandpa's Mathematical Puzzles), Narpavi Prasuram, Chennai, 2008. Joseph, *Iṉikum putir kaṇakkukaḷ* (The Sweet Mathematical Puzzles revealed in easy Tamil, Narpavi Prasuram, Chennai, 2008) and Joseph, *mūḷaikku ṭāṉik: putir kaṇakkukaḷ cey muṟaikaḷ* (Brain Stimulating Mathematical Puzzles), Narmada Pathippagam, Chennai, 2007.

[125] *Kaṇakkatikāram* (1783), verse 74, 114.

four?' This would involve the rule of five, already familiar to the student. There are numerous other variations of this kind which indicates the expression of a skill nurtured by the student or the *kaṇakkaṉ* himself, to display his virtuosity in computation.

But these are only fragments of such problems. There are others that involve much sophisticated computational skills, but the problems are always posed in the same tone, to excite and to listen to the prowess of the accomplished computational mind. The *Kaṇita Nūl* in fact has systematically collected one hundred problems of which fifty are in verse style, 25 in prose without exercises and the rest of the 25 accompanied by exercises in similar kind of problems.[126] This apart, the *Kaṇita Nūl*, as is mentioned in the previous chapter has devoted a separate section to the Gods, where each generic variety of such kinds of problems involving multiple proportion or linear equations *are* presented and solved. The Sarasvati Mahal's collected edition of *Kaṇakkatikāram*[127] has put together almost 200 problems of this kind and so does the *Āstāṉa Kōlākalam*. The classification of these problems that I have presented below are mine and this presentation is done with the aim to demonstrate variety in terms of techniques involved.

Cumulative Addition and Progression Techniques

Let me take one of the most typical problems in this variety. This particular problem is often repeated using different (quantities) numbers but using the same example in different manuscripts. A King once set up a beautiful garden in a town. There were 10 gateways to the garden. Once, he took an army of soldiers with him to the garden. When he reached the first gate, he stationed one-half of the soldiers there and took the rest to the second gate. There, he stationed one-half of the remaining soldiers and took the rest to the third and repeated the same till he reached the 10th gate. Then he entered the gate with the remaining men into the garden. When he was preparing to return, he found that there were ripe mangoes lying on the ground and took one for himself. Seeing this, the

126 *Kaṇita Nūl, Part II*, Chennai, 2005.
127 *Kaṇakkatikāram* (1998).

King's assistant took two. The man following the assistant three and the fourth man took four and this continued. When he reached the gates, the soldiers asked the King, 'Your Highness, everybody who followed you have got mangoes. What about us?' Hearing this, the King kept the mango that he had taken and ordered all the others to do the same. Then, he gave one mango each to every member of the army he took. The number of mangoes and the number of men accompanying the King were the same. Therefore, (a) how many people accompanied the King? (b) how many soldiers were each gate and at all the ten gates? (c) How many soldiers accompanied the King into the garden beyond the gates? and (d) How many mangoes did this number of people bring out of the garden?[128]In the original, the answer is immediately given in prose. Let me give the stated answer through the probable steps that would have yielded that answer. Since everybody who followed the King to the garden took one mango more than the previous person, starting from the King himself, we would get a series $1 + 2 + 3 + 4 + 5 + \ldots + n$. Now, if we take the number of soldiers stationed at the tenth gate to be one, then, the number of soldiers who followed the King would be $2^{10} = 1024n$. Now, this should be equal to $n (n + 1)/2$. Therefore, if

$1024 \times 2 = n + 1; n = 2048 - 1; n = 2047$. This will be the number of soldiers who actually followed the King into the garden and picked up the mangoes. Then, to get the total number of soldiers you again take $n + 2047$ and calculate the sum up to 2047, which is $(2047 \times 2048)/2 = 20,96,128$

Then, the number at the first gate = 20,96,128/2 = 10,48,064
Second gate, will be half of this, so, 10,48,064/2 = 5,24,032
Third gate, 5,24,032/2 = 2,62,016
Fourth gate, 2,62,016/2 = 1,31,008
Fifth gate, 1,31,008/2 = 65,504
Sixth gate, 65,504/2 = 32,752

128 For a variety of these kinds of problems, see *Kaṇakkatikāram* (1998), pp. 304–354. I have used the categories of modern techniques like recursion and matching problems rather than the conventional way in which such problems were recorded, which often involved the names of the objects in the context of problem solving, like mangoes, birds and pearls. The choice is to demonstrate the diversity in techniques present in the texts since in their originals they were written out continuously one after another, and often without any titles to such problems. Of course, this is a limitation given that we repeatedly caution ourselves not to use modern equations to represent problems from the past.

Seventh gate, 32,752/2 = 16,376
Eighth gate, 16,376/2 = 8,188
Ninth gate, 8,188/2 = 4,094
Tenth gate, 4,094/2 = 2,047

Therefore, the total number of soldiers would be 20 *laṭcattu* (lakhs) 96,128; the number of soldiers who went with the King into the garden and picked up the mangoes in a uniformly ascending fashion would be 2047 and the total number of mangoes will also be 20,96,128. There are several of these 'mango and the king' problems which all use the same method, which uses the sum of a series as a central element to the solution. However, in the answer to some problems[129] the number touches and goes beyond the unit *makākōṭi*.

In some other problems, different measuring units are put through the same method, but that which uses the sum of a series in fractions. There is also a commonly occurring sugarcane problem, 'if the 9 sections of one sugarcane are worth 9 *Kācu*, and if 9 persons eat the cane, how would each one of them pay for the cane in accordance with the section of the cane they ate?'

The method seems to be to calculate the sum up to 9 which is 45. So, the amount 9 *Kācu* is for 45 shares. For one share, it will be 1/45 × 9 = 1/5. So, the amount for the person who ate the last section of the cane = 1/5 × 9 = 1¾ +1/20. The amount for the person who ate the 8th section is 1/5 × 8 = 1½ + 1/10; likewise you calculate for all the nine sections of the cane. There are similar problems that deal with weights and volumes, which involve conversion of units into a basic unit and then computing the sum of the individual units involved. Thus we see how the common mathematical solution techniques used in the context of work are dressed up as problems, only seemingly for a popular consumption, but the method employed is the same. Ways of problem posing changed forms, not with the 'modern' intent of 'popularization' as scholars generally assume, but with a particular intent of establishing a professional virtuosity of the practitioner.

[129] The other similar problem of the same kind is the distribution of soldiers on different stairs of a temple tower in a particular fashion and asking for the number of soldiers in total and on each stair. These problems can be found in *Kaṇakkatikāram* (1998), pp. 304–360.

Residues of Fractions or Parts of Parts Problems

A King brought some lemons. He gave one-half to the courtesan, one-fourth to his brother, one-eighth to his wife, one-ninth to his son. Five lemons were left behind. How many lemons did he bring? The solution is given first (360) and then the computation at each stage. But the method is not stated explicitly. It could be as follows: If you take one out of four, there is 3; one out of eight, 7; one out of nine, 8, adding 3 + 7 + 8 gives 18, doubling 18, you get 36, and doubling the remaining 5, you get 10, now, multiplying 36 and 10, you get 360. Therefore, half of 360 = 180 lemons to the courtesan; one-fourth of 360 = 90 lemons to the brother; one-eighth of 360 = 45 lemons to the wife and one-ninth of 360 = 40 lemons to the son. The total of this adds up to 355 and 5 is the remainder.[130] A similar problem would explain the technique further.

One soldier had a few arrows in his kitty. He used 1/3rd of arrows on the opposite army; 1/4th on the chariots; 1/5th on elephants; one-sixth on the generals and 15 on the King. He was left with 6 arrows. How many arrows in total? The technique seems to be to compute the progressive sum up to 6: $(6 \times 7)/2 = 21$. Number of arrows on the King = 15 and the remainder is 6. Adding up all of these, that is 21 + 15 + 6 gives 42. Multiply by 10, you get 420. Now the respective number of arrows on the infantry, chariots elephants and the Generals will be 140, 105, 84, and 70. The total of these with the 15 on the King and the remainder 6 will give 420.

The other kinds of problems are those where while dividing a constant figure, the remainder increases in a constant fashion. For example, an old lady brought a few mangoes to sell. But the son of the King came and asked for one mango, which the lady refused. So, the brat snatched the mango and threw it away. When the old lady went to the King and complained, the King asked her for the number of mangoes she brought. She said, I don't know enough maths. But all I know is that, if I divided the total in terms of two, there will be one mango left.

[130] These problems are not strictly according to the classification of the editor of *Kaṇakkatikāram*, but cross over to other sections as well. However, for typical problems, one should see *Kaṇakkatikāram*, pp. 361–385. In *Kaṇita Nūl*, the last section devoted to the Gods, has seven problems and all of them can be taken as involving the techniques that characterize the problems discussed in this section. See *Kaṇita Nūl*, pp. 246–270.

If divided in terms of three, 2 left; in terms of four, 3 will be left; in terms of five, 4 will be left; in terms of six, 5 will be left and in terms of seven, nothing will be left. The answer is first given as 119. That is 119/2 = 59 + 1; 119/3 = 39 + 2; 119/4 = 29 + 3; 119/5 = 23 + 4; 119/6 = 19 + 5; and 119/7 = 17 and no remainder.

The other variation is the one when a figure is to be divided so that you always get a constant remainder. These problems are usually posed with a number of pearls to be divided in a particular order, so that you always get the remainder as one.

One *Ceṭṭiyār* once saved a few pearls and left it to be found by his sons after his death. When the first son divided the pearls in to two shares, there was one pearl left. The next one divided into three shares and one pearl was left. Likewise, till six shares, one was left. When it was divided into seven shares, nothing was left. The solution is given as 301. Because,

For 2 shares, 2 × 150 remainder 1
For three shares, 3 × 100 remainder 1
For four shares, 4 × 75 remainder 1
For five shares, 5 × 60 remainder 1
For six shares, 6 × 50 remainder 1
For seven shares, 7 × 43 and nothing left.

Matching Problems

This set of problems involves matching of either given quantities in a particular proportion to the number of objects so that both equal a particular number. For example, if a pumpkin costs 5 *Kācu*, brinjal costs 1 *Kācu* and bitter gourd costs ¼ *Kācu*, in what proportion will the total *Kācu* will also be 100 and the total number of the object be 100 as well? Again, the solution is given first without any explanation. That is, 15 pumpkins would cost 75 *Kācu*; 5 brinjals would cost 1 × 5 = 5 *Kācu*; and 80 bittergourds would cost 80 × ¼ = 20; therefore both the number of vegetables and the total *Kācu* will be 100 each. There are several problems of the same kind that involve volumetric measures and linear measures. The examples are often in terms of matching the number of three different animals to their respective prices in the market or matching clothes of various measures so that the total length and the number of different clothes equal 100.[131]

Exhaustion Problems

These problems are plenty in number and all of them are similar in form and usually involve the example of offering flowers from a temple pond to the Lord *Kaṇapati* in successive steps according to a given order so that there will be no flowers left at the end. This helps one compute quantities in such a way that one exhausts the entire sum. For example, let me state the following problem from the *Kaṇita Nūl*, which is very similar to those in *Kaṇakkatikāram*.[132] A priest brought a certain number of flowers to offer three *Kaṇapati* temples. When he reached the first temple, he poured water on the flowers. The number of flowers tripled. After offering them to the first *Kaṇapati*, he poured water again and the number multiplied by five times. After offering them to the second *Kaṇapati*, he poured water again and the number multiplied by 7 times. The number at the end was the same as offered to the second *Kaṇapati*. Then what is the number of flowers originally brought by the priest and what is the number of flowers he originally offered to each *Kaṇapati*?

The flowers,

Multiplied 3 times when poured water for the first time
Multiplied 5 times when poured water for the second time
Multiplied 7 times when poured water for the third time

The given method of solution goes like this. Take the primary number 1. Multiply the last said 7 with the second said 5 = 35:

Multiply this with the first said 3: $35 \times 3 = 105$.

[131] For these few problems and for the interesting examples used, see *Kaṇakkatikāram* (1998), pp. 386–392.

[132] These are familiarly called the 'Flower Problems' since all of them involve the example of offering flowers to the Lord *Kaṇapati*, also called the Lord *Vicṉēsvaran*. There are also other examples using the Goddess Sarasvati which often has some interesting twists in the problems, like if she assumes five forms and if those will have to be accommodated in the number of flowers in the pond without leaving any flower unoccupied.

Now, add $1 + 7 + 3 + 35 = 43$. This will be the original number of flowers brought by the priest. Because,

1. $43 \times 3 = 129$ and $129 - 105 = 24$
2. $24 \times 5 = 120$ and $120 - 105 = 15$
3. $15 \times 7 = 105$ and $105 - 105 = 0$

Distribution Problems and Magic Squares

These problems are very similar to the ones in the parts of parts or residues. Here, given a particular number of objects, it has to be equally divided or distributed uniformly into particular number of shares. There are several variations in these problems. Let me just illustrate a problem that uses magic square to find solution.[133] Once a *Ceṭṭiyār* took some pearls to the King. When the King asked for the cost, the *Ceṭṭi* said that the first one costs 1 *paṇam*, the second 2, the third 3, and so on so that, the 25th pearl costs 25 *paṇam*. The King says, I have 5 wives and distribute the pearls among them so that the number of pearls equals their cost as well. The solution given in the original is that the sum of numbers up to 25 using the progression is 325. Therefore, for the first share you give four pearls for 65 *paṇams* and proceed accordingly for the rest. A magic square is given for the same problem:

1	1	1	1	1	= 5
5	9	13	17	21	
25	4	8	12	16	
20	24	3	7	11	
15	19	23	2	6	
10	14	18	22	1	

That is for the first share, he will have to give the 5th pearl, the 9th, the 13th, the 17th, and the 21st, adding each of them will give 65. For the

[133] These problems are also typically found in all the texts and in almost all the variations of the problems of this section. The magic squares, however, can be found in *Kaṇakkatikāram* (1998), pp. 453–476.

second share, he will have to give the 25th, the 4th, and so on as in the square. Likewise, he will have to distribute the pearls so that the total will always be equal to 65 for each share. Followed by this is a whole series of problems that involve the computation of total sums given the various proportions of objects like pearls and their costs.

Of course, such problems have travelled all over the world and have become identified in other regions as the 'horse problem' or the 'hundred fowls' problem (like the one in the exhaustion problem section mentioned above).[134] It should not be surprising that in the same culture, two sets of practitioners could become familiar with a certain set of problems and proceed to engage with them differently. To adduce priority in the name of translation then subverts the social context of their practice. It prevents the possibility to engage with the localized character of translations despite the caste hierarchy, which limited communication. That two people of different castes could not sit together and contemplate ways of solving a problem, or go through the grind of the *Eṇcuvaṭi* together, is a fact of caste-based society. The mathematical knowledge within this culture of segregation can thus be engaged through the realm of practices. Each community would construct its own norms and virtues that would seep into their occupational practice as if inherited. That a pool of such problems could be made available for a public beyond the practitioners is pertinent to our discussion to situate transmission amidst hierarchies and not merely to look for the algebraic or the geometrical in premodern mathematical cultures.

This chapter has attempted to provide an overarching survey of the different kinds of sources available for a social history of mathematics. It has foregrounded the practitioner and his application of mathematical skills. It has also introduced the reader to the primary sources for such a history of mathematical practice in precolonial Tamil Nadu. In the following chapter, let us enter this practitioner's world to examine it in more detail.

[134] For historically pointing out this genre of the much mislabeled problems, see Jens Høyrup, 'The Sub-Scientific Heritage in "abbaco" Mathematics: Quasi-Algebra and Other Queer Species', First Part, *L'Educatizione Matematica*, XXII, Serie 7, Vol. 3, p. 35. http://akira.ruc.dk/~jensh/Publications/2001%7Bh%7D_Lasciti%20sotto-scientifici_S.pdf, Accessed January 5, 2015. See also, Jens Høyrup, 'Mathematics, Recreational and Practical', *Encyclopedia of the History of Science, Technology, and Medicine in Non-western Cultures*, Vol. 2, ed. Helaine Selin (New York: Springer Verlag, 2013): 1352–1356.

II
Mathematics of the Practitioner

The main task of the social historian of mathematics is to historically ground styles of mathematical reasoning, which are usually considered context free. The resources available for the historian to undertake this task from within the mathematical texts are usually sparse. Rarely do such texts reveal the social context that enabled the systematization of computational knowledge. Christopher Cullen notes that historians of mathematics keep looking for the 'mathematician' in cultures where such a socially distinct identity had no place, or for 'mathematical equations' in texts that did not follow such logic. In both instances, the questions asked by historians of mathematics have merely served as vectors of translation. For example, 'something similar to what could be equations' has constantly compelled the translation of 'mathematical information into modern symbolic notation'. Such translation may have helped historians find familiarity in the mathematical techniques, but it has robbed the techniques of their uniqueness.[1]

A prosopographical approach has been proposed as a possible way to relate texts to their historical contexts. This would allow us to look for skilled communities of practitioners, whose occupational and social profile could render the mathematical engagement historical.[2] But in the case of these Tamil mathematical texts under discussion the information available on the authors both within and outside the texts is too little to undertake such an exercise. The other possibility could be to identify layers of orientation of the mathematical structure of such texts which could help us identify contemporaneous social institutions and communities of

[1] Christopher Cullen, 'People and Numbers in Early Imperial China', *The Oxford Handbook of the History of Mathematics*, eds. Eleanor Robson et al. (New York: Oxford University Press, 2009), 591–592. One inspiring work that circumvents this problem of representation by staying close to the record which actually enables the historian to look at critical issues such as means of justification employed in problem solving can be found in Annette Imhausen, *Mathematical in Ancient Egypt: A Contextual History* (Princeton and Oxford: Princeton University Press, 2016).

[2] Ibid.

Mathematics and Society. Senthil Babu D., Oxford University Press. © Oxford University Press India 2022.
DOI: 10.1093/oso/9788194831600.003.0003

practitioners upon whom certain historical information is available. The context of work of the practitioner in the social hierarchy of production and distribution provides us with the space to explore the communication and systematization of mathematical skills. Thus we might begin by acknowledging that the orientation of specialized knowledge was conditioned by the social hierarchies under which such knowledge circulated. As we saw, one of the striking features of orientation of the three texts (*Kaṇakkatikāram, Kaṇita Nūl,* and the *Āstāṉa Kōlākalam*) is the scheme of classification they use to classify the computational field. Computation rules are not organized in terms of the types of rules to be employed to deal with the requirements of the computational context, but in terms of the objects involved in computation—Land, Grain, Rice, Gold, Stone, Wages, and so on. Computation rules are object centred and not classified by mathematical operation, such as rules for addition, subtraction, division, multiplication, squaring, and cubing. This distinct mode of classification points to a definite orientation to practice of particular occupational groups, but of course, only to be generalized as a scheme that someone has to learn in that social context of the Tamil region in the seventeenth and eighteenth centuries. In this chapter, I will show how these three texts inform two spheres of knowledge transmission—that of apprenticeship, wherein the work of practitioners was organized towards learning on the job, and in the *tiṇṇai* school.[3]

Orientation: Practical and Beyond

The *Kaṇakkatikāram*, *Kaṇita Nūl,* and the *Āstāṉa Kōlākalam* follow a scheme of classification of the computational arena that indicates the normative techniques employed to solve problems arising out of situations where in objects need to be measured, counted, and assessed. But is this merely a function of the textual organization or is it a schema that makes ready association with the work of the practitioner? It is important

[3] Even though the practice of apprenticeship was central to craft and artisanal work, not much discussed in these texts, the central figure of the revenue accountant's job involved a phase of apprenticeship, after passing through the elementary training in the tinnai school, along with every other students, the dynamics of which will be discussed in the next chapter on the curriculum and pedagogy of these schools.

to discern the practitioner to make sense of the orientation of the computational methods and problems presented in these texts. Measuring land, weighing gold, computing wages, measuring and distributing produce, estimating and computing time constitute the orientation of all three texts. Delineation of measures and their conversions and all kinds of problems involving them were subsumed within these sections. Problem situations determined the classification of the computational field. I will briefly point out typical problem situations using the 1783 manuscript of *Kaṇakkatikāram* to be able to identify the different actors involved in such situations—the people present in contexts who were involved in activities that were mathematical.

The titles of the sections themselves reveal how close the problem situations were rooted in the economic and social life of that society. They contain in them activities of different practitioners engaged in the production, distribution, and regulation of resources in the community. This chapter will try to argue that the mathematical practice of the practitioners in this tradition was grounded in political economy of resource distribution and remained central to that social order. It also points out how the canonical tradition's practices were distant from these transactions, and hence raise the question about the character of abstraction in mathematization in precolonial Tamil country by situating it in social segregation and fragmentation, without losing sight of how the exercising of authority conditioned modes of abstraction and generalization, through the particular occupational and social location of the different practitioners, be it the village accountant or the Brahmin astronomer.

In the *Kaṇakkatikāram's* section dealing with Land, there are thirty verses (77–107)[4] that deal with practical mensuration involving land, where the measuring rod is constantly present. The person who did the measurement was inevitably of a lower caste, one who would do the manual work. But the problems are addressed not to him, but to the accountant, who would be of a higher caste and who would do the mental computation based on the measurements.

In the next section on Gold, the first nineteen verses (108–127) deal with persons who deal with gold—assessing the purity of gold and selling

[4] *Kaṇakkatikāram*, eds. P. Subramaniam and K. Satyabama (Chennai: Institute of Asian Studies, 2007), 119–162. Hereafter *Kaṇakkatikāram* (1783).

it. In the next fourteen verses (128–142), we see problem situations where gold assumes the form of money and brings in cultivators as sharecroppers and tax payers, wage workers ploughing the land and other manual labourers, persons who had to share profit in proportion to income, and in a couple of problems, even salaried workers who receive money from the treasury.[5] Following this, there are twelve verses (143–155) in the section dealing with measuring produce, primarily rice. In problems that deal with the conversion of paddy into rice, the cultivator is constantly present trying to exchange rice with money using various units of capacity measures. But the interesting personality in this section is the person who actually pounds rice in a 'rule of three' type of problem about calculating how many breaths, in relation to the number of times pounded, would yield how much rice.[6] Verses 156 to 162 deal with problems of the stone mason carving out pillars and grinding stones.[7] Verses 163 to 166 bring up the job of the water regulator, or the person in charge of irrigating land from the tank using different number of sluices and the time it takes to do so.[8]

The next set of verses (167–198) deal with fractions. They present problems involving land and grain, involving proportions but they bring up multiple personalities—the agricultural labourer once more (except that here, his wages are in fractional quantities and land is measured in fractions), creditors involved in land-related transactions, the labourer who carries grains, the water lifter, the person who deals with commodities like oil, ghee, and milk, people of two settlements betting on a fund, people paying tributes, the money lender, the conch maker, the customs duty collector, the courier, the singer, the dancer, the person who assesses productivity of land, and the livestock trader—and even the gambler.[9] Almost all of the problems in these thirty-odd verses involve the problem of proportions using the rule of three, five, and seven. This particular manuscript of *Kaṇakkatikāram* has eight more verses and a few more problems presented in prose that are often classified as general

[5] *Kaṇakkatikāram* (1783), 164–225.
[6] Ibid., pp. 226–252.
[7] Ibid., pp. 253–264.
[8] Ibid., pp. 264–271.
[9] Ibid., pp. 271–336.

problems, about which we will discuss more in detail in the final section of this chapter.

It is interesting that a single mathematical text could bring in almost all actors involved in the economic life of the seventeenth- and eighteenth-century Tamil region through spheres of transaction that entailed measuring and counting. The carpenter making standard-sized planks from timber and the weaver dyeing clothes of particular strengths do not appear in this particular manuscript, but they do appear in the *Kaṇita Nūl*. Another interesting aspect in these texts is that the computations dealt with real world transactions in relation to land and its produce, which constitute the dominant concern; the world of the merchant or the trader is relatively less represented. The mathematics of the world of the merchant largely came under the rubric of 'general problems' or *potu kaṇakku*, or what I would argue has been misleadingly labelled 'recreational mathematics' in the last section of this chapter. I should mention at the outset that this is not 'commercial arithmetic', a common enough assumption for any kind that does not deal with the astronomical, in the Indian history of mathematics. If all the above economic actors were engaged in activities that involved computational moments as part of their working lives, can they be entitled to being called numerate?

Eighteenth-century Tamil society denied access to institutional education to the labouring caste groups with only the landed and the artisanal castes gaining access to what was called the *tiṇṇai* school, as we will see in the next chapter. But the *veṭṭiyāṉ*, who belonged to the untouchable and physically segregated caste was the person who physically measured land in the contemporary revenue administration hierarchy. Did he not know-how to count what he was measuring, holding the measuring rod, walking up and down tracts of land? Or was it only the person who he was reporting to, the village accountant, the immediate superior authority who would be numerate? Did the worker who measured grains not know how to deal with the measuring vessels and the counts that they yielded? Did not the water regulator, the *nīrkkāraṉ* (sometimes called the *kampukaṭṭi*), who regulated tank-based irrigation know how to keep time and assess extent of land in numbers? Would they have not learnt from within the family or on the job, just as the *kaṇakkuppiḷḷai* did, to cultivate their ways with numbers? What would constitute 'numeracy' in such a context, especially when modes of learning were in an oral environment and writing was only one instant in the learning process in that period? Or still further, how might we understand the notion of apprenticeship, which concerns itself with transmission of knowledge in relation to only certain trades and professions, or particular kinds of work?

How did these subaltern life worlds shape contemporary knowledge production, be it that of the local practitioner or of the dignified tradition? Could context-free knowledge emerge in a socially fractured society? To raise such a question is to propose that the history of knowledge in caste societies will have to reorient their central concerns towards the relationship between the mind and the hand in knowledge production in fundamental ways. The history of the practitioner's knowledge forms is but a beginning in this direction.

The Accountant as the Practitioner

The main actor, who stands above all the others, was the *kaṇakkuppiḷḷai*, or the accountant, the master calculator in the early modern Tamil country. He enumerated, assessed, and valued everyone's labour and produce, and fixed shares and entitlements, as an extension of distant state authority in the locality. He observed, comprehended, and provided a computational language to what others practised. The institution and the persona of the *kaṇakkuppiḷḷai*—variously called as the accountant, the scribe, or the *karaṇam*—have attracted much historical attention in recent times. While one stream has demanded of him a sense of history in the early modern period,[10] the other has characterized him as the quintessential knowledge intermediary during the colonial encounter in the latter half of the eighteenth century.[11] In the unfolding of eternal tension between the local and the universal in historical terrain, the *Kaṇakkaṉ's* literary prowess or his skill set has often been abstracted out of his political function in the local society—the powerful agent who sustained

[10] V. Narayana Rao, David Shulman, and Sanjay Subrahmanyam, *Textures of Time: Writing History in South India 1600–1800* (Delhi: Permanent Black, 2001).

[11] Phillip B. Wagoner, 'Precolonial Intellectuals and the Production of Colonial Knowledge', *Comparative Studies in Society and History* 45, no. 4 (2003): 783–814; C. A. Bayly, *Empire and Information: Political Intelligence and Social Communication in North India, 1780–1880* (Cambridge: Cambridge University Press, 1999).

the status quo and subsisted out of it, through conscious ways of cultivating his skills in the mnemonic arts, traversing the world of letters and numbers. Bhavani Raman's recent work *Document Raj* has unravelled this world of the *Kaṇakkaṉ* in the context of the early modern Tamil country.[12] In line with the subcontinental feature of the scribal office operating under the 'caste-kin formation', she emphasizes the centrality that the *Kaṇakkaṉ* held in the financial and record keeping aspects of administration in precolonial South India from the sixteenth century onwards.

The scribal office could be both delegated as well as hereditary. His primary job was to fix and collect revenue in return for entitlements to the revenue of a village or a cluster, or revenue shares in cash or grain or rent-free lands. But this differed with regions. In certain areas, they were entitled to revenue shares, while in certain others, they could be completely dependent on the inhabitants. But such rights were not in perpetuity and were subject to renewal, which meant competition among scribal families. This could also have meant that their skills and competence were often tested, compelled to improve skills, proficiency, and reputation. Scribes operated as agents of kings and influential households who tried to monopolize credit and fiscal networks, which made them very central to the expansion of fiscal domains to particular clusters in the eighteenth century. This enabled them to expand and consolidate their position in particular territories. For example, she informs us of the presence of sixty-six households of *Kaṇakkaṉ* scribes living in twenty-seven villages in the *jaghire* of Chingleput alone.[13] Their continuous mobility and accompanying fortunes inspired them to claim not just the status of a *jāti* but also normative claims to substantiate it through the recording of genealogical narratives. For example, a text found in Mackenzie's collection narrates the story of how the *Karuṇīkars* or the accountants came to settle in the Tamil region. It should be noted that our own authors, Karuvūr Nañcaiyaṉ of *Kaṇita Nūl* and Nāvili Perumāḷ of *Āstāṉa Kōlākalam*, ascribe their lineage to this *Karuṇīkar* clan. Therefore, the *Kaṇakkaṉ* effectively controlled and decided shares in produce, inheritance, land

[12] Bhavani Raman, *Document Raj: Writing and Scribes in Early Colonial South India* (Chicago: University of Chicago Press, 2012). I draw upon her work in this section to describe the social and occupational profile of the *Kaṇakkaṉ* in pre-colonial Tamil region.

[13] Ibid., pp. 29–33.

assessments, presided over local affairs and contracts, and assumed an important voice of evidence in matters of disputes.

The locality accounts of the Chingleput area published recently also provide us with a glimpse into this world of revenue assessment and collection.[14] These locality accounts were the result of a survey undertaken in Chingleput *jagir* in the years 1740–43 by the British company servant, Thomas Barnard, to assess the potential of revenue in this area. One of the first systematic surveys undertaken, this uses the *Kaṇakkaṉ*'s local administrative knowledge to delineate households in terms of their role in agrarian production and services rendered. Among several striking features of this corpus of information, what is of relevance to us is the overwhelming presence of the act of measuring, in the economic life of the locality and the glimpses it provides about the inner world of the *Kaṇakkaṉ*'s world of computation. From the various types of registers that he maintained, according to the demands of the annual revenue assessment, we can see how the *Kaṇakkaṉ*'s primary responsibility was to keep counting, measuring and marking land and its produce on the one hand and collecting part of produce as taxes and wages, on the other hand. Every year, he measured and marked the boundaries of the various types of village land and classified them in terms of boundaries and units in areas. He took stock of the land occupied by households, and the extent of land present in the form of water bodies, temples, wasteland, grazing land, houses, and their backyards and public roads. Every year he estimated the produce of different land parcels, assessed the actual production, divided the production in terms of rights and entitlements of the inhabitants, allocated shares to the producers, to the temple, to the families of the service caste, including for himself, divided quantities of produce among shareholders, took parts of produce as taxes and paid wages for labourers at the threshing floor. The act of measuring at the threshing floor—overseen by the *Kaṇakkaṉ*, but physically done by the *Veṭṭiyāṉ* or the *Tukkiri*—was hardly a happy place where everyone was content with

[14] M. D. Srinivas, T. G. Paramasivam, and T. Pushkala, *Thirupporur and Vadakkuppattu: Eighteenth Century Locality Accounts* (Chennai: Centre for Policy Studies, 2001). See also the unpublished doctoral dissertation of T. Pushkala who has reconstructed the accounts for a different set of localities using the same corpus, T. Pushkala, '*Cenkaṟpaṭṭu āvaṇaṅkaḷ – Camūkap Poruḷātāram*' (PhD Diss., Department of Manuscript Studies, Tamil University, Thanjavur, 1997).

the way the measurement was done. The grain heap in the measuring vessel, or the arbitrary fixing of the value of the *kalam*, *marakkāl* and the *paṭi* in terms of money, or the unit called *varākaṉ*, were not transparent processes of computation for the people involved, and incited discontent and anger. It was all about how many *kāṇi* of land, under whose control yielded how many *kalams* of grains and who got how many *marakkāls* and *paṭis* in terms of either assigned rights or established entitlements. The field deductions of shares on a routine basis kept the relation of proportions between units of measures very central to the *Kaṇakkaṉ's* job: a field of proportions that was pervaded with conceit and hatred, often for those who were receiving grains in assigned values.

In the year 1764, for the village Tirupporur, in the *Kaṇakkaṉ's vakai ēṭu*, note the grain produce from the revenue paying lands (*vārappaṟṟu*) and the grain produce from the revenue assigned lands (*maṇiyam*): for 65 *kāṇis* of Paddy, the produce was 848 *kalams*, 8 *marakkāl* and 5 *paṭis* of paddy and likewise for all other grains produced. So for the total of 81 and a half *kāṇi* of land, the total produce was 1160 *kalams*, 11 *marakkāl*, and 2 *paṭi* of all grains produced in that year. Then, the *Kaṇakkaṉ* began the business of deductions. First, were amounts to be deducted from the revenue assigned land: for a produce of 10 *kalams* and 8 *marakkāls*, the manual workers received a (*maṇiyam*) share at the rate of 8 *marakkāls* per *kalam*. Likewise, a whole series of deductions for each *maṇiyam* holder, followed by deductions for the service caste members were done in terms of rate of grain per unit of land. Then the *Kaṇakkaṉ* calculated value of the grain sale: For paddy at the rate of 3 *kalams* and 6 *marakkāls* for one *varākaṉ* (unit of money), 269 *kalams*, 1 *marakkāl*, and 3 *paṭis* of paddy was 76 *varākaṉ*, 32 *paṇam*, and 50 *kācu* and so on for each grain. Finally he collected cash revenue from the village merchants. Then the final revenue was calculated (*arutikkatan*), the share for the state and public works allocated, and his signature attested in the *vakai ēṭu*.[15]

This brief glimpse into the work of the *Kaṇakkaṉ* shows how the *Kaṇakkaṉ* was a settlement's revenue accountant whose 'skills of assessment, his ability to convert several disparate objects in to a single value' and his writing skills was 'more than a functional mastery over techniques of storage; it was a skill connected to the recognition of patterns

[15] Ibid., pp. 117–122.

and calibration of assessment through the dexterous conversion of matter and value. The *Kaṇakkaṉ* was a living concordance'.[16] A *Kaṇakkaṉ* cultivated and nurtured his skill through family-based apprenticeship, centred around kinship, and usually started off his career as an unpaid apprentice to relatives, where he laboured hard to augment his skills through the mnemonic mode, until he became the proficient master of computation. He was a political figure, invested with authority to measure, assess, and authorize and aligned with the landed upper caste elite of the settlement in maintaining registers of distribution of value to the labour of the different economic actors in the settlement.[17]

As the historian Sivasubramanian has recorded, the *Kaṇakkaṉ*'s job and reputation has identified the act of computation with certain virtues as well as the most vicious qualities.[18] It is very common among the Tamil-speaking public to identify the computational act, or the mathematical mind, as a manipulative one: a cunning mind that constantly schemes, plots, and destroys. Central to this perception is also the dislike the *Kaṇakkaṉ* incited by his role in aid of his master, the administration, or the rich landlord, the Zamindar, a common theme carried in popular culture. Consider the rather harsh usage that Sivasubramanian records from the people: *Kaṇakkaṉ cettāl piṇam, Kaṇakkaṉ āttāḷ cettāl maṇam* which means that if the *Kaṇakkaṉ* dies, it is just a matter of a corpse, but if his mother dies, then it is an occasion. If the *Kaṇakkaṉ* dies, people are relieved that it is just a matter of burial and get done with it, but if his mother dies then everyone has to be present so that they do not upset the

[16] Raman, *Document Raj*, 61.

[17] It is interesting that in the literature on scribal practices in the history of mathematics, the computational virtues of the accountant are often discussed in tandem with the kind of problems his job and training would involve, and only rarely the political implications of his practice, which is appropriately termed as 'numerate justice' by Eleanor Robson in the case of old Babylonian scribes. She presents the case of the scribe, Girini-isag criticizing his junior colleague Enki-manshum: 'You wrote a tablet, but you cannot grasp its meaning. You wrote a letter, but that is the limit for you! Go to divide a plot, and you are not able to divide the plot; go to apportion a field, and you cannot even hold the tape and rod properly; the field pegs you are unable to place; you cannot figure out its shape, so that when wronged men have a quarrel you are not able to bring peace but you allow brother to attack brother. Among the scribes you (alone) are unfit for the clay. What are you fit for? Can anybody tell us?', cited in Eleanor Robson, 'Mathematics, Metrology, and Professional Numeracy', *The Babylonian World* (2012): 418, doi:10.4324/9780203946237.CH29. But as we show here, such virtuosity was not always received in the same spirit by the subjects who had to be at the receiving end of his calculations.

[18] A. Sivasubramanian, *Aṭittaḷa Makkaḷ Varalāṟu* (Chennai: Makkal Veliyeedu, 2002). PAGE No?

Kaṇakkaṉ, making it a compulsory occasion. This sentiment resonates with another saying Sivasubramanian records that says if the *Kaṇakkaṉ* is upset with you, your land will also be upset. That is to say it is up to the *Kaṇakkaṉ* to define the boundary of your land and if you upset him he will mess with your land.[19] The hereditary institution of the *Kaṇakkaṉ* was abolished as recently as 1980. Despite having been the centre of revenue administration over several centuries and under different regimes and considering how hated he was all around, it is surprising that there are very few sources of documentation in the contemporary period even in Tamil.[20]

Kaṇakkatikāram texts need to be situated against this canvas. While the *Kaṇakkaṉ* could be our mathematical practitioner, he was also someone who used his specialized knowledge for very definite political purposes, in favour of the powerful. The orientation of the methods and problems in these texts then takes us to the heart of the *Kaṇakkaṉ's* computational practice. Before we discuss that, there are several places where one could find evidence to show that these texts were addressed to those students who took to specialist training after completing their elementary studies at the *tiṇṇai* school. I should remind the reader about how the two manuscripts of *Kaṇakkatikāram* refer to themselves as students' copies. The 1783 manuscript of *Kaṇakkatikāram* was used by four students, Gopala Naicken, Velayutham Pillai, Chinnama Naicken, and Thandavarayan, even though it was owned by Subramanyan and probably involved another person, Muthukkaruppan Pillai, who could have been another student or another scribe.[21] The EFEO (Pondicherry) manuscript, for instance, was copied in the 1860s from a printed book of *Kaṇakkatikāram*[22] by Arumuga Mudaliar, son of the famous Tamil pandit and reputed

[19] *Kaṇakkaṉ Vaḻakkāṟukaḷ* in ibid., pp. 98–99.

[20] M. Rajendiran, *Vaṭakarai – Oru Vamcattiṉ Varalāṟu* (Vandavasi: Agani Veliyidu, 2014). This novel published recently is probably one of the very few accounts on the changing roles and fortunes of people working in revenue administration from the nineteenth century till about the mid twentieth century. It is interesting that the author himself was part of the munsif family and went on to become an IAS officer and thought it necessary to record the history of his own family, as the title suggests.

[21] *Kaṇakkatikāram* (1783), 2.

[22] *Kaṇakkatikāram* EFEO – 0541, Leaf-5, Ecole Francaise d'Extreme Orient Collection, Pondicherry.

Teacher, Vedagiri Mudaliar.[23] It is clear that *Kaṇakkatikāram* was much in demand among teachers who took students after they graduated from the *tiṉṉai* schools and trained them in the art of computation. In fact, it could be reasoned that this genre of texts gained much credence among teachers probably from the eighteenth century onwards and continued to be in demand and active circulation well into the nineteenth century. The famous poet and scholar Vedanayakam Sastri copied a version of *Āstāṉa Kōlākalam* in the year 1807, probably with an intention to work on it; this indicates how these texts were circulating among reputed teachers.[24] Kāri Nāyaṉār, Karuvūr Nañcaiyaṉ, and Kūṭal Nāvili Perumāḷ, the authors of the texts, could have come from the *Kaṇakkaṉ* caste, and probably composed these texts with an aim to train potential *Kaṇakkaṉ* students.

But as we shall argue further, the variations and the character of certain manuscripts point us in a direction where the arts of computation of the *Kaṇakkaṉ* transcended their caste-kin network and came to be used by teachers who trained students in a kind of school, where one studied to pursue a career in accounting (what is called in Tamil generically as *kaṇakku eḻuta pōvatu*),[25] just as certain students after elementary training in the *tiṉṉai* school would decide to pursue studies in Tamil literature or grammar under specialized teachers. While this indicates the changing nature and relevance of the arts of computation over the eighteenth century, we notice how certain *Kaṇakkaṉs*, either as reputed accountants supervising their junior apprentices or as reputed teachers rewrote and revised these texts to suit their requirements.[26] The Guntur copy

[23] Vedagiri Mudaliar was a reputed Tamil Pandit, teacher who lived in the nineteenth century edited and wrote commentary for several Tamil texts. See M. S. Sampanthan, *Accum Patippum* (Chennai: Manivasakar Pathippagam, 1997).

[24] Titled *Kaṇakkuppustakam*, a manuscript is stored in the Collection of Private Papers of Vetanayakam Sastri at the Archives of the United Theological College, Bangalore. I say possibly intended because he completely reorganized the other most prevalent text of the times, the *Eṇcuvaṭi*, in line with changing times in the year 1807. We will discuss his work in Chapter 4.

[25] Literally this would mean to go writing accounts. As a saying this meant to go get trained in the job of becoming a *kaṇakkuppiḷḷai*. One popular reference is how the great Tamil scholar U. V. Swaminatha Iyer himself, after completing his *tiṉṉai* school in his own village, went to write accounts for a while before choosing to join his Tamil scholar-teacher, which determined his lifelong work and scholarship. See U. V. Swaminatha Iyer, *Eṉ Carittiram* (Chennai: U. V. Swaminatha Aiyar Library, 1990).

[26] This is particularly substantiated by Suryabooban's *Kaṇakkatikāram*. Except for a few initial verses on mensuration and conversion of measures, he devotes much of his attention to the

of *Āstāṉa Kōlākalam* belonging to V. Sankarappanar of Guntur in the Andhra region is remarkable on two counts:

(a) its thoroughly colloquial prose commentary which sounds as if the text was copied as the teacher was teaching, like notes from the classroom;
(b) its constant reference to the student to become a better *Kaṇakkaṉ*, encouraging to become proficient, and how following his instructions and methods, the student will definitely get there:

> Like Avvaiyar said, Numbers and Letters are like eyes, and like the saying, 'There are many ornaments but there is only one Gold', *Eṇcuvaṭi* is the source book of all computations. There are some who forget their *Eṇcuvaṭis* as soon as leaving school and take to writing accounts and face trouble. There are others who could tell solutions to any problem posed by the proficient, without any hesitation. Therefore, if you learn this concise text, no matter who the proficient testing you, you will gain reputation and shine in an assembly of accountants (*Kaṇakkuppiḷḷais*).[27]

In fact, in the rest of the text the commentary takes this task to heart and keeps rendering the *Eṇcuvaṭi* relevant to the demands of the job of the accountant, while at each instance, invoking the necessity to shine and gain reputation, but which comes only along with the ability to compute, correctly. In order to aid the student in the task, the commentator in this version goes at length to elaborate upon various techniques to find squares of both whole numbers and fractions, before he actually demonstrates how land area is to be computed. While introducing such techniques, he delineates categories of multiplication to arrive at squares and draws parallels with 'the poet who learns his techniques of composition

general problems, even versifying problems and procedure to some of the generic problems. See *Suryabooban Kaṇakkatikāram*, ed. Satyabama Kamesvaran (Thanjavur: Sarasvathi Mahal Library, 2007).

[27] Translation mine. See *Āstāṉa Kōlākalam*, ed. Satyabama Kamesvaran (Thanjavur: Sarasvati Mahal Library, 2004), 27. This is a collected edition of several other *Āstāṉa Kōlākalam* manuscripts in the same library but the source manuscript is R. No. 930, which was written for Sankarappanar of Guntur. Hereafter, this edition will be referred as *Āstāṉa Kōlākalam* (Guntur).

and identification of metre in poetry by learning texts like Tivākaram, it is also possible to solve any problem if one identifies the type of multiplication to be done'. Here then, he introduces certain mnemonic verses that will help identify the type of multiplication to be done. For instance, for squaring whole numbers,

nūṟuṭaṉ nūṟai māṟa nuvaṉṟiṭum nūṟuk kētāṉ
kūṟiya tāṉa mūṉṟāyk koṇṭiru varaikkum
āṟiṉil oṉṟu nīkka aintumuṉ tokaiyai māṟit
tēṟiya aintu tāṉam ceppiṭil kuḻiya tāmē

'If asked what is the *kuḻi* for 100 and 100, 100 × 100 = 10000. The *tāṉam* (place) for this is as follows: the place for 100: 1-10-100, therefore 3. The place for the other 100 is 3. Removing one place from the total 6 will give 5 and if you run this from 1 to 5 places: 1-10-100-1000-10000. Therefore the *kuḻi* for 100 and 100 is 10000'.[28]

This is fairly simple for similar kind of numbers, like 20 and 20 or 400 and 400, which he categorizes by the term *vittēṟu ilakkam*. If the numbers aren't similar like 400 and 6000, he calls them *māṟupākam* and enumerates techniques to find squares by identifying their places and running them with their products. As this gets complicated in the case of fractions (called *cilvāṉam*), he enumerates a table for identifying the *iṉam* (meaning, kind or in the arithmetic sense, multiples in terms of 10) of each standard fraction starting from *muntiri* to *mukkāl* (1/320 up to ¾) and demonstrates how to use this table in the context of multiplication of fractions and whole numbers, and then fractions with fractions.

This fairly elaborate section on multiplication trained the student in simple multiplication once he understood what multiples or *iṉam* were involved, a process assisted by the mental recall of tables such that 'whichever be the type, at that instant if you mentally recall or identify its equivalent place in the table and compute, the fellow accountants that you work with will hang their tongues in wonder'.[29] This entire exercise to constantly identify base-factors was not to indulge in the treatment

[28] Translation mine, ibid., pp. 29–30.
[29] Ibid., p. 43.

of numbers in relation to each other in abstraction, merely as numbers, but to assist in the computation of practical mensuration. This was important when land area was to be calculated using different measures, especially when square units of land had to be standardized in terms of *mā* and *vēli*, the extant land measures in use. While all other versions of *Kaṇakkatikāram* will begin with delineation of measures and then proceed to computational methods involving land, gold, grain, stone, weights and time, the author of this commentary spends a lot of effort to isolate numbers and elaborates on their properties in terms of their relationship to each other, organizes tables to that effect, demonstrates the procedure of finding squares using the tables and finally applies such exercises in the context of measuring land area. It is only after this that he proceeds like the rest of the *Kaṇakkatikāram* texts to the section on delineation of measures. Once that is done, he swiftly gets to the business of training the student by taking him back to the desk, armed with the *Eṇcuvaṭi*. In a completely new section, which is not found in any other texts, the text introduces '*Eṇcuvaṭi murittu kēṭṭal*'—problems involved in breaking up the *Eṇcuvaṭi*. A simple and elegant verse introduces the objective:

> *colliya eṇcuvaṭi vāykaḷ tōṟum*
> *tokai muṟiccu tāṉ kēṭka collak kēḷīr*
> *vallavarkaḷ coṉṉa lakkam taṉai tāṉattil*
> *vākāka niṟutti ratṉa curukkut tākkum*
> *nalla tokai mēl tāṉam naṭattik kūṭṭi*
> *naviṉṟu varum vāy taṉṉil nāṭṭu vīrāy*
> *allūrar īraintu maṭṭukkun tāṉ*
> *āmiraṇṭukku appāl mūṉṟākum tāṉē* (verse no. 24).

If you intersect the *Eṇcuvaṭi* at any point and learn to tell numbers, computation comes easily. Not just that, there are those quirky minds who will intersect the *Eṇcuvaṭi* horizontally as well as vertically and pose problems, that might involve the fourth and the sixth table at the same time. The same applies for the table of squares (*kuḻimāttu*) as well as the sum of products of each *vāy* (each table of multiplication in the *Eṇcuvaṭi*). If you fail to answer then they will think that you are not fit to become a *kaṇakkappiḷḷai* and curse you. Therefore, in order for you not to hear such abuses, learn the techniques as is explained here'.[30] For example, in the fifth table in the *Eṇcuvaṭi*, what is the sum of products from 1 × 5 = 5 up to 80 × 5 = 400?

Take 8 as the factor of 80 and the *paṭiyaṭi*[31] for which is 36. Taking 36 to two places, 36-360. Add this to the previous 36. Sum is 396. Multiply this by the *vāy* 5. 300 × 5 = 1500, 90 × 5 = 450, 5 × 6 = 30, hence 1980.

Therefore, the sum of products from 1 × 5 = 5 up to 80 × 5 = 400 is 1980.

Likewise you can tell the same from the first table to the tenth table. But this gets more complicated when it involves the fraction table in the *Eṇcuvaṭi*, for which additional techniques are required; accordingly, the commentator reminds the student to be prepared for the quirky, testing mind (*vikaṭamāka kēṭṭalum*). For example, he demonstrates the technique to find the sum from the *muntiri* (1/320) table up to *nālu mā* (1/5) and proceed till up to 600.

> Adding the series,
>
> 1/320+1/160+1/80+1/40+3/80+1/20+1/16+1/10+1/8+3/20+3/16+1/5,
>
> we get from these 12 numbers,
>
> ¾ + 1/5 + 1/160 + 1/320.
>
> Now, take 6 as the *iṉam* for 600.
>
> Add 1 to it, get 7. Half of this is 3 ½.
>
> Multiply this with the *iṉam*, 6.
>
> We get 21.
>
> Take this up to the third place: 21-210–2100=2331. Add 1 to this, it being the first table in the fractions and subtract it by the previous result,
>
> ¾+1/5+1/160+1/320
>
> Which is 2236 ¼ + 1/ 20 + 1/ 320 and is the required sum.[32]

Similar techniques are then discussed with respect to the tables involving capacity measures in the *Eṇcuvaṭi*, like the *nāḻi* table and the

[30] Ibid., pp. 82–83.

[31] *Paṭiyaṭi* means the sum of numbers in a sequence, of any given order, while *vāy* means the number for which the given table in the *Eṇcuvaṭi* is taken. Please note that the *Eṇcuvaṭi* mode of learning is also called *vāyppāṭu* (literally meaning recitation) and this *vāy* is taken to mean the nth table in the *Eṇcuvaṭi*.

[32] *Āstāṉa Kōlākalam* (Guntur), 88.

marakkāl table. This line of discussion leads the commentator to bring in problems involving arithmetic progression, including square numbers as well as geometric progression. The conscious pedagogic effort in this version of *Āstāṉa Kōlākalam* shows how such texts prepared the student trained in the *Eṇcuvaṭi* in the *tiṇṇai* school for the requirements of the job of an accountant. The *tiṇṇai* learning is taken over and is then tailored to particular skills that will make a good accountant, in a way building bridges between the school and the job. Not that such techniques are absent in other versions of the texts being discussed here. Problems involving summation of number series and the concept of finding products using the *iṉam* factor are commonly found, but only hidden among several other techniques, without any particular orientation that will make it easier for the student to identify the computational context in which such techniques could be useful. In fact a typical *Kaṇakkatikāram* text, as mentioned several times before, followed a system of classification of problem types according to what is being computed.

The idea of treating numbers independently from their association with practical measures is much less in the *Kaṇakkatikāram* where only one verse (present in most versions of the text) clearly relates units of measures to the idea of numbers. That is, units of land measures like *muntiri, araikkāṇi, kāṇi, mā* etc., are also simultaneously numbers in the Tamil number system. So are the volume measures like *nāḻi, kuṟuṇi, marakkāl, kalam* that could be similarly treated as numbers, as will be explained in the next chapter where we discuss the learning of the *Eṇcuvaṭi* in the *tiṇṇai* school and the structure of the *Eṇcuvaṭi* itself.[33] This verse clearly hints at conscious systematization by identifying three kinds of *tāṉams* (lit. meaning, place), which add up to 23 in total in Tamil computational system. Composed in the *veṇpā* metre, the verse is:

eṇṇaḷavu tāṉam irupattu mūṉṟavaṟṟuḷ
maṇṇaḷavu nāṉkiṉṟi yoṉṟumām – oṇṇutalāy

[33] For immediate reference, I request the reader to see Appendix III, which is a complete translation of the *Poṉṉilakkam*, the *Nellilakkam*, and the *Eṇcuvaṭi*, where the continuum between units of practical measures and numbers as seamless is evident.

ōrāṟu maintum orumūṉṟum ōriraṇṭum
cīrāṉa ēḻumeṉa ceppu.[34]

The prose commentary to this verse says that there are a total of 23 *tāṉams* in *kaṇakku* (computation).

> First is *eṇṇaḷavuttāṉam*, which is number places. They are of two types, each six and five. They are, 1, 5, 10, 50, 100, 500.
>
> The next five are:
> 1000; 10,000; 1,00,000; 10,00,000; and 1,00,00,000
> (*āyiram, pattāyiram, laṭcam, pattu laṭcam, kōṭi*)
>
> Second is called *nilavāittāṉam* (*nilam* = land, *vāi* = number, *tāṉam* = place) or what are *kīḻ aḷavai* or fractions. They are:
> 1/320, 1/160, 1/80, 1/20, ¼.
> (*muntiri, araikkāṇi, kāṇi, mā, kāl*).

Third is *nelvayttāṉam* (*nel* = paddy/grain; *vāy* = number, *tāṉam* = place). They are seven: *kalam, tūṇi, kuṟuni, nāḻi, uḻakku, āḻākku, ceviṭu.*

Of these twenty-three, 1/320, 1/160, 1/80, and 1/20 are inherent in all three types, which leaves the rest of the nineteen as distinct *tāṉams*. The division of types of quantities as numbers in their own right, and with respect to their place as basic units of measures in linear and capacity measures, constitutes the 23 types of places in the computational system. This aligns with the basic structure of the *Eṇcuvaṭi*, the number table book in its organization.

Nañcaiyaṉ, the author of *Kaṇita Nūl*, goes one step further and breaks away from the *Kaṇakkatikāram's* scheme of classification and introduces a new scheme, writing in the year 1693, where a separate section on numbers appear along with the *kōl* (linear measures, concerning land, primarily); *kāl* (volumetric measures), *tulā* (weights), *nāḷ* (time measures). This section has 14 verses, each verse corresponding not to problem types, but particular rules that guide the treatment of numbers, as distinct from their relation to measures. In fact, the first verse in this section qualifies

[34] *Kaṇakkatikāram* (1783), 104.

the number one with cosmological significance, as a way to point its fundamentally constitutive place in the Tamil number system.

One has its origins in *Om*, the *pranava mantra*. Nañcaiyaṉ says that there is nothing comparable to ONE in this earth, just like the Lord Shiva, the transcendent who dances in the burning ghat, the universal force propelling the world, whose head cannot be reached by anyone while not everyone can see what is below his feet. So, the number one, similar to the feet of Shiva would have its feet as ¾, ½, ¼, 1/20, 3/80, 1/40, 1/80, 1/160 and 1/320—the standard fractions. The head of Shiva for the number One will be 1, 10, 100, 1000, 10,000, 100,000 and 10,00,000.[35] After which in the rest of the section Nañcaiyaṉ, verse by verse deals with relationship between numbers in the fraction series, in the whole number series, the principle of *tāṉapperukkam* which is increasing values of numbers as multiples of ten, for both whole numbers and fractions; sum of products of numbers in a series, called *alakunilai*; sum of the products of sums in a number within a series called *paṭiyaṭi; paṭiyaṭi* for fractions; squares of whole numbers and fractions; sum of squares in a series; exponential numbers in a series and their sum. Interestingly, within this cosmological framework there is a surprising way through which the text frames 'the rule of three'. The rule of three is called the *muttokai vikaṟpam*, but it is not introduced as a general rule but as a problem type for calculating wages.

The teaching of numerical proportions and method to determine quotients was elaborated through wage problems.[36] This embedding is rather significant and we will return to it in due course. But for the moment, let me observe that in the elaboration of the rule of three, Nañcaiyaṉ's text reveals multiple orientations. We see how within the same tradition, there are multiple orientations like the Guntur *Kōlākalam* that tailors the computational world for the job while Nañcaiyaṉ attempts a scheme of generalization that will hold true, but still very much in the realm of practice—in mensuration and counting in context. In one, the *Kaṇakkaṉ* assumes the role of a persuasive teacher while in the other the *Kaṇakkaṉ* becomes the author of an elegantly composed mathematical text. More

[35] For the verse and the commentary, see *Kaṇita Nūl, Part I*, eds. P. Subramaniyam and K. Satyabama (Chennai: Institute of Asian Studies, 1999), 74. Hereafter referred as *Kaṇita Nūl* (1693).

[36] *Kaṇita Nūl* (1693), pp. 74–119.

interestingly, Suryabooban's *Kaṇakkatikāram* takes this into another direction by including a whole new section on calendrical computation, to include methods to compute time in relation to stars and sun signs in particular days and months. He also has an entire verse that acts as a guide to the night sky, to identify constellations by assigning them shapes of familiar things.[37]

These interesting variations point to a certain movement or flexibility within the tradition. It allowed for further systematization and refinement of methods of problem solving and adaptability to particular pedagogic environments. It also allowed the participant, space to elaborate upon any one particular section of interest, to focus and collate further information. But the core orientation remained towards the realm of the practitioner. Abstracting a separate section on numbers and attention towards their properties subject to various arithmetic operations that we see in the 1693 text definitely was an interesting development, from the perspective of mathematization, calling our attention to questions about generalization out of occupational practices. But even this remained very much premised upon the *Eṇcuvaṭi* and stayed close to the demands of practice.

The Centrality of the *Eṇcuvaṭi* to the *Kaṇakkatikāram*

The relationship between the *Eṇcuvaṭi*, a text from the *tiṇṇai* school, and the practitioner's computational work seemed to have remained important through the years. The centrality that the *Eṇcuvaṭi* occupies in each and every problem, in every single step in the execution of algorithms or extending the method to incorporate more problem situations, was dependent on training in it. Training in *Eṇcuvaṭi* provided the fundamental basis upon which the practitioner could engage with and improve his efforts to systematize his specialized knowledge. Given that the *Eṇcuvaṭi* training was institutionalized in the *tiṇṇai* schools, we can surmise that the school was central to the practitioner's mathematics. We will discuss

[37] *Kaṇakkatikāram* (Suryabooban), pp. 33–44.

in detail both the *tiṇṇai* school and the *Eṇcuvaṭi* in the next chapter, but here I would like to draw the reader's attention to some significant questions about the relationship between the school, the *Eṇcuvaṭi* and the *Kaṇakkatikāram* practice.

Was there a continuum between these three? Or in other words, did each one of the three take in things from each other? The school, as we shall see, continued to remain a central agency in the imparting training in recollective memory and in nurturing skills in the mnemonic computational arts and language till the late nineteenth century, despite continuous changes in and around its pedagogic world. The *Ariccuvaṭi* and the *Eṇcuvaṭi* remained two most important vehicles of training for the students in these *tiṇṇai* schools, which ensured that certain basic functional skills in language and arithmetic continued to be imparted to specific upper caste social groups in the eighteenth and the nineteenth centuries, if not earlier. The *tiṇṇai* school sustained *Eṇcuvaṭi* learning and hence by extension, sustained the *Kaṇakkatikāram* style of acquiring specialized knowledge. But did the practitioner give back anything to the school? Did elements of his specialized knowledge find their way back to the school? Did the school learn anything from the practitioner and in the process alter, or gain new problem-sets, methods or even pedagogic insights? Did the practitioner's work alter or reorient the school learning in any way? Could we ask, whether in the eighteenth century there was a constant process of reorientation between the school, expert practices and their changing roles in the social and political spheres?

It is very difficult to discern concrete instances that could lead us to a reasonable surmise of the changes in *Eṇcuvaṭi* texts. But clearly, the text's emergence in the *tiṇṇai* school, even if undatable, marked a very important shift in the world of practitioners. Another moment of change was the presentation of *Eṇcuvaṭi* in the form of the table. The reorganization of the text as a two dimensional representation of number facts in a predominantly oral environment of transmission marks a shift in the history of transmission of both elementary and specialized mathematical knowledge in premodern societies. We have no evidence to show when and how these happened. These two processes probably complemented each other while making possible the production of specialized knowledge. Specialist knowledge and the world of computing proportions perched itself upon the world of measures, a transition made possible and mediated by the *Eṇcuvaṭi*. The computational context of job training tested and honed further the training in the mnemonic arts imparted in the school through the *Eṇcuvaṭi* by demanding that computations be performed correctly and swiftly. The practitioner's continuous refinement of solutions required ever more problem types, as the application of the right method at the right instance provided the solution to a given problem, be it in the sphere of mensuration or proportions. The table book version of *Eṇcuvaṭi* was an essential resource to this mode of problem solving. The recollection of the appropriate table for the correct number in the context of the arithmetic operation involved made the solution of the problem possible. However varied the magnitude of the quantities involved, the tables enabled the practitioner to convert them into basic units and proceed further. This is why an ideal practitioner associated particular procedures with a problem type, backed with memory tables. Memory, then, was a virtue in this system. Memory, when combined with prudence in identification of the correct procedure to initiate problem solving, constituted a skill. This skill was considered worthy enough to be nurtured and developed, as if the society consciously decided to develop a particular expertise in its skilled labour. The predominant presence of problem types as distinct from rules[38] is a characteristic of the *Kaṇakkatikāram* texts. The problem construction or ways of problem posing were intended to train the practitioner in the skilful handling of methods at hand. The choice of the problems was conditioned by the familiarity with the stock of methods.

In this continuous process, these texts remained important pedagogic devices both at school and at work. The unification and coherence that these texts espouse in articulating the methods of problem solving

[38] See Jens Høyrup, 'Sanskrit-Prakrit Interaction in Elementary Mathematics as Reflected in Arabic and Italian Formulations of the Rule of Three—And Something More on the Rule Elsewhere', *Max Planck Institute for the History of Science, Preprint No. 435* (Berlin, 2012): 1, where he cautions against the prevalent tendency among historians of mathematics to conflate the problem type with a rule. But with respect to these texts, we often find that the both need not necessarily be in opposition to each other, as has been demonstrated in the case of differences in texts, above. However it would be an interesting exercise to explore this tension further in this tradition, as a dynamic between problem types and rules and what moments practical problems, using what means at hand, abstracted types into rules, as a case for further research. I thank Dorothy Ko for pointing out the necessity to draw attention to this important problem.

proceeded along with the demands at the workplace as well as in the pedagogic context, as we have seen in the case of the Guntur version of *Āstāṉa Kōlākalam*. This coming together of work place and pedagogic imperatives definitely points to the complementary relationship between the school and the work place; the work place simply took over the process of doing and learning in a different mode. Let me try and illustrate this using land related computations as a case in point in the *Kaṇakkatikāram*. In the context of computing area of land, the rule in verse is:

kallum kuḻiyum kaṇakkatil kaināṉkum
collum vakaikūṭṭi tuñcāmal - melliyalāy
aṉṉavaṟṟai pātiya tākki yaḷaviṟ kaḻittu
maṉṉiru mākāṇiyāl vāṭṭu.

When you have to measure *ciṟukuḻi*, measure the *kuḻi*, multiply it with *māttu* and say the *kuḻi*. If you further multiply this *kuḻi* with *mākāṇi* and by *muntiri*, you get the *nilam* and likewise all other problems of this type.[39]

This means that when it comes to land, there are two units of areas, *kuḻi* and *nilam*. *kuḻi* is the product of mean measures of length and breadth. The result has to be multiplied with what is called *mattu* (the commentary is not specific about what exactly this means; the editor of this text says it is height), but *mattu* here connotes a scale according to which certain square units of *kuḻi* becomes a unit of area. And from this to get the final extent of land, it has to be multiplied by 1/16 (*mākāṇi*) and by 1/320 (*muntiri*), which is again scaling the *kuḻi* into unit area.

To take a second example from the same text,

North *kōl* 15, South *kōl* 20, thus 35 *kōl*. Dividing this by 2 to get the mean measure, we get 17 1/2 . The east *kōl* 10 and the west *kōl* 8 will give the mean measure of 9.

Multiply 17 ½ and 9, we get 157 ½ .

This has to be multiplied by *mattu*, which is ¾ which is 118 1/8 *kuḻi*.

[39] *Kaṇakkatikāram* (1783), verse 79, 120.

This has to be multiplied by *mākāṇi*, which is 1/16. So, this yields, 7 ¼ + 1/8 + 1/40 + 1/160 *kīḻ* ½ .

On multiplying this by 1/320 again, this yields 1/20 + 1/40 + 1/160 + 1/320 *kīḻ* ¾ + 1/10 + 1/40 + 1/160 *nilam*.

This will be read as *māve araimā araikkāṇi muntiri kīḻ mukkāl irumā araimā araikkāṇi nilam*. So, what effectively happened here is measuring land in terms of this scale, which is ¾, and then arriving at the unit of *mā* land by multiplying it with *mākāṇi* and *muntiri*.

In the very next verse, the same rule is said in a different verse:

aḷanta kai nāṉkum aḷavaṟintu kūṭṭi
piḷantu periyataṉāl perukki – alantataṉai
maṭṭiṉāl tākki mākāṇiyil kaḻikka
ciṭṭāṟ kuḻiyeṉavē cāṟṟu.[40]

This *veṇpā* elegantly captures a rule of mensuration, which says measure (*aḷavaṟintu*) and add (*kūṭṭi*) the sides and divide (*piḷantu*) by 2 (to get the mean measure for each) and multiply both (*perukki*), multiply it with *mattu* (*mattiṉal tākki*), divide it by *mākāṇi* (*mākāṇiyil kaḻikka*) and pronounce the *kuḻi* as it appears. This is not very different as a method from the previous verse, but here, the *mattu* is taken as *kālē araikkāl*, which is ¼ + 1/8 and not ¾ as in the previous case.

The methods are the same but the problem variation allows for a multiplicity of standards through fraction conversions dependent on the dimension of the *mattu*, in this case determined by what is taken as the *mattu*, either ¾ or ¼ + 1/8. Such facility allowed for uneven dimensions of land. Indeed the following verses discuss the rules for measuring lands of different dimensions, in which all follow the principle of computing mean measures of the sides and multiplying it by the length of the diagonal (generically called as *naṭu aḷavu*: centre measure), or the perpendicular height for irregular quadrilaterals and triangular lands respectively. Again, the rule to compute the area of a pond brings in *mattu* in a different manner, which is the average height measured at different points

[40] *Kaṇakkatikāram* (1783), verse 80, 123.

in the pond. The point to note here is that the principle of mean measures remain constant across all types of land, but when to choose what factor as the *mattu*, to standardize or scale the area in terms of *mā* or *vēli* or *kāṇi*, is something that one learnt on the job, a skill that might not be entirely transparent to all inhabitants of the settlement.

This orientation very much remained the *Kaṇakkaṉ*'s area of expertise and constituted the core of the training for the *kaṇakkuppiḷḷai*'s apprentice or the student who passed out of *tiṇṇai* school and went on to learn accounts from a specialized teacher. The *Kaṇakkatikāram* enumerates all possible situations for the student in the process of measuring land, gives him the mnemonic verses to begin the computation, but the choice of *mattu* has to be chosen based on reality of the dimensions.[41] It enabled the student to face such varied situations and prepared him to apply the correct method at the correct juncture. When we consider that the measuring standards of land, using the foot-pole or the *aṭikkōl* were never constant, such ability acquires significance. Measuring standards constantly varied with regions and even with respect to the nature of rights over land. It could be a twelve-foot, sixteen-feet or even twenty-four-foot-pole and therefore, the *Kaṇakkaṉ* had to compute the area with a given foot-pole measure and then scale it with the required standard foot-pole as demanded by the administrative record. In the arithmetic sense, this often brought in problem situations, where, given the area and given the used foot-pole, either one had to find the area using another foot-pole, or, if one side was measured using one standard foot-pole (say twelve-foot) and the other was measured using another (say sixteen-foot), one had to arrive at the area. So the constant reference to varying standards of the foot-pole and the necessity to scale them into standard units of areas brought the rule of three into the centre of land-based computations. The coming together of practical mensuration and the method of rule of three in the *Kaṇakkaṉ*'s computational practice so strengthened his skillset that the act of physical measurement of the dimensions of the land became but a moment in the computational process, almost incidental, to the

[41] Ibid., pp. 123–158. The verses up to 105 discuss the various mensuration aspects of land measurement.

series of mental arithmetic operations that fixed the land into the revenue registers. The *Veṭṭiyāṉ* could have physically taken the foot-pole and measured the land himself, but the ability to proceed with scaling the land in terms of required units would have been possible only with formal training in the method of computations at the school through the *Eṇcuvaṭi* and at work. Both of course were denied to the *Veṭṭiyāṉ*, because of his lower place in the caste hierarchy.

The *Kaṇakkaṉ* and the *Veṭṭiyāṉ* worked in tandem, and both probably required each other's experience and skills, but the computing and authorizing of the results of that computation resided squarely with the *Kaṇakkaṉ*, a privilege borne out of his location in caste bound occupational hierarchy, and as a functioning authority in that political-economic order. One might argue then that he was then more proximate to the Brahmin computational astronomer in terms of his resources of knowledge at hand than with the sharecropper or the lower caste *Veṭṭiyāṉ*. Here we see, yet another instance of how the approach through practice could be more productive than the dualism of the Sanskrit and the vernacular would allow us.

The *Kaṇakkatikāram* honed the ability to identify a procedure quickly so as to enable the *Kaṇakkaṉ* to work in different problem solving contexts. In fact, it can be argued that the prevalence of diverse standards of measurement acted as an inspiration to draw upon more methods that would ensure accuracy and computational ease, not to forget correctness. This is not only true of land measures, but even more so of volume measures. The eighteenth-century locality accounts show that in the battles of the threshing floor and collection of revenue in kind, the act of measurement of volumes was not just merely sensitive, but very political and prone to contestations and conflict. The reduction of volume measures, when measured by different standards had to be standardized—the *ceviṭu, āḻākku, uḻakku, nāḻi, kuṟuṇi, marakkāl* and the *kalam*, the basic conversions for which the *Eṇcuvaṭi* prepares the student in the *tiṇṇai* school. The resources of recollective memory nurtured in the *Eṇcuvaṭi* learning at the *tiṇṇai* school was, thus, continuously called into the world of real world transactions and recording them in the computational registers of mathematical practice.

The intimate relationship between practical mensuration and computational processes, as I have outlined, implies that standardization of computation had to be possible in a context of great diversity in measurement; this was also a political act. In this sense, the practitioner's mathematics was not 'practical' but a power-laden practice. This means to demand from the practitioner a mode of contemplation, to ask of him generalized or abstract properties of geometrical objects like the square or the circle would be misleading, precisely because it was not within his orientation. By the same token, to look for traces of how the practitioner 'applied' theoretical knowledge, or to be specific, in this case, theoretical geometry, also misses the texture of this knowledge and its normative goals. Indeed, the historian of mathematics' search for the pure and the applied dichotomies in the mathematical practice of early modern cultures only meets the ends of an already anticipated discipline of 'mathematics' and pushes the practitioner's knowledge into the category of 'folk' knowledge or ethno-mathematics. The world of practical mensuration was not any less valid than the pursuit of disembodied knowledge, just because its orientation was not the quest for a 'transcendental geometrical blue print of the world'.[42] Because, as a rule, practical geometry, 'which aims at calculating, lengths, areas, volumes from already performed measurements, is not interested in geometrical construction, nor in the making of measurements'.[43] The textual orientation of the mathematical texts suggests that the skills of the expert were located in the world of concrete action, the measuring of paddy, the portioning of wages, the estimation of land area across a range of scalar and standard variants. But if the question for the historian of mathematics cannot be that of demarcating this world as one of mathematical folkways, then on what terms might we understand the orientation (or lack of orientation) to abstraction? In other words, why does the *Kaṇakkatikāram* corpus refrain from stating the rule as a rule, even as it operates within the normative parameters of rules that are explicitly elaborated in Sanskrit texts? Let me elaborate by returning to the example of the rule of three, a mathematical concept that is supposed to have originated in India and was explicated in Sanskrit texts since the seventh century.

[42] J. Bennett, 'Practical Geometry and Operative Knowledge', *Configurations* 6, no. 2 (1998): 198.

[43] Jens Høyrup, 'The rare traces of constructional procedures in "practical geometries"', *Filosofi Og Videnskabsteoripa, Roskilde Universtitetscenter*, 3, Raekke: Preprints 2006, Number 2.

The Rule of Three in Computing Proportions

The importance of the rule of three in Indian mathematical traditions is not that it is theoretically subtle, but that it is central to problem solving, for with this rule several problem types can be solved without the knowledge of a general theory of proportion.[44] 'The rule of three is a rule for solving linear problems of the type. If A corresponds to X, to what will B correspond? The rule states in one way or the other (but with this order of the arithmetical operations) that the answer is Y = (B × X)/A'.[45] The rule is also explained as 'process, which consists of writing down three given terms in a linear sequence (A – B – C), and then proceeding in the reverse direction, multiplying the last term with the middle term and then dividing their product with the first term (C x B / A)'.[46] I became interested in how the *Kaṇakkatikāram* corpus in all its variations conceived of the rule of three because of what might be revealed about the nature of the practitioner's mathematics. It seems to me that it is important to discern whether the *Kaṇakkatikāram* practitioner conceived of it as a rule or merely a problem type to address his various problem-situations because it provides us with an occasion to raise certain questions about the relationship between the Tamil *Kaṇakkatikāram* tradition with that of the Sanskrit one, or the practitioner's mathematics with that of the 'dignified' tradition. Sarma argues that the 'importance of this rule lies not in the subtlety of its theory as in the simple process of solving problems . . . With this rule one can easily solve several types of problems even without knowledge of the general theory of proportion'.[47]

The *Kaṇakkatikāram* texts are replete with problem types that involve the rule of three. Indeed, in each section, once the standards of measuring units are established in proportion to each other, the problem situations that follow are problems of proportions. The verses in each and every unique situation of problem solving tirelessly repeat the same principle of the rule of three using the terminology of the first, the middle and the last quantities—*muṉ, iṭai, kaṭai*. Be it in the case of direct or inverse

[44] Ibid.
[45] Høyrup, 'Sanskrit-Prakrit Interactions', p. 1.
[46] S. R. Sarma, 'The Rule of Three and Its Variations in India', *From China to Paris: 2000 Years Transmission of Mathematical Ideas*, eds. Yvonne Dold Samplonius et al. (Stuttgart, 2002): 134.
[47] Ibid.

proportions, we can see that the verses concerned themselves with the order of arrangement of the quantities in order for the rule to work. Very rarely do these texts state the generalized form of the rule that applies across the problems related to land, gold and grain measures.

One way to understand this tendency is to consider that the orientation in these texts was to identify the problem situation and solve it right away, and to aid that act of identification, the verses stated procedures that will help solve that problem only in that particular situation—and almost always end with this qualification by saying, 'follow this for all similar kind of problems'[48] by identifying their type. The following verse illustrates this:

> *aṭikkaṭiyun tāḻvēṟṟam āṅkaṟiya coṉṉa*
> *paṭippaṭiyē avvaṭiyai māṟi – vaṭukkaṇṇāy*
> *maṟṟavantāṉ coṉṉa aṭit tokaiyai piṟakkīyntu*
> *peṟṟa payaṉ pērvaḻiyē pēcu.*[49]

The verse says that if you encounter different foot poles used in the same parcel of land to compute its area, multiply the first given foot-pole with the given area, and with this product, divide it with the second foot-pole. Here, the situation is clearly mentioned, to help identify the procedure to be followed. So, if measured by a 16-foot-pole, the *kuḻi* is 256, if measured by 24-foot-pole, how much will be the *kuḻi*?

Yet, it is not that the rule of three is not elaborated as a rule at all. The term for the rule of three in Tamil—*muttokai viṉā*—(literally translated as three-quantity-question or problem of three quantities) occurs in the *Kaṇita Nūl* and is stated with an elaborate discussion of the various problems of this type in the *Āstāṉa Kōlākalam*. For example, in the problem of payment of wages in *Kaṇita Nūl*: 'If a person who worked for 12 days got 10 *paṇam*, how much will 8 days of work give him?' The problem is stated in the verse itself, and the last two lines give out the procedure which says, 'Keep the first 12 for now, multiply the middle with the last and now

[48] The Tamil phrase is *'ippaṭi varuvaṉa ellām kaṇṭu koḷka'*, which can be more closely translated as 'likewise identify all that comes'. Note the emphasis on identification.

[49] *Kaṇakkatikāram* (1783), verse 96, 143. *aṭikkaṭi*—feet by feet, *tāḻvēṟṟam*—difference, *paṭippaṭiyē*—one by one, *avvaṭiyai māṟṟi*—multiply the feet, *tāṉ coṉṉa aṭi tokaiyai*—with the product that you find, *piṟakkīyntu*—divide it with the other (foot-pole)

divide it with the 12 that you kept apart'.[50] It then follows this category of problems by consistently identifying them as *muttokai viṉā* in each section. In the context of land, it identifies this problem as *nila-viṉā*, the land question, and introduces a generic problem type in land, preceded by a verse whose second line instructs the learner to multiply the middle and the last and divide with the first (*'iṭaiyiṟ kaṭai cēr kuḻi perukki, muṉ vaitta atarku īyntu'*). But in the very next problem, it introduces a verse which instructs, 'Multiply the first and the last and divide by the middle' (*kaṭai talai māṟi iṭaiyataṟku īyntu*). The change in the sequence of the quantities in the two problems dictates the procedure for the solution. Here the rule of three is embedded in particular problem types.

In the *Āstāṉa Kōlākalam* unlike the *Kaṇita Nūl* the problems are explicitly elaborated as rule of three problems. This text distinguishes between problem types and procedures entailed by the rule of three. It marks the difference in procedure by naming them differently—*muttokai viṉā* (as the *Kaṇita Nūl* does) for the direct case and *kaṭaittalai viṟpūṭṭu*[51] (which is not in *Kaṇita Nūl* as a name for the category). It lists generic problems for both kinds to identify the difference and solves a series of problems for both kinds. Then it goes on to categorize problems that involve multiple proportions involving the rule of five, the rule of seven, the rule of eleven by demonstrating problem-sets for each of these. The *Kaṇakkatikāram* and the *Kaṇita Nūl* also have problems that involve multiple proportions and the rule of five and seven but not categorized with specific names like *aintokai viṉā, eḻu tokai viṉā* and so on.

Jens Høyrup suggests that the ordering of the quantities in a sequence is important to the rule of three. And then he traces how various Sanskrit authors have gone about discussing the rule of three, including Aryabhata, Mahavira and Bhaskara and Brahmagupta who all follow a standard terminology:

A: *pramana* (measure)	X: *phala* (fruit)
B: *iccha* (wish)	Y: *icchaphala* (fruit of wish)

[50] *Kaṇita Nūl*, verse 26, 111.

[51] *kaṭaittalai viṟpūṭṭu* denotes the imagery of a locked bow string that has the last and the first as its two ends.

Now these authors have each given the rule in one way or the other, pointing out how the first and the last quantities will have to be similar while the middle one will have to be of a different kind. This distinction is crucial for Høyrup and he contends that the argument for identification of similarity in the quantities involved would have come from a 'vernacular environment', in that he distinguishes the economic and vernacular world of transactions from the world of astronomy. Mahavira (of the ninth century) to him, discerns this important factor in his work, because of his orientation of not being an astronomer like the rest of the Sanskrit authors. It is probable that he would have got this rule from the world of commerce, grounded in a vernacular mathematical tradition. Høyrup notes that Mahavira makes the similarity cause central to the operation of the rule of three in his *Ganitasarasangraha*. 'That similarity is mentioned by Mahavıra is a first argument that the concern with similarity originated in a vernacular environment (in economical transactions its relevance is obvious, in astronomical pure-number calculations less so); that Bhaskara I introduces the observation in connection with an (commercial) example that points in the same direction'.[52] In the practitioner's mathematical tradition as found in the *Kaṇakkatikāram*, we see the repeated presence of the rule in operation but not the rule in itself. There is only one verse that details the similarity clause mentioned by Høyrup, interestingly not in the *Kaṇita Nūl* or in the *Āstāṉa Kōlākalam* but in *Kaṇakkatikāram* itself, which does not provide the nomenclature for the rule.[53]

[52] Høyrup, 'Sanskrit-Prakrit Interactions', 4.

[53] In *Kaṇakkatikāram* (1783), verse 168, p. 273, states:

antamum ātiyum ōriṉamē yāmākil
cantataṉain tāṉākki tākkiyapiṉ - muntokaikku
peṟṟa payaṉai piṟaḻāmal īntatē
poṟkoṭiyāy piṉṉiṟukkum poṉ

An even better formulation appears in another manuscript (R. No. 6176, p. 273), where the same verse is composed as:

antamum ātiyum ōriṉamē yākil
antamuṭan avviṭaiyai tākka – vanta tokai
attokai ātikku īyntu poruḷataṉai picakāmal
poṟkoṭiyāy piṉṉiru poṉ

The first version in the first line says, 'If the first and the last are of the same species (*iṉam*)', the second version very clearly says the rule itself: 'if the last and the first are of the same species, multiply the last with the middle and divide this product with the first (*ātikku īyntu*)'. The significance of identification of what is similar is germane to the operation of the rule, as the rest of the procedure is merely a mechanical application. But then, this verse appears after many preceding

Do we take this as an indication of a natural progression in the practitioner's tradition where after solving problem after problem, it inevitably arrived at a generic clause of similarity? Did repeated 'drilling' give rise to a generality of a rule that would yield a significant idea, which then clarified the practice itself? An affirmative answer would allow us to consider abstraction in the Tamil corpus as an autonomous possibility from Sanskrit. And yet, we could also ask why *Kaṇakkatikāram* refrains from declaring rules, especially when the Sanskrit corpus had done so from the seventh century. We could ask why the *Kaṇakkaṉ* remained uninterested in rule-making, and invested only in problem-making and rule-following.

The rule of three is as universal as a mathematical rule can get, in that it can be found in almost all cultures around the world. Hence it occupies for Høyrup a window to the world of transmission of not the theoretical type, but the practitioner's type, in mathematical knowledge.[54] I would argue that our questions should not lead us to a quest for the original invention of the rule of three. Rather, the task should be to identify the nature of the interaction between the vernacular and the theoretical traditions in each of these cultures that might cut across languages and texts. To be sure, the practitioner's orientation towards the 'know-how' may not necessarily always entail the 'know-why', simply because he was not interested in contemplation but only in correct computation. However, both worlds of computation, be it that of the *Kaṇakkaṉ* or that of the computational astronomer, did share the same set of mathematical techniques, each to their own end. Both did use the rule of three, as practitioners in cultures in the rest of the world through centuries did. S. R. Sarma points out that the application of this rule in the context of astronomical calculations was crucial to the Sanskrit practitioners,[55] but the presentation of the rule itself within the Sanskrit canon has mostly been through the idiom of so called commercial arithmetic, as in the *Ganitasarasangraha* or as in *Lilavati*. Aryabhata uses the rule of three primarily in the context

verses where the idea of similarity is not markedly present. Nor is it in the rest of the verses that deal with similar problems.

[54] For how pervasive the rule of three was in different culture areas involving the vernacular and the high traditions, see Høyrup, 'Sanskrit-Prakrit Interactions', and Sarma, 'The Rule of Three and Its Variations in India'.

[55] Ibid.

of astronomical computations, like in the case of finding the mean position of a planet from the number of its revolutions or in the context of spherical astronomy to deal with problems in case of 'latitude-triangles'. It forms the basis of computations for dealing with trigonometric ratios. Nilakantha Somasutva (born AD 1444) in his commentary on Aryabhata 'says that entire mathematical astronomy is pervaded by two fundamental laws: by the law of the relation between the base, the perpendicular and the hypotenuse in a right angled triangle and the Rule of three'.[56] Bhaskara I, in his commentary on Aryabhata again was the first to demonstrate the application of the rule of three by providing seven kinds of problems or examples and the methods to solve them. They are (1) price and quantity of sandalwood, (2) price and weight of ginger, (3) price and quantity of musk also with fractions, (4) time taken by a snake in entering a hole, (5) mixed quantities, (6) partnership, and (7) partnership expressed as fractions. Later other authors like Sridara and Mahavira 'created independent topics of these variations and formulated separate rules for each of these variations'.[57]

The application of this rule in measuring land, counting grains, and distributing wages was not the central concern in the dignified Sanskrit tradition. Probably it is this non-concern towards the everyday world of computation which rendered that mode of theorization privileged. But then is this a problem of these different practitioners, or is it that their practice was essentially embedded in a social and political distribution of labour? What would such a division of labour mean for the ways in which mathematization could proceed? It is impossible to consider these matters without taking seriously the social fragmentation that caste hierarchies fostered. Therefore, mathematization in caste societies would also have to be studied with a particular awareness of how it is uncritically possible to pick and valorize only one way of theorizing as that entire culture's way of theorizing. It is the modes of theorizing by those who reconstruct the past which renders cultural privilege and textual power, reifying theory-building or theorem-making as the most honourable pursuit. Once this is done, we are left eternally chasing the problem of how and why practice did not become theory. Even more easily, such reconstructions sustain

[56] All these examples are cited in S. R. Sarma, 'The Rule of Three and Its Variations', 141.
[57] Ibid., pp. 143–144.

binaries and the cultural hierarchies within knowledge making. Having said this, we also need to ask, with the same awareness, to what extent the contemporary practitioners themselves were aware of the hierarchies and privileges under which they were making knowledge and doing practice. To what extent did caste fragmentation allow for such questioning?

The difference in orientation of the *Kaṇakkaṉ* and the Brahmin astronomer was, of course, substantial. In fact, most canonical Sanskrit texts do not follow the classification based on their objects of computation, like the *Kaṇakkatikāram* does. Their classification was rule-based. Rules were stated and problems came in to demonstrate the rules. In *Kaṇakkatikāram*, problems followed problems, and the presence of the rule was subservient to the algorithm, like in the case of the similarity clause of the rule of three, buried deep somewhere among so many other problems of the same type. Mahavira's *Ganitasarasangraha* and Bhaskara's *Lilavati*, two of the most popular and widely circulated Sanskrit texts both follow rule-based classification. For instance, Mahavira's *Ganitasarasangraha* begins by stating the various terminologies of measurement of space, time, grain, gold, silver, other metals; names of operations in arithmetic, rules of each operation with respect to zero, positive and negative quantities, and the names of the notational places. It then proceeds with the statement of rules of arithmetic operations, followed by illustrations, which are problems posed (without solutions) with respect to the eight operations (*parikarman*): multiplication, division, squaring, square roots, cubing, cube root, summation and subtraction. The typical model is to pose the general statement of the rule, with problems posed as often pedantic exercises involving numbers rather than objects. Then come the rules for operations with fractions, their various types, problems involving fractions followed by the chapter on rule of three, proportional division, measures of areas, shadows etc. In each of the sections dealing with the above, problems were subsumed under rules.[58] *Lilavati* of Bhaskara II similarly begins with the eight operations of arithmetic, fractions, ciphers, followed by miscellaneous rules for inversion, supposition, rule of concurrence, problems concerning squares, and rules for assimilation and proportion. This was followed by

[58] *The Ganitasarasangraha of Mahaviracarya With English Translation and Notes*, ed. and trans. M. Rangacarya (Madras: Government Press, 1912).

the section on mixtures which include rules for interest, purchase and sale, and permutations and combinations. Next is the section on arithmetic and geometric progressions, followed by geometrical treatment of plane figures, excavation of solids, stacks, saw, mound of grain, shadow of gnomon, the pulverizer and the combination of digits.[59] The world of the examples in these works served the generalization of the rule, where as for *Kāri Nāyaṉār*, *Karuvūr* Nañcaiyaṉ and *Nāvili Perumāḷ*, the examples themselves were concrete problems to meet the requirements of that particular computational instance.

That is probably why the tone in these texts is also very distinct. One of the interesting differences between the Tamil and Sanskrit texts is the form of address. In the *Lilavati* the address is one of constant challenge: 'If you are a mathematician', 'Oh, you trader, tell me!' In the *Kaṇakkatikāram* tradition it was always an invitation: 'You can do this', 'Here is how to do it'. These distinct registers of challenge and invitation in the two traditions are not merely a function of language and its poetics, but indicate particular attitudes associated with notions of mathematical competence. Bhaskara's engagement with the world of proportions and time and his yearning to capture means to manipulate them are presented in the language of commodities and their exchange to derive a rule. For *Kāri Nāyaṉār* on the other hand, the world of proportions in land and grains presented concrete problems for which methods need to be discerned. The examples chosen connote the differing orientation: if *Kāri Nāyaṉār* wishes to solve the problem of irrigating land from available water in a tank, for Bhaskara it is the time taken to fill the cistern of a fountain. One is focused on the redistribution of resources in a social landscape; the other focused on the movement of liquid and its relationship to time. The social operation of knowledge reveals one, the *Kaṇakkaṉ*, geared to and embedded in the redistribution of resources through social fragmentation, and the other, that of Bhaskara, to be an abstract consideration of matter but an abstraction enabled by social fragmentation. The mathematics employed and used was similar, but the orientation that guided each practice was different. Each orientation was shaped by its specific role in the social organization of knowledge. The Sanskrit astronomer's

[59] *Lilavati of Bhaskaracharya*, trans. H. R. Colebrooke and ed. H. C. Banerjee (Allahabad: Kitab Mahal, 1967).

priority was with the realm of celestial bodies while for *Kaṇakkatikāram* it was agrarian production.

By suggesting that the difference in the traditions might be organized through the context of their development and their use or role in society, I am by no means suggesting that the traditions did not share a certain ecology. Each spoke in different languages, yet operated in similar oral environments. The nature of oral transmission in Sanskrit tradition—the Sanskrit verse and its distinct function in the mathematical context, the use of number names and the facility it offered and the constraints it posed—has been much discussed.[60] In the *Kaṇakkatikāram* tradition, what constitutes its fundamental significance is the fact that leaf after leaf remains a running record of how computation proceeded orally. No step in the algorithm is left to imagination, every single step was recorded. Not just that, the very process of adding, subtracting, multiplication and division was written down without missing a step. Arithmetic operations proceed in context, not away from it, conditioning the nature of arithmetic involved. In effect, computation involved proceeding step by step, aloud. The execution of algorithm had to proceed in the open, wherein the other person, if present, would be able to follow the procedure. Computation was simultaneously a kind of communicative knowledge.

The mnemonic function of the verse in a subculture of specialist knowledge demanded certain qualities in language; the problems of the prosody, metre and the prose commentary then could arguably be shared by both the traditions in this case. The purpose of writing, of communication and the audience for each was conditioned by the nature of the circulation of these knowledge types in society. The Sanskrit astronomer's priority was with the realm of celestial bodies while for *Kaṇakkatikāram* it was agrarian production. Both were specialist knowledge practices that circulated within respective communities of practitioners, determined by and situated in social hierarchies—ritual power and bureaucratic

[60] Kim Plofker, 'Sanskrit Mathematical Verse', *The Oxford Handbook of the History of Mathematics*, eds. Eleanor Robson and Jacqueline Stendhal (New York: Oxford University Press, 2009), 519–536. See also, Pierre Sylvian Filliozat, 'Ancient Sanskrit Mathematics: An Oral Tradition and a Written Literature', *History of Science, History of Text, Boston Studies in Philosophy of Science*, Vol. 238, ed. Karine Chemla (Netherlands: Springer 2005), 137–157; Michio Yano, 'Oral and Written Transmission of the Exact Sciences in Sanskrit', *Journal of Indian Philosophy* 34, nos. 1–2 (April 2006): 143–160.

control. The *Kaṇakkaṉ*'s role as an accountant and the *Kaṇakkaṉ*'s work as a teacher both complemented each other, but his reach was within the local. Perceptions about his competence as an accountant were shared locally. Sivasubramanian narrates several locally popular accounts, wherein the *Kaṇakkaṉ* as the accountant was essentially a cunning, vindictive type, to the extent that people wouldn't stop beating even his corpse in the graveyard.[61] Along with the fear and the hatred towards his authority to attest local transactions, what accompanied such distrust and hatred towards his work was also his ability to quantify and abstract physical, material properties of land and labour in order to assess them economically for the purpose of state-making. This close association between the power to abstract (not transparently) and quantify, rendered his skill suspect and prone to the subjective, especially when the avenues for contesting his modes of quantification and abstraction was limited to local non-literate practitioners. However, the Brahmin astronomer, even if present locally as a scholar or a teacher or even as a sanctified astrologer pursued his celestial interests, which did not directly impinging on the lives of the local public, and his computational prowess or ability remained within the realm of his family and kin, more so when he had to assume the role of a teacher. Therefore historically, the activity of teaching to one's own kin, family or members of one's own caste in ritually sanctified places would also help petrify one mode of pursuing knowledge (computational astronomy) as almost sovereign, even though in material terms, this sovereignty was circumscribed by individual and state patronage, like in the case of Sanskrit *tols*. This also implies that there were two distinct competencies, one subject to constant social scrutiny and the other not. The celestial pursuit of the Brahmin astronomer and the bureaucratic pursuit of the *Kaṇakkaṉ* both involved computational ability, but the way in which mathematization proceeded in these two realms was unmistakably influenced by that caste society even as the texts produced and reproduced caste difference.

To be sure, the historicist anxieties of the historians of Sanskrit mathematical tradition, their quest for markers of change or its absence over centuries preoccupy the historian of Tamil mathematics too. Kim Plofker's

[61] For this stark tale and the story associated with it, please see Sivabsubramanian, *Kaṇakkaṉ Vaḻakkāṟukaḷ*.

concern about the limitations of the mnemonic verse in its possibility to express the 'intuitive' process of her practitioner, coupled with the terse prose commentary that left little room for the followers of this tradition to identify with actual thought processes of the working mathematical mind, to pick up pieces and make progress, compels her to take notice of the role that language and caste could have played in the communities of Sanskrit mathematical tradition.[62] In the context of her discussion on Sanskrit commentaries, she reasons that,

> developing one's own mathematical intuition, one's ability to perceive truth, is also important: if you need to have every inference explicitly justified for you, may be you are just not a very good mathematician. Hence perhaps, the role of explicit proofs in mathematical texts remained flexible: a demonstration might be presented or omitted, depending on the author's decision about its necessity or appropriateness in a particular context. It is the mathematician's responsibility to know why a rule is true but not inevitably the author's responsibility to prove it. The price of this flexibility and autonomy seems to have been the occasional loss of crucial mathematical information when rules were transmitted without accompanying *rationale to fix their meaning securely* (emphasis mine).[63]

Minkowski's troubled quest in taking forward his 'historicist foot' into the terrain of the Sanskrit astronomer's practice on the other hand is driven by search for a 'research programme' or at least a semblance of it, given the continuity of the great tradition.[64] But I would venture to suggest that the world of the regional practitioner's context of work is a significant entry point, which can actually help even bring the Sanskrit tradition down to the realm of social practices, and can help render it amenable to historical scrutiny.[65] I would argue it is impossible to posit

[62] Kim Plofker, *Mathematics in India*, 173–216.

[63] Ibid., p. 215.

[64] Christopher Minkowski, 'The Study of Jyotiḥśāstra and the Uses of Philosophy of Science', *Journal of Indian Philosophy* 36, nos. 5–6 (2008): 587–597. See also Christopher Minkoswki, 'Astronomers and Their Reasons: Working Paper on Jyotisḥśāstra', *Journal of Indian Philosophy* 30, no. 5 (October 2002): 495–514.

[65] The recent reminder that even Sanskrit literary practitioners writing from the regions addressing local audiences were not taken all that seriously even though 'these works reveal a vital

the case of abstraction or transcendence in Sanskrit as a sign of universalism when we consider the social hierarchies that shaped and that were produced by the skills of abstraction. Be it the accountant-scribe or the astronomer, or even school based training, communication was oriented towards those who were authorized to be eligible to participate in distinct spheres of activity. These were essentially power laden acts. For the *Kaṇakkaṉ*, the mnemonic function of the verse embodied a movement from concrete measuring activity into a rule of know-how for a fellow practitioner—signalling a constant traffic between practice, the school and the profession. However, caste hierarchy would determine who that practitioner would be. This means that we should not be surprised that few aspired to move from 'know-why' to 'know-how'.

Plofker legitimately worries that the role of demonstration in Sanskrit mathematical practice cannot be treated as a substitute for orality or as a derivative of that mode of practice, as is often taken by historians. This leads her to look for qualities of 'intuition' in the practice of 'non-rigorous method of mathematical inference', which could have simultaneously rendered that manner of doing mathematics 'strengthened or weakened'[66] or something that resided in the individual brilliance of the mathematician. This is probably bound by the historian's confounded search for a reasonably universal yardstick for what constituted mathematical practice. If this is further compounded by lack of evidence about the social conditions of that practice, is uncovering mathematical techniques from the practitioner—framing practice under the eternal binary of the theoretical and the applied—the last resort for the historian of mathematics? In the case of the *Kaṇakkaṉ* traditions, the mathematics of the measuring rod and the measuring vessel determined how elastic the computational rhythms could be between meeting the requirements of computation and the yearning to communicate—and communicate elegantly—such techniques to the trainee. There was not an ever-expanding horizon of

and organic relation to the crystallizing regional traditions of the subcontinent and to emerging vernacular literatures', means that they were also speaking and living with two different languages. See Yigal Bronner and David Shulman, '"A Cloud Turned Goose": Sanskrit in the Vernacular millennium', *The Indian Economic and Social History Review* 43, no. 1 (2006): 1–30.

[66] Kim Plofker, 'How to Appreciate Indian Techniques for Deriving Mathematical Formulas?' *Mathematical Europe: History, Myth, Identity*, eds. Catherine Goldstein, Jeremy Gray, and Jim Ritter (Paris: Edition de la Maison des Sciences de l'Homme, 1996), Vol. 62, 55–64.

mathematics in front of them. They only had ways to achieve competence, or even to show off their virtuosity. Could this way into the world of the *Kaṇakkaṉ* inform the inquiry into the practices of the astronomer?

John Warren in 1825 was awestruck by how a Tamil *munshi* who calculated 'a lunar eclipse by means of shells placed on the ground, and from tables memorized from artificial words and syllables'. In 1952, even Otto Neugabeur, the historian of the exact sciences who was reading Warren, found it interesting.[67] It is a different problem for us to ask why no historian of mathematics considered it worthwhile to investigate what and how the Tamil *munshi* was doing and where he acquired such techniques. But apropos our present discussion, this anecdote indicates the possibility of a hierarchical and entangled world of mathematical practices of the practitioners, but a world that was not kind to shared learning opportunities. The binaries of theory-practice and pure-applied that the history of knowledge has sustained, however, can only limit the explorations of the nature of such borrowing at the local level, especially through the study of curricular transactions in places of higher learning such as the Sanskrit *tols* in comparison to learning spaces of the accountant and the working spaces of the *veṭṭiyāṉ*.

In this chapter so far, we have seen how the task of spatially and socially situating the *Kaṇakkatikāram* in the early modern Tamil region has actually taken us beyond the constraints of such binaries, or even the binary of the nation-region or Sanskrit and Tamil. Closely following practice and its ethos could take us closer to it and enable us to look at the world around it to find contours of give-and-take, which were conditioned by caste society rather than by any prior distinction between knowledge forms. There could be several ways in which mathematization proceeded but whether they did so or not depended on the orientation allowed by socially segregated spheres of access to knowledge and its practice.

By not approaching the problem of mathematical knowledge as located in practices but rather as located in distinct language traditions (Tamil and Sanskrit), historians of mathematics have focused in effect on how the traditions translated from each other, while continuing to code capability in terms of reasoning rather than social context in which the dignified tradition's difference from the practical was established.

[67] Cited in Høyrup, 'Sanskrit – Prakrit Interactions', 3.

The problem of translation as the historians of science have used it thus makes the social redundant and the *knowledge form* the foremost determinant, thereby privileging one form over the other. Hence the world of the local practitioner and his ways of learning and working with mathematics has been occluded. Treating the texts not as disembodied pursuits of transcendental knowledge but as records of practices requires 'a shift in focus from the world of ideas to the world of action, from thinking to doing'.[68] The problem of time—what got transmitted when—and what were the routes and who were the agents of such transmission process is by itself a straightforward problem when considered in its own right, in history writing. But when weighed down by parochialism of the nation, or the obsession with priority (who did what first?) has only sustained an equally parochial effort to look for 'scientificity' in past practices or even for that matter, the postcolonial intellectual's quest for different selfhoods. The practitioners themselves were probably not afraid of translation and borrowing, when it was within the order of their working lives, even if they were only village clerks. What remains important to ask, however, is to what end such borrowing happened—to teach, to work or to even perform?

The *Kaṇakkaṉ*, the student, and the *tiṇṇai* school teacher—with their own sets of virtuosity and social legitimacy—pursued the arts of computation. But it is very difficult to imagine their practice without the training in the *Eṇcuvaṭi*, the quintessential Tamil table book, that enabled each and every step in problem solving. It is to the working of the school in which the table book was drilled into the students that we need to turn our attention to. This will help us ground the context-free computational principles and tie them to social practices—not to undertake an outrageously externalist task in the history of mathematics, but to prevent further alienation of practice from the teaching and learning of mathematics.

[68] Similar voices could be heard in the European context as well, See Jim Bennett, 'Practical Geometry and Operative Knowledge'.

III
Memory and Mathematics in *Tiṇṇai* Schools

Our exploration of the history of mathematics began with a study of mathematical texts in circulation in the Tamil region in the seventeenth and eighteenth centuries. Then, we saw how the practitioner that these texts trained had to have a thorough grounding in memory-based skills. Such skills were nurtured in the *tiṇṇai* schools of the Tamil country through primers like *Eṇcuvaṭi*. This chapter will discuss the learning practices in these institutions in detail.

Just as it was impossible to study the mathematical knowledge of *Kaṇakkatikāram*, *Kaṇita Nūl*, and *Āstāṉa Kōlākalam* and their practitioners in isolation from the hierarchical and socially fragmented landscape, the *tiṇṇai* school and its practices, too, require us to take into consideration the social field in which they operated. The *tiṇṇai* school's environs and the nature of its instruction cannot be viewed in isolation from its structures of support in the community, roles, and relationships of the students and teachers within and outside the school, and its rituals and mode of functioning. These social relationships also shaped the curriculum in these institutions with respect to the learning of language and mathematics. We will look at these in turn before focusing on the pedagogy of language and mathematics using the *tiṇṇai* texts that we have at our disposal. Our final goal will be to detail the relationship between this pedagogy and the nature of arithmetic practice in the community, providing us with the basis to explore systems of dialogue between skills and practice in circulation across and through caste hierarchy with that of the *tiṇṇai* curriculum. This journey through the *tiṇṇai* school will help us, in our concluding reflection, to discuss the role that the *tiṇṇai* pedagogy of mathematics

Mathematics and Society. Senthil Babu D., Oxford University Press. © Oxford University Press India 2022.
DOI: 10.1093/oso/9788194831600.003.0004

played in the cognitive and social dimensions of the *Kaṇakkatikāram* style of mathematical practice.

What Do We Know About the *Tiṇṇai* Schools?

The primary sources related to *tiṇṇai* schools are quite scant. The manuscript and print archive containing the Tamil texts are products of the curriculum practiced in these schools. But very few biographical accounts mention the school itself. A lot of oral lore about the schools often consists of disjointed memories based on hearsay, while the British colonial archive, especially educational records, contains mostly statistical information. We know nothing of the school's antiquity in the Tamil region. No inscriptions available in Tamil mention the *tiṇṇai* schools. This, of course, may not mean that they were absent in history; instead, it reveals their scale and probably structures of local patronage unlike in the world of monastic and temple-centred learning supported by individual and state patronage. However, we know these schools were not unique to the Tamil country and seem to have been very common institutions almost all over southern Asia and probably across the Bay of Bengal. Some European travel accounts in the seventeenth century have accounts of such institutions in the Tamil country. The only detailed engagement of their presence was documented by the British Educational Surveys in the beginning of the nineteenth century, in Bengal and Madras and later in Bombay and Punjab. See Image 3.1 showing a *pathshala* at work in Varanasi in the nineteenth century.

A recent account of the history of education in South India based on a detailed study of inscriptions from 400 AD to 1300 AD finds no evidence of the presence of Tamil elementary institutions of learning. The inscriptions mention *kaṭikai, maṭam, akrakāram*, and *sālai,* all of which catered to Vedic and Sanskrit education. These were patronized and sponsored in different ways by the ruling elite and were connected to monastic centres, meant mostly for the education of Brahmins.[1]

[1] S. Gurumurthy, *Education in South India Ancient and Medieval Period* (Chennai: New Era Publications, 1979).

Image 3.1 Pathshala learning in progress with children writing on sand along with the loud recitation of a student guiding them, monitored by the single teacher. A school in Varanasi in the nineteenth century. Courtesy: https://commons.wikimedia.org/wiki/File:A_private_teacher_in_one_of_the_indigenous_schools_in_Varanasi_(c._1870).jpg, accessed on 20 October 2018.

These were exclusive institutions teaching the Vedas, Sanskrit, theology, law, logic, medicine, and astronomy. One of the earliest records of the elementary *tiṇṇai* kind of schools in South India can be found in a Portuguese traveller, Peter Della Vạlle's travel writings, when he toured Malabar in the year 1623.[2] In the eighteenth century, Thomas Barnard, an engineer by profession was entrusted by the East India Company to undertake a household survey of the Chingleput District of Madras Presidency to assess the revenue potential for the Company, which resulted in a huge corpus of village-level revenue accounts in the form of

[2] Peter Della Valle, 2-11-1623, in *The Travels of Sig. Peter Della Valle: A Noble Roman Into East India,* 1665, 110–111, cited in Dharampal, *The Beautiful Tree: Indigenous Education in Eighteenth Century India* (Delhi: Biblia Impex, 1983), 260.

palm-leaf manuscripts. These manuscripts provide a detailed account of the revenue administration and institutions already in place in the villages of the district when the survey was conducted during the years 1767–1774.[3] Pulavar Kannaiyan, who has worked extensively with these manuscripts, now stored at the Tanjore Tamil University, mentions that there are a few references to the village 'Tamil teachers' being paid grants in kind, as a particular percentage of the total produce on an annual basis.[4]

Some years after the Barnard Survey, Thomas Munro, as Governor-General of Madras Presidency, ordered a detailed survey of indigenous schools in the year 1822, which culminated in the year 1826. Munro's report on the survey's findings became the basis for his initiatives to improve indigenous education. Dharampal, the Gandhian scholar, used Munro's survey along with that of W. Adam in Bengal, Elphinstone in Bombay, and G. Leitner in Punjab in his project to document the nature of indigenous education in the precolonial period. His project sought to validate Gandhi's claim, in his debate with Philip Hartog, that British rule uprooted indigenous education in India and hence literacy actually declined. This older debate brought out the British surveys of indigenous education out into the public. Dharampal argued in social and economic terms to show how the British were responsible for destroying a well-established indigenous system of education, by just letting them 'stagnate and die', through fiscal measures that affected the village society on the one hand, and by sheer 'ridicule' and insensitivity of that tradition on the other.[5]

B.S. Baliga, a Madras archivist, revisited the same debate in the 1970s.[6] During his tenure in the Madras Archives, he tried to verify if literacy actually declined during the period 1822–1931 in the light

[3] This survey in two villages was recently reprinted. See M. D. Srinivas, T. K. Paramasivam, and T. Pushkala, *Tiruppōrūr maṟṟum Vaṭakkuppaṭṭu: Patiṉeṭṭām Nūṟṟāṇṭu āvaṇaṅkaḷ* (Chennai: Centre for Policy Studies, 2001).

[4] Pulavar Kannaiyan, 'Revenue Administration in Madras', Unpublished Notes, n.d., p. 24.

[5] See Dharampal, *The Beautiful Tree*, particularly his Introduction, 1–79.

[6] B. S. Baliga, *Literacy in Madras 1822–1931, Studies in Madras Administration*, Vol. 2 (Madras: Government Press, 1960), 58–81.

of the Gandhi—Hartog debate and if the British government could be charged with having done so. Baliga, using archival sources, primarily correspondence between the Presidency and District collectors, showed that during the period 1822–1881, literacy declined by using the data on the number of children in all schools, including the *tiṇṇai* schools, and contrasting it with the number of children in the school-going age in the total population. However, during the period, 1881–1931, Baliga used the annual returns of the Director of Public Instruction and several other measures taken by the government after the Wood's Despatch (1850) such as the grants in the aid system and the results grant system, etc. Here, he showed that the number of children of school-going age had actually increased and that elementary schools under the supervision of the Directorate of Public Instruction had, in fact, increased. In that sense, for him, literacy did not decline and the British could not be blamed for eroding literacy; rather he argued that they succeeded in assimilating and fostering the *tiṇṇai* schools, resulting in better coverage. Despite the different assessments of the fate of the school, both Baliga and Dharmapal, like Gandhi and Hartog, equated the *tiṇṇai* curriculum with providing literacy, in the conventional sense of reading and writing. Suffice here to say that, for all this, the *tiṇṇai* schools were, however, recognized only in statistical frames, and no effort was made in understanding their modes and rhythms of functioning.

P. Radhakrishnan's project in the 1980s reviewed the same set of British surveys to bring out aspects of caste-based discrimination in these schools.[7] His concern was to look at 'differentiation in the participation of education and the role of the caste system in working out such a differentiation', because according to him, 'from Vedic to village education, is involved a process of Brahminic ascendancy in the bureaucratic hierarchy and subsequently to restrict literacy to lower classes, to guard their interests'. The discriminatory nature of the patronage extended to the indigenous *tiṇṇai* schools vis-à-vis the Sanskrit *tols*, expensive fee-based *tiṇṇai*

[7] P. Radhakrishnan, 'Caste Discrimination in Indian Education I: Nature and Extent of Education in Early Nineteenth Century India', *MIDS Working Paper No. 63* (Chennai 1986). Also see a condensed version of the project in P. Radhakrishnan, 'Indigenous Education in British India: A Profile', *Contributions to Indian Sociology* 24, no. 1 (1990): 1–29.

schools vs. free Sanskrit education, absence of a mural dimension, limited periods of study, and the limited nature of the curriculum are identified as realms of discrimination structured into the organization of these schools.

A more recent study of the Bengali *pathsalas* by Poromesh Acharya profiles the Bengali variant of the *tiṇṇai* schools.[8] Acharya's account is different from the above works, in that it tries to address the nature and orientation of the *pathsala* curriculum in relation to the society, which supported the teacher and the schools. Calling these the 'three – R' schools, Acharya says that these institutions flourished during the sixteenth to the eighteenth centuries. They were widespread, decentralized, with a curriculum that was oriented towards 'practical' competence by following a 'rote method' in the teaching of reading, writing, and arithmetic, a curriculum that was sustained by the community and the teacher, providing them a sense of 'spontaneity', which the British failed to appreciate.[9]

In sum, the scholarship on the *tiṇṇai* school has relied not just on British accounts, but also on the very terms of British documentation when it comes to the task of understanding the curriculum and pedagogy of these schools. Such perceptions were conditioned by a particular understanding of what constituted 'learning' at the elementary levels of a scheme of education. The *tiṇṇai* curriculum had to be perceived in relation to such frames of understanding, perpetuating a stereotype, characterizing them as 'practical' or 'reading, writing, and arithmetic' schools. But the task is to attempt a reconstruction of the *tiṇṇai* mode and rhythm, now that we know a bit more about the content of the curriculum, nature, and organization of the texts that were products of this curriculum, accompanied by distinct modes of pedagogic practice, that was so central to their rhythm.

It is important to dwell within the *tiṇṇai* curriculum, its pedagogy, and its ways of operation in practice. What is also important is to gain a

[8] Poromesh Acharya, 'Indigenous Education and Brahminical Hegemony in Bengal', *The Transmission of Knowledge in South Asia: Essays on Education, Religion, History and Politics*, ed. Nigel Crook (Delhi: Oxford University Press, 1996), 98–118.

[9] Sourced from Archaeological Survey of India Collections: India Office Series (Volume 46), taken in c. 1870 by Brajo Gopal Bromochary.

glimpse of a typical Tamil village that would have sustained these institutions. Also, a certain picture of the nature of mathematical practices that were in circulation among the communities in the village becomes necessary if any sense has to be made of the goals and orientation of the *tiṇṇai* curriculum. So we begin our journey in the environs of the locality that sent its children to be schooled in the *tiṇṇai*.

The Local Community as Measuring Public

At the time of extensive documentation of the Tamil schools, in the early nineteenth century, Tamil localities in which they were found were spatially organized by caste hierarchy. The typical Tamil village of this time, as we can see from the eighteenth century locality accounts, comprised of a distinct division of labour. Social groups contributing to the economy performed distinct occupational roles in relation to land and commerce, and these ties were regulated by a revenue and ritual structure. Spatial segregation of the various communities, especially manual labouring caste groups, was common. Numerical entities—quantities, estimation, measurement, planning, and control—were integral features of regulation and embodied in the structure of taxation, forms of tribute, in agricultural practices, in the use of labour and in payment of wages. Transactions involving the exchange of food grains in particular depended on occupational roles, the contribution of labour, services offered, and social status of the participants involved.[10] The number thus had a deep life in social and political practice.

For example, when it came to land revenue administration, the following representatives were involved whose *job was to estimate, measure and control*:

- *Kaṇakkar* (accountant);
- *Veṭṭiyāṉ* (assistant to accountant and the one who actually measured land);
- *Tukkiri* (guard and assistant);

[10] M. D. Srinivas, et al., *Eighteenth Century Locality Accounts*, 24–30.

- *Talaiyāri* (village assistant);
- *Nīrkkāraṉ* or *Kampukaṭṭi* (one who regulated water for irrigation) and
- *Paṭiyāḷ* (manual labourer).

There were other service caste groups in the same village who were related to the agrarian production processes and received their share in distinct percentages of the total produce out of the different kinds of land and norms of taxation:

- *Pāḷaiyakkārar* (village headman);
- *Vaṇṇār* (washermen); *Nāvitar* (barber);
- *Kuyavar* (potters); *Terupperukki* (sweeper);
- *Tēvatāci* (courtesans);
- *Taṭṭāṉ* (goldsmith or blacksmiths);
- *Taccaṉ* (carpenter);
- *Kammāḷar* (artisans, also a generic caste name), etc.

Allocations of grain were made to each of these groups from the total produce of the land in the village, notwithstanding the sphere of day-to-day transactions that involved counting, measuring, computing, estimation, planning, with objects of work and commodities. Occupational engagements warranted a cognitive negotiation with quantities, estimations and related computations primarily by those who manually laboured for their wages and returns, not to mention those groups who used their labour. The culture of labour and entitled returns, in parts of well-defined whole(s), defined the daily lives of the labouring classes compelling them to know and engage with practices that were mathematical. It is this material context of an agrarian and mercantile social order which fostered a constant and everyday measurement of labour and its returns in which we must place institutions of schooling called the *tiṇṇai* schools. The school was an arena of social reproduction that ordered knowledge, especially mathematical knowledge and its distribution. Its authority is derived from its capacity to sanctify ritually and through its social exclusion certain modes of knowledge formation and its transmission. This intimate exercise of power play at the heart of the pedagogic virtue cultivated within the precincts of the school and it was felt by those who could not enter its boundaries.

Introducing *Tiṇṇai* Schools

'*Tiṇṇai*' in Tamil means a veranda-like space in a traditional Tamil house,[11] usually outside, for people to gather, talk or rest. The schools got this name because they functioned usually in such spaces, the *tiṇṇai* of a household that usually belonged to that of the teacher, or of a local notable, or even under the shade of a tree or that of the local temple. The British hence gave them the name '*pyal*' schools, sometimes even spelt as '*pial*' meaning, '*veranda* schools' (for a visual characterization of the school, see Image 3.2). These were single-teacher schools, situated not in all the villages, but one in three to four villages, when the children could

Image 3.2 A pyal School near Vepery, Madras in the 1860s.
Courtesy: https://sites.google.com/site/thumbòochetty/EARLY-LIFE, accessed on 20 October 2018. Used under the Creative Commons License from the original source http://dsal.uchicago.edu/

[11] For the spatial configuration of a traditional Tamil household and its intricacies, see Robert Dulau, *Nakaramum Vīṭum Vāḻumiṭattiṉ Uṇarvukaḷ* (Pondicherry: French Institute of Pondicherry, 1992).

be in a walking distance of seven to eight miles.[12] It was entirely managed by the teacher, catering to the students of the upper and the middle caste groups that included the cultivating castes, but not the manual labouring caste groups.[13] However, they were not like the Sanskrit schools that were meant exclusively for Brahmins. While most of the Sanskrit schools were patronized by land grants, the *tiṇṇai* schools hardly had any grants, and education involved an expense, to be incurred by the families of the children, paid straight to the teacher, in cash and in kind, on a periodical basis.[14] The complexion of the institution varied in accordance to the nature of the village, for instance, in a village dominated by merchant groups, it was almost an exclusive institution managed by the community, like the *Nakarattār* community did, in training its younger generation.[15]

The *Tiṇṇai* Teacher

For the *tiṇṇai* teacher, age was no criterion. What mattered was his ability in teaching, entirely guided by his own experience. It was usual then for him to model himself on his own teachers and scope for improvement and innovation in teaching was entirely dependent on how sympathetic he was to the students. He was generally considered to be a knowledgeable individual, whose skills would improve with experience and age, 'the longer you were a teacher, the better you were'. His professional ethos, however, was not dependent on the caste he belonged to, but more in terms of his ability to teach and play socially assigned roles in the village. He was not a free floating individual, but had to function entirely

[12] S. Sivalingaraja and S. Sarasvati, *Pattoṉpatām Nūṟṟāṇṭil Yāḻppāṇattu Tamil Kalvi* (Colombo: Kumaran Putthaka Illam, 2000), 15.

[13] U. Vē. Cāmināta Aiyar mentions in his biography that his *tiṇṇai* school teacher, Narayana Iyer, in his village, taught students from among the peasants as well as from the *akrakāram*, the Brahmin residential area in the village. See U. Vē. Cāmināta aiyar, *Eṉ Carittiram* (Chennai: U. V. Swaminatha Aiyar Library, 1990), 55.

[14] See A. D. Campbell, 'Note on Indigenous Education', Proceedings of the Madras BoR, TNSA, 25 August 1823, 958, nos. 32–33: 7167–7187.

[15] See P. Annamalai, *Nakarattār Kaṇakkiyal* (Chennai: Manivasakar Pathippagam, 1988), 92. *Nakarattārs* are also known as *Nāṭṭukkōṭṭai ceṭṭiyārs*, a well-known trading community, known for their overseas trade in the South East Asian countries, and their sophisticated skills in book keeping and accounting in Tamil.

within the circumscribed territory of the village, constantly watched by the people, who respected him, used his skills but also constantly evaluated him. He was dependent on them as well, for his sustenance was entirely based on the income he drew from the fee paid by the families of the children, and the periodical payments in kind, that were meant to be given to him, on special occasions, festivals, on the beginning of new lessons, on the day of initiation into school, etc. On average, he earned about four rupees and eight *annas* in a month,[16] but this highly varied depending on the village and region in question. His usual payments in kind involved fruits, edible oil, fuelwood, paddy, or rice (the rich usually paid him rice).[17] But payment in money also was predominant. Apart from the nominal fee he collected, some sources say that he earned extra money on holidays, called *vāvukkācu,* about a quarter of a rupee. On festival days in a year, children would sing and dance in special costumes in front of each house, when the families were obliged to offer money or kind, called the *maṇampu* money, that usually took care of the marriage-related expenses of the teacher's family.[18]

Certain other accounts also claim that the teacher would sell palm-leaf manuscripts for a price, on-demand, of significant texts, mostly engaging the senior students as scribes for the job. There is one story of how the students were sent to the weekly market with palm-leaf manuscripts, where they were supposed to sell them and earn money for the sake of the teacher.[19] Another account says that it was also usual for the families of the children to do free labour in the land of the *tiṇṇai* teacher, if he owned any, so that he could cultivate it without having to pay for the labour in wages.[20]

Certain ancillary income also came in by the social roles he played in the village. He was usually the most easily accessible scribe in the village, who by his virtue of knowledge to read and write, and as a 'knowledgeable' individual, also in most instances became an arbiter of local disputes,

[16] This figure is computed for the 1820s by P. Radhakrishan for the Madras Presidency. See Radhakrishnan, *Caste discrimination in Indigenous Education*, 51–55.

[17] Cāminàta Aiyar, *Eṉ Carittiram*, 56.

[18] Ibid.

[19] Personal recollection of Mr K. Venkatachalam, who hails from a small village in the Chengam Taluk in Tiruvannamalai District of Tamil Nadu. Mr Venkatachalam himself is a scholar in Tamil mathematics, who taught me the rudiments of the subject.

[20] Sivalingaraja and Sarasvati, S., *Yāḻppāṇattu Tamil Kalvi*, 51.

fixed time for auspicious occasions like time of seeding and harvest or roofing the house and also temple related affairs. Some of them also played the role of a local medical practitioner and astrologer, which always returned him some income. He in this sense was an integral member of the community. However, he couldn't afford to antagonize them in any way, for his life was entirely dependent on the patronage extended by the families, notwithstanding the fact that he often had to work for it. But as far as the school was concerned, he seems to have had a free hand in running the day-to-day affairs of it, where the children were considered to be his entire responsibility. He handled the curriculum and pedagogy of the school, entirely on his own by deciding its routine, setting its rhythm. He could be a scholar himself, who could compose literature in verses, but the most common teacher of the *tiṇṇai* school would be somebody who would guide the students until the elementary stages of learning, beyond which stage, he would invariably suggest specialist teachers in the vicinity for scholarly learning in Tamil. In that sense, he was one significant link for the circulation of scholarly networks in a region, which was alive, by constant search for teachers by the students, committed to such learning. In another sense, he was also a medium for the circulation of Tamil literary and grammatical texts, epics, and even mathematical texts; in effect, a conduit between patrons and scholars and scribes. His reputation also was dependent on which network he belonged to, often determined by the reputation of the teacher, under whom he was trained, like the teacher *paratēci* of *Vrittacalam*, who U. Vē. Cāmināta Aiyar mentions as an important link in a network of teachers covering three to four districts.[21] His professional virtuosity invariably came from the reputation from within the community and his own self-tutored or imitated ways of life, conditioned by his commitment to the profession of teaching, like Catakopan Aiyangar, who genuinely believed that teaching, magnified and enhanced knowledge, and to gain that 'pleasure', he wouldn't mind 'teaching a pole kept in front of him' while he would go on narrating his lessons.[22]

Tamil texts like the *Naṉṉūl* even set the standards for a virtuous teacher as the one who has knowledge in the order of a mountain, patience like the earth, and from whom emanates fragrance as from a flower, while dealing

[21] U. Vē. Cāminata Aiyar, *Eṉ Carittiram*, 100.
[22] Ibid., p. 75.

with his students.[23] It was not always that the teacher gained such a high esteem among all sections of the village. He was also a favourite subject for satire and ridicule, probably more among those sections to whom access to his education was denied. For example, he was a preferred choice of subject, in a genre of theatre, based on satire, apparently popular in the regions under the Maratha rulers, in and around Thanjavur. In one such play,[24] the teacher himself becomes a narrator and vents out his plight, interspersed also with the proud proclamation of his virtues:

> I am Canmuka Narayana Tamotara Vattiyar.
> There are children in this village to eat,
> but not many to learn ...
> Mine was the only school in the entire fort area.
> Everybody learnt in my school, and knew of no other.
> Even people from outside desired to study with me,
> learnt all the skills but still behave like this ...
> Ten schools have come up now.

He then takes pride in his ability to deal with several subjects, to any number of students, and proceeds:

> I don't get a measure of money, not even a cow-dung cake.[25]
> No holiday fee. No holidays at all. I let them all play.
> Will have to keep writing on the palm-leaf all the time.
> Have to read all the time.
> I write volumes of texts.

[23] Sivalingaraja and Sarasvati, S., *Yālppāṇattu Tamil Kalvi*, 51.

[24] *Vikaṭam* is the generic name in Tamil for satire. A pandit had put together a collection of plays, where the subjects of satire begin with the school teacher, the local policeman, the medicine man, the head man, the revenue officer, the petty trader, the nomad, the beggar woman, the pandit, the clown, the *sittar*, and other such characters in the village. Such short monologues often come in during intermissions of performances, to keep the interest of the audience intact, when often the character called the *kaṭṭiyakkāran* (almost like a comedian, but an intelligent one at that, free to ridicule whomsoever he wants). The free translation of the play involving the schoolteacher is taken from that collection, published recently, but the original compiler is not known. See C. K. Deivanayakam, *Palajatika Vikaṭam* (Thanjavur: Sarasvathi Mahal Library, 1986), 1–8.

[25] In the original, it's mentioned as *varaṭṭi*, which has been edited as fuel wood, but we know that *varaṭṭi*, that is cow-dung cake was given as payment in kind, once a week, to the *tiṇṇai* teacher.

I hold the hands of the monitor and write.
Even if the tiny tots assemble, I can make them all recite in unison.
I don't care for people's money.
It is my own volition to teach.
With good temperament, I teach how to read texts.
Teach valuable skills daily, out of my own memory,
while all the gods, stand to protect me.
Children should be god-fearing.
They need memory. Need clarity. Need determination.
Even if paid for it, they should not turn to evil.
At the break of dawn, they should start with their pack of palm-leaves,
Sharply recite from memory all that they studied.
Must know the morals, clear off all that is vulgar, and even break the stammer'.[26]

The *Tiṇṇai* Student

The clientele for the *tiṇṇai* school teacher were the children of the families that could spare their labour. It usually meant that the priestly communities, the cultivators, merchants, and even artisanal castes sent their children to learn with a teacher. The child would normally find a teacher within the village, but might have to walk to the next one, if he wasn't available locally. The student–teacher ratio in a typical *tiṇṇai* school was supposedly in the range of nine to twelve for a teacher in the Madras Presidency but went up to thirty-six in the nineteenth century.[27] One does not know how the teacher, in the assemblage, treated children of various social backgrounds particularly in the absence of a mural dimension to the institution. Children were usually admitted at the age of five. The day of the admission was a special occasion, for the children in the school as well as for the family, for it involved a ritual called *vittiyāppiyācam* or *vityārampam*. On that day, the admission of the child was marked by a procession, when either the teacher went to the child's house, or the child

[26] For other detailed surveys of this kind, see Bhavani Raman, *Document Raj Writing and Scribes in Early Colonial South India* (Chicago: University of Chicago Press, 2012).
[27] Radhakrishnan has meticulously calculated the different ratios in different periods, using the British surveys, See Radhakrishnan, *Caste Discrimination in Indigenous Education*, 70–79.

was taken to the teacher (may be was dependent on the socio-economic status of the family) and conducted a ritual, that usually involved making the child recite the Tamil alphabet and write them on a heap of rice, which would later be sweetened and distributed to all the children and neighbours. The teacher however would get his share, normally a new pair of clothes, rice, vegetables, and some money. But once admitted, then the child was at his mercy, for those eight to nine hours of the child's presence in the school. In certain other cases, probably for slightly older children, who were either taught by parents or relatives at home, if were to be admitted, the teacher would evaluate the capability of the child in clarity of pronunciation and retentive memory, before he takes him into the school. But this would have been the case for very few teachers, who were in demand.[28]

The *tiṇṇai* school was meant for boys. Girls were not allowed into them. Though some observers in the nineteenth century mention that girls of particular castes like the *Kaikkōḷars* and the courtesans were educated, that was nevertheless not along with the boys. Even there, interestingly, girls would be taught 'to read and write' but not arithmetic.[29] Once admitted, the students were not divided into sections according to their age groups, but with respect to their ability in progressing to stages of learning. This would usually be the case for the whole of the student's stint with the *tiṇṇai* school. This raises an interesting issue on what exactly the notions of childhood were in that society. A learner always ready to be trained in cultivating memory, with enough dexterity to be able to write from day 1, a monitor, and even as an errand-boy, all at the same time, within the framework of the institution. But we find no evidence to show that there was a syllabus design that was sensitive to the age groups of the children, though there is a clearly laid out plan of things in the learning of language and mathematics, which will be discussed soon, in this chapter. The best student becomes the *caṭṭāmpiḷḷai*, or the monitor,

[28] Sivalingaraja and Sarasvati, S., *Yāḻppāṇattu Tamil Kalvi*, 18.

[29] Evidence given by Mrs Brander, Inspectress of Girls Schools, to the Madras Presidency Committee of Education, *Evidence Taken Before the Madras Provincial committee*, Madras, 1882, 9. She says that in few places, girls do learn along with their brothers. The next evidence presented by Mrs R. M. Bauboo to the committee however says that girls were not at all allowed in the *tiṇṇai* schools, see Ibid., p. 13. For more on the status of girls' education in the indigenous mode and later in the nineteenth century, see Sita Anantharaman, *Getting Girls to School: Social Reform in the Tamil Districts 1870–1930* (Calcutta: Stree, 1996).

who substitutes for the teacher in several ways in the teaching-learning process of the school. So it was important that the children keep the monitor in good spirits, because the modes of punishment, were particularly harsh in these institutions: *kōtaṇṭam* was the name of the punishment, where the student's legs would be tied to a pulley and hung upside down; *kutirai ēṟṟam* or horse riding, where the 'deviant' will have to carry another student on his back; kneeling down for long hours, not to mention the whims of the teacher's rod, which clearly ruled and reigned high in the minds of the students.[30] There was also the constant pressure on the child to deliver the fee to the teacher, on particular days of the week or the month, at the discretion of the teacher or as a custom in the village. In some cases, the children were also often employed not only in the household chores of the teacher but, even on the land of the teacher, if he had some.[31]

The *Tiṇṇai* Curriculum

There was no standardized curriculum set for these schools across regions. It varied widely, depending on the region and the language of instruction. There was no uniformity either, in case of the duration of learning for a *tiṇṇai* proficient to move out. It varied between three years and ten years from the time of admission of the child at the age of five, whereas in the case of the Sanskrit schools the duration was dependent on the branches of learning.[32] The orientation of the curriculum across regions was, however, local. It wasn't meant to equip anybody for any particular occupational role, nor was it meant to create scholars out of the *tiṇṇai* students. However, it was definitely meant to enable a student to take up any occupation including the literary profession, once he had completed the course of instruction in the *tiṇṇai*. The fundamental goal was to enable the children in the village to become competent and skilled

[30] U. Vē. Cāmināta Aiyar claims out of his own experience that the rule of the rod helped skills in memory. He also recounts the nature of punishment meted out to students. Cāmināta Aiyar, *Eṉ Carittiram*, 57.

[31] Sivalingaraja and Sarasvathi, S., *Yāḻppāṇattu Tamil Kalvi*, 51.

[32] Radhakrishnan, 'Caste Discrimination in indigenous education', 86, where he has compiled the various information collected from the reports of the district collectors, as part of the Munro survey.

participants in all the transactions of letters and numbers, within the village or outside of it. Its aim was not to enable them to compose poetry but to write practical letters and petitions, in proper and correct Tamil. It wasn't meant to enable the students to write commentaries on texts that he studied in the *tiṇṇai* school but its goal was to commit all such texts to memory, place them in the context of the lessons based on those texts provided by the teacher—so that he did not feel out of place when any of the text was under discussion within the village. It was important that the *tiṇṇai* student know and relate himself competently to such transactions. In a similar manner, the curriculum was meant to enable the students to count, compute and reduce quantities and measures—to deal with numbers and measures with able skills and competence.

Interestingly, the curriculum blended together language and number learning together, using pedagogic strategies that were rooted in 'memory as a modality of learning', and not just a tool or a technique, that was incidental in the process of 'acquiring knowledge'. Learning in the *tiṇṇai* mode, then meant, a competent engagement with practice, being a legitimate participant in local transactions, with a say in the community of the measuring public. The skills and competence were personal, in the sense of a demanding cognitive engagement and a personal memory, occasioned by situations to be dealt within acts of estimation pertaining to practices within the household or even in productive activities, say estimating expenses for a good yield after the payments to be made. But skills and competence would be recognized as such only when displayed in public. They had to be legitimated in the public, within the community—a normative value of proficiency—that has to attain its credibility in the society, and outside the institutions of the *tiṇṇai* school. In a way, the curriculum of the *tiṇṇai* school rested upon this process of gaining credibility and legitimacy among the local measuring public, for its own sustenance. Skills and competence as knowledge would be possible only when they were performed or displayed in public, among equally credible practitioners of the craft and participants in similar practices, within the community.[33]

[33] This was the potential space for traffic between the *kaṇakkaṉ's* practice and the local public. From the common pool of problems that each provided, mathematization proceeded both at school and in the public.

It trained the student in the practice of writing—although the exercise of writing within the *tiṇṇai* curriculum was only to supplement the memory mode of learning—on palm-leaves, using different kinds of stylus, for different ways of writing, varying with purpose, not to mention the training involved in preparing the palm-leaves, by seasoning them to make them fit enough to write on, and to preserve them. There was neither certification involved, nor a stipulated period of time; it was up to the student to become proficient through this course of instruction, to the satisfaction of the teacher, and if at all it mattered, to his parents. Once he completed this level of training, depending on the parents and the opinion of the teacher, the student had options to go in for specialized learning in the branch that he chose to, with unique teachers with a high reputation in such branches of learning. Or he could simply choose to become an apprentice as a scribe, or an accountant in the local revenue establishment, or a book keeper with a merchant, where learning on the job would add to his repository of skills, which had been ensured in the *tiṇṇai* course of instruction.[34]

The learning of Tamil normally involved a beginning with *Ariccuvaṭi*, the language primer, which is structured to start with the learning of the Tamil alphabet, recognition and writing of monosyllabic words, then bisyllabic words, sentences, paragraphs, and stories in the end. Other texts like the *Ātticūṭi* and *Koṉṟaivēntaṉ*, Cāmināta Aiyar says, were meant to familiarize the children with alphabets. The child usually started out from the teacher's book, they didn't have to use these texts like textbooks. The beginning was to make him recognize the sound-form of a letter, as pronounced by the teacher or the monitor, following whom, he was supposed to recite it aloud ('practicing the tongue', as it is commonly called in Tamil), followed by the act of writing the graphic form of the letter, assisted by the monitor or the teacher, on a heap of fine sand or rice husk, laid out in front of him. To hear, repeat, see the letter and finally write, ensuring the ear-tongue and eye coordination was the procedure. Pronunciation was central in the introduction of alphabets, where loud recital defined the ability to

[34] The life of Cāminātā Aiyar would be a typical example, even though his father seemed to have played a very active role and struggled to make his son succeed in the plans that he had made for him.

write correctly. Once this stage was cleared, then the real training in alphabetical notation, involving combinations of vowels and consonants began, using the various graphic representations, often done by holding the hands of the child. Here again memory was central, with the use of the tongue.[35]

The Tamil alphabetical structure interestingly is also called the *neṭuṅkaṇakku* (meaning literally, the long math or the long computation), which a Tamil scholar has argued, is designed to integrate hearing, speech/pronunciation, and the visual sense altogether, in phonetic measurements, aided by memory as a modality in practice.[36] Vocalization, visualization, retention, and recollection through repeated exercises of recital and writing were central to the memory mode of learning language at the elementary level, where the texts in use were constituted and structured to aid this process.[37] In this mode, writing functions as an aid to the memory mode of learning. Gopal Iyer says that the students memorized what the pundits had written, but copied what they composed, and wrote after dictation when elegance, measure, form, and clarity became the virtues in the craft of writing. For language, the curriculum then used *Ariccuvaṭi* (language primer), *Ātticūṭi* (proverb book), *Koṉraivēntaṉ* (moral lessons), *Nikaṇṭu* (a form of Tamil dictionary), *Piḷḷaittamiḻ* (devotional poetry),[38] and so on, often decided by the teacher.

The *tiṇṇai* math curriculum was very similar to the language component.[39] As mentioned earlier, it did not aim for its students to end up writing mathematical treatises, but to gain basic competence in counting and manipulation of numbers as quantities, as measures in their transformations, in specific contexts. Familiarity with the Tamil number system, the numerical notation, the multiplication tables involving integers, fractions, and measures, the notation for measures of volume,

[35] Sivalingaraja and S. Sarasvati, *Yāḻppāṇattu Tamil Kalvi*, 36–38.

[36] T. V. Gopal Iyer, *Tamil eḻuttum ēṭum* (Thanjavur: Tamil University Publications, 1990).

[37] An interesting parallel but with a complete absence of notation and hence an entirely oral tradition with similar means of memory and practice, until recently, was the south Indian Carnatic music tradition.

[38] For an excellent introduction to this genre of poetry, see Paula Richman, *Extraordinary Child Poems From a South Indian Devotional Genre* (Honolulu: SHAPS Library of Translations, 1997).

[39] On the issue of language learning in the *tiṇṇai* school, see Bhavani Raman, *Document Raj*.

weight, time, and area; problem solving involving the four operations; rule of three, reduction of measures, tables of squares, the Tamil calendar, elementary skills in account keeping, were all structured into the way mathematics was organized in the *tiṇṇai* curriculum. A thorough grounding in these skills would enable the *tiṇṇai* student, to participate in the practices involving the constituents of the measuring public. *Poṉṉilakkam* (Tamil number primer), *Nellilakkam* (Measures primer), *Eṇcuvaṭi* (Tamil tables), *Kuḻimāttu* (Table of squares) were the texts used for this curriculum.

Mathematics and the *Tiṇṇai* Routine

There are no uniform accounts about the exact nature of the daily routine of a *tiṇṇai* school. One account says that a child went to school 'while the cock crows, takes an hour for breakfast and a two hour break for lunch and remains in the school until sunset; the morning was spent in the recitation of new lessons and memorizing the arithmetic tables while in the forenoon he is occupied with copywriting and arithmetic; the afternoons in copying new lessons and in taking new lessons from the teacher'.[40]

Another account says that the children spent about nine hours in the school. Three hours in the morning (6–9 am) devoted to elderly boys to prepare their lessons while the beginners wrote alphabets and multiplication tables on the sand with the help of monitors and in the absence of the teacher. Between ten to one in the forenoon, advanced boys wrote a copy set as instructed by the teacher, and in the afternoon 2–5 pm were the busy hours when the teacher wrote lessons in a palm-leaf book, heard the lessons being repeated, and taught what was written by him in their books, while the young and the less advanced boys were attended to by the monitors. After all the boys had had their lessons, all stood in line before the teacher and the multiplication tables of fractions and integers, names of Tamil years, etc., were repeated by each boy in turn. The teacher

[40] T. Chelvakesavaraya Mutaliar, 'Tamil Education Address Delivered to the Students of the Teachers' College, Saidapet', *MCC Magazine*, January, 1901, 392.

then prescribed homework, usually a problem to be solved orally in the case of advanced students.[41]

U. Vē. Cāmināta Aiyar in his biography recounts his *tiṉṉai* school days as follows: to school at five in the morning, recited the lessons of the previous day, not always in the presence of the teacher but he would anyway listen, sitting inside his house. After 6 am, the children went for a bath, where they carried sand from the riverbed, replaced the old sand on the floor; those who were meant to write, practiced on the sand with their fingers, while the rest memorized. At nine, children went for breakfast and returned in an hour where punctuality had to be strongly adhered to, when the monitor listened to the students reciting from memory; lunch at 12 noon, classes resumed at 3 in the afternoon and ran up to 7 pm. After the lessons, the teacher would tell the names of a flower or a bird or an animal to each one, which was to be remembered. Usually, when children reached home, they repeated the words or the verses to be remembered to their parents, which was meant to enhance memory. The next day, at five, the children got back to school, usually accompanied by an elderly member of the family.[42]

The Learning of Mathematics

Just like the Tamil alphabet, children began their lessons in mathematics with the learning of the Tamil numerals. The process began with the monitor pronouncing the number, which the student would recite, following after the monitor. The monitor then introduced the graphic symbol for that number in the Tamil notation,[43] which the students had to recognize, associate with the number name, and while reciting, write it by themselves, all in unison, first on the sand. Often the monitor would also hold the hands of the beginners, assisting them in the process. This

[41] Evidence submitted by the Deputy Inspector of Schools, Hosur, to the Madras Provincial Committee of Education, *Report of the Madras Provincial Committee of Education, Part II Evidence*, Madras, 21.

[42] U. Vē. Cāmināta Aiyar, *Eṉ Carittiram*, 55–56.

[43] Tamil had a well standardized notation for its numerals. Its development is briefly discussed in the Annexure II, A Brief Note on Tamil Numerical Notation.

would continue until the students acquired familiarity with each number, in terms of their name and symbol, stepping into the first process of committing himself to know numerical notation. Each number would be made familiar in an ordered pattern, as recorded in the text, called the *Poṉṉilakkam* (Image 3.3), which was the elementary number primer in Tamil. This was not a textbook in the modern sense, but functioned like a manual, which wasn't given to the students beforehand. However, each student in the process of learning numerical notation, created his own manual, when he gained sufficient skill to write confidently on a palm-leaf, acquiring a book for himself in the process, his first *ēṭu* or *cuvaṭi*, as it is known in Tamil. When he reached that stage, the student was proficient in the Tamil number system, called *muntiri ilakkam.*

The number system in Tamil had three layers:

- Numbers from ***one and above***, up to a crore were grouped as *Pērilakkam* or *Pēr Eṇ* (literally Large number).
- The second group was called the ***middle number group***—*Iṭai Eṇ* or *Kīḻvāy Ilakkam* also known as *mēlvāy ciṟṟilakkam* (meaning middle numbers or small numbers, in the literal sense). These comprised the fractions from 1/320 leading up to one, that is one divided into 320 parts. So they proceeded farther by adding 1/320, repeatedly, until reaching one. The significant units that occurred in this additive series were the following:
  - *Muntiri* (1/320)
  - *Araikkāṇi* (1/160)
  - *Kāṇi* (1/80)
  - *Araimā* (1/40)
  - *Mukkāṇi* (3/80)
  - *Mā* (1/20)
  - *Mākāṇi* (1/20 + 1/80 or 1/16)
  - *Irumā* (2/20)
  - *Araikkāl* (1/8)
  - *Mummā* (3/20)
  - *Mummākāṇi* (3/20 + 3/80)
  - *Nālumā* (4/20)
  - *Kāl* (1/4)

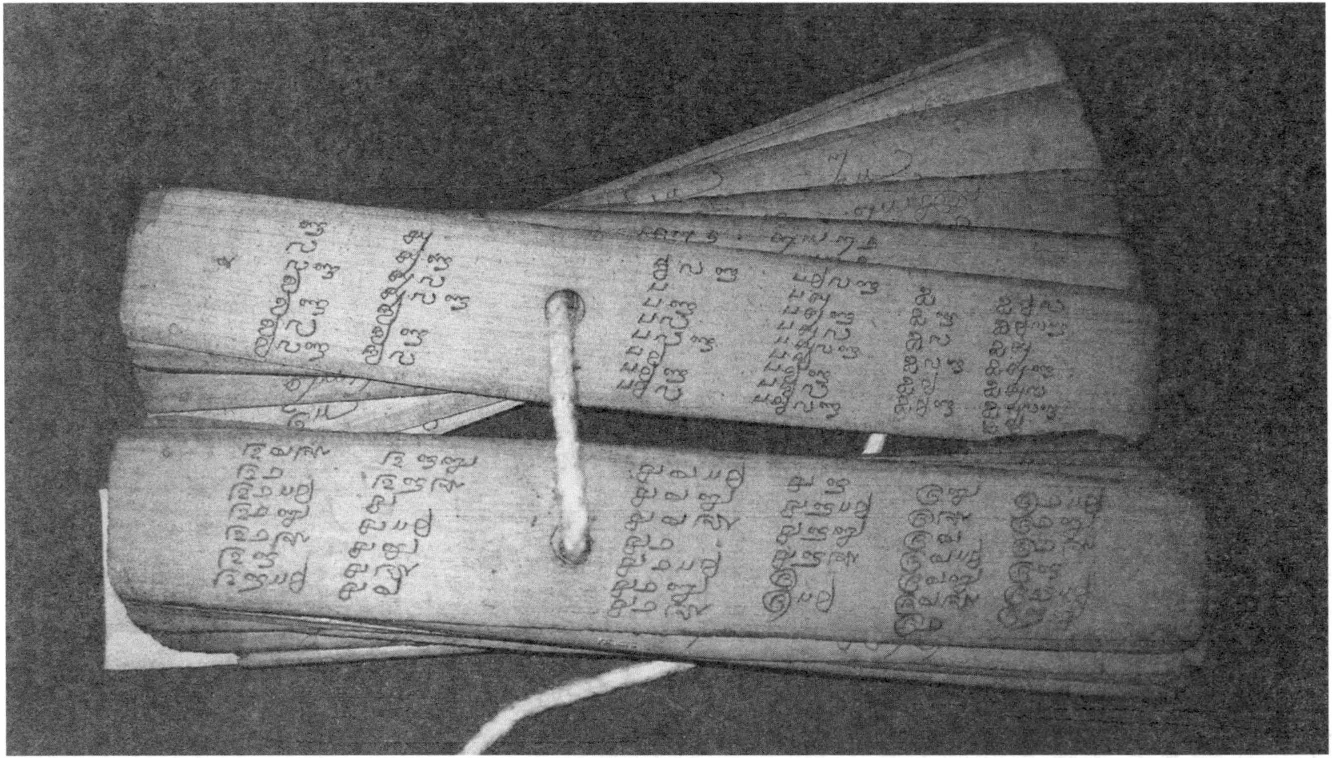

Image 3.3 A manuscript of *Poṉṉilakkam*. Courtesy: Manuscript Collections, French Institute of Pondicherry.

- *Arai* (1/2)
- *Mukkāl* (3/4) and
- *Oṉṟu* (1)

Each of these numbers had standardized notation in Tamil.

- The third group was called the ***small number group***—*Ciṟṟeṇ* or *kīḻvāy ciṟṟilakkam* which comprised fractions from the number (1/320 × 1/320) up to 1/320. This *muntiri* = 1/320 was taken as one, and further divided into 320 parts, and was called *kīḻ muntiri* (*kīḻ* meaning below) and the series proceeds as *kīḻ muntiri* (1/320 × 1/320); *kīḻ araikkāl* (1/320 × 1/160); *kīḻ kāṇi* (1/320 × 1/80) and so on until *kīḻ mukkāl* (1/320 × ¾).

All these three layers were structured as an additive series. Crucially, the significant numbers in the series became standard through frequent use, and these were simultaneously numbers as well as units of measures. *Thus the number theory and standards taught in the school drew from and sustained social reproduction patterns.* For example, *muntiri, kāṇi*, and *mā* were all units of land measures. In fact, all the standard fractions in the middle series and the small number series stood for standard measures of land, except for *mā* which was also a unit for gold. The units thus become numbers, too. The students would then be taught to distinguish between their use as units and as numbers.

The second aspect important in *Poṉṉilakkam* was that all the standard fractions were expressed in terms of each other. This was called the *varicai* or series in Tamil, and they were *muntiri varicai, kāṇi varicai*, and *mā varicai*. This helped in learning fractions—as numbers, as quantities, as familiar units—all of which could be represented in relation to each other, but distinguished by distinct notational forms.[44]

What added significance to the representation of the number series, along with the fact that they were additive and expressed as iterations, was also that they were represented as tables, in rows and columns, a structural device in representation, significant in the memory mode of learning. The

[44] See Annexure III for the complete translation of the *Poṉṉilakkam*.

two-dimensional representation of numbers in a tabular form would immediately situate itself as memory images, visualized in a system of medians and reference points. A closer look at the structural organization of the *Poṉṉilakkam* would reveal this feature. For example, the middle series began with *muntiri*, and continued until you reached the next standard fraction, which was *araimā* as shown in Table 3.1.

Table 3.1 The *muntiri* series

Significant units	Additive factor	Sum
Muntiri		*Araikkāṇi*
Araikkāṇi		*araikkāṇiyē muntiri*
Araikkāṇiyē muntiri		*Kāṇi*
kāṇi	*muntiri*	*kāṇiyē muntiri*
kāṇiyē muntiri		*kāṇiyē araik kāṇi*
kāṇiyē araik kāṇi		*kāṇiyē araikkāṇiyē muntiri*
kāṇiyē araikkāṇiyē muntiri		*araimā*

Then continue till one reaches the next standard fraction, which is *mukkāṇi*, as shown in Table 3.2.

Table 3.2 The *muntiri* series until *mā*

Significant units	Additive factor	Sum
araimā		*araimā muntiri*
araimā muntiri		*araimā muntiriyē araikkāṇi*
araimā muntiriyē araikkāṇi		*mukkāṇi*
mukkāṇi		*mukkāṇiyē muntiri*
mukkāṇiyē muntiri	*muntiri*	*mukkāṇiyē muntiriyē araikkāṇi*
mukkāṇiyē muntiriyē araikkāṇi		*mukkāṇiyē araikkāṇi*
mukkāṇiyē araikkāṇi		*mukkāṇiyē araikkāṇiyē muntiri*
mukkāṇiyē araikkāṇiyē muntiri		*mā*

To illustrate the working of the series, the following figure 3.4, would be helpful to demonstrate its additive character.

Then *mā* proceeded in an iteration, when it would be added to all the above numbers in a series, until the next standard fraction was reached,

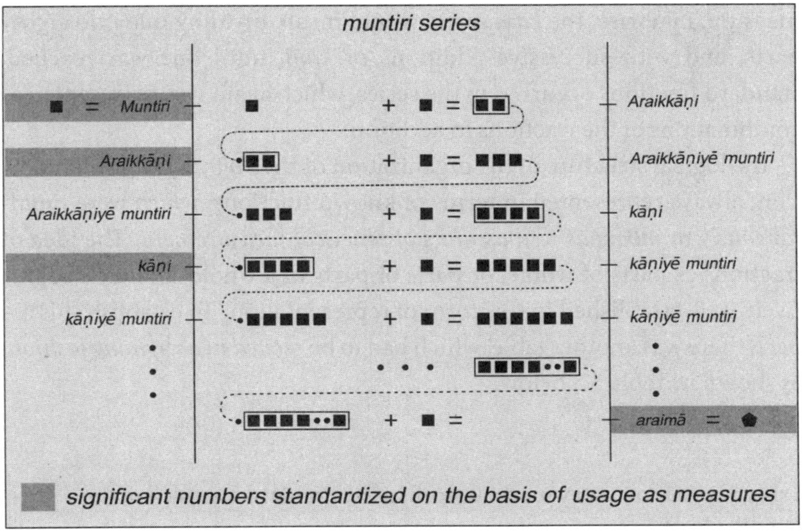

Image 3.4 The working of the *muntiri* series in the *Poṉṉilakkam*. Courtesy: Ganesh Gopal, French Institute of Pondicherry for making the illustration.

which was *mākāṇi*, which would then add itself to all the previous combinations to reach *irumā*, then the series proceeded to reach *araikkāl*, then until *mummā*, followed by *mummākāṇi*, *nālumā*, *kāl*, *arai*, *mukkāl*, and finally one. After one, it would be added to *kāl* to yield *oṉṉē kāl*, then to *arai*, which was *oṉṉarai*, then with *mukkāl* to yield *oṉṉē mukkāl*, then two, and so on until the standard integers occurred, to begin the series of large numbers, or the *pērilakkam*. This constituted the process of learning the *muntiri ilakkam*.[45]

The *mā varicai*, or the *mā* series, on the other hand, began with *mā* (1/20), and after successive additions with *mā*, until one was reached, the same set of fractions were obtained in iteration. Again *mā*, which was one divided into twenty parts, could be represented as a series involving the standard fractions. Twenty *mā* was equal to one *vēli*, in a land measure, thus that series became immediately familiar in a context of practical

[45] Please refer to the translation of the entire *Poṉṉilakkam* provided in the Appendix to understand the working of the series crossing all standard fractions to reach whole numbers and above.

measure. Likewise, the *kāṇi* series would mean, dividing one into eighty parts, and with successive additions of *kāṇi*, until one was reached, standard fractions occurred in the series, which again was represented as combinations of the fractions in addition.

The logical structure of the organization of the *Poṉṉilakkam* was addition, always represented in terms of known fractions, *which were simultaneously numbers as well as units of practical measurement*. The idea of fractions as parts of whole, or parts of parts in a whole, could be cognitively well-established in this form of representation. To establish this aspect, there was another table, which had to be *recited in a rhyming fashion*, as shown in Table 3.3 below:

Table 3.3 The memory mode at work in the standard fractions of the *Poṉṉilakkam*

Memory mode	Modern notation
Mukkāl āvatu nalu paṅkil mūṉṟu	*¾ is 3 parts in 4*
Arai āvatu iraṇṭu paṅkil oṉṟu	*½ is 1 part in 2*
Kālāvatu nalu paṅkil oṉṟu	*¼ is 1 part in 4*
Nālumā āvatu aintu paṅkil oṉṟu	1/5 is 1 part in 5
Mummākāṇi āvatu paṭiṉāṟu paṅkil mūṉṟu	3/16 is 3 part in 16
Mūṉṟumā āvatu irupatu paṅkil mūṉṟu	3/20 is 3 parts in 20
Araikkāl āvatu eṭṭu paṅkil oṉṟu	1/8 is one part in 8
Irumā āvatu pattu paṅkil oṉṟu	1/10 is 1 part in 10
Mākāṇi āvatu paṭiṉāṟu paṅkil oṉṟu	1/16 is 1 part in 16
Orumā āvatu irupatu paṅkil oṉṟu	1/20 is 1 part in 20
Mukkāṇi āvatu eṇpatu paṅkil mūṉṟu	3/80 is 3 parts in 80
Araimā āvatu nāṟpatu paṅkil oṉṟu	1/40 is 1 part in 40
Kāṇi āvatu eṇpatu paṅkil oṉṟu	1/80 is 1 part in 80
Araikkāṇi āvatu nūṟu aṟupatu paṅkil oṉṟu	1/160 is 1 part in 160
Muntiri āvatu muṉṉūṟu irupatu paṅkil oṉṟu	1/320 is 1 part in 320
Kīḻ mukkāl āvatu āyirattu irunūṟṟu eṇpatu paṅkil mūṉṟu	3/1280 [1/320 × 3/4] is 3 parts in 1280
Kīḻ kāl āvatu āyirattu Irunūrru eṇpatu paṅkil oṉṟu	1/1280 [1/320 × 1/4] is 1 part in 1280
Kīḻ nālumā āvatu āyirattu Ārunūṟu paṅkil oṉṟu	1/1600 [1/320 × 4/20] is 1 part in 1600

Table 3.3 *Continued*

Memory mode	Modern notation
Kīḻ mummākāṇi āvatu aintāyirattu nūrru irupatu paṅkil mūṉṟu	3/5120 [1/320 × 3/16] is 3 parts in 5120
Kīḻ mummā āvatu āṟāyirattu nānūṟu paṅkil mūṉṟu	3/6400 [1/320 × 3/20] is 3 parts in 6400
Kīḻ araikkāl āvatu iraṇṭayirattu ainūṟṟu aṟupatil oṉṟu	1/2560 [1/320 × 1/8] is 1 part in 2560
Kīḻ irumā āvatu mūvāyirattu irunūṟu paṅkil oṉṟu	1/3200 [1/320 × 1/10] is 1 part in 3200
Kīḻ mākāṇi āvatu aiyarittu nūṟṟu irupatil oṉṟu	1/5120 [1/320 × 1/16] is 1 part in 5120
Kīḻ orumā āvatu āṟāyirattu nāṉūṟil oṉṟu	1/6400 [1/320 × 1/20] is 1 part in 6400
Kīḻ mukāṇi āvatu irupattu aintāyirattu āṟunūṟil	1/25600 [1/320 × 3/80] is 3 parts in 25600
Kīḻ araimā āvatu paṉiraṇṭu āyirattu eṇūṟil oṉṟu	1/12800 [1/320 × 1/40] is 1 part in 12800
Kīḻ kāṇi āvatu irupattu aintāyirattu āṟu nūṟil oṉṟu	1/25600 [1/320 × 1/80] is 1 part in 25600
Kīḻ araikāṇi āvatu aimpatti ōrāyirattu irunūṟil oṉṟu	1/51200 [1/320 × 1/160] is 1 part in 51200
Kīḻ muntiri āvatu pattu nūṟāyirattu iraṇṭāyirattu nāṉūṟṟil oṉṟu	1/102400 [1/320 × 1/320] is 1 part in 102400

Actually, this marked the end of the fractions, and the beginning of whole numbers in the order of the *Poṉṉilakkam*. Each and every number in all the series mentioned above, then, was memorized in that particular order, in the same pattern of integrating the sound of the number name, visual recognition of the symbol, loud recital, and writing, with concurrent testing at each level by the monitor or the teacher. Such an extensive system of fractions when represented as addition-based iterations, then become the organizing basis to learn numbers in the memory mode of learning. There were also separate sessions as mentioned above, where the children would stand up and recite the entire series in unison, loudly in front of the teacher, one series after the other, repeatedly, day after day, until the logic of addition as the basis of number organization could be cognitively internalized along with the process of building memory registers for the numbers in a particular order. This would finalize the memory learning of the elementary number series in Tamil, called the

Poṉṉilakkam[46] (*poṉ* = gold; *ilakkam* = number place, in the literal sense), denoting a particular order of numbers, as quantities.

Another *tiṇṇai* text was the *Nellilakkam* (*nel* = paddy; *ilakkam*—number place) which was a number series that took the units of Tamil capacity measures as numbers and proceeded along similar lines as that of the *Poṉṉilakkam*. Here, the standard numbers that occurred in the series were the standard units for grain measures in Tamil. This series, then, also was organized on the principle of iterations of addition, where the basic unit of grain measure, the *ceviṭu would* become the number to be added repeatedly until the highest unit, the *kalam was* reached. The standard units of the grain measure, that occurred on the way from *ceviṭu* to *kalam* were *ceviṭu, āḻākku, uḻakku, uri, nāḻi, kuṟuṇi, patakku, tūṇi, and kalam.*[47] In a similar pattern, all these units that occurred below the unit *kalam*, would be represented in combinations with each other, paired by addition, as demonstrated in Table 3.4 below.

Table 3.4 The *ceviṭu series in the Nellilakkam*

Significant units	Additive factor	Sum
Oru ceviṭu		*iru ceviṭu*
Iruceviṭu		*mucceviṭu*
Mucceviṭu		*nālu ceviṭu*
Nālu ceviṭu		*oru āḻākku* (hence, one *āḻākku* = five ceviṭu)
Āḻākku	*ceviṭu*	*āḻākkē oru ceviṭu*
---		---
āḻākkē nālu ceviṭu		*Uḻakku* (hence, five *āḻākku* = one *uḻakku* or ten *ceviṭu* = one *uḻakku)*
uḻakku		*uḻakkē oru ceviṭu*

46 *Poṉṉilakkam* and *Nellilakkam* were usually combined into one *cuvaṭi* or book, and are available as palm leaf manuscripts even today in several collections, abundant in the Government Oriental Manuscripts Library in particular. I consulted an entire set of such manuscripts in the Library of the French Institute of Pondicherry. They were also printed in Tamil press, from the first half of the nineteenth century. For example, see *Poṉṉilakkam, Nellilakkam*, published by Ramasamy Mutaliar, Chennai, 1845. This text was printed in Tamil for the use of the students of a school in Bangalore run by the Caturveta Siddhantha Sabha, an organization that pioneered the publication of Tamil literary and pedagogic manuals in the 1840s.

47 See Annexure III for the complete translation of the *Nellilakkam*.

And so on, until one reached the next unit, the *uri* which was five *uḻakku* or fifteen *ceviṭu*. This would continue until the next unit kept occurring as representations of additions of *ceviṭu*, *āḻākku*, *uḻakku*, until *nāḻi* was reached, which was represented as additions of *ceviṭu*, *āḻākku*, *uḻakku*, and *uri*; then *kuṟuṇi*, which was represented as additions of all the preceding units, then *patakku*, *mukkuṟuṇi*, *tūṇi* and finally *kalam*. After *kalam*, it still proceeded as *kalam* in addition with fractions until ten *kalams*, after which it became a regular whole number series when the standard *kalam* remained until one thousand *kalam* was reached, which marked the culmination of the *Nellilakkam* series.[48]

It should be remembered that each of these units had distinct notational forms and were written as such, while here for the sake of clarity, their names were written and not the symbols. The *Nellilakkam* provided in the Annexure has both the name and the Tamil notation for each unit. Although there is no information for the time taken by a student to become proficient in *Poṉṉilakkam* and *Nellilakkam*, it seems that this alone took about two years to complete, that is to attain a stage when each student, after completely committing to memory the entire series of the *Poṉṉilakkam* and *Nellilakkam*, would actually *write* his *own book, on palm leaves, out of his own memory, without assistance from the teacher or the monitor.*[49] This also marked a process by which *natural memory ability was trained into a cultivated memory*, where reading and writing were only incidental to the learning process,[50] not ends in themselves.

In many ways then, we can read the organization of the number system and its focus on fractions as a sort of abstract or a mirror of a social world which turned around the relations between fragments, the shares one had in land, temple honors, or the relations of hierarchical reciprocity that

[48] Please refer to the translation of the *Nellilakkam* in the Appendix III for the working of this series.

[49] Subbiah Cettiar, an elderly gentleman in the Cettinadu area was trained in a *tiṇṇai* school during his younger days, who said that the completion of *muntiri ilakkam* took about two years. This was said to Prof Subbarayulu, in a personal interview, at his native village, *Attankuti*, 14 January 1989.

[50] Carruthers argues that memory was a native talent, that was merely confirmed by practice, and that it could actually be improved upon, through modes of organization of symbols in particular ways, like 'division and composition, for order most secures the memory'. See Mary Carruthers, *The Book of Memory: A Study of Memory in Medieval Culture* (Cambridge: Cambridge University Press, 1990), 70.

laid the foundation of virtuous generosity or obligation. Mastering the relationship between numbers was to gain an incalculable form of social acumen.

Mastering the *Eṇcuvaṭi*

The *Eṇcuvaṭi*[51] was the quintessential Tamil multiplication table book.[52] These books were so central to the life of the *tiṇṇai* school rhythm that they prompted an early observer to call them as 'multiplication schools'.[53] The *Eṇcuvaṭi* was a compilation of several kinds of multiplication tables. All the numbers learnt during the course of *Poṉṉilakkam* and *Nellilakkam* would be subjected to multiplication with each other, to yield an entire set of tables that was to be committed to memory. The organizing basis of the *Eṇcuvaṭi* was multiplication, represented in a tabular format, to secure an order, helping memory. There were several layers of multiplication tables:

First, multiplication tables of whole numbers involving whole numbers, beginning with one, and usually proceeding up to ten. For example, the first table appeared as in the following Table 3.5.

Second, multiplication tables of whole numbers with fractions, or in other words, each standard fraction in the middle series of the *Poṉṉilakkam* was multiplied with whole numbers from one to ten. For example, the *muntiri* table (as shown in Table 3.6) looked like this:

Third, multiplication tables of fractions with fractions: that is, each standard fraction in the middle series of the *Poṉṉilakkam* was multiplied with each other and represented in tables. For example, the *mukkāl* (3/4) table was as shown in Table 3.7:

Fourth, multiplication tables of fractions in the grain measures series as discussed in the *Nellilakkam* series would be multiplied with whole numbers from one to ten and represented as tables. For example, the first unit *ceviṭu*'s table is shown as in Table 3.8:

[51] For a complete translation of the *Poṉṉilakkam*, the *Nellilakkam* and the *Eṇcuvaṭi*, please refer Appendix III.

[52] See Annexure III for the complete translation of the *Eṇcuvaṭi*.

[53] In a long excerpt from the Walker of Bowland Papers, on the character of the 'native schools', they were called as multiplying schools. See Dharampal, *The Beautiful Tree*, 261.

Table 3.5 The first table of multiplication in the *Eṇcuvaṭi*

Memory mode	Numbers	Multiplication factor	Product
Oṉṟu	1		*1*
Pattu	10		*10*
Iraṇṭu	2		*2*
Irupatu	20		*20*
Mūṉṟu	3		*3*
Muppatu	30		*30*
Nāṉku	4		*4*
Nārpatu	40		*40*
Aintu	5		*5*
Aimpatu	50	Oṉṟu (1)	*50*
Āru	6		*6*
aṟupatu	60		*60*
Ēḻu	7		*7*
eḻupatu	70		*70*
Eṭṭu	8		*8*
Eṇpatu	80		*80*
Oṉpatu	9		*9*
Toṇṇūṟu	90		*90*
Nūṟu	100		*100*

Mallikai yaintu malarntapū toṇṇūṟu koḷḷuvā raivar paṟittu - alakunilai 595
'five jasmine buds bloomed into 90 jasmines, shared by five' *alakunilai* 595

Fifth, multiplication tables involving fractions in the middle series of the *Poṉṉilakkam* with that of the fractions in the *Nellilakkam* series, represented as tables. For example, the table for the unit *nāḻi* is shown in Table 3.9:

Below each table, there was a Tamil verse in a prosodic form. It functioned as a mnemonic to remember a number, which was the sum of the products of that particular table. For example, in the first table given, the verse using jasmine buds was to denote the number 595, the sum of the products of the first table. Each and every table had a prosodic verse, denoting the sum for it, and when sung aloud, they had a rhyme that caught onto memory pretty quickly: yet another instance where the association between prosody and memory was established. Here is an instance where we can see that in a

Table 3.6 The multiplication table for *muntiri* in the *Eṇcuvaṭi*

Memory mode	Numbers	Multiplication factor	Modern notation
Muntiri	1		1/320
Araimā araikkāṇi	10		1/40 + 1/160
Kālē mākāṇi	100		1/4 + 1/20 + 1/80
Araikkāṇi	2		1/160
Mākāṇi	20		1/20 + 1/80
Araiyē araikkāl	200		1/2 + 1/8
Araikkāṇiyē muntiri	3		1/160 + 1/320
Orumāvē mukkāṇiyē Araikkāṇi	30		1/20 + 3/80 + 1/160
Mukkālē mummākāṇi	300		3/4 + 3/20 + 3/80
Oru kāṇi	4		1/80
Araikkāl	40		1/8
Oṉṉē Kāl	400		1 + 1/4
Kāṇiyē araikkāṇi	5	Muntiri	1/80 + 1/320
Mummāvē araikkāṇi	50		3/20 + 1/160
Oṉṉaraiyē mākāṇi	500		1 + 1/2 + 1/20 + 1/80
Kāṇiyē araikkāṇi	6		1/80 + 1/160
Mummāvē mukkāṇi	60		3/20 + 3/80
Kāṇiyē araikkāṇiyē Muntiri	7		1/80 + 1/160+ 1/320
Nālumāvē kāṇiyē araikkāṇi	70		4/20 + 1/80 + 1/160
Iraṇṭē mummāvē mukkāṇi	700		2 + 3/20 + 3/80
Araimā	8		1/40
Kāl	80		1/4
Iraṇṭarai	800		2 + 1/2
Araimāvē muntiri	9		1/40 + 1/320
Kālē araimāvē Araikkāṇi	90		1/4 + 1/40 + 1/160
Iraṇṭē Mukkālē Mākāṇi	900		2 + 3/4 + 1/20 + 1/80
Mūṉrē araikkāl	1000		3 + 1/8

Malarpattu pōteṭu vāṉiramapa vākavilai nāṉkē kompiraṇṭē vēroṉṟē vēriṉ mutaloṉṟē muntiri vāykku – alakunilai 18½ 1/5 1/40 1/160 1/320

memory-based learning system, a prosodic verse acted as a mnemonic to remember an entire table. The prosody, when occasion demands, would act like a trigger to recite the entire table, at once. Also, such verses would lend meaning to the mnemonic only in a context. It was called as *alakunilai*, in

Table 3.7 The multiplication table for *mukkāl in the Eṇcuvaṭi*

Memory mode	Numbers	Multiplication factor	Modern notation
Mukkāl	1		¾
ēḻarai	10		*7+½*
Ēḻupattu aintu	100		75
Oṉṉarai	2		1+½
Patiṉaintu	20		15
Nūṟṟaimpatu	200		150
Iraṇṭēkal	3		2+¼
Irupattu iraṇṭarai	30		*22 + ½*
Irunūṟṟu irupattu aintu	300		*225*
Mūṉṟu	4		*3*
Muppatu	40		*30*
Munnūṟu	400		*300*
Mūṉṟē mukkāl	5		*3 + ¾*
Muppattu ēḻarai	50		*37 + ½*
Muṉṉūṟṟu ēḻupattuaintu	500	*Mukkāl*	*375*
Nālarai	6		*4 + ½*
Nāṟpatti aintu	60		*45*
Nānūṟṟu aimpatu	600		*450*
Aintēkāl	7		*5 + ¼*
Aimpatti iraṇṭarai	70		*52 + ½*
Ainūṟṟu irupattu aintu	700		*525*
Āṟu	8		*6*
Āṟupatu	80		*60*
Āṟunūṟu	800		*600*
Āṟēmukkāl	9		*6 + ¾*
Āṟupattu ēḻarai	90		*67 + 1/2*
Āṟunūṟṟu ēḻupattu aintu	900		*675*
Ēḻunūṟṟu aimpatu	1000		*750*

Nālvar kaṇikaiyar nāṉmāṭak kūṭaliṟ ṟēroṉpa tēṟit teruvē kaṭāvēṟi āṟāvā teṉṟu vilakkiṉāṉ cāletirē kāloṉṟu kaikoṇṭa toṉṟu. Alakunilai – 4496¼

Tamil meaning 'position that points'; *alaku* = pointer and *nilai* = place or position. There is another function to these verses, where in some higher order texts, that were discussed in the first chapter, like the *Kaṇakkatikāram*, where summation of series are dealt with, these mnemonics came in very useful. This mnemonic also served an additional function of verification. Because,

Table 3.8 The multiplication table for *ceviṭu* in the *Eṇ cuvaṭi*

Memory mode	Numbers	Multiplication factor	Product
Oru ceviṭu	1		*1 ceviṭu*
ōrulakku	10		*1 uḻakku*
Irunāḻiye ōruri	100		*2 Nāḻi and 1 uri*
iru ceviṭu	2		*2 ceviṭu*
ōruri	20		*1 uri*
Ainnāḻi	200		*5 Nāḻi*
mucceviṭu	3		*3 ceviṭu*
ōr muvuḻakku	30		*1 muvuḻakku*
Ēḻunaḻiye ōruri	300		*7 Nāḻi and 1 uri*
Nāṟceviṭu	4		*4 ceviṭu*
Oru Nāḻi	40		*1 Nāḻi*
Oru kuṟuṇiye irunāli	400		*1 kuṟuṇi and 2 Nāḻi*
ōr āḻākku	5		*1 āḻākku*
Orunāḻiye ōruḻakku	50		*1 Nāḻi and 1 uḻakku*
Oru kuṟuṇiye nānāḻiye ōruri	500		*1 kuṟuṇi, 4 Nāḻi and 1 uri*
ōrālākkē oru ceviṭu	6	*ceviṭu*	*1 āḻākku and 1 ceviṭu*
Orunāḻiyē ōruri	60		*1 Nāḻi and 1 uri*
Oru kuṟuṇiyē ēḻunāḻi	600		*1 kuṟuṇi and 7 Nāḻi*
ōrālākkē iru ceviṭu	7		*1 āḻākku and 2 ceviṭu*
Orunāḻiyē mūvuḻakku	70		*1 Nāḻi and 1 mūvuḻakku*
Oru patakkē orunāḻiye ōruri	700		*1 patakku, 1Nāḻi and 1 uri*
ōrālākkē mucceviṭu	8		*1 āḻākku and 3 ceviṭu*
Irunāḻi	80		*2 Nāḻi*
Oru patakkē nānāḻi	800		*1 patakku and 4 Nāḻi*
ōrālākkē nāṟceviṭu	9		*1 āḻākku and 4 ceviṭu*
Irunāḻiyē ōruḻakku	90		*2 Nāḻi and 1 uḻakku*
Oru patakkē aṟunāḻiyē ōruri	900		*1 patakku, 6 Nāḻi and 1 uri*
Mukkuṟuṇiyē Orunāḻi	1000		*1 mukkuṟuṇi and 1 Nāḻi*

'*alakunilai oru kalamē nāṉku patakkē ainnāḻiyē oru mūvuḻakkē ōrāḻākku*' (which is *one kalam, four patakku, five nāḻi, one mūvuḻakku and one āḻākku*)

Table 3.9 The multiplication table for *nāḻi in the Eṇcuvaṭi*

Memory mode	Numbers	Multiplication factor	Product
Orunāḻi	*1*		*Nāli*
Mūvuḻakku	*¾*		*1 Mūvuḻakku*
ōruri	*½*		*1 uri*
ōrulakku	*¼*		*1 uḻakku*
ōrālākkē mucceviṭu	*4/20*		*1 āḻākku and 3 ceviṭu*
ōrālākkē iranṭraiccevitu	3/20 + 3/80		1 *āḻākku* and 2 ½ *ceviṭu*
ōrālākkē oru ceviṭu	3/20		1 *āḻākku* and 1 *ceviṭu*
ōrāḻakku	*1/8*		*1 āḻākku*
narceviṭu	*2/20*	*nāḻi*	*4 ceviṭu*
Iranṭaraiccevitu	*1/20 + 1/80*		2 ½ *ceviṭu*
iru ceviṭu	*1/20*		2 *ceviṭu*
Oṉṉaraiccevitu	*3/80*		1 ½ *ceviṭu*
oru ceviṭu	*1/40*		1 *ceviṭu*
araicceviṭu	*1/80*		½ *ceviṭu*
Kāl ceviṭu	*1/160*		¼ *ceviṭu*
Araikkāl ceviṭu	*1/320*		*1/8 ceviṭu*

Aṟupattiranṭākun tāmaraippūviṟ kuṟukūli yaiṅkuṟuṇi munnāḻi yeṉparē maṟumoḻi kāṭciyavar – alakunilai 62 kaḷam 5 kuṟuṇi 3 nāḻi.

if a particular product was required in a situation of problem solving, say *kāl* and *araikkāṇi*, the repeated exercises in memory would immediately yield that product in the context of the particular stage, in the algorithm of problem solving. If verification became necessary, then such verses would again function as mnemonics to trigger the tables, so that the particular product—*kāl* and *araikkāṇi*—would be verified by checking the entire algorithm and providing the solution; this was because, 'accuracy comes about through the act of recreating in memory the complete occasion of which the accurate quotation is a part of'.[54]

If the entire table set had to be memorized there was another very crucial resource that had to play an inevitable role—language and rhyme.

[54] See Carruthers, *Book of Memory*, 61.

All the tables in the act of memorization went through the process of a rhythmic singing aloud, with the monitor setting the tune in the beginning, but later on almost universally followed by all the students of the *tiṇṇai* schools. For example, the first table would be sung as

> *ōr o<u>nn</u>u o<u>nn</u>u* (one and one is one),
> *paitto<u>nn</u>u pattu* (ten and one is ten),
> *īr o<u>nn</u>u iraṇṭu* (two and one is two),
> *irupatu o<u>nn</u>u irupatu* (twenty and one is twenty) and so on until
> *nū<u>r</u>o<u>nn</u>u nū<u>r</u>u* (hundred and one is hundred),

followed by the reciting of the mnemonic verse, sung as

> *'mallikai aintu malarnta pū toṇṇū<u>r</u>u koḷvar aivar pa<u>r</u>ittu' alakunilai 595.*[55]

Though the entire task of memorizing all the tables appears a monumental one, we should remember that in the given context, even language learning proceeded in gradual stages, tending towards the composition of verses as the aim. Learning language and learning mathematics were dependent on prosody and meter, elements that were essential for building Tamil verses. All the learning, including literature, grammar, styles—all were learnt through forms of prosody, and a learned man was one who would immediately recognize the form of meter used in a particular verse and himself compose another in response to it. Texts like the *Na<u>nn</u>ūl*, for instance, were manuals that were not guidebooks to attain mastery in the art of composition but practical manuals, which guided to write properly. This association between language learning and the learning of numbers was so integral to the *tiṇṇai* pedagogy, to which it was a natural resource, put to good advantage.

So the process of committing entire tables would proceed step by step, practicing to write on sand would also occur either simultaneously or in the time allotted for that purpose. A Portuguese traveller, Peter

[55] It is not uncommon today to hear such rhyme while students memorize multiplication tables. But what is of significance is to have set rhymes for the entire set of tables in the *Eṇcuvaṭi*.

Della Valle, travelling in the Malabar area of South India in the year 1623 captured a typical *Eṇcuvaṭi* class and recorded it. Observing four boys learning the *Eṇcuvaṭi*

> … after a strange manner, which I will here relate. They were four, and having all taken the same lesson before the Master, to get that same by heart, and repeat likewise their former lessons, and not forget them, one of them singing musically with a certain continued tone, (which hath the force of making a deep impression in the memory) recited part of the lesson; as for example, 'one by itself makes one'; and whilst he was thus speaking, he writ down the same number, not with any kind of pen, nor in paper but with his finger on the ground, the pavement being for that purpose strewed all over with fine sand; after the first had wrote what he sung, all the rest sung and write down the same thing together. Then the first boy sung, and writ down another part of the lesson … and so forward in order. When the pavement was full of figures, they put them out with the hand, and if need were, strewed it with new sand … and thus they did as long as exercise continued; in which manner, they told one, they learnt to read and write … which certainly is a pretty way. I asked them, if they happen to forget or be mistaken in any part of the lesson, who corrected them and taught them, they being all scholars without the assistance of any Master; they answered me, and said true, that it was not possible for all four to forget or mistake in the same part, and that they exercised together, to the end, that if one happened to be out, the other might correct him.[56]

Here we see how repetition in a context of mutual instruction proceeds through recognition of sound of a number by hearing its name, reciting after loudly, and writing it cognitively associating the sound with a symbol, in association with two numbers in a relationship, involving multiplication, in the memory mode of learning. Again, vocalization and visualization stand central. Likewise, each table was committed to memory. Each table, then, became distinct lessons. For instance, if one table was

[56] Cited in Dharampal, *The Beautiful Tree*, 260.

memorized in a day, through repeated practice, the next day morning, that particular table had to be recited as the first thing in the morning, or else in the forenoon sessions, when the teacher himself would supervise students taking turns to sing that table. When memorization proceeded in distinct parts, in a well-designed order, it also helped avoid the problem of overloading of memory. These sessions of reciting the previous day's lessons, (called as *muṟai collutal*—meaning reciting in order, in the literal sense) included not just the language lessons based on the *Ariccuvaṭi*, but also the tables of the *Eṇcuvaṭi*. It is not surprising then that the learning of the *Eṇcuvaṭi* was one continuous process throughout the course of instruction of the *tiṇṇai* schools, as Subbiah Cettiar testifies.[57] Of course, there would have been plenty of occasions to commit error, but those were occasions, marked by moments of recollective loss, that could have been due to 'improper imprinting in the first instance'. Therefore the option was to carefully imprint, and by repletion and practice ensure that they are in the 'long-term memory'. The ethos of this mode of learning was not to 'tire memory' by trying to memorize too much at a time, or too quickly –

> ... however large the number of things one has to remember, because, all are linked to one another, all join with what precedes to what follows, no trouble required except the preliminary labour of memorizing.[58]

Once memorized and stored in the long-term memory, assisted by the rhythms of a language that help in associating facts with words that have concrete meaning (that is why it is interesting to look at the fact that each and every number had a meaning, in the context of any kind of transaction, within the community), the ability to recollect was strengthened. Representations in an order like the tables further assisted recollection, which gave rise to the possibility of identifying a median (one easy number in the middle of a table, say five, fifty, five hundred) so that both sides from that point could be remembered and recollected well. Even though logical constructions involving numbers of this order are universal (in contrast to words, that require habit and repeated practice

[57] Subbbiah Cettiar, Personal Interview with Prof. Subbarayalu, January, 1989.
[58] Carruthers, *Book of Memory*, 61–62.

for recollective memory), in the pedagogic practice of the *Eṇcuvaṭi*, we find a situation where language played a central role, integrating itself strongly to number learning, when not a single number name would appear strange to a child growing up in a community that survived on measuring on a day-to-day basis.

Towards the end, the students also committed to memory the various conversion tables involving measures of weight. Reduction of measures again proceeded through repeated exercises of memorizing the conversion tables. Some of the nineteenth-century *Eṇcuvaṭi*s published in the region, had to devote more and more pages to these conversion tables because the units of conversion between the local and the newly introduced set of units in all realms kept expanding.

Knowing Myths and Facts

The tables in the *Eṇcuvaṭi* were followed by a long section called the *Varucappirappu* (literally meaning the birth of a year), which is but a series of lists, meant to be memorized. These rather long lists of 'lists' seem to familiarize the student with names of all kinds of entities that would normally be known to anybody growing up in a Tamil village. The meticulous way in which these lists appear to have been constructed, involving names, however, should not mislead us to conclude that the students were compelled to memorize more. There was a distinct possibility that each of these lists would have been an occasion for the teacher to actually teach the children about worldly affairs, spending long hours on these lists, narrating stories, interpreting the lore associated with these names. Someone like Catakopan Aiyangar, the teacher of Cāmināta Aiyar, immediately invokes a sense where it is not that difficult to imagine him going for days on end, narrating lessons based on these lists. What all did these lists contain? A selection is presented here, to provide us with a sense of them—the four *yukams*; the sixty years, twelve months; the fifteen *titis*, seven days of a week; auspicious and inauspicious times of a day; names of the twenty-seven stars; twenty-seven *yōkams*; sun signs; planets; directions; heavenly guardians; the eight famous cities; vehicles of the gods; wives of the gods; mythical names of snakes; the seven heavens and the seven gallows; the mythical islands; oceans; tastes; smells; emperors; avatars of various gods; diseases and so on and on. The representative sample here provides us with a glimpse of probable nature of the sessions that would have been part and parcel of the *tiṇṇai* schools.

Learning the *Kuḻimāttu*

The last section in the learning of mathematics in the *tiṇṇai School* was the learning of tables of squares, called the *Kuḻimāttu*. *Kuḻi* is a square unit for the measure of land, whose higher units were *mā, kāṇi* or *vēli* in certain regions. A basic unit of length in the measurement of land is the *kōl*, meaning a rod, which can be 12 ft, or 18 ft or 24 depending on the region in question. A square unit, namely the *kuḻi* was obtained by squaring a rod measure. In *Kuḻimāttu*, students memorized the table of squares. There were two sections here,

(a) *perukuḻi* (lit. meaning large measures), involving measures in whole numbers, beginning with 1 and ending with the square of 32 and
(b) *ciṟukuḻi* (meaning small measures), beginning with the square of *mākāṇi* (1/20 + 1/80), *araikkāl* (1/8 × 1/8), *kāl* (1/4); *arai* (1/2), *mukkāl* (3/4), *oṉṉēkāl* (1 + ¼); *oṉṉarai* (1 + ½); *oṉṉē mukkāl* (1 + ¾); *iraṇṭēkāl* (2 + ¼) . . . up to ten.

Interestingly in the text of the *Kuḻimāttu*, we get an idea of how students learnt multiplication as an operation as well. For instance, in the table of the *perukuḻi*, the squares of the whole measures up to ten are listed, but on reaching 11, the square of 11 is listed in the table 3.10, as follows:

Table 3.10 The calculation of the square of 11 in the *Kuḻimāttu*

Multiplication of factors		Product	Cumulative sum
10	10	100	100
10	1	10	110
10	1	10	120
1	1	1	121
Thus Total is			121

And the similar pattern is followed until the square of 32. We see how multiplication is performed, by the identification of the number into two easily recognizable parts (bringing upon closer resemblance to the order in *Eṇcuvaṭi*, in the process), when it becomes a series of addition. In *ciṟukuḻi*, again, this can be demonstrated for instance, in the case of the square of say, *mūṉṟē mukkāl*, as shown in Table 3.11 below:

Table 3.11 The calculation of the square of *mūṉṟē mukkāl* *(3 + 3/4)* in the *Kuḻimāttu*

Multiplication of factors		Product	Cumulative sum
3	3	9	9
3	3 × ¾	2 + ¼	11 + ¼
3	3 × ¾	2 + ¼	13 + ½
¾	¾	½ + (1/20 + 1/80)	14 + (1/20 + 1/80)
Thus Total is:			14 + (1/20 + 1/80)

During the actual process of memorizing, it is recited loudly step by step, for example, the above square will proceed in the following manner:

mūṉṟē mukkālukku kuḻi
mūṉṟum mūṉṟum oṉpatu
mūṉṟum mukkālum iraṇṭēkāl — *niṟpatu patiṉoṉṉē kāl*
mūṉṟum mukkālum iraṇṭēkāl — *niṟpatu patiṉmūṉṟē kāl*
mukkālum mukkālum araiyē mākāṇi — *niṟpatu patiṉāṉkē mākāṇi*

Here we see in the multiplication of fractions, the product, and the number are separated in terms of recognizable fractional units, and how multiplication proceeds as a series of additions. The *Kuḻimāttu*, then equipped the learner to deal with land measures and the computations of the area of land in all variations.

Problem Solving in *Tiṇṇai* Schools

As mentioned previously when a typical daily routine of a *tiṇṇai* school was discussed, the morning sessions were usually spent on memorizing and practicing the various tables. In the afternoon, probably the most active session of the day, in the school, teachers taught the students the lessons that they memorized in the forenoon in case of language learning, rendering meanings to words they had memorized. In the case of mathematics, problem solving was the mode by which the entire exercise of memorizing tables was rendered meaningful, wherein, skills of recollective and associative memory were called upon in an algorithmic context. Problems were posed as word problems, as these are known in the modern sense. Problems usually involved operations of addition, subtraction, multiplication, and division, reduction of measures involving the rule of three even though there were not separate tables for addition or subtraction. The word problems, posed orally, were meant to be computed mentally, though initially the process of solving proceeds by each student reciting each step aloud, to be heard by the whole class, monitored by the teacher. This is familiarly known in Tamil as *manak kaṇakku*,[59] meaning mental computation.

It would have been quite possible that if each distinct tables were separate lessons, that were memorized in the morning, practiced in the forenoon, then the problem-solving sessions in the afternoon involved training the skills of associative and recollective memory, involving those tables currently in practice. The Maratha theatre performance that we discussed in the context of the *tiṇṇai* school teacher has such a scenario narrated that would substantiate this. The play continues after the teacher vents out his plight and misery, yet his pride in leading a virtuous life. As if to substantiate his claims over virtuosity, the teacher tries to demonstrate the ability of his students in the skills that he trained them in.

He calls out the name of the student: Hey *Muttukumāra pavatē rācāli*, read!

STUDENT: What to read, sir?

TEACHER: Read the *araikkā* lesson (*araikkāl*, that is the table for the fraction 1/8).

[59] U. Vē. Cāmināta Aiyar, *Eṉ Carittiram*, 56. He says that the sessions involving problem solving in the *tiṇṇai* school were meant to enhance the skills of mental computation, which when combined with the skills in learning the tables would be of use to anybody well equipped to become traders or accountants.

STUDENT: All lessons sound like that *araikkā* only. Quarter lesson, half lesson, three quarter of a lesson, anyway, there will never be a full lesson, to hear from you, right?

TEACHER: Read you little boy!

STUDENT: What to read, *ātticcūṭi*, this and that?

TEACHER: Great, how is it that you are telling me names of words (*muṟai collutal*)?

STUDENT: No, I am reading the book sir, not telling you words.

TEACHER: [To the audience] See how this guy fares. [Points to another] Why don't you read?

STUDENT: What to read sir? *Ambikai mālai* or *mōtira muppatu*?

TEACHER: This boy is keen only to tell me words, not to read. [Looks at another student] What was the name of the flowers I told you yesterday?

STUDENT: *Makiḻampū, māmpū, mallikaippū* (names of flowers).

TEACHER: [To another student] What were the flowers for you?

STUDENT: *Tāmaraippū, tāḻampū, tāmarattāmpū* (names of flowers).

TEACHER: [To another student] Hey, what was the problem given yesterday?

STUDENT: One *kuḻi* for one, ten and a quarter for one; cancel the eight, add two, mix, stir and multiply in the mouth to give it to eleven people.

TEACHER: [To another student] What was the problem for you?

STUDENT: *Nālē araikkāl* is one banana. *Kālē araikkāl* is one banana. How much is the money?

TEACHER: Hey, you there, give me the rod, at this rate, you all will read fifty books in fifty years.

Monitor and the students: We have read the whole of *Kaṇakkatikāram, Eḻuttatikāram, Patiṉeṭṭām Perukku Pāṭṭu*, all of it sir![60]

Although the above scenario was meant to make fun of the plight of the *tiṇṇai* teacher and the way he handled his institution, what is significant to us is the information it gives us about the practice of taking tables as lessons, when the teacher asks the student to tell the 'lesson' of *araikkāl* (1/8) table. Subsequently, we also get to know a bit about the way problem-solving sessions would have been conducted in these institutions. The problems that occur in the script above were meant to

[60] C. K. Deivanayakam, ed. *Palacataka vikaṭam*, 5–6.

incite humour, and do not make any mathematical point. But it shows how problems were posed—demanding more than one arithmetic operation at the same time, involving more than one variable. Also, in the second problem, the banana problem, we get to see how the recollective memory based on tables would have been tested in an algorithmic context. Here, the student had to associate the particular table, and in that context, identify the product and proceed to compute. We also learn that it was a common practice for the teacher to give homework, either given as a list of names to be memorized like the names of the flowers mentioned in the script, Cāmināta Aiyar also confirms. Along with words to be memorized, problems were given as homework as well. Problem solving then happens outside the school, in an entirely non-institutional context, where the elderly and the parents are involved in the process. The next morning, the answers to the given problems were discussed, repeated, and then it was back to the business of memorizing the tables.

In this mode of learning, then, the student would have to draw on recollective memory to score well. Memory enabled a quick solution for solving an algorithmic problem that usually involved more than one variable and arithmetic operation at the same time. This was in effect the essence of computing. Associating the table in memory of a particular number, with the variable to be dealt with in the problem, at a particular stage of an algorithm became an issue. Recollection triggered a process, which can be represented as a series of steps, like:

(a) recognition of the variable in the problem,
(b) setting off the algorithm,
(c) recollection from a sequence or a table,
(d) association with the algorithm and solving the problem,
(e) addition to the repository of skills, and
(f) conceptualization as part of a system of algorithms.

In this mode, sets of rules were built up from recall, and the principal purpose would be to recognize and organize likeness, when verses, prosody, and tables aided the process of learning. The associative nature of memory thus became crucial in the context of arithmetic operations, involving transformations. But interestingly the texts contain no explicit mathematical representation of the process of transformation anywhere, and no reference to the relatedness of arithmetic operations. For example, multiplication of fractions, when represented in terms of addition of fractions, definitely involved factorization in several stages. But an explication of those processes is not elucidated in the texts. This points to two possibilities. It means first of all, that the texts we discussed here, the *Poṉṉilakkam*, *Nellilakkam*, *Eṇcuvaṭi*, and *Kuḻimāttu* (this being an exception, for here we saw how squaring a number was taken up) were primers that set off the process of learning. Secondly, language use was a very important factor in the problem-solving context. Mathematics and language were interrelated. For example, for addition-based operations, the '*yē*' sound became the signal to recognize it as addition (e.g. *Kāṇi* + *muntiri* will be *kāṇīyē muntiri*) but when multiplication was involved, the absence of the '*yē*' sound would mark the process involved as that of multiplication and not as addition (e.g. *Kāṇi* × *muntiri* will be *kāṇi muntiri*).

Language learning and number learning were integral to each other in the *tiṇṇai* mode. Language did not only assist in problem solving, but was also central, in a cognitive sense, to the execution of an algorithm. For students used to mental computation, the pattern, the recital of each step of execution, was imperative. If the word, *māṟa* (which signified multiplication) occurred, the table series in question would immediately come to mind. Again, it was the knowledge of numbers in the language of Tamil that aided in the process of computation at each and every step. Terms like *taḷḷa*, *īya*, meant, for instance, to cancel, to divide, which merely as arithmetic operations, in abstract sense would not have helped in the proceedings of an algorithm, when number names and the operations to be performed were all known as only cognitively rooted, semantically loaded terms. Even though the comedian in the script above makes fun of the way problems are posed in the schools, when he says, 'cancel the eight, add the two, mix it well, stir and multiply it in the mouth' he exactly signifies the way language plays around in the context of problem solving.

Problems posed for solving within the *tiṇṇai* were linked to problems outside the school, too. It is likely that the problems that *tiṇṇai* students trained in were part of a common pool of problems in which the larger social fabric would have partaken in. These were the riddles and aphorisms outside the *tiṇṇai* institution. On the other hand, the same set of accumulated problems, in active circulation within the community served well to cultivate computing skills relating themselves to the pedagogic strategies inside the *tiṇṇai* school. The school in that sense was permeable with society. Its transactions happened in concurrence and participation of the patrons who supported it, not merely in economic terms, but actually roping in their skills into the functioning of the school itself. These skills remained as knowledge within the society, from which members of all the strata in the society partook, including those who had no exposure to the training in reading and writing.

The value that emerges as central to the functioning of this mathematical landscape was not the speed and accuracy of computation as much as the value of 'prudence'. Intelligence, in the context of problem solving, would mean not speed and accuracy, but precise recollection. It was the act of recollection from the organized order of the *Eṇcuvaṭi* or to put it another way, the *Eṇcuvaṭi* itself was constituted in that particular order as a system of mnemonics. The ability to recollect may be natural, but the procedure itself is formed by habit and practice, rendering the mnemonic organizational structure as a system of heuristics in the process. Then recollection becomes synonymous to reasoning, and even interpretation.[61]

When the students finally wrote down their memorized *Eṇcuvaṭi* on palm leaves, the practice marked the final stages of learning when each own their set of manuals, beginning with the *Poṉṉilakkam*, *Nellilakkam*, the *Eṇcuvaṭi* and the *Kuḻimāttu*. In a way, a whole process of dealing with mental representations gives birth to the written form, where writing helps memory rather than gaining a significance for itself, in this pedagogic practice. Writing then adds to the memory images, not in a simply abstract manner but as affective images. Writing in the *tiṇṇai* mode, on the other hand, also makes the student eligible for an occupational role, say that of a scribe, or at least for an apprenticeship with the local revenue official or the trader, where learning on the job would add further experience to the repository of his skills, fine-tuned in the *tiṇṇai* mode. In the

[61] Carruthers, *The Book of memory*, 60–64. Another important study, that point to a more organic theory of remembering, which posited the significance of active recollection as construction is that of Bartlett's pioneering work, '... In fact, if we consider evidence rather than presupposition, remembering appears to be far more decisively an affair of construction rather than one of mere reproduction'. See F. C. Bartlett (1932). *Remembering: A Study in Experimental and Social Psychology* (Cambridge: Cambridge University Press, 1995). I thank Simon Schaffer for drawing my attention to this work.

process, the student became a fitting member of the measuring public, as a competent individual to partake in the several modes of transactions involving land and labour within the local community.

Tiṇṇai Curriculum, Pedagogy, and Caste

So far, we have had a glimpse into the world of the *tiṇṇai* pedagogy, in relation to the learning of arithmetic, with the help of the texts or the manuals. But what do these texts tell us about the nature of relationship between the mathematical practices in the community, the *tiṇṇai* curriculum, its pedagogy, and the society itself?

One way would be to think of the whole set of arithmetic representations, almost obsessed with tabulations of quantities, measures—always being transformed into each other, always associated with skills to manipulate them both within the institutional setting and outside—was common to everybody, despite their social status or occupational role, 'educated' or 'uneducated', manual labourer or clerical labourer. They were all 'aware' of the kind of mathematical manipulations involved, deeply imbued in the common language familiar to them, very much cutting across the caste hierarchy. That is why the occasions when the members of the local community interacted with each other, in very informal ways, involved subtle moments of challenge to each other. Testing each other's 'proficiency' or shall we say 'prudence' was always the most social of the occasions, say during festivals, a special function in a household, or even a visit to the temple. The most common form of such an interaction would be an elderly person posing to the younger lot, in a ridiculing fashion, mockingly, a set of problems, and asking them to come out with the solution. It was then that the learning of the *tiṇṇai* was under test, often bringing in the competence of the local teacher into public evaluation. His teaching, his skills and competence come into the sphere of recognition, gaining credibility or otherwise, out in the open, when it was upon the *tiṇṇai* students to display and perform in public.[62]

[62] Sivalingaraja and S. Sarasvati, *Yāḻppāṇattu Tamil Kalvi*, 71–72. This is the only account of the *tiṇṇai* schools, that recognized this dimension to the curriculum and its orientation.

There is another story to be told here. In the list of occupational groups mentioned in the beginning of this paper, there were three personalities associated with the administration of land in the revenue bureaucracy: the *Veṭṭiyāṉ*, the *Tōṭṭi*, and the *Nīrkkāraṉ* or the *Kampukaṭṭi*. These occupations were customarily confined to the 'untouchable' castes, who were physically segregated to the far end of the village society. They would have never touched an *Eṇcuvaṭi* in their life. But it was the *Veṭṭiyāṉ* or the *Tōṭṭi* who would take up the measuring rod and engage with the physical and cognitive act of measuring the land through mensuration. On the other hand, the learned *Karaṇam* or village accountant would record the measures in writing, in codes specified by a system that trained his skills, the beginning place to which was the *tiṇṇai* school. The *Nīrkkāran*, a person who would own nothing and would inevitably be poor, was entrusted with the task of regulating the distribution of irrigation water, which involved computation of time, motion and area to be irrigated in accordance with the sluices of a tank at his disposal. However, the *tiṇṇai* curriculum would deal with such situations in the problem-solving mode. But these were situations that the *Veṭṭiyāṉ* and the *Nīrkkāraṉ* lived with and cognitively engaged with as part of their manual work. But they were denied a place in the *tiṇṇai* school.

The socially thick world of numeracy, measurement, and calculation provokes another question regarding arithmetic representations. If arithmetic representations were products of standardization that evolved out of concrete practices involving work and labour, then how must we narrate the history of standardization? Did the standardization proceed at the behest of a centralizing state, or was led by the labourers? The contests and negotiations around measurement could produce two very contradictory histories. We know nominally that when a state decided to standardize, as when a King altered the standard of the measuring rod (say, from a 12-foot to a 24-foot rod), it was an act intended to gain legitimacy for his rule. The intention was to alter things down to the level of the village, establishing authority and control from a distance.[63] But it was the people like the *Veṭṭiyāṉ* and the *Nīrkkāraṉ* who negotiated with such interventions, learnt them, and manipulated them. These practices would make their way into the school, which appropriated them into another

[63] Y. Subbarayulu, *Studies in Cola History* (Chennai: Surabhi Pathippakam, 2001), 31–40.

sphere of learning and turned them into 'knowledge'. The knowledge thus textualized in the school—in the memory mode—was then disseminated to the students, who were not the only ones knowledgeable in it and who would perform the tasks of the *Veṭṭiyāṉ* and the *Nīrkkāraṉ*.

The orientation of the curriculum made it a form of mediation between the world of courts and royal edicts and the world of rods and ploughs. The arithmetic representations and the *tiṇṇai* mode of problem solving were oriented towards the range of socio-economic transactions where memory-based pedagogic strategies ensured a sense of competence in skill and functionality.

Based on the preceding discussions, it can be argued that the memory mode of learning in a cognitive sense and the problem-solving strategies would help train a learner to comfortably handle a text like the *Kaṇakkatikāram*, with proficiency, with additional guidance. The learners were supposed to go looking for specialized masters, who might not be available in the immediate vicinity. But if he was interested, and if the family could afford the cost of such teaching, a student always had the option to move to where it was available.

It might be problematic to consider the *tiṇṇai* school as a romanticized ideal, as scholars like Dharampal have done because they are of, by, and for the community. To Dharampal, the proximity of the school to the community means closer scrutiny of the teacher and greater participation of the parents. But this proximity also had its problems. For one, if a teacher branded a student as a failure, the teacher in turn also got blamed for it. Also, the *tiṇṇai* school did not offer everyone in the community the possibility of going on to higher learning. The social distribution of skills was determined by access and denial.[64] Teachers periodically demanded payment and transition to higher stages of learning—for example, graduating from writing on the sand to palm—leaves—was marked by rituals that demanded higher fees. The failure to pay such amounts could lead to the humiliation of the student in the school and his family outside the

[64] Peter Damerow outlines a conceptual framework to understand the evolution of numbers as cognitive universals, in a scheme where he identifies distinct historical stages in the development of logico-mathematical thought. But the place for social distribution of abilities rooted in experiences of work and labour that would have contributed to similar processes seems very limited in his framework. See Peter Damerow, *The Material Culture of Calculation A Conceptual Framework for an Historical Epistemology of the Concept of Number*, Preprint 117 (Berlin: Max Planck Institute for the History of Science, 1999).

school. Caste was also an organizing principle to the school, where exclusion of certain social groups was inherent to its functioning.[65] Thus social divisions and discriminations outside the school were reflected and reinforced within them.

The forms of punishment within the *tiṇṇai* school were severe, and it was a common knowledge that the rod ruled in the *tiṇṇai* school. The distance to school was often a barrier because not every village had a *tiṇṇai* school, and children often had to walk seven to eight miles to reach it.

Given these problems, did the *tiṇṇai* school offer everyone the possibility to pursue higher mathematical learning and abstract reason? It is clear that abstraction per se was never the explicit agenda of the *tiṇṇai* schools. The school remained like any other institutional site of education, within the publicly sanctioned goals of institutionalized learning in the contemporary society. Not unlike many other pedagogical sites associated with modern education the *tiṇṇai* too, was circumscribed socially and functional in its orientation. And yet, it would be unfair to dismiss the *tiṇṇai* curriculum as completely functional. Several aspects of the *tiṇṇai* curriculum fostered creativity and play and a more integrated approach to learning language and computing.[66] There were forms of affective learning and expression embedded in these modes of linking text to life, such as reading and appreciating literature. That these did not foster other possibilities because of the deep processes of social fragmentation that the school sustained is clear. But the inadequacy of a modern pedagogical reform mindset in addressing this problem is also clear when we

[65] Radhakrishnan, 'Caste Discrimination in Indigenous Education', has extensively documented this aspect.

[66] An important study that questions the distinction between functionality and creativity, which could be useful in this context is that of Jean Lave when she engaged with adult workers shopping in American super markets and tailors in Liberia to suggest 'that calculation and measurement procedures are generated in situationally specific terms which both reflect and help to produce the specific character of activities in daily life. At the same time, the values embodied in the standardized forms of quantitative knowledge discussed here, especially values of rational objective utility, appear to be resources employed expressively in everyday practice. A politics of knowledge is thus embodied in mundane transformations of knowledge and value through activity constituted in relation with its daily settings', see Jean Lave, 'The Values of Quantification', *The Sociological Review* 32 (1984): 88–111. Her extended work Cognition in Practice is of equal relevance to us as well, as we discussed in first chapter in the context of relationship between practical measures and construction of numbers. I thank Simon Schaffer for pointing to the relevance of her work in the context of this book.

turn to the ways in which colonial officials, reformers, and missionaries tried to reshape the *tiṇṇai* school.

It is here that the story of the transition of the *tiṇṇai* schools upon their contact with the techno-economic complex of British colonialism becomes interesting. This is not because it heralds modernity that displaces tradition. If concepts, skills, reasoning, ways of abstraction were all immersed in the 'functional' *tiṇṇai* mode of learning, then what sort of modernity was in progress in Tamil South India? Was this modernity inherently shaped first by the social fragmentation of its experience and then overlaid by the limiting remit of liberal individualism introduced by British pedagogic intervention? Was there a peculiar and enduring potential convergence between aspects of the former—namely the functional reasoning of problem solving, that could be perceived and articulated with, and encompassed by, the frame of liberal individualism of nineteenth century Europe?

Politics at the heart of the struggle over *tiṇṇai* curriculum was based on narrow perceptions of a tradition that could at best callously engage with a tradition, but remain seriously rooted in a power structure. The tinkering with the *tiṇṇai* schools did not effectively change them through the nineteenth century. They were made irrelevant when the social ethos which sustained them changed, during the early decades of the twentieth century. It is to this nineteenth-century story that we will turn to in the next chapter.

IV

Mathematics Pedagogy for a Public

The Colonial Transition

The *tiṇṇai* mode of learning encountered its first critics during the late eighteenth and the early nineteenth centuries as a result of the colonial and missionary efforts in education. We are highly dependent on the colonial archive and to a lesser degree on the missionary archive to reconstruct the dynamics of this encounter. The description of the *tiṇṇai* in these sources has bias. From the very beginning, the revenue officials of the East India Company viewed the *tiṇṇai* school with contempt, seeing it as an institution that cultivated mechanical memory, memorization without understanding, or what was already termed as rote memory. One of the chief problems, in consequence, is that the existing records about the *tiṇṇai,* which were written by both the British and the local elite, present *tiṇṇai* schoolteachers as requiring reform.

How did the *tiṇṇai* school teacher experience the changes advocated? What strategies did he adopt? How did his values and professional virtuosity change? Did his conception of learning and knowledge alter, when the school inspector urged him to shift, to follow a rigidly defined, 'cut and dry' curriculum? That curriculum was heavily dependent on textbooks, in the production and organization of which he had no role? Or was he 'prudent' enough to see the content of the new curriculum, subjecting himself to the demands of highly bureaucratic machinery, which lured him with financial incentives or threatened him with consequences, not to his liking?

It is difficult, if not impossible, to answer these questions directly because the sources at hand—authored by school inspectors, revenue officials, missionaries, and the newly educated upper-caste elite—always present the school teacher as resolutely intransigent to and incapable of change.

Mathematics and Society. Senthil Babu D., Oxford University Press. © Oxford University Press India 2022.
DOI: 10.1093/oso/9788194831600.003.0005

Yet the resilience of the *tiṇṇai* through the nineteenth century is clear. Although the colonial state tried to appropriate the *tiṇṇai* school to bring it into the net of a 'liberal' education scheme and criticized the *tiṇṇai* curriculum for its 'rote memory', the *tiṇṇai* school system refused to yield to the hegemony of textbooks and examinations. In practice, memorization haunted even the institutions of modern education. For the majority of the young children who passed a multitude of exams, and for the millions of children who failed but nevertheless had been through the grind of colonial education, the resources of recollective memory nurtured in the *tiṇṇai*, manifested as mechanical memorization, formed an enduring foundation of their student lives.

The historians of education have been unable to critically address the *tiṇṇai*'s influence in modern education. They have been sensitive to the compulsion to learn European knowledge (primarily literary rather than scientific) in a foreign language, in institutions in which evaluations and classroom organization were thoroughly insensitive to the cognitive needs of young learners.[1] But this story of self-alienation under colonial rule cannot fully elaborate the struggles and possibilities experienced in pedagogic environments. To understand the transformation in mathematical knowledge and the canvas upon which numeracy was reconfigured, our history of mathematics must describe the exclusions and inclusions of the new paradigm of modern mathematical competence and innovation. We need to understand how agents in the school experienced and responded to the new colonial environment. The story of transition in the nineteenth century is not a simple one of colonial intervention and response, or for that matter, of an unchanging tradition at work. The *tiṇṇai* school teacher and his mathematics curriculum nurtured a basic and impressive computational competence. This is why *tiṇṇai or* practitioner mathematics was both credible but inadequate for colonial officials and hence an object of reform.

[1] Krishna Kumar, *Political Agenda of Education: A Study of Colonialist and Nationalist Ideas* (New Delhi: Sage, 2005). For the ideological orientations of the colonial education project, see Gauri Viswanathan, *Masks of Conquest: Literary Study and British Rule in India* (New Delhi: Oxford University Press, 1998).

Some studies make the 'local' speak in the institutional history of primary education.[2] Nita Kumar's study of education makes an important contribution in this regard. The British engagement with these myriad local traditions turns out, in Kumar's estimation to be shallow, because it fails to consider the nature of the local practices. Indeed Kumar recuperates the creative afterlives of skills deemed pedagogically inadequate by attending carefully to local traditions. Her work describes resilient practices and ideas, articulated by occupational groups and various communities in Benares. These communities not only participated in colonial modern education but also established their own institutions and arrangements.[3] Kazi Shahidullah's history of the persistence of the Bengali pathshala teachers,[4] and the study of schooling in the Tamil region of Sri Lanka by the Sivalingarajas provide us an interesting account of the history of modern interventions in schooling. The latter underscores how consistent missionary effort supported by the Portuguese and the British produced individuals and institutions and created varied and distinct local practices.[5] These studies show us that the story of modernity in education was not uniform. They also imply that it might make sense to drop the separation of traditional schooling and modern schooling in our discussion of mathematics pedagogy. But the tense entanglement of different normative expectations of pedagogy outlined by these scholars cannot be read as illustrating the grafting of one knowledge type upon another.[6]

[2] For very useful and standard works for the history of education in India, see Syed Nurullah and J. P. Naik, *A Students' History of Education in India (1800–1961)* (Bombay: Mac Millan & Co., 1962). Also, Aparna Basu, *Essays in the History of Indian Education* (New Delhi: Concept Publishing Company, 1982).

[3] Nita Kumar, *Lessons From Schools: The History of Education in Banaras* (New Delhi: Sage Publications, 2000).

[4] Kazi Shahidullah, '"The Purpose and Impact of Government Policy on Pathshala Gurumohashoys in Nineteenth Century Bengal" and Poromesh Acharya, "Indigenous Education and Brahminical Hegemony in Bengal"', *The Transmission of Knowledge in South Asia Essays on Education, Religion, History, and Politics*, ed. Nigel Crook (Delhi: Oxford University Press, 1996), 98–134.

[5] Sivalingaraja and Saraswathi Sivalingaraja, *Pattoṉpatām Nūṟṟāṇṭil Yāḻppāṇattu Tamil kalvi* (Chennai: Kumaran Putthaka Illam, 2000).

[6] This is suggested as a way to understand the emergence of modern mathematics education in India, that draws upon curricular transactions in textbooks and their translations along with distinct attempts at experiments and innovations, as in the case of Master Ramachandra in Delhi College and the huge translation factory of sorts established by Col. Jervis at Bombay which resulted in the production of translated textbooks in Marathi and Gujarati, including the works of Augustus De Morgan. See Dhruv Raina, 'Mathematics Education in Modern India', *Handbook on the History of Mathematics Education*, eds. Alexander Karp and Gert Schubring (New York: Springer, 2014), 376–383.

One kind of knowledge was not grafted upon another. In the case at hand, the reform of the *tiṇṇai* in the Tamil context, the problem was not that the terrain of the *tiṇṇai* and its practitioners were incapable of engaging with the call of modernity creatively. Rather a series of pedagogic possibilities were articulated during the course of the colonial period, especially during the first half of the nineteenth century. They were limited at the same time.

I will detail these as efforts to create and imagine a public for mathematical knowledge. The making of this public involved the creation of a mathematical pedagogy imagined for general circulation. This articulation of a public did not just operate as a form of institutional dissemination through the machinery of colonial education alone but was also worked-out in the institutions of the family and kinship. This chapter will show how the creation of markets around pedagogy, namely in textbooks and jobs, went alongside the continuing resonance of social fragmentation. Through these complex dynamics, a series of possible mathematics for general circulation were explored in a variety of sites. I begin by explaining why in the nineteenth century, a need arose to articulate a mathematics for general circulation.

Colonial Transition: The Reshaping of Computation

The axis of the transmission of computational knowledge was reshaped in the nineteenth century with the consolidation of the Company's rule through the establishment of property in land and the range of demands this initiative imposed on social and economic terrains. It is certainly true that transactions around the assessment of produce, credit, entitlements, and exchanges of a commercial nature were well established in South India before the East India Company's ascendance. Indeed, as we saw, the expertise of the *Kaṇakkaṉ* and the practitioner's mathematics was secured by this world at least by the seventeenth century, if not earlier. But the East India Company's investment in revenue management rested on securing private property in land through the regular maintenance of records, legible surveys, and easily convertible and accessible measurements and these interventions changed the topography in which numeracy operated.[7] The establishment of private property in land brought with it concomitant changes to the meaning of production, labour, and their counting and assessment.

The revenue-based entitlements and the labour quotient in assessing produce shares became two distinct entities in a different order of numbers, inscribed in a statistical register that was tied to a regime of property rights. As Raman notes, the land was counted in terms of per unit of labour—the labour of a plough through the new unit of acre. The already existing measurements were made commensurate to this new method of assessment. But at the same time, land value or its produce could be viewed in isolation from the inputs of cultivation. This is how a new mode of deploying numerical knowledge in the context of the ryotwari survey 'abstracted labor from hierarchical reciprocity and rendered it into a standard input for two goals; in so doing, it brought forth a new regime of property'.[8] The *Kaṇakkaṉ* remained central to this new ryotwari organization but his expertise had to articulate with a new regime of field-based assessment and measuring practices and the statistical orientation of recordkeeping. The statistical work brought in by the Company state[9] was both reliant on the *Kaṇakkaṉ*'s expertise but it was also fostered to discipline his practices.[10] The number had a new place in the political and social imaginary. It attested to the development of a new type of computational activity that was no longer the mode of proportional measurement. Instead, it had an absolute value which could now be dis-embedded from matter and the social relations of production. From the *Kaṇakkaṉ*-mediated proportional assessment, this new regime of assessment standards changed the map of localized skills. The measurement of land was no longer a mean measure of all sides of land only, which the *Kaṇakkatikāram* trained the student for, but now,

[7] On the changes wrought in recordkeeping by this investment in revenue management see Bhavani Raman, *Document Raj: Writing and Scribes in Early Colonial South India* (Chicago: University of Chicago Press, 2012).

[8] Ibid., p. 71.

[9] For a discussion on the emergent relationship between statistics and state building, or what was political arithmetic, see Theodore M. Porter, *The Rise of Statistical Thinking 1820–1900* (Princeton: Princeton University Press, 1986). In the context of colonialism, see U. Kalpagam, 'The Colonial State and Statistical Knowledge', *History of the Human Sciences* 13, no. 2 (2000): 37–55. See also, Mary Poovey, 'Figures of Arithmetic, Figures of Speech: The Discourse of Statistics in the 1830s', *Critical Inquiry* 19, no. 2 (1993): 256–276.

[10] Raman, *Document Raj*, 23–82 especially Part I on Scribal Practices

it required a different statistical order of numeracy and modes of mensuration. The acre displaced the *aṭikkōl*, which as we saw in the first two chapters was central to the mathematics of the practitioners. This foot-pole was soon succeeded by the measuring chain and its number of links and the processes of triangulation which contributed to the making of territorial scale in property, cementing the connection between measurement and state power.[11]

The new apparatus of property required a new mode of mathematical engagement. It is telling in this context that the Company's first intervention in mathematical pedagogy was not the *tiṇṇai* school but the establishment of new survey schools. Started in 1804 and attached to the Madras Observatory, the survey school was supported by the Government and later directly managed by the Board of Revenue in the 1820s. This school was meant to train a class of native servants to assist Engineers and Surveyors.[12] The Company recruited its survey school student from the Anglo-Indian orphanage of Madras city. These boys were considered ideal surveyors and drafters—teachable and removed from the social world of revenue shares and local politics. The kind of expertise shaped in the survey school was intended to create new agents who were to be independent of the world of the *Kaṇakkaṉ*. Although the survey school created a new layer of measuring expertise that the colonial state could use, local notables in consort with the *Kaṇakkaṉ*s strived to re-mould and obstruct early efforts at surveying.[13] The newly trained and disinterested survey agents alone were not enough to sustain the intervention in revenue management. Graduates of the survey school,

[11] For mapping and territoriality in the making see Mathew Edney, *Mapping an Empire: The Geographical Construction of British India, 1765–1843* (Chicago: University of Chicago Press, 1997). Also, U. Kalpagam, 'Cartography in Colonial India', *Economic and Political Weekly* 30, no. 30 (1995): PE87–PE98. From the perspective of the history of mathematics, this relationship is explored in Serafina Cuomo, 'Divide and Rule: Frontius and Roman Land-Surveying', *Studies in History and Philosophy of Science Part A* 31, no. 2 (2000): 189–202.

[12] For a brief account of the beginnings of the school and how it became the foundation for the establishment of the Civil Engineering College in Madras, with the then priority of irrigation and public works, see, 'Minute by Colonel Sim, On the Formation of a School for Civil Engineering, January 1842, Appendix Z', in *Selections From the Records of the Madras Government, Papers Relating to Public Instruction*, Madras, 1855, pp. clxii–clxxiii.

[13] Nilmani Mukherjee, *The Ryotwari System in Madras, 1792–1827* (Calcutta: Firma K. L. Mukhopadhyay, 1962). See also, Nilmani Mukherjee and Robert Eric Frykenberg. 'The Ryotwari System and Social Organization in the Madras Presidency', *Land Control and Social Structure in Indian History*, ed. R. E. Frykenberg (Delhi: Manohar, 1979), 217–25. Also, see Raman, *Document Raj*.

moreover, could not provide all the skills required for the new template of statistical knowledge.

Colonial surveys—from the Barnard Survey in the 1760s to the making of the ryotwari settlement in the provinces of the Madras Presidency in the early decades of the nineteenth century—enlisted locally available computational skills for quantifying and classifying productive resources. Everything local that was measured and counted had to be recorded in new types of registers. The information compiled on palm leaf had to be transcribed into statistical tables in English so that information could travel out of the settlement into the office and out to the metropolis. The early decades of the nineteenth century thus saw a huge increase in the manpower of the revenue establishment ranging from measurers, calculators, and compilers during the *jamabandi*, the annual revenue settlement exercise. In order to incorporate and discipline the *Kaṇakkaṉ*'s computational records into the new survey system and transform them into new artefacts for empire-wide circulation, the Company began to draw on agents other than its survey school graduates. It increasingly relied on the expertise of the Maratha Brahmans, even as it concurrently searched for an expert whose skills could match the demands of statistical compilation.

By the 1820s, a number of changes were underway. The new revenue knowledge form changed the significance of the number for the measuring public. Land and produce assessment was no longer a localized affair. The assessment written into new registers were annually assessed and settled at an office distant from the locality. This meant that the traffic between the *Kaṇakkaṉ* and the office was not only always under suspicion by the upper echelons of the revenue administration but was equally, if not more, suspect in the eyes of the local measuring public. Previous land-related computations, as we discussed earlier, could have been an expert practice, but the basis of measurement and its results were familiar to the public. But now, land area, its produce, and the taxation associated with it all were in register-based numbers, not entirely visible and transparent. This meant, for the public, an additional layer of interpretation of these numbers, which again, brought in an additional level of dependence on someone who could understand numbers.

Colonial officials often attributed their inability to secure legible surveys to corruption that in their opinion was a sign of moral turpitude and required a total reform of education. The cultivators in turn found their own scrutiny of *Kaṇakkan* inadequate as he was now a powerful agent of the colonial state. But in the process, the locally credible modes of computation with respect to revenue assessments centred around proportions of land, grains, and entitlements were reordered into absolute measures, which came to determine the labour processes of producers and workers. The setting up of machinery to redefine skills to align with the production of absolute values went along with the expansion of commodity production through land ensured by the securing of private property. This coming together of the regimes of calculation of absolute values and that of rights-based private property provided the context for new alignments of local computational expertise with that of new modes of revenue extraction. It also provided a place for a range of intermediaries to facilitate the transaction between producers and workers with the new authority, among which the village accountant and the school teacher were very central as we proceed through the nineteenth century.

There was another aspect to this change in the place of the number in society. The requirements of the ryotwari survey and assessment system were such that in addition to the *Kaṇakkaṉ*'s much needed computational skills, other skills were in great demand. This created a job market at various levels of offices all the way up to the district collectorate. The annual assessments required a variety of measuring and writing expertise. This rapid expansion of the job market for the most part was supplied with kin-based informal recruitment from upper-caste families who still relied on apprenticeship. The familial space honed new skills. The jobs moreover tended to be precarious; employees could be rapidly hired and fired. Entry into the job market that serviced ryotwari assessment was uncertain and cut-throat and mediated completely by caste and kin connections.[14] It was in this context that existing rules and methods of problem solving, akin to the tradition, had to align themselves to the new knowledge of surveying. The practitioner continued to be important to the new regime, but his skills and expertise had to change and align in tune with the requirements of the new dispensation. The consistent anxiety felt by the Company bureaucracy articulated itself on the morality plane, but the skill base and the expertise of the practitioner could not be dislodged.

[14] On this see Raman, *Document Raj*.

Hence a language of reform was articulated in the early decades of the nineteenth century. It is here that we can start tracing the efforts that sought to build a mathematical pedagogy for general circulation, which would swing between the need for skills as a concrete requirement for the colonial state as well its need for the rhetoric of education for the public.

Mathematics for a Public: Early Possibilities, 1800–1840

Some of the earliest efforts to engage with the changed place of the number were by Protestant missionaries and Tamil pandits associated with the College of Fort St. George. The mission establishment over the eighteenth century had largely followed *tiṇṇai* mathematical practices but had already begun to invert its schema. It was a scheme that taught the rules first and the problems later—unlike in the *tiṇṇai* mode and in *Kaṇakkan* apprenticeship where rules were subsumed under problem solving. Around the time of the early survey efforts of the Company, mission mathematics emphasized the transcribing of numbers rather than mental computation. In mission schools, students were encouraged not to write numbers as an aid to recollective memory, but to write them in a particular order, as part of the process of computation. This was not writing down the numbers in arithmetic operations in a single line, as they might be recited, that is, when there was a necessity to write, as in the case of writing manuals like the *Kaṇakkatikāram*.

Numbers now had to be written in columns, one below the other to start the operation itself.[15] Writing down arithmetic operations decisively shifted the terms of the new mathematics pedagogy in mission schools. The *tiṇṇai* system was based on the capacity to recall a sequence of numbers learned via the *Eṇcuvaṭi*. The *tiṇṇai* method trained the student to recall number in a specific context to solve a problem. This was why the proportions (relations between numbers) were so tied to concrete relations to matter to social contexts. The mission system too required recall

[15] Column based addition and subtraction by the method of carrying over was very much part of the Bell—Lancaster system. For a discussion on how it actually worked see David Salmon, ed. *The Practical Parts of Lancaster's Improvements and Bell's Experiments* (Cambridge: Cambridge University Press, 1932).

but the student was trained to recall number 'facts' as they engaged in addition and subtraction in columns. If the new regime prioritized grammar and neat writing as education, in the case of arithmetic it had to be rule-based, step-by-step computation, where numbers were merely numbers, not necessarily quantities of measures (as in the *Nellilakkam*), and relational entities (as in the *Eṇcuvaṭi* mode). Now they stood alone and assumed meaning only during the proceeding of the arithmetic operation on the slate or paper. The treatment or the cognitive engagement of numbers as facts marked one of the fundamental shifts in the constitution of a public for the new modes of mathematical computation.

We can observe a range of experiments in missionary sites for the creation of new mathematical publics. Early examples include the Bell system that was tried out in various Madras missions, other experiments occurred in the mission schools of Jaffna,[16] as well as in the Church Missionary Society's schools in Tirunelveli.[17] These were well underway by the 1820s. These missionary-led initiatives on occasion generated considerably creative re-workings of *Eṇcuvaṭi* traditions. These were rich with possibility but constrained or subverted and at times erased by historically power-laden hierarchies. Consider, for instance, Vedanayakam Sastri's[18] reform of the *Eṇcuvaṭi*. Sastri called his text the

[16] For some of the early experiments and the context of the work of American Mission in Jaffna, please see Sivalingaraja and Sivalingaraja, *Yāḻppāṇattu Tamil Kalvi*, 2000. But their best works are evident in the Tamil arithmetic textbooks that they published, which used Tamil numerical notation, used the *tiṇṇai* idioms and the *Eṇcuvaṭi* mode or problem solving, retained the significance of memory recall and still introduced arithmetic practice with pen and paper. However, it we should not forget that for most of these efforts, it was only a strategic step, to shift to European arithmetic. See, Balar Kanitam, *An Elementary Arithmetic Combining Many of the Peculiarities of the European and Tamil System* (Jaffna: American Mission Press, 1849). Its preface says, 'Those who are at all conversant with the educational process in the country will readily appreciate the importance of giving the characters and methods of operation according to both English and Tamil system'.

[17] For a brief summary of educational work by the CMS in the Tirunelveli region, especially under Rhenius, see the Letter from Rev. C T Rhenius to the Board of Revenue, Proceedings of the Madras Board of Revenue (BoR), Tamil Nadu State Archives (TNSA), 1 March 1830, nos. 21–22, Vol. 1231, pp. 2615–2621 when he was asking for sanction for land for his schools. Also, see his report in *Church Missionary Record*, Vol. IV, September, 1833, p. 200. UTC Archives. In this report he mentions the adoption of the Bell's system in all the CMS schools, provided there were enough children, where arithmetic practice was taught along with the use of palm leaves and memorizing catechism. Interestingly, when asked why the practice of hiring heathens as schoolmasters was to be continued, Rhenius responded that the missionary ought to 'take the people as they are and not as they ought to be'.

[18] Vedanayakam Sastri was an important figure in the early nineteenth century world of Tamil Christianity, who was trained by the German missionary Rev. C F Schwartz, who also

Eṇ Viḷakkam.[19] He tried to alter the very structure of the *Eṇcuvaṭi* so that the concept of number defined its very learning process, instead of numbers in relation to each other memorized for recall in a defined order, under the recollective memory mode. *Eṇ Viḷakkam* was meant to render the *Eṇcuvaṭi* obsolete and equip the student to deal with numbers as abstract quantities. But this was not a complete break from the traditions of recollection because Sastri intended the numbers to be learned in relation to each other, using techniques of recollection. Sastri wanted the static *Eṇ—Cuvaṭi* (literally the Number—Text) to become the dynamic *Eṇ Viḷakkam* (literally, Number—Explained). The *Eṇ Viḷakkam* however was never published. It still lies buried in a box at the UTC Archives in Bangalore, as a handwritten manuscript that probably never entered the world of active circulation.

Such efforts to reimagine mathematics for the public did not really take off in these early decades of the nineteenth century. For one, missionaries intended their schools, where much of this early creativity occurred and for which someone like Sastri may have composed his textbook, only as a way to transition to formal European-style schooling.[20] This effort proceeded to fragment the student body. For example in many mission schools, like in language training, mathematics was demarcated for different publics. The Tamil *tiṇṇai* teacher taught *tiṇṇai* arithmetic and the European master teaching the modern arithmetic, albeit in the

taught the wards of the Thanjavur Maratha kings. His contribution to Tamil letters by way of adopting Tamil literary genres like the *paḷḷu* and the *kummi* for the preaching of Christianity. See Indira Vishwanathan Peterson, 'Between Print and Performance: The Tamil Christian Poetry of Vedanayaka Shastri and the Literary Cultures of Nineteenth Century South India', *India's Literary History, Essays on the Nineteenth Century*, eds. Vasudha Dalmia and Stuart Blackburn (Delhi: Permanent Black, 2004), 25–59.

19 Vedanayakam Sastri, *Eṇ Viḷakkam*, Handwritten Manuscript, VPC-VNS 29, UTC Archive. The preface to this *Eṇ Viḷakkam* was written as a dialogue between a student and the author, Sastri himself. The student asks: 'Already we are subjected to the pain of memorizing the *Eṇcuvaṭi*, why impose on us one more and carry further pain? Sastri: No. Why do you need the *Eṇcuvaṭi* when you are learning *Eṇ Viḷakkam*? This contains all that is in the *Eṇcuvaṭi*. I have only separated it into distinct parts and added new elements to reform it. I didn't do much more'. Student: If that is so, I shall happily carry forward your lessons, Aiya'.

20 'Native ciphering is a subject of study in the seminaries and when they are thoroughly grounded in it, we intend to direct their attention to the European system', Report from the CMS Schools, Tirunelveli, *Proceedings of the Church Missionary Society, 1823–1824*, p. 145, UTC Archives. The previous year's Report actually says, 'the native schoolmasters are hopeless, only hope for a European system to work is to make the boys trained in our schools to become the assistants', *Proceedings of the Church Missionary Society, 1822–1823*, p. 235, UTC Archives.

same school, for different classes and castes of students. In the schools of Rhenius and that of Charles Schmidt in the CMS schools of Tirunelveli,[21] concurrent teaching[22] of Tamil *tiṇṇai* arithmetic for the lower castes and the English arithmetic for the upper castes meant the cultivation of two life careers rather than the converging of a universal knowledge that would break caste barriers to yield an ideal knowledge type, to be absorbed by an ideal company state. The lower caste students went on to become butlers and domestic servants whereas their Veḷḷāla counterparts became clerks in the revenue establishment.[23] The Bell system (see Image 4.1 for a visual understanding of the Bell system of monitorial instruction) as it was localized in England inspired utilitarian visions of controlled learning in the name of efficient, factory style of schooling.[24] This utilitarian uptake was prompted by the necessity to deal with the rising radicalism of the emerging working class,[25] to contain which, education was considered an effective tool.

[21] 'On Plan of Instruction in Tinnevelly Schools', Ibid., where he says since the natives consider ciphering a very important subject and since 'I have not had time to acquaint myself with the system, left it to the Tamil school masters'. But in the following year, when he tried teaching modern Arithmetic to the boys of the sixth class, 'with a view to ascertain their talents and prepare them for an instruction in Geometry as I had then the idea of competing our seminaries with the most promising boys of the Central School; but I soon found out that their understandings were not prepared for this science and hence discontinued it', p. 233.

[22] Of course, we know that the model of concurrent teaching was a widely known strategy across the various Presidencies in the teaching of modern science. For an interesting case of the teaching of Astronomy, see Rajiv Tiwari, 'A Transnarrative for the Colony: Astronomy Education and Religion in Nineteenth Century India', *Economic & Political Weekly* 41, no. 13 (2006): 1269–1277.

[23] S. Manickam, *Studies in Missionary History: Reflections on a Culture-Contact* (Madras: Christian Literature Society, 1988).

[24] For a discussion of the complex processes and response to the reception and localization of the Madras System of Tuition in England, see Simon Schaffer, 'How Disciplines Look', *Interdisciplinarity: Reconfigurations of the social and natural sciences*, eds. Andrew Barry and Georgina Born (London: Routledge, 2013), 57–81. Also on the history of this travelling pedagogic system, see Jana Tschurenev, 'Incorporation and Differentiation: Popular Education and the Imperial Civilizing Mission in Early Nineteenth Century India', *Civilizing Mission in Colonial and Postcolonial South Asia: From Improvement to Development*, eds. Carey A. Watt and Michael Mann (London: Anthem Press, 2011), 93–124; Jana Tschurenev, 'Diffusing Useful Knowledge: The Monitorial System of Education in Madras, London and Bengal, 1789–1840', *Pedagogica Historica* 44, no. 3 (2008): 245–264. For a different perspective from educational theory, see David Hogan, 'The Market Revolution and Disciplinary Power: Joseph Lancaster and the Psychology of the Early Classroom System', *History of Education Quarterly* 29, no. 3 (1989): 381–417.

[25] For this perspective towards the history of mathematics education in England, see Leo Rogers, 'The Mathematical Curriculum and Pedagogy in England 1780–1900: Social and Cultural Origins', *History and Epistemology in Mathematics Education, Proceedings of the First European Summer University Montpellier* (Montpellier: Irem De Montpellier, 19–23 July 1993), 401–412.

Image 4.1 Monitorial system at work in the nineteenth century Europe. Courtesy: Wikimedia Commons. Source: https://upload.wikimedia.org/wikipedia/commons/7/75/Monitorial_education_system_Bell-Lancaster_19th_century.png) accessed on 23 October 2018.

In the South India mission context, the monitoral principle however was widely adopted to teach the catechism and cultivate spiritual order efficiently. Even here, as it has experimented with the native children, there was an increasing discomfort about the very idea of 'emulation' central to the Bell system, because it was considered that 'this systematic and deliberate rousing and fermenting of ambition and pride, those most powerful and dangerous passions of man, is directly counteracting all religious instruction … the system carried on with consistency and energy prescribed is admirably calculated to produce excellent soldiers and sailors, but ... not soldiers of Jesus'.[26] This was not about the global circulation of a pedagogic knowledge in transit, which of course is an interesting phenomenon to acknowledge, but the ways and manners in which such pedagogy was localized by each agency need to be considered, as it helps us in understanding the operative part of the pedagogic practice. Thus the mission school was not so much a space of hybridity or grafting but a space for maintaining, sustaining, and entrenching social fragmentation. This perhaps offers one reason why Sastri's textbook was never seen worthy enough to publish in the textbook market. There was no market for a creative combination of different traditions.

Let us consider the case of another text, Pantulu Ramasamy Naicker's *Kanitadeepikai*, probably the first printed arithmetic textbook in Tamil published by the 'grammar factory' of the Fort St. George College in the year 1825.[27] Different practitioners participated in the making of this book: Major De Havilland, a French hydraulic engineer trained in modern mathematics,[28] Elathur Subramanya Sastriar, a proficient of Surya Siddhanta, trained in the Sanskrit tradition and the Tamil Head Master of the College, Tandavaraya Mudaliar. The *Kanitadeepikai*[29]

[26] Rev. Schmidt, Report on Tinnevelly Schools, *Proceedings of the Church Missionary Society*, 1822–1823, p. 235. He did try and start teaching European mathematics to the same class of students under the tinnai mode, but soon he stopped it, he said, when he found that they were not prepared to enter that arena of learning. But then he did report that he followed the Bell's method for religious instruction and found the monitorial principle useful only to the extent of boys correcting each other's faults. However, we do know that the Bell's system was found to be useful and efficient to teach catechism and Gospel, for its early history, see Elmer H. Cutts, 'The Background of Macaulay's Minute', *American Historical Review* 58, no. 4 (1953): 824–853.

[27] For a very interesting collection of work on the College of Fort St. George or what is now known as an 'explosion in the grammar factory', see Thomas R. Trautman, ed., *The Madras School of Orientalism Producing Knowledge in Colonial South India* (Delhi: Oxford University Press, 2009).

[28] Major De Havilland was an important personality in Company's Madras, and seems to have taken an active role in several projects including designing several public buildings, exploring navigational paths in the city and in the seas and probably his most important role was his coordination of the Company's attempt to standardize weights and measures, an attempt that started as early as 1804 and took about forty years before an 'imperial decree' from the Company's headquarters promulgated the use of English weights and measures as the standard. This is a story in standardization and state making as much as it is a story of both practitioners and public becoming subjects of a different political economic order of measures. This is a work in progress and hopefully would help us in dwelling into the details of the contexts of change in the first half of the nineteenth century with respect to mathematical practices.

[29] Pantulu Ramasamy Naicker, *Kanitadeepikai* (Madras: Madras School Book Society, 1825). I am grateful to the scholar, Venkatachalam of Chengam for sharing the copy of this book.

aligned Tamil numerical notation in line with the place value system. It marked a clear break in the mode of Tamil arithmetic representation of numbers. According to Naicker, the language of computation was chosen to be a mixture of Sanskrit words and *kotuntamil*, so that the book could be used by everyone and therefore tried to 'cure' a 'deficiency' in Tamil numerical notation.[30] It is difficult to believe that Naicker and his colleagues were unaware of the *Eṇcuvaṭi* which used commonly known spoken words for arithmetic operations in Tamil, which had cognitive proximity to a native Tamil speaker: like *kūṭṭa*, *kaḻikka*, *perukka*, and *vakukka* for addition, subtraction, multiplication, and division, respectively. Even for rules like the rule of three, it had terms like the *muttokai vinā* but in Naicker's scheme of language, it had to be *kuṇanam, kuṇaṇīyam, kuṇitam* (for the terms involved in multiplication) *cōtakam cōttiyam* (for subtraction), *pācciam, and pācakam* (for dividend and divisor). Even the multiplication table to him would be called *kuṇana paripācai*, not *perukkal vāyppādu*. This probably marked the beginning of a long history of using technical words in the sciences, especially in translation. But in this case, the immediate cognitive distancing brought in by the use of strange terms, would have probably rendered the learning of arithmetic a seriously technical business, wherein, arithmetic manipulation involved distant, abstract quantities, not the locally familiar and the immediate language of the *Eṇcuvaṭi*.

The *Kanitadeepikai* offered a different blend from Sastri. It could have successfully alienated the learner from the familiar territory of the *Eṇcuvaṭi* and seamlessly merged with the modern learning of arithmetic. In doing so, the publication of this book also marked certain fundamental reorientation in the presentation of mathematical textbooks in the vernacular. In case of Tamil, it changed the Tamil numerical notation and modernized it, by integrating the symbol for zero into it. Earlier, the number ten in Tamil, as we discussed in Chapter 1, was represented by the symbol, ய and one hundred was ள. Now, Naicker introduced the notation of one and zero adjacent to each other, and ten became க0, and one hundred became, க00, and so on. His book also marked the beginning of an era in the format of arithmetic textbooks in Tamil, when the

[30] 'Since Tamil lacks appropriate terms and even if translated, they are tough and therefore using a mixture of Aryan and *kotuntamil*', Ibid., p. 5.

classification of arithmetic learning now was based upon the four arithmetic operations as distinct from the Tamil mode of traditional classification based on *Poṉṉilakkam* (in the order of gold), *Nellilakkam* (in the order of grains: measures as numbers), and *Nilam* (land: area or squares). Numbers now stood alone, as entities now to be operated with rules, and through specific steps and processes, to achieve certain results, where in, the arithmetic operation becomes the prime mover and remained so since then. Interestingly, in order to make the public abide by these new changes, Naicker called upon divine authority, seemingly impatient at persuading his public and seeking recourse to the authority of rules. While introducing place value, with the notion of units, tens, and thousands using the symbol for zero, which was absent in the Tamil symbol for numbers, but very much part of the number names, Ramasamy instead of explaining the linkage between number names and symbols and how zero helps, simply said, 'take it as the rule of God', evocative of the beginning of a rule-based, procedural arithmetic in mathematical pedagogy.

But Naicker's *Kanitadeepikai* did not really gain traction. Naicker was searching for public for new mathematics, but this public for him was only possible with the blending of Sanskrit and Tamil notational practices. This turn is intriguing given that the question of language for public circulation (like the growth of Cutcherry Tamil[31]) was in fact enmeshed with Persianate idioms during the same period. Thus for someone like Naicker, the re-imagination of the public for mathematics was clearly constrained by his fidelity to ritual and sacrality, represented by Sanskrit, rather than the material practices of the *tiṇṇai*. Why was this the case? We also need to consider the dynamics of the textbook market for which Naicker wrote his text. His book was part of the textbook publication project of the Fort St. George College that coincided with the Company's move to intervene in education beyond the Survey school. The Company had by the end of the second decade of the nineteenth century begun to attribute the failures of the ryotwari survey to a general lack of education and particularly a lack of education among its revenue servants. This frustration on the one hand, as I mentioned earlier, led to a greater

[31] For a discussion on cutcherry Tamil, see Raman, *Document Raj*. Also Hephzibah Israel, 'Cutcherry Tamil vs. Pure Tamil: Contesting Language Use in The Translated Bible in the Early Nineteenth Century Protestant Tamil Community', *The Postcolonial Bible Reader*, ed. R. S. Sugirtharajah (Malden: Blackwell, 2006).

reliance on the Maratha Brahmans to oversee the survey, but it also led to significant interventions in the education system. The Madras Governor Thomas Munro was singularly important in this regard.

Thomas Munro based his governance on the principles of co-option of selected elements in the native society. He advocated that the Company enlist the loyalty of elites and Brahmins, offering them a new and very different kind of social status.[32] A closely structured community, with flexible skills combined with the lure of a promising opportunity, set off by a process of state-building, was continuously forced to come to terms with establishing authority and ways to enforce loyalty.[33] This feature had a significant influence on education. Munro documented the existing systems of pedagogy,[34] namely the *tiṇṇai* school, in order to deem them inadequate so that he could institute a new set of schools to recruit and train students exclusively for Company employment. Munro's new schools were to operate at the level of the District or Tahsil (sub-district) and were called Tahsildari-Collectorate schools. They were to be run on systematic lines, almost as a counter to the *tiṇṇai,* and they were to use printed paper textbooks rather than palm leaf. Munro directed the Fort St. George College to provide the textbooks.

Naicker's *Kanitadeepikai* was one of these textbooks. Naicker's articulation of a potential public notation built on a curious mix of Sanskrit and *Kotuntamil* ('vulgar' Tamil) therefore addressed Munro's project. By its very nature, we can see that the *Kanitadeepikai* was constrained by the objective of the colonial state and embedded in the hierarchies of caste. Given the few number of Tahsildari/Collectorate schools, the market for Naicker's text was limited. Not more than 200 copies were printed and it is hard to discern when and how it was used in the classrooms.[35]

[32] Letters and Records of Munro, *Ceded Districts, 1805–1806*, Public Sundries, Vol. 122, TNSA. Also, *Minutes of Sir Thomas Munro*, 3 August 1825, Madras, Public Sundries, Vol. 129, para 20, TNSA.

[33] Robert Frykenberg, 'Modern Education in South India, 1784–1854: Its Roots and Its Role as a Vehicle of Integration Under Company Raj', *American Historical Review* 91, no. 1 (1986): 37–65.

[34] This exercise is what is known as the Munro survey, documented in Dharampal, *The Beautiful Tree: Indigenous Education in Eighteenth Century* (New Delhi: Biblia Impex, 1983).

[35] *Minutes of Meetings, 1823–1839*, Volume 1, The Madras School Book Society Papers, MSBS-1, UTC Archives. Singarachari, the collectorate school teacher in Cuddalore sent a request for school books which he said is 'absolutely required for efficient teaching' to which the College Board responded by sending an entire set of books to all the collectorate schools in the entire Presidency, among which was included Ramasamy's Arithmetic. Public Consultations, TNSA, 6 September 1833, Vol. 614, nos. 16–17, pp. 3453–3455.

In fact, Munro's scheme seems to have triggered off a textbook market. Several individuals tried to write books and sought approval from the Government and the Madras School Book Society, asking for recognition and patronage. This inevitably brought in personal networks and favours in order to promote one's book. Despite this, there was no guarantee that the author might get a response from the authorities.[36] Moulvee Mohammad Irtaza Alee Khan, an official at the Court of Sadr and Fouzdari Adalat submitted in 1823 a manuscript in Persian on the sciences of Arithmetic, Algebra, and Geometry called 'Nakoodool Hisab' along with another book on the 'Mohammaden Law of Inheritance'. While the law book was printed immediately, his maths book was rejected, with the response that the printing press was busy printing books for the Madras Army.[37]

Munro's school experiment failed. It turns out that Munro had struck a compromise. In the much talked about Munro Minute of 1826, he chose not to disturb the *tiṉṉai* arrangement at all. Recruits to his schools had to graduate from the *tiṉṉai* first. He modelled his intervention not as a mode of pedagogic reform but as a way to install a bureaucratic arrangement of power that could monitor easily and hence assume control of pedagogic outcomes.[38] It was political exigency that marked the beginning of modern education. Priorities were set to make a system of revenue extraction, work by all means. The collectorate and the tashildari schools were also bound to fail, for want of teacher trainees, who were supposed to come to the Madras city to be trained in the College and sent back to each collectorate. Almost all district collectors wrote back to Munro saying that the Brahmins would not favour the option of becoming a teacher when they could get a job in the local cutcherry. The Annual Report of the Central School cited a contemporary Tamil proverb to that effect: 'Not the Shastras, but a knowledge of English is what the Brahmins now regards the best'. Most of the collectorate trainees had some relationship with

[36] See *Proceedings and Letters, Madras School Book Society, 1854–1856*, MSBS-2, UTC Archives, for various such requests and how the Society members went about deciding on their publication.

[37] 'On Request to the Government to buy a Persian Mathematical Work', Public Consultations, TNSA, 9 November 1827, Vol. 555, nos. 19–20, pp. 4483–4486.

[38] Minute by Sir Thomas Munro, 25 June 1822, in Appendix A, *Selections From the Records of the Madras Government Papers Relating to Public Instruction*, Madras, 1855, pp. iii–iv.

someone working at the revenue establishment. Those who decided to come started their journey with modern mathematics in the Presidency School, under the leadership of Venkatachalam Mudaliar with the available copy of Charles Hutton's *Course of Mathematics*. But after eight years that witnessed several students opting out for better jobs, the judgement on the collectorate school trainees was that they were not ready to teach mathematics. This was not because they could not learn mathematics. It was because they were more interested in options that would pay better. The Board's observation about the students is telling, 'They only have 'sufficient knowledge to enable them to give instruction in the first rules of that science ... The study of Mathematics, the Board regrets to observe, has become almost altogether neglected—the advantage to be derived from this branch of science seem to be regarded by the great bulk of students as too remote to offer a sufficient inducement for the direction of their time and attention to it and in the acquirement of a general nature and of more practical utility in their time of life they have seen a greater promise of substantial return'.[39]

The case of the tahsildari schools was considered even worse than the existing *tiṇṇai* schools, which had far better and reputed teachers while the teachers to the tahsildaris were recruited from the personal networks of the cutcherry officials and the people were not particularly interested in these schools.[40] Throughout this ill-fated experiment, the cutcherry apparatus recruited largely from the circuits of family apprentices who had *tiṇṇai* training or the mission school, which, as we saw catered to the job market by streaming its students along caste and linguistic lines. Munro's failed effort had entrenched further the legacy of hierarchical schooling that would define the colonial educational policy for a very long time. In this model, the urban, higher schools teaching in English would receive all the modern pedagogic resources and possible innovations while training job aspirants for upper castes, while the local tahsildari-like schools, which anyway were only poor imitations of the

[39] *Annual Report on the Progress of Native Education*, Public Consultations, TNSA, 8 February 1833, Vol. 609, nos. 15–16, p. 591.

[40] A. D. Campbell, 'On Native Education'. *Madras Journal of Literature and Science* (April, 1836): 110–116.

tiṉṉai, would produce a labour force that could aspire for jobs and end up as domestic labour in European households.[41]

Around this time, the teaching of mathematics itself was going through profound transitions. In England, in 1831, Augustus De Morgan[42] published his work on mathematics education, *On the Study and Difficulties of Mathematics*. In this book, he formulated a critique of the Bell Lancaster system and literally lambasted the pedagogy: the Bell system, to him, broke down arithmetic into a multitude of rules, many of them so unintelligible that they could be 'Hebrew'. Pupils were not expected to understand the reasons for rules but merely to be able to apply them. Teachers were scared to teach such principles, for to do so required knowledge and understanding. Therefore, it was much easier to teach rules and various books of worked-out solutions to avoid any troublesome questions. As a result, after several years of working meaningless and useless questions by the slates, he argued that the student left the school as a 'master of few methods, provided he knows what rule a question falls under'. The Bell Lancaster system condemned the majority to the rote learning of half-digested gobbets of information.[43] In effect, memorizing the rules to carry out each case, a student had to only recognize which case a given problem fell under, and apply the

[41] There were at least two instances when the admission of pariahs into the schools became an issue and the Government decided against the pariahs as a matter of political decision when it said that it would put the entire experiment in jeopardy, if the rest of the teachers and the students would get offended. In fact, interestingly it wrote to the other Presidencies to seek counsel in the matter and both Bombay and Calcutta approved of the Madras intent and suggested opening separate schools if necessary. See the trail following the issue of 'On a Pariah into College', Public Consultations, TNSA, 24 January 1834, Vol. 618, nos. 24–25, p. 177. For the Calcutta response which actually said that such a case did not arise in Bengal and for the response from the Secretary of the Native Education Society in Bombay, which went even further and said that 'no boy of the lowest caste has ever applied for admission', see Public Consultations, TNSA, 1 April 1834, Vol. 620, nos. 9–11, pp. 906–910.

[42] Through the London-based Society for the Diffusion of Useful Knowledge Augustus De Morgan's reform initiative sought to move British education away from the classical education scheme of the Cambridge and Oxford approach and published new textbooks and manuals for the teaching of Arithmetic and Algebra in the 1830s. The University of London, to which he belonged, was also part of this wider political initiative to move away from the elitist classical education model. For De Morgan, it was important that arithmetic teaching commence with a clear explanation of methods of numeration, illustrated by reference to other systems besides the decimal, and supported with the use of counters. See Augustus De Morgan, *The Study of Mathematics Part I and II* (London: Society for the Diffusion of Useful Knowledge, 1830).

[43] Geoffrey Howson, *A History of Mathematics Education in England* (Cambridge: Cambridge University Press, 1982), 89.

appropriate rule, a game of manipulation based on matching problems to rule.[44]

De Morgan's critique was quite appropriate to the Indian colonial context as well. The failure of Munro's Collectorate Schools and the lack of adequate school teachers made the *tiṇṇai* a focus of colonial and reformist ire. The inability of the village teacher to help liberate the student from the clutches of 'mechanical memory', which this experiment was supposed to make possible, was to remain a consistent complaint from the colonial establishment for the rest of the century. However, in practice, given the operations of the market of recruitment, the Company continued to rely on the *tiṇṇai* school and they continued to multiply. This proliferation of *tiṇṇai* as part of a colonial compact with revenue collection is one way of understanding the resilience, if you like, of the *tiṇṇai* pedagogy in mathematics. Indeed we can see that rather than creative textbooks, the nascent textbook market when it began to boom catered largely to the *tiṇṇai* curriculum. Printed *Eṇcuvaṭis* were now made available to the *tiṇṇai* school *teacher*, sponsored by the small town publishing ventures, supported by agencies like the Caturveta Siddhantha Sabha, and from centres like Chidambaram, Tanjavur, and Kumbakonam, by those trying to resist the missionaries. Ironically, even the printing presses fostered by Tamil pandits of the Fort St. George College catered to this market. It is probable that the print runs of the *tiṇṇai Eṇcuvaṭis* may have supported their more rarefied literary endeavours.

Thus far, we have seen how efforts to articulate mathematics for general circulation in Tamil region were generated by colonial transitions but also simultaneously constrained. It is clear that these efforts occurred well before the institution of a formal education department. They emerged in the context of the revenue survey that ran both on informal recruitment and an incipient textbook market that came up to serve the needs of recruits and others who made up the mathematics public. Some additional layers of complexity came about from the 1840s, when the colonial government changed tactics to further reform its revenue inefficiencies and manage the market for jobs, textbooks, and schools. These markets shaped the nature of the mathematics public.

[44] C. Philips, 'Augustus De Morgan and the Propagation of Moral Mathematics', *Studies in History and Philosophy of Science* 36 (2005): 105–133.

Mathematics for a Public and the Problem of Scrutiny/Assessment, the 1840s Onwards

From the 1840s, two changes marked the audiences for mathematics: one change was in the realm of measurement that was increasingly standardized and had an impact on all manner of people including the labouring poor. The other change was a change in the nature of a formal education policy to regulate and certify schools. The latter in particular must be understood not as a direct intervention in education but as a system of regulation through a calibrated framework of aid and certifications through inspections and examinations as well as syllabi that shaped the orientation of pedagogic efforts in South India. Both these efforts can be understood as forms of scrutiny that shaped the outcomes of mathematical pedagogy.

The standardization of all weights and measures in the great reforms of record keeping[45] and the use of new modes of accounting with the use of Arabic numerals that were made compulsory unfolded through the 1840s but culminated after about ten years in the 1850s.[46] This weight of English on the Tamil world was not so much a process of grafting, again, but further differentiation. It was a massive and important intervention in the social world of numeracy. The story of the transition from the native measures to British standards was a rather long and painful tale. The world of metrological practice in South India did not change with a single stroke of pen.

The attempt for standardization of weights and measures in the various Presidencies under the East India Company is a long and complex story, which involved concerns of political economy of course, but the terms of the debate on ways to settle the issue of standardization was

45 There were a series of measures to call this a great reform, there was a survey to assess how much of the revenue establishment had people who were related to each other by birth or by marriage so as to ascertain 'interests' and to make efforts to stop it. There was also an effort to take stock of the amount of records stored in each establishment and decisions were taken with respect to their storage and preservation. Then there was the transition to the English numerals and the abolition of Marathi as a language of recordkeeping, accompanied by a very concerted attempt towards standardization of weights and measures.

46 It should be noted that in many districts, records were kept in at least two languages, Tamil and Marathi and in places like the North Arcot, in Persian as well. The first such request was made by the Collector of Nellore in 1840 who wanted this transition and considered it possible given that the 'commonest village curnum could attain a perfect knowledge of the English numerals in a few hours and indeed many of those Gentoo, Maratta and Tamil are so similar in form to ours that the transition will hardly be perceived'. To support his case, he drew up a sheet graphically representing the numerals in each South Indian language along with English. *Proceedings of the Madras BoR*, TNSA, 30 April 1840, Vol. 1704, nos. 83–84, pp. 5629–5631.

often constructed through idioms of mathematical exactitude and how appropriate it could be for practical needs of commerce. Colonel TB Jervis in Bombay and FW Ellis in Madras seemed to be the early protagonists of this debate, which probably was prompted by the Madras Company's administration's initiative on the issue of standardization, as early as 1802.[47] Several pamphlets and treatises were written in a long and protracted debate for almost two decades.[48] Curiously, a petition of grain merchants made it urgent for the Company to intervene, when they demanded a course of standardization, which triggered a process that involved a host of establishments including the Police, Customs, and Collectors. While in 1825, the Company's response was to intervene in a way that subjected the use of measuring instruments to periodical scrutiny by retaining the native measures,[49] it continued an elaborate exercise from then through the 1830s and 1840s, through the formation of several committees, and culminated in a final exercise in 1851 with a decisive shift to the British standards.[50] This is a completely different project, which is waiting to be written to tell the story of how the material world of measuring and weighing was brought under political control that did not merely stop with the realm of recordkeeping, which it did, and hence directly shaped the arithmetic curriculum for the rest of the century, but more significantly, determined the day to day lives of an entire population, the measuring public, as it were.[51] This was also the case with native almanacs, the time-keepers in the world of the measuring public, where,

[47] *Proceedings of the Madras BoR*, TNSA, 25 January 1802, Vol. 309, no. 21, p. 883.

[48] For a brief but an interesting summary of these debates, see C. E. Gover, *Indian Weights and Measures. Their Condition and Remedy* (Madras: W. Thomas, 1865).

[49] See *Reports Submitted to the Commissary General on Weights and Measures in Use in Several Districts*, Public Consultations, TNSA, 11 November 1825, Vol. 533B, nos. 7–8A, pp. 3670–3738. This had an even earlier precedence, when the Collectors were asked to send physical models of all measuring instruments to Major De Havilland (the French hydraulic engineer and co-author of Pantulu Ramasamy Naicker's *Kanitadeepikai*), a process that lasted from 1821 to 1823. See Proceedings of Madras BoR, TNSA, 1823, Vol. 1011, no. 60, pp. 1326–1328.

[50] This massive exercise left volumes over the years, but for the final resolution, see List of Papers with respect to Weights and Measures as listed in Assay Master to the Chief Secretary of Government, *Proceedings of Madras BoR*, TNSA, 24 March 1851, Vol. 2278, pp. 4264–4271.

[51] This is a work in progress. In fact, it needs to be pointed out that the long history of standardization as an exercise in the political economy of knowledge practices needs to go even further back, because such attempts were not only initiated by the Company suddenly in the early nineteenth century but very much part of state making processes in the history of South India. We have just begun a project to make an historical atlas of metrological practices in south India from the ninth to the fifteenth centuries to begin with. Concurrently, we will be studying the debates of the early nineteenth century.

however, it was felt that non-intervention was best since it would cause extreme inconvenience and that there 'would be no other way to compare the native and European dates'.[52] A survey of the people who could convert to the writing of English numerals in the cutcherry offices conducted soon after, evoked very mixed results. Though this took the native revenue servants by storm, threatening many people's careers and lives, it could be roughly estimated that on an average, about fifty per cent could make the transition possible, given a time of three months to do so, aided by lithographed sheets of English numerals.[53]

Many struggled and there were representations from among the native officials in the bureaucracy trying to argue that the efforts could end up being counterproductive, not as a case against the new system but they brought in the image of a local public, who would not be able to understand the records and therefore would become more apprehensive. On top of this, they also argued that with very bad writing and illegible figures, the initiative could compound the task further.[54] But there was no going back and there were people like Subba Row and Narasinga Row in the North Arcot cutcherry who faced the risk of dismissal.[55]

Again it was the upper-caste family network that responded best to the pressures and change. One could almost visualize how each family would have mobilized around the concerned individual to train him in the use of English numerals, working hard with the litho sheet helping him to be successful within three months. The family remained the most efficient site for

[52] Extracts from the Minutes of Consultation dates 24 January 1837, *Proceedings of the Madras BoR*, TNSA, 6 February 1837, Vol. 1545, nos. 5–6, pp. 957–958. Not only were the Tamil and Telugu almanacs asked to be printed continuously but the office of the Native Astronomer of the College establishment was given the responsibility to coordinate 'time-keeping' with the revenue and judicial officers by periodically sending them these printed almanacs.

[53] The Governor actually felt that the system of pointing of large sums of lakhs and crores, rather than by hundreds of thousands, and millions according to the English system of notation, for example, 3,75,00,000 instead of 37,500,000. System of counting by lakhs may be convenient, nor in the term objectionable either as a written or an oral expression, but the Governor in Council thinks that at least in its printed reports, one has to conform to the European system. See 'On Discontinuing Mahratta as the Language of Revenue', *Proceedings of the Madras BoR*, TNSA, 13 November 1854, Vol. 2445, nos. 11–12, pp. 15336–15350. A circular then was issued to all the *District Collectors: Proceedings of Madras BoR*, TNSA, 16 November 1854, Vol. 2446, no. 9, pp. 15545–15547. This brought in swift response from almost all the collectors with mostly welcoming the measure and a few with apprehensions.

[54] For the Memorandum by Seshaiah, the Naib Sheristadar, who was a proficient of the Madras University working at the Masulipatnam collectorate, see *Proceedings of the Madras BoR*, TNSA, 28 July 1855, Vol. 2484, nos. 654–655, pp. 12205–12218.

[55] *Proceedings of the Madras BoR*, TNSA, 28 May 1855, Vol. 2473, no. 84, pp. 8317–8320.

adaptation to the new expectation. So, this also tells us how personalized spheres of the family and kinship remained the primary sphere of knowledge transactions, tailored towards particular jobs in the market. It proved itself efficient too, because, at the end of this exercise, we see how there were no causalities reported in the transition to the English numerals.

For a teacher of mathematics or the writer of textbooks, this demand of the colonial state for literacy in English notation meant that in practical terms English notation had to be directly translated into Tamil, leaving very little space for creative play or traffic. Thus a whole new segment of a book market emerged to fulfil the demand of this new world of numeracy, the daunting array of tables of conversions from the native ones into the English measures of all kinds. The printing of these ready-reckoners with conversion tables now became necessary in all revenue and trading establishments, not to mention the little shop keepers, artisans and merchants. This transition to the new world of measures assumed its own life as an integral part of the learning of mathematics, where the shift from the world of Tamil measures like the *aṭikōl, marakkāl*, the *palam, the varākaṉ and the nāḻikai* into their corresponding standard British measures were now compulsory learning both for everyday transactions with the state and in society as well as in the classroom and the examinations. The learning of the rule of three that constituted the world of the practitioner's mathematics, as we saw in the *Kaṇakkatikāram* tradition had to meet the new counterparts. A new set of tables replaced the *Eṇcuvaṭi*. The textbook market emerged to fulfil this demand for English notation. The earliest 'English style math textbooks' like that of Colenso's *Arithmetic*, Barnard Smith's *Arithmetic* were now adapted to the Indian world, which basically meant for large parts, just accounting for these conversions as standard exercises. These fields of conversions and notations fundamentally defined the world of the Anglo vernacular learning.

An examination and scrutiny system developed concomitantly to manage and cultivate the new norms. An ardent disciple of Thomas Munro, Sir Arbuthnot, ordered a survey on the lines of the Newcastle commission in England in 1850s. His survey was not really a success—few collectors responded to his circular and the data generated remained incomplete. But the survey however incomplete, established the spread of missionary schools in the urban centres of the hinterland with teaching in English and Arithmetic, Algebra, Euclid, Plane and Spherical

Trigonometry and Mechanics. The survey, secondly, also listed the curriculum in use in these schools of all kinds, not as components of mathematics pedagogy to be learnt but by the use of particular textbooks. The textbooks defined the curriculum, collapsing learning with printed textbooks[56] and showed clusters of mathematics pedagogy emerging in towns like Tanjore, Kumbakonam, Masulipatnam and Tirunelveli,[57] where a set of elite schools called the Provincial schools were supported by the Government to nurture what the government felt was a remarkable 'aptitude' for the learning of mathematics. These incidentally were also centres where caste hierarchies were extreme in schooling.[58] And finally the survey documented what we can now anticipate given our account of early history of Munro's 'compact': the proliferation of *tiṉṉai* schools, along with a huge proliferation of a distinct category called 'private tuition', which prepared aspirants for the educational tests introduced during the 1840s which were to be the mainstay of revenue and University establishment. In effect, Arbuthnot's counting of the *tiṉṉai* provided once again an opportunity for the colonial government to revisit *tiṉṉai* reform on the one hand and estimate, at the same time, the demand for a textbook industry as the means through which to create broad-based pedagogic intervention. The survey was underway when the important 'Wood's Despatch' of 1854 espoused and legitimated non-violent interference as a foundation of colonial governance of education and heralded the move to establish a comprehensive system of national

[56] *Papers Relating to the State of Education in the Provinces Subject to the Government of Madras* (Madras: Government Press, 1854). The entire survey with returns from each district is collated in this volume.

[57] To the extent that the Collectors responded by furnishing details of the curriculum, textbooks in use and subjects taught, we could see, not just the proliferation of mission schools, but that proliferation concentrated in very particular centres, teaching British math textbooks in English medium of instruction. For the details of this emerging pattern in the 1850s, see *Papers Relating to the State of Education, 1854*, ibid, This is significant, considering the fact that we could already discern a pattern of hierarchy in schooling.

[58] Caste based exclusion in the schools were repeatedly a problem. In Kumbakonam for instance when one pariah student was admitted, all the rest of the 128 Brahmin students threatened to quit the school. See Annual Report of the Cumbakonam Provincial School dated 7 May 1855, in Appendix D, *Selections from the Records of the Madras Government Report on Public Instruction in the Madras Presidency, 1854–1855*, Madras, 1855, pp. ci–cviii. It is the same school, which later developed in to what was called the 'Cambridge of South India' and produced a generation of fine scholars and teachers of mathematics in the second half of the nineteenth century. This relationship between the centres of excellence in mathematics and its relationship to caste, in particular the Brahmin centres of learning requires further exploration, in order to reconstruct a meaningful social history of mathematics in India.

education.[59] Taking the Despatch and the discussion of Arburthnot's survey together we can conclude that they paved the way for a colonial educational bureaucracy. This bureaucracy was heavily centralized, and sought to extend its control right into the classroom. Textbooks (and hence certification of textbooks as well as sponsorship of textbooks) became the vital medium of this control and curriculum prescription for eligibility of grant in aid, the guiding frame of authority. Minimal enrollment forced innovations within the grant in aid, on a continuous basis, like the salary grants system, the payment by results system or the combined system of both salary and results, all meant to convert the *tiṇṇai* into the modern fold.

The textbooks became more like instruments of extension of the colonial authority rather than mere pedagogic devices. An elementary curriculum was forged that would emphasize the necessity of training students in methods of arithmetic problem solving, while the problems themselves were to be tailored to local necessities. These will be typically word problems that followed exercises involving numbers.[60]

An entire series of public examinations in the colonial state's consistent effort to create a recruitable public took on from the early 1840s, which was also modelled on the British tests for civil services. These tests with their rigid prescription of the curriculum made the first generation of the educated middle class from among the Brahmins and the Veḷḷālas qualified for clerical service. The number of examinations kept increasing as a means of certification as much as a way for the University to financially sustain itself. But the mass production of qualified people for government jobs had to be soon kept under check, which resulted in further grades of public examinations and high rates of failure.[61] Education as a means of public employment was the dominant norm which was very rarely

[59] See Syed Nurullah and J. P. Naik, *A Student's History of Education in India 1800–1965* (Bombay: Mac Millan & Co., 1969), 115–125 for a discussion on the features and implications of this Despatch.

[60] I consulted a whole set of textbooks during the course of the study, a selected list of which is provided in Appendix IV. The story of the changes in the features of the math textbooks through the nineteenth century deserves a separate study.

[61] As a response to this growing sentiment, the University examiners thought it necessary to fix a minimum in each subject: at least 1/4th of total marks and half of the whole to pass in each subject, without compromising on standards, as they say, 'the candidates should be required to show an accurate knowledge of vulgar and decimal fractions, and proportion in the paper in Arithmetic'. See 'Report on the UCS Exams for 1873–1874', Madras Department of Education G.O., TNSA, dated 27 August 1874, nos. 28–29.

questioned during this period. The academic function for this important role in society was to be provided by the itinerant educationists and the University teachers in their role as examiners. Students also responded to this system by developing their own means of negotiation. The matching of examination syllabus with marked out portions within the prescribed textbooks then meant very narrow spaces for actual learning. This simply required hard work. This in practice meant doing as many pages as possible in limited time by committing them to memory. Learning mathematics was not immune to this new mode of memorization. By repeated practice, the student learned problem solving by writing them down, again and again, till each step was memorized in the procedure, including the final solution, for each and every problem in the textbook. Even more, if problems involving decimal fractions in the Arithmetic syllabus were too demanding on memory practice, students would focus on those portions that could be easily remembered through such practice. This constituted the day to day engagement with modern mathematics for the student and the aspirant for jobs, which culture of learning by the 1870s, would be commonly described as the culture of cramming.[62]

Interestingly enough, the office of the *Kaṇakkaṉ* was protected from this new world of assessment. *Karaṇams* were required to know English notation but they did not have to pass an examination. In the 1880s, when the University proposed a test for village *Karaṇams*, the government summarily rejected the proposal arguing that the *Karaṇam* had to have local

[62] The Collector of Coimbatore's report was quite poignant and is worth mentioning, reflective of the sentiment of the emergent culture in that time. Talking of the misfortune of the schoolmasters that they must work at such high pressure to obtain results and position for their schools in written and oral exams, 'to pass a standard and work up to the textbooks till the contents can be transferred to paper is the object, and the precocious Indian youth is stimulated till his brains are addled and a reaction follows. It is not recollected that the growth of the mind, like that of the body is slow, and that over exertion and stimulus have a reactionary effect, but if prize boys be produced, and a large pass list is produced by what is certainly 'cram', the end is supposed to be attained. I have seen and heard pages of books learned by heart, and on passing to a page not learned, have noticed the most egregious blunders in even ordinary words. Minds are not exercised in thinking, there is no time allowed for that development. The questions from the book must be asked and answered, and nothing beyond. Common objects of life are unnoticed and unknown. A whole school in Karoor did not know what a tadpole was, they swarmed in their paddy fields . . . I cannot think this healthy education, which I take to be a calling forth of the powers of mind in observation and reasoning from it, and not only the memory these forced boys turn into schoolmasters and the evil goes on'. See 'Order on Coimbatore Collector's Report on Certain Defects in the System of Education pursued in the Generality of Schools', Madras Department of Education, G.O., TNSA, dated 28 December 1874, nos. 27–29.

knowledge which could not be certified by an exam.[63] Again it was the familial training kept within caste networks that precluded the realization of a public mathematics from entering the lowest level of revenue apparatus. The *Karaṇam* remained a politically important institution throughout the nineteenth century and did not have to pass through any of the modern qualifying processes of testing his computational ability. Local knowledge—a knowledge which might have been parleyed by many members of local society—was not entirely the monopoly of the hereditary *Kaṇakkaṉ* and it was completely commensurate with other orders of reform mathematics that were in circulation among the upper castes. While the *Kaṇakkan* eluded in this peculiar way the grasp of scrutiny and examination, how did the *tiṇṇai* school and the *tiṇṇai* master fare?

Negotiating Scrutiny and Modes of Memory: Reconciliation with the *Tiṇṇai* Teacher

An effective combination of public competitive examinations, 'a cut and dry curriculum' and a heavy textbook culture meant that the *tiṇṇai* schools found themselves little hope to survive as agencies of education on their own terms. The story of the *tiṇṇai* teacher in the second half of the nineteenth century can only be described in terms of his negotiation and struggle with the new forms of scrutiny that came to bear on his work. This was the scrutiny of the edifice of the colonial state's inspection and examinations to which his skills had to respond. The assessments by the colonial state were so much about certification that the upper-caste notables who sought the teacher's services often incorporated its norms: failure and success in public examinations for example, as a way to hold the teacher accountable to her social world. Entangled with this scrutiny came a very messy and ambivalent discourse about the work of memory in the school—indeed the school teacher of mathematics, in the *tiṇṇai* or otherwise, occupied a central place in the constant struggle between two modes of memory. This constant struggle between the two

[63] 'On Educational Tests for Curnums and Village Headmen', Madras Department of Education G.O., TNSA, dated 6 September 1881, no. 288.

modes of memory, we should remember, was left to be sorted out by the *tiṇṇai* teacher himself. The resources that were supposed to come into his aid were abysmal for the entire century. So how did the school and teacher survive?

Tiṇṇai teachers did last, not out of volition or as resistance to post-Kantian rationality,[64] but they lasted because of ways in which they negotiated the colonial state's scrutiny. The main authority to enforce this scrutiny was the figurehead of the School Inspector, a product of the grant-in-aid system and the ever-expanding educational bureaucracy, whose job was to ensure that the state money was well spent and that the *tiṇṇai* school *teacher* shifted to the new curriculum. His continuous journeys on 'bad roads and bad bullocks', when he was covering about a school in every 100 miles, for about 100 days in a year was the chief conduit for the all-important moment of colonial encounter—meeting with the *tiṇṇai* school master and asking him to enrol into any of the grant-in-aid schemes. Even then, by the late 1860s, the Inspectorate was asked to focus on the aided schools, so that the government money did not go waste. The rest of the schools merely were to be touched upon along the way, agreed the DPI to the complaint of high workload by the First Division Inspectors from all Districts.[65] The *tiṇṇai* however survived undisturbed. The possibility of the School Inspector's moment of encounter was highly limited not merely because of his heavy workload, which probably was the case, but he was also ironically burdened by his caste status. If the Inspector was of higher caste, which he normally was, and the poor *tiṇṇai* school master was not to his preference in terms of caste, he would park his bullock cart outside the village and transact knowledge. On the other hand, if it was an upper-caste neighbourhood, his caste affinities with the local upper-caste elite would come into play, where in either the local elite would heed to his enlightening wishes on the basis of caste affinities or he would tinker his terms of enlightenment based on how local caste

[64] Sanjay Seth, *Subject Lessons: The Western Education of Colonial India* (Durham: Duke University Press, 2007).

[65] Even though the heavy work load of the School Inspector was a very common complaint that the Director of Public Instruction received, the response was to increase the manpower of the Inspectorate, but increasingly at a lower grade and salaries. For instance, a new division of Inspecting Schoolmasters was created whose job would double up as a teacher and a school inspector. For one such complaint, see Madras Department of Education, G.O., TNSA, dated 15 October 1866, nos. 42–43.

realities, as told to him, by the local elite.[66] Knowledge transactions were determined by caste realities, the new knowledge by itself could not reach out, transcending caste.[67]

Let's reflect a little more on the moment of inspection. It is likely that the inspector on his annual visit, strapped for time and resources probably had a fleeting encounter with the un-aided school. Given that he was usually an upper-caste man, it would be reasonable to assume that, if he chose the meeting place, it would have been at the house of an upper-caste notable or on the outskirts of the village if the travelling inspector happened to be a Brahmin or an upper-caste and if the *tiṇṇai* teacher was of the lower caste. The constantly changing grant-in-aid rules and assessment regimes, the introduction of public examination one after the other, let us not forget, were always aimed at the urban aided schools and their children.[68] What was offered to the *tiṇṇai* teacher was that the grant would pay him a pittance of money if he created students who could pass. A pass in arithmetic was rewarded the most at the rate of Rs. 1.60, 1.80, 2.00, and 3.00, respectively, for the first four primary classes.[69] The *tiṇṇai* teacher may have as a result of the operation of inspector escaped the colonial state that split much ink on his inadequacies. But he did not escape the scrutiny of his student's parents, who increasingly, thanks to the commodification of education, asserted their scrutiny in terms of consumer demands. Essentially, the commercial transaction in education made the *tiṇṇai* teacher accountable to the local caste elite. They blamed the teacher for failing to achieve the extraordinarily high standards of the examination system. Teachers were asked to compensate for the student's failure by paying the money from his own pocket. Or even worse, if the upper-caste elite agreed to start a school in the village at the

66 This is probably not an out of place comment to remind ourselves that the very basis of kinds of 'extension work' that descended down in to the poor little village had to, or allowed itself to be conditioned by the compulsions of the dominant caste. The case of agricultural extension or even modern day science popularization would be welcome cases to explore.

67 Testimony of Cecil M. Barrow, Principal, Kerala Vidyalaya, Calicut with 13 years experience in education in the Madras Presidency, *Evidence Taken Before the Madras Provincial Committee*, 1882, p. 97.

68 Nita Kumar pleads for the case of the provinces in discussions regarding colonial education and how distant it was, as much as how education was transpired through or limited by caste, family and gender. See Nita Kumar, 'Provincialism in Modern India: The Multiple Narratives of Education and Their Pain', *Modern Asian Studies* 40, no. 2 (2006): 397–423.

69 For the various standards of the results grant system in the grant in aid code, see *Report of the Madras Provincial Committee*, Appendix B, pp. 179–207.

behest of the Inspector, the *tiṇṇai* schoolmaster was made to teach only the children of their families. Or, they made him the personal 'writer' for their family and put up a show of a school at the next visit of the Inspector.

The roving school inspector appears to have often detested the very thought of having to meet the *tiṇṇai* school master, thinking he was merely doing him a favour by disbursing the results grant money to the teacher. These money transactions brought in blackmail and fraudulent encounters in the transmission of knowledge. Take the case of Tandava Rao, a *tiṇṇai* schoolmaster under the results grant, who made students pass his exams in his name so that he could get all the money.[70] Or the other case of the Malabar inspecting schoolmaster who was prosecuted and sentenced to imprisonment for fifteen months, when caught in his attempt to blackmail the *tiṇṇai* schoolmasters in his purview and extort money from them.[71] The upper-caste scrutiny of the *tiṇṇai* school which took on the norms of the consumer demands was not a mere internalization of the norms of the colonial state. The upper castes nurtured an apathy towards colonial educational intervention, in a politically defensive gesture. In addition, some of them also argued that colonial education bred incompetence. In the case of languages, particularly, a mere smattering of English would be appreciated or writing legibly in good handwriting, and dictation and correct spelling would invoke immediate excitement for the local public.

But in the case of mathematics, we should remember that it was always performing the computation in public, where the local scrutiny of the student was unrelenting. Or consider a situation, where the *tiṇṇai* schoolteacher and the *tiṇṇai* school student would continue to do mental computation and solve problems before the same public. In the case of a result grant school (a new arrangement in school under the old teacher), the knowledge of the student was found wanting at the moment of performance, because he now had to necessarily use pen and paper to do simple problems—count and add and subtract, using the column mode.

[70] Report of the Deputy Inspector of Schools, Coimbatore District, Madras Department of Education, G.O., TNSA, dated 30 November 1869, pp. 60–61.

[71] Reported by Garthwaite, the Chief Inspector of Schools, Malabar on his feedback to the Director of Public Instruction on the work of the Inspectorate. See *Annual Report of the Department of Public Instruction for the Year 1879–1880*, Madras, 1881.

The nature of local numeracy, which did not have to use pen and paper or slate and chalk to compute, found the computational ability of the new student to be abysmally low and incompetent. This ridiculing of the modern math student in the locality for his incompetence and inability to compute was very strongly felt which reflected in the perception towards colonial education itself.[72] The tension between pedagogic norms was not played out as a struggle between the local—functional orientation of the *tiṇṇai* vis-a-vis the outward-looking, procedural, rule-bound learning of arithmetic. It was a tension about the learning of modern procedural arithmetic, irrespective of the fact whether it could have actually led to ability in theorem building, at the best of its moments of transaction.[73] But the interplay between the orientation towards theorem making in the learning of mathematics and the locally felt necessity of useful mathematics was persistent, at least for the public in the provincial hinterland, yet to be bitten by the lures of the new job market.

How do we then understand the relationship between the perception of usefulness in the learning of mathematics among different publics? The *tiṇṇai* school teacher navigated the scrutiny of the state and dealt with the pressures of his upper-caste clientele in the settlement through the 1880s. The problem between the teacher-practitioner, the modernizing bureaucracy, and layers of caste society resolved itself interestingly in the 1880s, when the *tiṇṇai* school and its teachers were incorporated into Government's policy in positive terms –in favourable assessments of his competence. The possibilities for a different public for mathematics manifested ironically by the 1880s in the incorporation of the *tiṇṇai* schoolmaster into the fold of the colonial apparatus. Because, a consensus was reached about the pedagogic importance of his arithmetic teaching for the education system. The other reason was political. The colonial state considered that the local public would approve of its method of education only when they saw arithmetic problem solving work and demonstrate itself within in the locality. How do we understand this shift

[72] This was a recurrent theme of discussion in most of the testimonies presented before the Provincial Committee on Education, where many argued for leverage to the *tiṇṇai* schools and its teachers. A clear line of argument emerged around this time in the local perceptions among the elite and the parents about how useless the modern curriculum is for them. See *Evidence Taken Before the Madras Provincial Committee on Education*, Madras, 1882.

[73] For an interesting contemporary discussion on the relationship between the *tiṇṇai* arithmetic and modern arithmetic, see Charles Gover, *Survey of Education in Madras*, Madras, 1871.

underway in the 1880s, a mere thirty years after the school teacher was reprimanded and made a figure of ire?

From the 1880s the colonial state staged a rapprochement with *tiṇṇai* schools. The native upper-caste elite, which had shown signs of becoming a 'civic community' with inherent contradictions and biases was also trying to formulate a critique of the colonial state's educational initiatives, but from very much within the colonial premises. The Education Commission of 1882, which was supposedly lobbied for by the missionaries to keep the centralizing spree of the state in check, turned out to be disappointing as far as the missionaries were concerned, but provided a space for the anxiety regarding the *tiṇṇai* schools to be voiced in the very high echelons of power. The remarkable force by which the *tiṇṇai* compelled the state to reconcile with it was given credibility almost entirely by its strength in the arithmetic teaching. The turn towards the local public and the recognition of its consent to make modern education possible was evident in the statements of the majority of those who testified before the Madras sitting of the Hunter Commission. Take the case of Rev. Louis St. Cyr, a Catholic missionary of the Madurai Jesuit Mission, who confessed that the *tiṇṇai* mathematics pedagogy was 'doubtless less perfect and easy than the European methods but they appear to please them more ... I have met with several headmen of villages, with curnums of the Government who, though they had been taught European methods of calculating in Protestant schools, preferred using their old methods'.[74] There were even more voices coming from very important members of the Government. H. S. Thomas, Second member of the Madras Board of Revenue stated that 'the agricultural classes pay nine-tenths of the money available as funds for education, but very few of them seek middle or higher education ... they need no conic sections to drive a plough or hydraulics to milk a cow', which the present curriculum insists upon them and in failing there, denies education to those classes.[75] There were even more radical voices, D. Duncan, a Scotsman, Professor and Principal of the Presidency college who had come to serve in India with high recommendations from the University of Aberdeen argued that education

[74] Evidence of Rev. Louis St. Cyr, *Evidence Taken Before the Madras Provincial Committee*, p. 121.

[75] Ibid., p. 260.

cannot be divorced from the task of improvement in the physical and economic conditions of the people and that communities should decide their own course of education. He argued that in the 'conditions of an indigenous, complex and many sided civilization … a cut and dry rigid system imposed on the country once for all from without' and without catering to the varied wants of a country, all one could innovate upon are 'refined ways of torture' in the name of examinations and evaluation and explicitly argued to leave the business of teaching deductive logic and arithmetic to the natives.[76] The *tiṇṇai* master's proficiency in that mode of arithmetic was recounted, celebrated, almost with a sense of nostalgia. Ironically, this nostalgia came not from the educational establishment but from the employers: the railways, the chambers of commerce, the banks, revenue, public works, in short the employers were lamenting how the first generation of employees who came out of the traditional system of education was so efficient in all trades, especially in bookkeeping and mathematics. The present generation of high school and middle school graduates despite going through the grind of multiple public examinations, which do help in providing certification for us to employ on public standards, can't do simple addition properly.

Having reconciled to such a scenario, the state with a renewed vigour sent out its army of inspectors to assimilate the *tiṇṇai* schools and incorporate their arithmetic into an altered curriculum. This meant that the local community's idea of relevant education had to be contended with, for it was clear that the people wanted arithmetic in the old, memory mode, making the state yield. In effect, this meant making mental arithmetic yet another subject along with numeration and the four operations of arithmetic problem solving; just that now, it would be called bazaar arithmetic.

The sudden increase in the numbers of schools in the official registers starting from the 1880s was not because the *tiṇṇai* teachers started following the new arithmetic books but because the inspecting system could now 'record' them as schools. As a result, the hitherto invisible *tiṇṇai* schools, came out in the open, and were made to subject themselves to this bureaucratic process of assimilation, providing a moral boost to the logic of the colonial state, further legitimizing its agenda

[76] Ibid., pp. 32–48.

of privatization and devolution of control to the local fund boards and the municipalities. At the turn of the century, there was a dramatic rise in the number of the primary schools under the purview of state inspection.[77] While the rest of the policies remained intact, an entire generation of students grew up with a fear of failure and uncertainty. This effectively packaged the *tiṉṇai* arithmetic as an addendum to the slate or pen and paper arithmetic. Starting with the rules and procedures of problem-solving recollection was then a crutch to navigate textual proficiency. Memorization of tables was a matter of choice, but it continued along with that of rule-based problem solving. Oral or mental arithmetic as it was known would be an exercise that could aid rule-based problem solving. It assumed a new name, 'bazaar mathematics'. Exercises in bazaar mathematics were confined to conversions of weights and measures, which meant learning new tables and memorizing them. But bazaar mathematics was not just the *Eṇcuvaṭi* in a new form. It was also not recollective memory as the very mode of learning. Memorization in this new form was not trained and honed as interpretation. Memorization became an aid to modern arithmetic. It was not prudence that was the preferred virtue as in the case of *tiṉṇai* arithmetic, but speed and diligent following of rules, which would help arrive at the results, became the normative value for students to imbibe. Thus, *tiṉṇai* arithmetic was assimilated into the modern.

In the meantime, by the 1880s state monopoly over textbooks was given up. A nascent Tamil textbook industry had emerged. Tamil merchants were also busy organizing a network of clerical professionals and teachers, who would compete with each other to partake in the new business of writing, editing, and publishing textbooks for money. Textbook writing also emerged as a profession.[78] The era of translations survived and the free exposition for the author, however, was restricted to the writing of preface for the textbooks. Often these prefaces also became spaces for picking up issues, for ridicule, and most importantly, spaces for hard selling and aggressive marketing for the same arithmetic syllabus as

[77] See B. S. Baliga, *Studies in Madras Administration, Vol. II* (Madras: Government Press, 1960) for a neat summary of the changes in the number of schools entering the official registers of the Department of Public Instruction, which was sudden and very large in number, in every passing year after the Hunter commission's Report and recommendations.

[78] On this see, A. R. Venkatachalapathy, *The Province of the Book: Scribes, Scribblers and Print* (Delhi: Permanent Black, 2011).

prescribed in the grant-in-aid code, shown in the Table 4.1.[79] The hitherto invisible *tiṇṇai* that had eluded the bureaucracy and the inspector raj, in the meantime, started to appear in the annual returns of the Department of Public Instruction from the late 1880s. From this time, the DPI put out a curriculum of arithmetic that was mixed enough to make it legitimate in front of the local *tiṇṇai* patronizing public along with some space for the *tiṇṇai* schoolmaster to teach.

Table 4.1 Arithmetic curriculum in the Madras Presidency during 1881[80]

Name of the examination	Class and marks	Arithmetic standards required
The Higher Examination for Women	Compulsory; Maximum 90 and Minimum 30	The four simple and compound rules, reduction, vulgar and decimal fractions, simple and compound proportion, practice, extraction of square root, interest
	Optional (Mathematics); Max 80 and Min 20	Euclid—The first two books with easy deductions Algebra—Addition, Subtraction, Multiplication, Division, Involution, and evolution of algebraic quantities and simple equations with easy deductions
The Special Upper Primary Examination	Compulsory; Max 80 and Min 26	Four simple and compound rules, reduction and vulgar fractions (English figures must be used, and the candidate must be acquainted with the principal Indian weights and measures)
Examinations under the Results system	First (Lowest Standard); Max 16	Notation and Numeration to four places of figures, Simple addition of numbers of four figures in five lines. (English figures must be used in this as well as in the higher standards)
	Second Standard; max 24	Notation and Numeration to seven places of figures. Multiplication table to 12 times 16. Four simple rules
	Third Standard (Vernacular); Max 32	Easy questions in the compound rules and reduction, restricted to Indian weights and measures, and money tables published by the DPI Easy mental arithmetic restricted to the simple rules

[79] Similar to the new protocols of literary publishing explored by A. R. Venkatachalapathy, Ibid.

[80] This table shows the Standards required for the various public examinations and the terms of evaluation for each. Compiled from *A Description of the Actual State of Education in the Madras Presidency on the 31 March 1882*, Madras, 1882.

Table 4.1 *Continued*

Name of the examination	Class and marks	Arithmetic standards required
	Fourth Standard: Max 48	Miscellaneous questions in the compound rules and reduction, easy questions in vulgar fractions Mental arithmetic applied to bazaar transaction In Vernacular schools, the questions will bear exclusively on the Indian tables published by the DPI, including the native multiplication table of integers and fractions marked A, and the table used in native bazaars marked B
	Fifth Standard, Max 56	Simple and compound rules, reduction, vulgar and decimal fractions Mental arithmetic applied to bazaar transactions
	Sixth standard; Max 48; now with the head Mathematics	Arithmetic- as for the fifth std, with the addition of Practice and Simple Proportion Euclid—Book I, to the end of the 16th proposition
The Middle School Examination (Seventh Standard)	Branch D: Arithmetic: 110 marks	The compound rules, Reduction, Vulgar and Decimal Fractions, Practice, Simple and Compound Proportion (English figures must be used and the candidate must be acquainted with the Indian weights and measures and the English tables of money, of Troy weight, of Avoirdupois weight, of Linear, Square and Cubic measures, and of Time)
	Branch E: Mathematics, 90 marks	Euclid, Book I (50 marks) Algebra, to the end of Fractions (40 marks) Symbols permitted by the Madras University may be used
The Upper Primary Examination	Branch B: Arithmetic (compulsory) 40 + 10	a) To work miscellaneous questions in Reduction, the Compound rules and Vulgar fractions b) Mental Arithmetic applied to bazaar transactions
Lower Primary Examination	Arithmetic, 40 marks	To work sums in the first four rules of arithmetic, simple and compound, including easy miscellaneous questions

Was this a successful curriculum, a form of hybridity or engraftment and did it foster a mathematics public? The reconciliation with the *tiṇṇai* curriculum was in stages even as the rate of failure increased in the various examinations and the number of dropouts in them rose. The increasingly visible and vocal intelligentsia, thanks to the emerging print world, started talking about the tyranny of exams, the rule of textbooks, and growing unemployment. By the end of 1890s, there were concerted attempts on behalf of the missionaries and the emerging Tamil intelligentsia to thwart the Examination Raj. Cramming, many of them argued, was the most significant evil of education. By the turn of the century, cramming, the new term for rote memory or mechanical memory had assumed commonplace:

> cramming full of undigested and un-assimilated odds and ends of information of various kinds, his memory fagged with the strain it has undergone and his understanding not merely undermined but left much of its elasticity destroyed . . . there is a greater facility and accuracy in the more mechanical processes of arithmetic and mathematics . . . the evil is in the air, cram to pass; due to follies of teaching geometry and algebra when the student is unable to use his understanding in preparing to be examined have driven him to rely on memory and mechanical imitation.[81]

Law-abiding learners of mathematics were created not through vocal recital, but with slate and chalk now helping memory and rule following. Memory ruled in the learning of mathematics. Most of those who came from the *tiṇṇai* tradition into the modern arena of mathematics could not cope. But there were an exceptional few who blended the two traditions, and who seemed to have managed to figure out the nuances: people like V. Krishnamachariar, Subramaniam Sastri, Arumugam Navalar from Jaffna and the like, who attempted writing textbooks and later became well-known pedagogues. Innovations did not mean much, playing around with examples, employing relevant linguistic strategies in textbooks, and attempts to integrate the *Eṇcuvaṭi* mode of learning tables in line with the modern demands of problem solving.

[81] *MCC Magazine*, October 1899, pp. 217–227.

But far from being a figure under attack, the *tiṇṇai* master also benefited from this new world of transactions. He had the resources to study modern math himself and subject himself to recruitment examinations if he did not want to remain a school teacher. The option of becoming a schoolmaster as the last resort in one's career in the nineteenth century also conditioned the way mathematical learning or any learning for that matter could proceed. If the *tiṇṇai* teacher or the village schoolmaster was good, then he would obviously have a crack at the different examinations and opt-out of the village and the harassment of the Inspectorate.

So, how was mathematics faring towards the turn of the century in the districts of Madras, amidst all these conditions which it could not have transcended?

The distance between the agenda of theorem-building mathematical competence in the school arithmetic education and its reception by the local public was a very important factor that conditioned the emergence of colonial schooling itself. The colonial officials had to depend on the same *tiṇṇai* teacher, who was the quintessential cultivator of recollective memory in order to make this liberation possible. This constant struggle between the two modes of memory, we should remember, was left to be sorted out by the *tiṇṇai* teacher himself. As far as the student was concerned, he constantly tried to innovate to deal with the tyranny of examination. Pammal Sambanda Mudaliar, whose name is synonymous with modern theatre in Madras, narrates his encounter with modern mathematics, which captures the daily life of a student's tryst with the theorem-making agenda of modern mathematics. Here, he narrates his encounter with the study of Trigonometry during his F.A. examinations:

> In this class a mathematics book called Trigonometry arrived. To be honest, it never agreed with my mind. If someone asks me today, what is Sin Theta or Cosine Theta, I will not know how to answer. It is not surprising then that I stood last in the exam. In this exam, all the marks of the students of our class were handed over to Professor Poondi Ranganatha Mudaliar by our Mathematics Professor, Chakravarti Ayyangar. He started reading each one's marks aloud in the class. The well scoring students, Jagadeesan, Thirunarayanachari, Singaravelu received the appreciation of 'very good'. I then realized what was waiting

> for me. I was the last in the list. I had scored 23 marks out of 100. (This also was like the Euclid paper). 'Sambandam, 23 marks', he read out and said, 'Sambandam, you used to be a good student when you were young'. That is all he said. But I burst into tears.
>
> That same evening, the moment I reached home, apprehensive of passing the FA Examination, I thought of a solution. I brought out the Trigonometry book and started copying the Book Work section of that book, like an 'iyattittan rider'. I did this everyday so that I memorized and by the time I sat for the examination, I had done this for fourteen times. As a result, even though I did not understand the meaning of what I had been writing, if asked any problem from the Book Work section of that book, I could recite it aloud without mistake! I followed the same strategy with Algebra and gained prowess at it. When I appeared for the University exam for FA in December, I wrote all the Book Work, finished the paper well before time and returned home. Due to God's grace, I passed.[82]

This experience captures the life of a student of mathematics at the turn of the century Madras. Was this the case without exception? Of course, there were exceptions. M. T. Naraniengar, who also passed through the same system of education became one of the first Indians to take to research in the field of Coordinate Geometry had a completely different experience with Mathematics. To him it was so intimate of an encounter and so personal to life itself that he authored a paper called the 'The Geometrical Projection of the Life of a Vaishnavite Brahmin', where he geometrically reconstructed not just his life, but of the ways of life and rituals of his caste.[83] Were these two experiences merely a case of individual life choices that modern mathematics made possible? But then, that is another story.

[82] Pammal Sambandam, *En Suyasarithai* (Chennai: Sandhya Patippagam, 2012). Translation mine.

[83] M. T. Naraniengar, 'The Geometrical Projection of the Life of a Vaishnavite Brahmin', *Mathematics Student*, 1917.

Conclusion

Mathematics and Its Images of the Public

A focus on the practitioner of Indian mathematics can help us pose new questions of knowledge circulation. It is often asked how people imagine mathematics. This book has tried to reconstruct the publics that mathematics tried to imagine for itself—through its practitioners such as the school teacher and its textbooks. In this history of practice, it has focused on two significant moments in the mathematization of Tamil South India—the times of the *Kaṇakkatikāram,* a widely used practitioner's text, during the seventeenth and eighteenth centuries, and during the colonial encounter of the nineteenth century. By committing to the history of practice, we have been able to see how mathematics was embedded in social relations. Mathematization, the processes through which we can chart numeracy, opens up channels of looking into how various practitioners like the *Kaṇakkaṉ*, the *tiṇṇai* schoolmaster, the student, the colonial educational official, and the measuring public, worked with mathematical techniques. The measuring public comprised the laypeople who encountered numbers in their everyday life as they learned artisanal crafts and trade, or as they laboured on fields, sold vegetables, or carried sacks of grain. In the nineteenth century, there emerged an anxious new class of job aspirants and parents, for whom schooled mathematics was essential for mobility. This created different trajectories of mathematization for these two different publics.

The diversity of mathematical practices developed in relation to these different publics compelled us to engage each trajectory of mathematization in relation to its material histories, embodied by labour, caste, habits, and rituals. This has allowed us to rethink the ways in which mathematics and its publics have come to interact with each other through processes that entailed idealization of knowledge, hierarchization of schooling, and

Mathematics and Society. Senthil Babu D., Oxford University Press. © Oxford University Press India 2022.
DOI: 10.1093/oso/9788194831600.003.0006

discrimination of access. In this open-ended conclusion, I want to reconstruct the nature of the public that was imagined for mathematics.

The *Kaṇakkatikāram*'s Public

The first two chapters showed how the practitioner's skills imparted in the *Kaṇakkatikāram* tradition were nurtured at the *tiṇṇai* school and at work. These skills had social value and were accorded dignity. What mattered was not their mere possession, but their expression, too. They had to be performed in front of an audience. The *Kaṇakkatikāram* imagined a public and invited that public into its folds with a promise that it would make them 'clever' or 'prudent', able to face challenges in daily life and remain unintimidated when confronted by experts such as accountants. What was striking in this tradition was the gesture constantly made to its public. The mnemonic verses of the tradition were not just literary ornamentation of technical content, but a persuasive way to employ language to relate to the public. There were, at times, efforts to hard-sell mathematics, but the tradition also tried to convince its public that learning mathematics was desirable.

These gestures expressed the ideals associated with mastering computational procedures. In the *Āstāṉa Kōlākalam*, one of the more accessible mathematical texts aimed at accountants, the author said that although it was common to forget mathematical tables after finishing school, it was also equally common that there were people who were intelligent and felt comfortable when confronted by 'an assembly of a hundred mathematicians'. Public display of proficiency in computation was presented as a worthy pursuit. So, both the 'computationally weak'[1] and the 'intelligent'[2] were to benefit from the author's work, but the only difference would be that the intelligent one would acquire 'the fragrance of a golden flower'![3]

One of the versions of Kāri Nāyaṉār's *Kaṇakkatikāram* loudly proclaimed virtuosity for the computationally proficient. It says that the *vāttiyār*, the teacher who masters the *Kaṇakkatikāram*, could be

[1] '*Arivil mandamanavan*', *Āstāṉa Kōlākalam*, ed. Thirumalai Sree Saila Sarma (Madras: Government Oriental Manuscripts Library, 1951), 1.

[2] *Yuktikaran*, Ibid.

[3] Ibid.

compared to an axe as sharp as the *vajra ayutam*,[4] a weapon of Lord Indra powerful enough to split open a torso.[5]

Mathematics also provided the practitioner with exclusive qualities, in relation to its public. The author of the text *Kaṇita Nūl* talks about certain mathematical virtues in a series of verses[6]:

> The world stands merged with the science of numerals. The study of numerals is like an attempt to scale the *Mēru* mountain, while the study of letters is like climbing a post standing on quicksand. There are two kinds of knowledge – that of the numerals and of the letters. There are three kinds of treatises – (*mutal, vaḻi, cārpu*) original, derivative and adoptive. There are four effects of learning – ethics, wealth, pleasure and salvation. There are six kinds of defects associated with mathematical practice – (*kuṉṟal*) underestimation; (*kūṭṭal)* overestimation; (*kūṭṭiya tokai kāṭṭal*) wrong consolidation, (*māṟukoḷak kūṭṭal*) self-contradiction; (*vaḻut tokaip puṇarttal*) defective usage and (*mayaṅka vaittal*) creating confusion or dilemma. There are seven kinds of virtues associated with mathematical practice – refusal to concur immediately; accepting others' proposition and clarifying mistakes; standing by one's own proposition; choosing the right view among differing opinions; ability to point out others' mistakes; and the ability to differentiate between one's work and that of others'. There are eight devices of understanding – addition, subtraction, multiplication, division, comprehension, and identification of unique distinction, ability to differentiate and to explain or articulate. Finally there are three kinds of students – the first rate, second rate and the third rate. The first rate is like the mythical bird called the *acuṇam*, which would fall dead the moment it hears a discordant note in music; the second rate is likened to an eagle, which surveys its prey before picking on it; and the third rate is like a hen, which keeps picking on garbage till it finally gets something useful. [Translation mine]

[4] *Vajra Ayutam*, the legend goes that it was made out of the backbone of a sage, *Dadhichi* and given to Lord Indra, a very powerful weapon.

[5] *Kaṇakkatikāram—Tokuppu Nūl*, ed. K. Satyabama Kamesvaran (Thanjavur: Sarasvathi Mahal Library, 1998), 4.

[6] *Kaṇita Nūl: A Treatise on Mathematics, Part I*, eds. P. Subramaniam and K. Satyabama (Chennai: Institute of Asian Studies, 1999), 66.

Engagement with the world of numbers was considered a worldly enterprise, more privileged than engagement with letters. Learning mathematics was like scaling the mythical mountain, *Mēru*. Learning maths was tough, but it gave direction and was reliable because the Gods resided in the *Mēru* mountain. The learning of letters was like a post that seemed conquerable, yet was slippery and uncertain like standing on quicksand.

This tradition of mathematics also distinguished a critical apparatus between attitude and judgement for practice. While refusal to concur, accept, or clear mistakes in others' propositions and to stand by one's own were marks of attitude, virtues like choosing the right view, ability to point out others' mistakes and differentiate between one's own work and that of others all pertain to judgement. The distinction between attitude and judgement, along with demands of rationality and consistency, provide us with a set of critical ideals that a practitioner of this mode of mathematics could attain. These norms were part of a system of ideals that *Kaṇakkatikāram* held up for its public. Therefore, of the three types of students categorized in the text, the first one is so fine so as to be possessed with a sense of proportion and harmony. The second type was highly discerning, with a sense of practical intelligence and judgement. The third could be anyone who would enter this tradition and display sheer perseverance.

The professional virtuosity of the teacher or the preceptor and the acknowledged possibilities of any learner or participant in this tradition to be superior, intelligent, or be persevering could only apparently point to a hierarchy of virtues. But when taken along with the system of arithmetic practice in question, it could be read as different options available for anyone to partake in this practice, because ultimately the goals anyway are ethics, wealth, pleasure, and salvation. Such an ethos in the realm of seeking knowledge also shows us how this knowledge could transcend the immediate and reach out for something more—a better aesthetic or a higher spiritual quest like scaling the '*Mēru*'. In this mode *Kaṇakkatikāram,* then, was possibly not a free knowledge for all but strongly connotes the advantages of sophisticated forms of computation, yet grounded in the local and the functional, while emphasizing the affective and aesthetics of knowledge practice. That is to say, the tradition provides ample evidence of a critical and reflective apparatus, a theory of practice that endows a sense of dignity to itself.

But then again, the hierarchy of virtues notwithstanding, such gestures of invitation and pathways to salvation offered by the practitioner of the *Kaṇakkatikāram* were also the way in which he could make himself distinct, making his knowledge expert and useful to the machinery of power. This, as we repeatedly saw, was even further compounded by a practitioner's operations in a caste society and the forms of scrutiny to which he subjected the local public. The language of invitation to engage with the computational world then helped only in enhancing his professional virtuosity which made possible a public, which could then, only aspire for knowledge, but may not be able to get there, given the social conditions in which such gesturing and performance assumed shape.

Mathematics, the British Public, and Colonial Education

We move from the commercial and agrarian ethos of the early modern world of the *Kaṇakkatikāram* to a particular moment in the early nineteenth century. The Tamil *tiṇṇai* school's regime of pedagogy in recollective memory enmeshed with principles of Scottish political economy and were imbibed by Andrew Bell.[7] He reorganized the monitorial system to resemble idealized forms of the factory system in such a way that the principles of manufacturing would be the same in schools. Bentham's utilitarian ideology, which had its role in the making of British colonial policy in the early nineteenth century, praised Bell's invention as 'the most useful of all products of inventive genius, printing excepted, that this globe has ever witnessed and that it may be applied to the highest branches of useful learning'.[8] For its 'profit maximization and expense minimization', the division of labour in the monitorial principle was rather revealing to the

[7] Andrew Bell, *The Madras School or Elements of Tuition comprising the Analysis of an Experiment in Education Made at the Male Asylum, Madras, with Its Facts, Proofs and Illustrations* (London, 1808).

[8] Cited in Simon Schaffer, 'Indiscipline and Interdisciplines: Some Exotic Genealogies of Modern Knowledge', p. 15, http://www.hse.ru/data/2011/11/13/1272007743/Schaffer.2010.Indiscipline_and_interdisciplines.pdf, Accessed on January 5, 2015.

utilitarian ideologue. For Bell himself, the monitorial system was 'like the steam engine or the spinning machinery, it diminishes labour and multiplies work, but in a degree which does not admit of the same limits and scarcely of the same calculations, as they do'.[9]

As Schaffer argues, this was a 'machine utopia' of a specific form, simultaneously a showroom and a classroom. Each school was to be divided into sets of classes, with more junior inmates subjected to more advanced pupils; each stage was meticulously registered; each lesson was divided into brief segments; under the 'place-capturing principle' each member of each class moved around the tightly disciplined space of the class room; and the whole was under the surveillance of an inspector, 'whose scrutinizing eye must pervade the whole machine' under a 'never-ceasing vigilance'. Samuel Coleridge considered Bell's monitorial system to be a 'vast moral steam engine' and advocated that it be adopted throughout the British empire.[10] Arguably, Bell transformed the monitorial ethos of *tiṇṇai* learning that sustained the *Kaṇakkatikāram* tradition and situated it in a different system of virtues in England. (see Images 5.1 and 5.2 for a visual arrangement of the two systems). Blessed by the Church of England, Bell's 'moral steam engine' was brought by the British missionaries to India, and used as a crucial element of their evangelical work.

Around the same time, the nature and purpose of a liberal system in British higher education was evolving. In particular, it was important for the British mathematical community in the early 19th century to tell the British public what mathematics could offer them. William Whewell, scholar, mathematician and an influential public figure in England, argued that mathematics was all about the cultivation of the mind, in contrast to the exercising of the body in the popular education movement of Bell's system. The objective of a liberal education was 'the whole mental development of man' and mathematics was best suited for that purpose. There were two opposing views about mathematics in England at the time. One held that,

> it is the most admirable mental discipline; that it generates habits of reasoning, of continuous and severe attention, of constant reference

[9] Ibid., p. 16.
[10] Ibid., p. 17.

Image 5.1 A *Tiṉṉai* school in 1930s Pondicherry. Courtsey: Pondicherry Past and Present, Photo Archives, French Institute of Pondicherry.

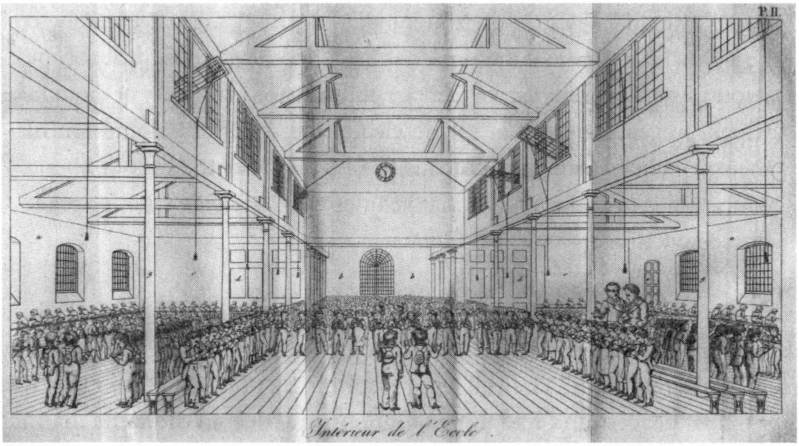

Image 5.2 Andrew Bell's National School in Holborn in 1811. This image is sourced from book L'enseignement mutuel by Dr. Bell, J. Lancaster and others, Translated by Joseph Hamel, Paris, 1818.

> to fundamental principles. On the other side, it is asserted that mathematical habits of thought unfit a man for the business of life – make his mind captious, disputatious, over subtle, over rigid – that a person inured to mathematical reasoning alone, reasons ill on other subjects, seeks in them a kind and degree of proof which does not belong to them, becomes insensible to moral evidence, and loses those finer perceptions of fitness and beauty, in which propriety of action and delicacy of taste must have their origin.[11]

But for Whewell, mathematics was an example and an exercise in exact reasoning. The whole purpose of education was to trace securely the necessary consequences of assumed principles:

> Men's minds are full of convictions which they cannot justify by connected reasoning, however reasonable they are. Nothing is more common than to hear persons urge very foolish arguments in support of very just opinions and what has been said of women is often no less true of the sex which pretends to have the more logical kind of head – namely, that if they give their judgment only, they are not unlikely to be right, but if they add their reasons for it, those will most probably be wrong. There prevails very widely an obscurity or perplexity of thought which prevents men from seeing clearly the necessary connexion of their principles with their conclusions ... therefore the task of liberal education is to make his speculative inferences coincide with his practical convictions.

Cultivating the mind and exercising the reasoning faculty was best done by mathematics, and not even by logic. While logic was reasoning by rule, mathematics to Whewell was reasoning by practice. Reasoning was a practical process and had to be taught by practice, in the same manner as fencing, riding, or any other practical art. The student should be able to

> conduct his train of deduction securely, yet without effort, just as in the riding school, the object is that the learner should proceed firmly and

[11] William Whewell, *Thoughts on the Study of Mathematics as Part of a Liberal Education* (Cambridge: J. & J. J. Deighton, 1836), 3.

> easily upon his stead ... the horseman, tries to obtain a good seat rather than to describe one, and rather avoids falling than considers in how many ways he may fall. To cultivate logic appears to resemble learning horsemanship by book.[12]

Habitual exercise, continuity and concentration of thought, and the quick sense of demonstration were virtues for a strong British character and mathematics was the ideal subject to cultivate these virtues. Arguing for reforms in British university system of teaching mathematics, and enrolling the support of the British public in the process, Whewell argued that products of such a reformed learning process would make the best professionals, in particular, the best lawyers and law makers. Deduction, steadiness, and perseverance through the practice of reasoning and to proceed from the first principles towards the singular truth and attain firm conviction, along with the ability to see fallacies and not to yield to them, was the system of virtues that British maths was offering its public in the name of liberal education in early nineteenth-century Britain.

It is striking that these Victorian virtues were not very different from that of the normative ideals of the *Kaṇakkatikāram* tradition. Both normative visions gestured to an ethos of learning mathematics conceived as a system of practice, for anyone to participate in. However, we have seen how such ethos materialized in the mathematical practices of these two different cultures in the colonial nineteenth century for the teacher and student practitioners in the colony. Through a sustained culture of hierarchical schooling, the learning of mathematics under colonial conditions allowed for difference and discrimination. Claiming to liberate a population from the clutches of mechanical memory, the colonial machine institutionalized mechanical imitation, which as a mathematical experience translated into a routine of physical labour in learning for the student-aspirant throughout the nineteenth century. Repeated practice of systematic copying down of exercises—to be able to remember for a regime of assessment that was not oriented to provide for knowledge, but was tailored to meet the requirements of state building—underpinned the basis of mathematical experience for the colonial subject. Whewell's offer to the public, a facility to 'cultivate the mind' through mathematical

[12] Ibid., p. 6.

experience, transposed into a facility to exercise the body in the act of memorization.[13]

Perhaps most importantly, the existing contours of caste difference resonated through this experience and made possible different experiences, depending on caste status, in both the *tiṇṇai* as well as in the urban centres of privileged learning. That mathematization could proceed along such different trajectories for individuals and for communities may not be a function of mathematics in itself, as we saw while discussing the rule of three in Chapter II. The learning in *tiṇṇai* schools, elaborated in Chapter III, showed how the divergent trajectories could depend on the transmission of mathematics. That is how mathematics could speak in different languages to different publics.

We have already seen, in Chapter IV, how this divergence sharpened under colonial rule. Even today, when professional mathematicians and maths popularizers are working on dissemination and creating a public of their own, they are not being able to critically reflect on the conditions of alienation embedded in colonial maths teaching.

What makes ways of making a public possible? And what purpose does this serve? The social experience of not merely constructing the values associated with competence and merit, but the act of negotiating and living with such values, has always been associated with certain ideals of doing mathematics. Mathematics for the school, mathematics for the competitive examination, mathematics for aptitude tests, mathematics for IITs, and of course the 'mysterious practices' of the distant, working

[13] Interestingly, Whewell's critics in England, like the great Edinburgh philosopher William Hamilton, wrote in 1836 that 'every step in mathematical demonstration calls forth an absolute minimum of thought . . . The routine of demonstration in the gymnastic of mind may, indeed, be compared to the routine of the treadmill, in the gymnastic of the body' and by this, Hamilton reckoned Whewell was the evil mathematical propagandist for mechanical routine. See W. R. Hamilton, 'A Review of Rev. William Whewell's Thoughts on the Study of Mathematics as a Part of Liberal Education', *Edinburgh Review* 62 (1836): 218–252. Whewell himself reckoned mechanical routine was the sin of analytical mathematics, like that of Charles Babbage, and insisted that geometrical demonstration was the unique method of true mental training: 'in the one case, that of geometrical reasoning, we tread the ground ourselves, at every step, feeling ourselves firm and directing our steps to the end aimed at. In the other case, that of analytical calculation, we are carried along as in a rail-road carriage, entering at one station and coming out of another, without having any choice in our progress in the intermediate space . . . It may be the best way for men of business to travel, but it cannot fitly be made part of the gymnastics of education', in Whewell, *Liberal Education*, 1845, p. 41. I thank Simon Schaffer for this nuance in the debate in contemporary England and I reproduce his personal communication to me in this note.

mathematician herself. The social lives of mathematics then go beyond the question of diversity and into that of social difference.

The recognition of this difference and its concomitant practices of power enables us to enter the world of the public. The practices pry open the contradictions in the modes of theorizing—between the folk and the expert, between pure and applied maths, between theory and practice, and between the national and the regional. Such binaries are manifested acutely in the divisive social conditions of caste society.

Re-thinking beyond the binaries will require the invention of a critical apparatus that contends with the histories and practices of the public, which are embroiled in caste, language and social organization of power. This would offer insights into some contemporary challenges in mathematics education and rescue the learning of mathematics from the rule-bound, problem-solving mode and reconcile it with the dense demands of everyday computations. It would allow for the joy of mathematics as play, as performance. For this to happen, we need a clear look at the possibilities of crafting a mathematics that could preempt its own subversion. But we also have to desist from demarcating knowledge between theory and practice and subject this language of binaries to historical and political scrutiny. Making mathematics Indian or Tamil renders it into a mathematics of the past. This is a colonial view that can only be subverted by giving a new history to a living mathematics and increasing the possibility of its circulation beyond the cram centres that make up the market of mathematics today.

APPENDIX-I

Numbers, Weights, and Measures in the Tamil System

Errata

Page No.	Row	Column	Should Read as :
228	1st	2nd	pattu nūṟāyiram
228	7th	4th	patumam
228	8th	2nd	patumam
229 (2nd table)	1st	2nd	4 ½ times
230	text between tables		The larger measures are then converted in terms of the smaller, beginning with the unit of kūppiṭu as the base:
230 (2nd table)	5th	1st	cāṇ
232	text between 1st and 2nd table		There is a slight variation in the measures used in Kaṇakkatikāram
232 (2nd table)	3rd	2nd	1 mañcāṭi
233	5th	1st	100 nei
233 (1st table)	15th	2nd	1 kalam
236 (3rd table)	1st	2nd	4 cāmam
236 (3rd table)	2nd	1st	4 cāmam

Table 1: Numbers

The tables below show the standard denominations of both the fractions (*kīḻtāṉam*) and whole numbers that were commonly in use.

Place value	Name of Numbers in words	Tamil notation used	Modern notation
1	*oṉṟu*	௧	1
2	*pattu*	௰	10
3	*nūṟu*	௱	100
4	*āyiram*	௲	1000
5	*patiṉāyiram*	௰௲	10000
6	*laṭcam*	௱௲ (லட்சம்)	100000
7	*pattu laṭcam*	௰௱௲ (பத்து லட்சம்)	1000000
8	*kōṭi*	௱௱௲ (கோடி)	10000000
9	*pattu kōṭi*	௰ கோடி	100000000
10	*nūṟu kōṭi*	௱ கோடி	1000000000
11	*āyiram kōṭi*	௲ கோடி	10000000000
12	*patiṉāyira kōṭi*	பதினாயிர கோடி	100000000000
13	*nūṟāyira kōṭi*	நூறாயிர கோடி	1000000000000
14	*pattu nūṟāyira kōṭi*	பத்து நூறாயிர கோடி	10000000000000
15	*makā kōṭi*	மகா கோடி	100000000000000

There are still higher denominations noted, but they are mentioned as multiples of kōṭi as an unit. They proceed like this:

1	pattu nūrāyiram	ten times	kōṭi (one crore)
2	kōṭi	ten times	makā kōṭi
3	makā kōṭi	ten times	caṅkam
4	caṅkam	ten times	makācaṅkam
5	makācaṅkam	ten times	vintam
6	vintam	ten times	makāvintam
7	makāvintam	ten times	patuman (also called camuttiram)
8	patuman	ten times	kumutam
9	kumutam	ten times	cintu
10	cintu	ten times	makācintu
11	makācintu	ten times	veḷḷam
12	veḷḷam	ten times	makāveḷḷam
13	makāveḷḷam	ten times	piraḷayam
14	piraḷayam	ten times	makāpriralayam
15	makāpiraḷayam	ten times	cañcalam
16	cañcalam	ten times	makācañcalam
17	makācañcalam	ten times	valampuri
18	valampuri	ten times	makāvalampuri
19	makāvalampuri	ten times	taṇpaṉai
20	taṇpaṉai	ten times	makātaṇpaṉai
21	makātaṇpaṉai	ten times	kaṇvalai
22	kaṇvalai	ten times	makākaṇvalai
23	makākaṇvalai	ten times	aṉantam

Fractional units

Serial no.	Name in Tamil	Notation in Tamil	Modern notation
1	*muntiri*	𑿀	1/320
2	*arai kāṇi*	𑿁	1/160
3	*kāṇi*	𑿂	1/80
4	*arai mā*	𑿄	1/40
5	*mukkāṇi*	𑿆	3/80
6	*oru mā*	𑿈	1/20
7	*vīcam*	𑿉	1/16
8	*reṇṭu mā*	𑿋	1/10
9	*arai kāl*	𑿌	1/8
10	*mummā*	𑿍	3/20
11	*mūvīcam*	𑿎	3/16
12	*nālu mā*	𑿏	1/5
13	*kāl*	𑿐	¼
14	*arai*	𑿑	1/2
15	*mukkāl*	𑿓	¾
16	*Oṉṟu*	௧	1

There are further lower denominations which are:

nuṭpa muntiri	*4 1/2 times*	*immi*
immi	*10 ½ times*	*kīḻ muntirikai*
kīḻ muntirikai	*320 times*	*mēl muntirikai*
mēl muntirikai	*2 times*	*araikkāṇi 1/160*
araikkāṇi	*2 times*	*kāṇi 1/80*
kāṇi	*4 times*	*mā 1/20*
mā	*5 times*	*kāl ¼*
kāl	*2 times*	*arai ½*
arai	*2 times*	*One 1*

Table 2: Standard Units of linear measure

8 atoms	one micro-strand of cotton
8 micro-strands of cotton	one hair tip
8 hair tips	one grain of fine sand
8 sand grains	one white mustard seed
8 white mustard seeds	one gingili seed
8 gingili seeds	one grain of paddy
8 paddy grains	one viral (could mean finger)
12 viral	one cāṇ (1 span)
2 cāṇ	one mu<u>l</u>am
2 mu<u>l</u>am	one ci<u>r</u>u kōl
4 ci<u>r</u>u kōl	1 peruṅkōl or cemporkōl
500 peruṅkōl	1 kūppiṭu tūram (extent to which a person can be heard)
4 kūppiṭu	1 kātam
4 kātam	1 yōca<u>n</u>ai

The larger measures are then converted in terms of the smaller, beginning with the unit of *kuppitu* as the base:

kātam	4 *kūppiṭu*
peruṅkōl	2000
ci<u>r</u>ukōl	8000
mu<u>l</u>am	16000
span	32000
viral	384000
nel	3072000
Eḷḷu	2 crores and 45756000

Table 3: Weights

Standards of various units of weight measures used in the Tamil system:

Weight of one grain of paddy is called *oru mā*.

2 *orumā*	1 *piḷavu*
2 *piḷavu*	1 *kuṉṟi*
2 *kuṉṟi*	1 *mañcāti*
2 *mañcati*	1 *Paṇaveṭai*
10 *Paṇaveṭai*	1 *Kaḻañcu*
15 *Kaḻañcu*	1 *Palam*
20 *Palam*	1 *eṭai*
2 ½ *eṭai*	1 *niṟai*
2 *niṟai*	1 *tulām*.

In terms of the unit *tulām*,

One *tulām* will be equal to:	2 *niṟai*;
	5 *eṭai*;
	100 *Palam*;
	1500 *Kaḻañcu*;
	15,000 *Paṇaveṭai*;
	30,000 *mañcāṭi*;
	60,000 *kuṉṟi*;
	1,20,000 *piḷavu* and
	2,40,000 grains of paddy.

There are also other standards based on the same units:

nel	1/16 *vāy*;
piḷavu	1/8 vāy;
kuṉṟi	¼ vāy;
mañcāṭi	½ vāy;
paṉaveṭai	1 vāy and
kaḻañcu	10 *vāy*.[1]

There is a slight variation in the measures used in *Kanakkatikaram*[2]:

Weight of one grain of paddy *vīcam*

2 *vīcam*	1 piḷavu
2 *piḷavu*	1 *kuṉṟi*
2 *kuṉṟi*	*mañcāṭi*
5 *mañcāṭi*	1 *kāl Kaḻañcu*
4 *kāl Kaḻañcu*	1 *Kaḻañcu*
2 *Kaḻañcu*	1 *kaicā*
4 *kaicā*	1 *Palam*
100 *Palam*	1 *niṟai*
2 *niṟai*	1 *tulām*
20 *tulām*	1 *pāram*

A different manuscript in the *Kaṇakkatikāram* genre, also shows how standards were fixed in terms of weights of particular objects. For instance,

300 *palam* of sandal	1 *tulām*
40 *palam* of camphor	1 *kutiram*
300 *palam* of akil	1 *lōkkiam*
40 *palam* of turmeric	1 *vīcai*
600 *palam* of pepper	1 *pāram*

Table 4: Volume Measures in the Tamil System

100 *maṉam*	1 *pukai* (smoke)
100 *pukai*	1 *pāl* (milk)
100 *pāl*	1 *taṇṇīr* (water)
100 *taṇṇīr*	1 *nei* (ghee)
100 *ghee*	1 *celam*
100 *celam*	1 *vintu* (semen)
100 *vintu*	1 *tuḷḷi*
100 *tuḷḷi*	I *turuvam*
100 *turuvam*	1 *ceviṭu*
5 *ceviṭu*	1 *āḻākku*
2 *āḻākku*	I *uḻakku*
4 *uḻakku*	1 *nāḻi*
8 *nāḻi*	1 *kuṟuṇi*
4 *kuṟuṇi*	1 *tūṇi*
3 *tūṇi*	1 *kalam*.

The same set defines the standard for the common unit *Ceviṭu* in terms of objects:

23,400 mustards	1 *ceviṭu*
2,880 gingili	1 *ceviṭu*
360 paddy grains	1 *ceviṭu*
360 *kaṇam*	1 *ceviṭu*
320 pepper	1*ceviṭu*
180 *tuvarai*	1 *ceviṭu*

A different manuscript defines units differently:

30 *marakkāl* of *tuvar pākku* (betelnuts)	1 *cumai*
48 *marakkāl* of pepper	1 *pāram*
140 *marakkāl* of tamarind	1 *pāram*

Another variation is:

17 *palam maṇ* (sand)	1 *nāḻi*
20 *palam*	*nāḻi maṇal*
11 ¼ *palam*	*nāḻi nel* (paddy)
12 ½ *palam*	*nāḻi arici* (rice)
16 *palam*	*nāḻi uppu* (salt)

Kaṇita Nūl

9 grains of paddy	1 *tuḷḷi*	9 *nel*
8 *tuḷḷi*	1 *turuvam*	72 *nel*
5 *turuvam*	1 *ceviṭu*	360 *nel*
5 *ceviṭu*	1 *āḻākku*	1,800 *nel*
2 *āḻākku*	1 *uḻakku*	3,600 *nel*
2 *uḻakku*	1 *uri*	7,200 *nel*
2 *uri*	1 *nāḻi*	14,400 *nel*
8 *nāḻi*	1 *marakkāl*	1,15,200 *nel*
2 *marakkāl*	1 *patakku*	2,30,400 *nel*
2 *patakku*	1 *tūṇi*	4,60,800 *nel*
3 *tūṇi*	1 *kaḷam*	13,82,400 *nel*

In terms of *Kaḷam*, a commonly used measure,

1 *kaḷam*	3 tūṇi;
	6 *patakku;*
	12 *marakkāl;*
	96 *nāḻi;* 192 *Uri;*
	384 *uḻakku;*
	768 *āḻākku;*
	3840 *ceviṭu.*

Then some of the conversion tables are given, where *tāṉa perukkam* or multiples of ten are used. For instance, the *tāṉa perukkam* for *Nāḻi* will be:

10 *nāḻi*	1 *marakkāl*, 2 *nāḻi*
100 *nāḻi*	1 *kaḷam*, 4 *nāḻi*
1000 *nāḻi*	10 *kaḷam*, 5 *marakkāl*

Tāṉa perukkam or higher denominations for *Marakkāl* will be:

10 *marakkāl*	
100 *marakkāl*	8 *kaḷam*, 4 *marakkāl*
1000 *marakkāl*	83 *kaḷam*, 4 *marakkāl*

Higher denominations for *Kaḷam* will be:

10 *kaḷam*
100 *kaḷam* and
1000 *kaḷam*

Table 5: Measures of Time

The different units and their standards are given below:

2 *kaṇṇimai*	1 *kai noṭi*
2 *kai noṭi*	1 *māttirai*
2 *māttirai*	1 *kuru*
2 *kuru*	1 *uyir*
6 *uyir*	1 *kṣaṇikam*
12 *kṣaṇikam*	1 *vināḻikai*
60 *vināḻikai*	1 *Nāḻikai*

Other set of units from a different *Kaṇakkatikāram* manuscript:

2 *kaṇṇimai*	1 *māttirai*
2 *māttirai*	1 *kai noṭi*
2 *kai noṭi*	1 *cuṣpiram*
4 cuṣpiram	1 cuṭcanam
12 *cuṭcanam*	1 *vināḻikai*
60 *vināḻikai*	1 *Nāḻikai*

Another set of units from another manuscript:

7 ½ *nāḻikai*	1 *camam*
4 *camam*	1 *poḻutu*
2 *poḻutu*	1 *nāḷ* (day)
30 *nāḷ*	1 *tiṅkaḷ* (month)
12 *tiṅkaḷ*	1 *varuṣam* (year)

Another set of units from a different *Kaṇakkatikāram* manuscript:

If 108 lotus flowers are stacked up and pierced with a needle, four units of time taken for something (what is not known) to melt from one petal to the other is called a *kaṇam*;

8 *kaṇam*	1 *kāṭṭai*
8 *kāṭṭai*	1 *meṭṭai*
8 *meṭṭai*	1 *tuṭi*
4 *tuṭi*	1 *māttirai*
360 *māttirai*	1 *vināḻikai*
60 *vināḻikai*	1 *nāḻikai.*

It should be noticed here that except for the standard, 60 *vināḻikai* 1 *nāḻikai*, all the other standards differ.

Kaṇita Nūl states a different set of standards. It says that the time taken for the batting of eyelid or the snapping of two fingers is equivalent to a māttirai, which is the basic unit similar to one second. Time taken to breathe once is also called a māttirai.

6 *māttirai*	1 *vināḻikai*
5 *vināḻikai*	1 kaṇitam
12 *kaṇitam*	1 *nāḻikai*
7 ½ *nāḻikai*	1 *cāmam*
4 *cāmam*	1 *poḻutu*
2 *poḻutu*	1 *nāḷ* (day)
15 *nāḷ*	1 *pakkam* (fortnight)
2 *pakkam*	1 *mātam* (month)
2 *mātam*	1 *rutu*
3 *rutu*	1 *ayaṉam*
2 *ayaṉam*	1 *āṇṭu* (year)

Therefore, one year contains 2 *ayaṉam*, 6 *rutu* and 12 *mātam* or months, 24 fortnights or *pakkam*, 360 days, 720 *poḻutu*, 2880 *cāmam* and 21,600 *nāḻikai.*

APPENDIX-II

A Brief Note on Tamil Numerical Notation

A Note on Tamil Numerical Notation

Tamil numerals, like the Tamil alphabets are supposed to have been derived from the cave and the *Aṣōkā* or the *Brahmi* numerals[1]. Both epigraphic and paleographic evidence have suggested that by about the late *cōḻā* and the late *pāṇṭyās*, the numerical symbols have attained standardization into forms that continued to be in use[2]. This system of notation has been used in stone inscriptions, copper plates and through the palm leaf manuscripts. The geographical extent of the usage of this notation is also significant because, across political and territorial boundaries, this notation seems to have persisted for long.

In the Tamil system, separate symbols are formed for numbers from one to ten. There was no separate notation for zero in Tamil and hence, the notation for ten, hundred and the thousand are denoted by single figures: ten = ௰ ; hundred = ௱ ; thousand = ௲ . The tens, hundreds and the thousands are expressed by prefixing the signs for the units to the left side of the figure representing the order. The use of zero is not found in Tamil and hence, a number like 2225, in Tamil notation will be written as - ௨௲௨௱௨௰௫ , that is, 2(1000) + 2(100) + 2(10) + 5. Large numbers however, will be expressed as words, like 10^{15} will be called as *makākōṭi* and written as a combination of symbols and words, as in, ௱௱௲கோடி.The table shows the symbols of the numbers from one to *makākōṭi*, written in various combinations using the twelve signs available, and as multiples of ten in 15 steps. These systems seem to have been well in practice and were also used in computations. But in latter times, there seems to have been a change in the way numbers were written. The difference between the old and the latter method is shown below:

In the old method,

11 will be written as ௰ ௧
101 as ௱ ௧
241 as ௨௱ ௪௰ ௧
2441 as ௨௲ ௪௱ ௪௰ ௧

In the latter method, there seems to have been a change more akin to the Arabic system and these are mostly found in the palm leaf manuscripts. Palm leaf manuscripts are generally dated to the seventeenth century. In this method,

11 will be written as ௧ ௧
21 as ௨ ௧
241 as ௨ ௪ ௧ etc.

Symbols for fractions are extensively notated in the Tamil system. Some degree of standardization has been in vogue for the fractions ranging from 1/320, called a *muntiri* in Tamil to ¾, called a *mukkāl*. As given in the table, there are some fifteen symbols commonly used in the manuscripts for the fractions between 1/320 and ¾. Moreover, symbols are also found for lesser magnitudes, up to 1/1075200, called as *immi*, in Tamil. If one wants to classify further, then, one could still come up

---

[1] T. A. Gopinatha Rao, Travancore Archeological Series, Vol. I, Methodist Publishing House, Madras, 1910-1913, p. 211.

[2] "...the earliest known examples (about 1400 A.D.) are precisely of the same form as those still in use". A. C. Burnell, Elements of South Indian Paleography from the Fourth to the Seventeenth Century A.D. Being An Introduction to the Study of South Indian Inscriptions and Manuscripts, Indological Book House, Varanasi, (1878), 1968, p. 68.

with at least a three-tiered layer of fractional units, tending towards the micro-units. But what could have been the possible reason for such a small magnitudes of fractions and even a clearly demarcated system of notation for them? There is one epigraphic explanation available, which is worth consideration.

During the 11th century, the peak time of the *cōḻās*, there was an elaborate attempt at standardization of measures. One of the most evident aspects of this process is that, the land was classified in accordance with the quality as well. This was called the *maṭakku muṟai*, where a large measure of land, in terms of the new standardization would either become too big or too small when contrasted against the normal system of linear measures. That is a 10 *kuḻi* area of an uncultivable green pasture land, would become say, one-fifth of a *kuḻi* in the new system, where as the same area of a cultivable wetland would measure, say only one-half of the original measure. The micro-units of fractions could have been in use because of this new system where fractional units would have to be probably reduced further into secondary and tertiary levels. This interpretation was enabled by the prevalence of a large number of such tertiary level fractional units in the inscriptions of the eleventh century and after[3]. The use of the fractions must have continued even much after if not in all the subsequent administrative structures of the states, at least in some restricted spheres, enough to retain the notation for them. The same notation is what one finds in the palm leaf manuscripts of the sixteenth and the seventeenth century and even in the *Tiruppōrūr* and the *Vaṭakkuppaṭṭu* survey records in 1776.

Apart from numbers there is also an extensive system of notation developed for different kinds of measures – linear measures, measures of capacity, weight and time. Though the standards for these measures varied widely on a regional basis, the notation for these multitudes of measures seems to be common. For example, the standard measure of a yardstick differed from *Toṇṭaimaṇṭalam* region to the *Koṅku* region, and they further varied even within the same region[4], however, the notation used remained the same. The common usage of the notations signifying a fair degree of uniformity across the various regions of the Tamil speaking areas definitely point towards standardization, the time of its occurrence and the reasons for which are not yet well studied.

Tamil measure	**Notation**
A. Linear Measure	
nel	நெல்
kuḻi	குழி
vēli	வேலி

3 See Y Subbarayalu, South India under the Cholas, Oxford University Press, Delhi, 2012

4 Such huge variations in the standards of weights and measures were to cause much anxiety and effort to the British, as they spent the first five decades of the nineteenth century trying to figure out some method to standardize these measures. The story of standardization of weights and measures under the company rule is an area waiting to be explored in detail.

Tamil measure	**Notation**
B. Volume Measures	
ceviṭu	[illegible]
āḻākku	[illegible]
Uḻakku	[illegible]
uri	[illegible]
nāḻi	[illegible]
paṭi	[illegible]
marakkāl	[illegible]
kalam	[illegible]
C. Weights	
nel	[illegible]
paṇaveṭai	[illegible]
kaḻañcu	[illegible]
palam	[illegible]

There are no signs for the different arithmetical operators in the Tamil system. In the manuscripts, the verses use particular words and in the prose commentary that follows, just a hyphenation mark is used to denote all the operators. They were to be recognized depending on the context in which the marks were used.

5

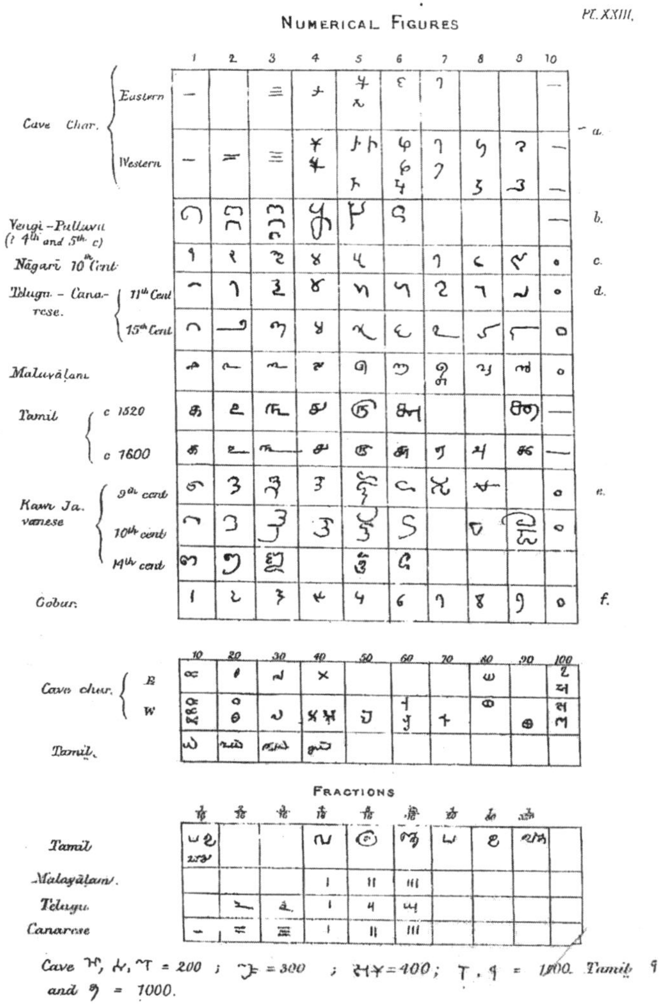
Numerical Figures
Pl. XXIII.
Cave Char. Eastern
Western
Vengi-Pallava (? 4th and 5th c)
Nāgarī 10th Cent.
Telugu.-Canarese. 11th Cent
15th Cent
Malayālam
Tamil c 1520
c 1600
Kawi Javanese 9th cent
10th cent
14th cent
Gobar.
Cave char. E
W
Tamil.
Fractions
Tamil
Malayālam.
Telugu.
Canarese
Cave = 200 ; = 300 ; = 400 ; = 1000. Tamil and = 1000.

---

[5] A.C. Burnell, Elements of South Indian Paleography from the Fourth to the Seventeenth Century A.D. Being An Introduction to the Study of South Indian Inscriptions and Manuscripts, Indological Book House, Varanasi, (1878), 1968, p.

APPENDIX-III

Poṉṉilakkam, Nellilakkam, Eṇcuvaṭi

Errata

Page No. in Book	Row	Column	Should Read as :
245	23rd	1st	Orumā Araimā Araikkāṇiyē Muntiri
246	3rd	1st	Irumā Kāṇiyē Muntiri
	4th	1st	Irumā Kāniyē Araikkāṇi
	5th	1st	Irumā Kāniyē Araikkāṇiyē Muntiri
	19th	1st	Mummā Orukāṇiyē Muntiri
	20th	1st	Mummā Orukāṇiyē Araikkāṇi
	21st	1st	Mummā Orukāṇiyē Araikkāṇiyē
247	29th	1st	Kālē Orumā Kāṇiyē Araikkāṇi
248	15th	1st	Kālē Mummā Kāṇiyē Araikkāṇi
251 (2nd table)	18th	1st	Kīl Kāl āvatu āyirattu Irunūṟṟu Eṇpatu paṅkil oṉṟu
261	12th	1st	Uḻakkē oruceviṭu
261	28th	3rd	1 nāḻi, 3 Uḻakku and 1
273	24th	2nd	Burning 5 times a lamp with 3 legs brought in 50 bees of which 5 went in search of flowers
274	30th	2nd	Kōṭimaṭavārtam kuṉṟupōl māḷikaimēl pāṭap
298	6th	4th	Kīl Orumā
300	17th	4th	Nāṟkalamē orupatakku
307	4th	4th	ōruḻakkē iru ceviṭu

This Appendix contains the translation of three number primers that were used in the *tiṇṇai* schools. In the translation, we have retained the original Tamil notation and number words on the left and provided the translation in modern numerical notation on the right. We have used the term "memory mode" for the Tamil notations and words to denote the fact that they were recited aloud and written simultaneously as part of the pedagogic practice in the *tiṇṇai* schools.

We have used the following printed editions as sources for the translation.

1. *Poṉṉilakkam Nellilakkam. Ivai catuvēta cittānta capaiyaic cārnta peṅkulūr aracamānakaram vittiyācālai vittiyārttikaḷiṉ poruṭṭu cila upāttiyāyarkaḷ muṉṉilaiyiṟ paricōtittu vi. Irāmacāmi mutaliyāral vittiyā vilāca vaccukkūṭattiṟ patippikkappaṭṭaṉa. kurōti, māci* (1845).
2. *Eṇ Cuvaṭi parivāy varuṣap piṟappu. Ivai peṅkuḷūr aracamānakaram vittiyā cālai vittiyārttikaḷiṉ poruṭṭu puracai aṣṭāvatāṉam capāpati mutaliyār muṉṉilaiyiṟ paricōtittu pu.kantappa mutaliyāral tamatu vittiyā vilāca accukkūṭattiṟ patippikkappaṭṭatu. Vicuvāvicu. Cittirai* (1845).
3. Keṭṭi Eṇcuvaṭi, accessed at http://www.tamilvu.org/library/kettiensuvadi/ketti_en_suvadi.pdf

We have also corroborated the translation with the following original palm-leaf manuscripts.

1. The catalogue number of the Tamil University, Thanjavur manuscript is, 2290 - ENSUVADI-TAMIL-1778-B02290.
2. The catalogue number of the Tamil University, Thanjavur manuscript is, 1504 - ENSUVADI-TAMIL-1191-B01504.

Pon̲n̲ilakkam

Kāppu

Kaṇṇan̲ marukan̲ kaṇapatiyait toḻa

Veṇṇīya lakka meḷitā varumē

Memory mode	Tamil notation	Modern notation
Cir̲r̲eṇ		**Small Numbers**
Aticāram		
Immi		
Kīḻ muntiri	கீழ் வத	1/320 x 1/320
Kīḻ araikkāṇi	கீழ் ஈ	1/320 x 1/160
Kīḻ kāṇi	கீழ் 8	1/320 x 1/80
Kīḻ Araimā	கீழ் சு	1/320 x 1/40
Kīḻ Mukkāṇi	கீழ் து	1/320 x 3/80
Kīḻ Orumā	கீழ் ப	1/320 x 1/20
Kīḻ makāṇi	கீழ் ப8	1/320 x 1/16
Kīḻ Irumā	கீழ் ஐ	1/320 x 1/10
Kīḻ araikkāl	கீழ் ஷ	1/320 x 1/8
Kīḻ mummā	கீழ் ஸ	1/320 x 3/20
Kīḻ mummākāṇi	கீழ் ஸ	1/320 x 3/16
Kīḻ nālumā	கீழ் ஹ	1/320 x 1/5
Kīḻ kāl	கீழ் வ	1/320 x ¼
Kīḻ arai	கீழ் உ	1/320 x ½
Kīḻ mukkāl	கீழ் ஞ	1/320 x ¾
Iṭai Eṇ		**Middle Numbers**
Muntiri	வத	1/320
Araikkāṇi	ஈ	1/160
Araikkāṇiyē muntiri	ஈ வத	1/160 + 1/320
Kāṇi	8	1/80

Kāṇiye Muntiri	ஒ வத	1/80 + 1/320
Kāṇiye Araikkāṇi	ஒ ர	1/80 + 1/160
Kāṇiye Araikkāṇiyē Muntiri	ஒரவத	1/80 + 1/160 + 1/320
Araimā	சு	1/40
Araimā Muntiri	சு வத	1/40 + 1/320
Araimā Araikkāṇi	சு ர	1/40 + 1/160
Araimā Araikkāṇi Muntiri	சுரவத	1/40 + 1/160 + 1/320
Mukkāṇi	தூ	3/80
Mukkāṇiyē Muntiri	தூ வத	3/80 + 1/320
Mukkāṇiyē Araikkāṇi	தூ ர	3/80 + 1/160
Mukkāṇiyē Araikkāṇiyē Muntiri	தூரவத	3/80 + 1/160 + 1/320
Orumā	ப	1/20
Orumā muntiri	பவத	1/20 + 1/320
Orumā Araikkāṇi	ப ர	1/20 + 1/160
Orumā Araikkāṇiyē muntiri	பரவத	1/20 + 1/160 + 1/320
Oru Mā Oru kāṇi	ப ஒ	1/20 + 1/80
Oru Mākāṇiye Muntiri	பஒ வத	1/20 + 1/80 + 1/320
Oru Mākāṇiye Araikkāṇi	பஒர	1/20 + 1/80 + 1/160
Oru Mākāṇiye Araikkāṇiyē Muntiri	பஒரவத	1/20 + 1/80 + 1/160 + 1/320
Orumā Araimā	பசு	1/20 + 1/40
Orumā Araimā Muntiri	பசு வத	1/20 + 1/40 + 1/320
Orumā Araimā Araikkāṇi	பசு ர	1/20 + 1/40 + 1/160
Orumā Araimā Arikkāṇiye Muntiri	பசுரவத	1/20 + 1/40 + 1/160 + 1/320
Orumā Mukkāṇi	பதூ	1/20 + 3/80
Orumā Mukkāṇiyē Muntiri	பதூ வத	1/20 + 3/80 + 1/320
Orumā Mukkāṇiyē Araikkāṇi	பதூர	1/20 + 3/80 + 1/160
Orumā Mukkāṇiyē Araikkāṇi Muntiri	பதூரவத	1/20 + 3/80 + 1/160 + 1/320
Iru mā	ஐ	2/20
Irumā Muntiri	ஐ வத	2/20 + 1/320
Irumā Araikkāṇi	ஐ ர	2/20 + 1/160

Irumā Araikkāṇiyē Muntiri	ஐ ரு வத	2/20 + 1/160 + 1/320
Irumā Oru Kāṇi	ஐ உ	2/20 + 1/80
Irumā Kāṇiye Muntiri	ஐ உ வத	2/20 + 1/80 + 1/320
Irumā Kāṇiye Araikkāṇi	ஐ உ ரு	2/20 + 1/80 + 1/160
Irumā Kāṇiye Araikkāṇiyē Muntiri	ஐ உ ரு வத	2/20 + 1/80 + 1/160 + 1/320
Irumā Araimā	ஐ சு	2/20 + 1/40
Irumā Araimā Muntiri	ஐ சு வத	2/20 + 1/40 + 1/320
Irumā Araimā Araikkāṇi	ஐ சு ரு	2/20 + 1/40 + 1/160
Irumā Araimā Araikkāṇiyē Muntiri	ஐ சு ரு வத	2/20 + 1/40 + 1/160 + 1/320
Irumā Mukkāṇi	ஐ க்ஷ	2/20 + 3/80
Irumā Mukkāṇiyē Muntiri	ஐ க்ஷ வத	2/20 + 3/80 + 1/320
Irumā Mukkāṇiyē Araikkāṇi	ஐ க்ஷ ரு	2/20 + 3/80 + 1/160
Irumā Mukkāṇiyē Araikkāṇiyē Muntiri	ஐ க்ஷ ரு வத	2/20 + 3/80 + 1/160 + 1/320
Mūṉṟu Mā (or) Mummā	ங	3/20
Mummā Muntiri	ங வத	3/20 + 1/320
Mummā Araikkāṇi	ங ரு	3/20 + 1/160
Mummā Araikkāṇiyē Muntiri	ங ரு வத	3/20 + 1/160 + 1/320
Mummā OruKāṇi	ங உ	3/20 + 1/80
Mummā Orukāṇiye Munitiri	ங உ வத	3/20 + 1/80 + 1/320
Mummā Orukāṇiye Araikkāṇi	ங உ ரு	3/20 + 1/80 + 1/160
Mummā Orukāṇiye Araikkāṇiyē Muntiri	ங உ ரு வத	3/20 + 1/80 + 1/160 + 1/320
Mummā Araimā	ங சு	3/20 + 1/40
Mummā Araimā Muntiri	ங சு வத	3/20 + 1/40 + 1/320
Mummā Araimā Araikkāṇi	ங சு ரு	3/20 + 1/40 + 1/160
Mummā Araimā Araikkāṇiyē Muntiri	ங சு ரு வத	3/20 + 1/40 + 1/160 + 1/320
Mummā Mukkāṇi	ங க்ஷ	3/20 + 3/80
Mummā Mukkāṇiyē Muntiri	ங க்ஷ வத	3/20 + 3/80 + 1/320
Mummā Mukkāṇiyē Araikkāṇi	ங க்ஷ ரு	3/20 + 3/80 + 1/160
Mummā Mukkāṇiyē Araikkāṇiyē	ங க்ஷ ரு வத	3/20 + 3/80 + 1/160 + 1/320

Muntiri		
Nālu Mā	𑿏	4/20
Nālumā Muntiri	𑿏𑿀	4/20 + 1/320
Nālumā Araikkāṇi	𑿏𑿁	4/20 + 1/160
Nālumā Araikkāṇiyē Muntiri	𑿏𑿁𑿀	4/20 + 1/160 + 1/320
Nālumā Kāṇi	𑿏𑿂	4/20 + 1/80
Nālu mā Kāṇiyē Muntiri	𑿏𑿂𑿀	4/20 + 1/80 + 1/320
Nālumā Kāṇiyē Araikkāṇi	𑿏𑿂𑿁	4/20 + 1/80 + 1/160
Nālu mā Kāṇiyē Araikkāṇiyē Muntiri	𑿏𑿂𑿁𑿀	4/20 + 1/80 + 1/160 + 1/320
Nālumā Araimā	𑿏𑿄	4/20 + 1/40
Nālu mā Araimā Muntiri	𑿏𑿄𑿀	4/20 + 1/40 + 1/320
Nālumā Araimā Araikkāṇi	𑿏𑿄𑿁	4/20 + 1/40 + 1/160
Nālumā Araimā Araikkāṇiyē Muntiri	𑿏𑿄𑿁𑿀	4/20 + 1/40 + 1/160 + 1/320
Nālumā Mukkāṇi	𑿏𑿆	4/20 + 3/80
Nālumā Mukkāṇiyē Muntiri	𑿏𑿆𑿀	4/20 + 3/80 + 1/320
Nālumā Mukkāṇiyē Araikkāṇi	𑿏𑿆𑿁	4/20 + 3/80 + 1/160
Nālumā Mukkāṇiyē Araikkāṇi Muntiri	𑿏𑿆𑿁𑿀	4/20 + 3/80 + 1/160 + 1/320
Kāl	𑿐	¼
Kālē Araikkāṇi	𑿐𑿁	¼ + 1/160
Kālē Kāṇi	𑿐𑿂	¼ + 1/80
Kālē Kāṇiyē Araikkāṇi	𑿐𑿂𑿁	¼ + 1/80 + 1/160
Kālē Araimā	𑿐𑿄	¼ + 1/40
Kālē Araimā Araikkāṇi	𑿐𑿄𑿁	¼ + 1/40 + 1/160
Kālē Mukkāṇi	𑿐𑿆	¼ + 3/80
Kālē Mukkāṇiyē Araikkāṇi	𑿐𑿆𑿁	¼ + 3/80 + 1/160
Kālē Orumā	𑿐𑿈	¼ + 1/20
Kālē Orumā Araikkāṇi	𑿐𑿈𑿁	¼ + 1/20 + 1/160
Kālē Orumā Kāṇi	𑿐𑿈𑿂	¼ + 1/20 + 1/80
Kālē Orumā Kāṇiye Araikkāṇi	𑿐𑿈𑿂𑿁	¼ + 1/20 + 1/80 + 1/160
Kālē Orumā Araimā	𑿐𑿈𑿄	¼ + 1/20 + 1/40

Kālē Orumā Araimā Araikkāṇi	𑿐𑿈𑿄𑿁	¼ + 1/20 + 1/40 + 1/160
Kālē Orumā Mukkāṇi	𑿐𑿈𑿆	¼ + 1/20 + 3/80
Kālē Orumā Mukkāṇiyē Araikkāṇi	𑿐𑿈𑿆𑿁	¼ + 1/20 + 3/80 + 1/160
Kālē Irumā	𑿐𑿋	¼ + 2/20
Kālē Irumā Araikkāṇi	𑿐𑿋𑿁	¼ + 2/20+ 1/160
Kālē Irumā Kāṇi	𑿐𑿋𑿂	¼ + 2/20+ 1/80
Kālē Irumā Kāṇiyē Araikkāṇi	𑿐𑿋𑿂𑿁	¼ + 2/20+ 1/80 + 1/160
Kālē Irumā Araimā	𑿐𑿋𑿄	¼ + 2/20+ 1/40
Kālē Irumā Araimā Araikkāṇi	𑿐𑿋𑿄𑿁	¼ + 2/20+ 1/40 + 1/160
Kālē Irumā Mukkāṇi	𑿐𑿋𑿆	¼ + 2/20+ 3/80
Kālē Irumā Mukkāṇiyē Muntiri	𑿐𑿋𑿆𑿀	¼ + 2/20+ 3/80 + 1/160
Kālē Mummā	𑿐𑿍	¼ + 3/20
Kālē Mummā Araikkāṇi	𑿐𑿍𑿁	¼ + 3/20 + 1/160
Kālē Mummā Kāṇi	𑿐𑿍𑿂	¼ + 3/20 + 1/80
Kālē Mummā Kāṇiye Araikkāṇi	𑿐𑿍𑿂𑿁	¼ + 3/20 + 1/80 + 1/160
Kālē Mummā Araimā	𑿐𑿍𑿄	¼ + 3/20 + 1/40
Kālē Mummā Araimā Araikkāṇi	𑿐𑿍𑿄𑿁	¼ + 3/20 + 1/40 + 1/160
Kālē Mummā Mukkāṇi	𑿐𑿍𑿆	¼ + 3/20 + 3/80
Kālē Mummā Mukkāṇiyē Araikkāṇi	𑿐𑿍𑿆𑿁	¼ + 3/20 + 3/80 + 1/160
Kālē Nālumā	𑿐𑿏	¼ + 4/20
Kālē Nālumā Araikkāṇi	𑿐𑿏𑿁	¼ + 4/20+ 1/160
Kālē Nālumā Kāṇi	𑿐𑿏𑿂	¼ + 4/20+ 1/80
Kālē Nālumā Kāṇiyē Araikkāṇi	𑿐𑿏𑿂𑿁	¼ + 4/20+ 1/80 + 1/160
Kālē Nālumā Araimā	𑿐𑿏𑿄	¼ + 4/20+ 1/40
Kālē Nālumā Araimā Araikkāṇi	𑿐𑿏𑿄𑿁	¼ + 4/20+ 1/40 + 1/160
Kālē Nālumā Mukkāṇi	𑿐𑿏𑿆	¼ + 4/20+ 3/80
Kālē Nālumā Mukkāṇiyē Araikkāṇi	𑿐𑿏𑿆𑿁	¼ + 4/20+ 3/80 + 1/160
Arai	𑿑	½
Arai Kāṇi	𑿑𑿂	½ + 1/80
Araiyē Araimā	𑿑𑿄	½ + 1/40

Araiyē Mukkāṇi	ஒகூ	½ + 3/80
Araiyē Orumā	ஒப	½ + 1/20
Araiyē Orumā Kāṇi	ஒப8	½ + 1/20 + 1/80
Araiyē Orumā Araimā	ஒபகு	½ + 1/20 + 1/40
Araiyē Orumā Mukkāṇi	ஒபகூ	½ + 1/20 + 3/80
Araiyē Irumā	ஒஉ	½ + 2/20
Araiyē Irumā Kāṇi	ஒஉ8	½ + 2/20 + 1/80
Araiyē Irumā Araimā	ஒஉகு	½ + 2/20 + 1/40
Araiyē Irumā Mukkāṇi	ஒஉகூ	½ + 2/20 + 3/80
Araiyē Mummā	ஒ௩	½ + 2/20 + 3/20
Araiyē Mummā Kāṇi	ஒ௩8	½ + 3/20 + 1/80
Araiyē Mummā Araimā	ஒ௩கு	½ + 3/20 + 1/40
Araiyē Mummā Mukkāṇi	ஒ௩கூ	½ + 3/20 + 3/80
Araiyē Nālumā	ஒ௪	½ + 4/20
Araiyē Nālu mā Kāṇi	ஒ௪8	½ + 4/20+ 1/80
Araiyē Nālumā Araimā	ஒ௪கு	½ + 4/20+ 1/40
Araiyē Nālumā Mukkāṇi	ஒ௪கூ	½ + 4/20+ 3/80
Mukkāl	ஞ	¾
Mukkālē Kāṇi	ஞ8	¾ + 1/80
Mukkālē Araimā	ஞகு	¾ + 1/40
Mukkālē Mukkāṇi	ஞகூ	¾ + 3/80
Mukkālē Orumā	ஞப	¾ + 1/20
Mukkālē Orumā Kāṇi	ஞப8	¾ + 1/20 + 1/80
Mukkālē Orumā Araimā	ஞபகு	¾ + 1/20 + 1/40
Mukkālē Orumā Mukkāṇi	ஞபகூ	¾ + 1/20 + 3/80
Mukkālē Irumā	ஞஉ	¾ + 2/20
Mukkālē Irumā Kāṇi	ஞஉ	¾ + 2/20 + 1/80
Mukkālē Irumā Araimā	ஞஉகு	¾ + 2/20 + 1/40
Mukkālē Irumā Mukkāṇi	ஞஉகூ	¾ + 2/20 + 3/80
Mukkālē Mummā	ஞ௩	¾ + 3/20

Mukkālē Muṁmā Kāṇi	𑿓𑿍𑿂	¾ + 3/20 + 1/80
Mukkālē Mummā Araimā	𑿓𑿍𑿄	¾ + 3/20 + 1/40
Mukkālē Mummā Mukkāṇi	𑿓𑿍𑿆	¾ + 3/20 + 3/80
Mukkālē Nālumā	𑿓𑿏	¾ + 4/20
Mukkālē Nālumā Kāṇi	𑿓𑿏𑿂	¾ + 4/20+ 1/80
Mukkālē Nālumā Araimā	𑿓𑿏𑿄	¾ + 4/20+ 1/40
Mukkālē Nālumā Mukkāṇi	𑿓𑿏𑿆	¾ + 4/20+ 3/80
Onru	௧	1
Onrē Orumā Kāṇi	௧𑿈𑿂	1 + 1/20 + 1/80
Onrē Araikkāl	௧𑿌	1 + 1/8
Onrē Mu Mākāṇi	௧𑿍𑿆	1 + 3/20 + 3/80
Onrē Kāl	௧𑿐	1 + ¼
Onrē Kālē Orumā Kāṇi	௧𑿐𑿈𑿂	1 + ¼ + 1/20 + 1/80
Onrē Kālē Araikkāl	௧𑿐𑿌	1 + ¼ + 1/8
Onrē Kālē Mu Mākāṇi	௧𑿐𑿍𑿆	1 + ¼ + 3/20 + 3/80
Onnarai	௧𑿑	1 + ½
Onnaraiyē Orumā Kāṇi	௧𑿑𑿈𑿂	1 + ½ + 1/20 + 1/80
Onnaraiyē Araikkāl	௧𑿑𑿌	1 + ½ + 1/8
Onnaraiyē Mu Mākāṇi	௧𑿑𑿍𑿆	1 + ½ + 3/20 + 3/80
Onnē Mukkāl	௧𑿓	1 + ¾
Onnē Mukkālē Orumā Kāṇi	௧𑿓𑿈𑿂	1 + ¾ + 1/20 + 1/80
Onnē Mukkālē Araikkāl	௧𑿓𑿌	1 + ¾ + 1/8
Onnē Mukkālē Mu Mākāṇi	௧𑿓𑿍𑿆	1 + ¾ + 3/20 + 3/80
Iraṇṭu	௨	2
Iraṇṭē Kāl	௨𑿐	2 + ¼
Iraṇṭarai	௨𑿑	2 + ½
Iraṇṭē Mukkāl	௨𑿓	2 + ¾
Mūnru	௩	3
Mūnrē Kāl	௩𑿐	3 + ¼
Mūnrarai	௩𑿑	3 + ½

Mūṉṟē Mukkāl	௩ ஞ	3 + ¾
Nālu	௪	4
Nālē Kāl	௪ வ	4 + ¼
Nālarai	௪ உ	4 + ½
Nālē Mukkāl	௪ ஞ	4 + ¾
Aintu	௫	5

Oṉṟukku / In terms of One

In Tamil memory mode	**English translation**
Mukkāl āvatu nālu paṅkil mūṉṟu	¾ is 3 parts in 4
Arai āvatu iraṇṭu paṅkil oṉṟu	½ is 1 part in 2
Kāl āvatu Nālu paṅkil oṉṟu	¼ is 1 part in 4
Nālumā āvatu aintu paṅkil oṉṟu	1/5 is 1 part in 5
Mu Mākāṇi āvatu patiṉāṟu paṅkil mūṉṟu	3/16 is 3 part in 16
Mūṉṟuma āvatu irupatu paṅkil mūṉṟu	3/20 is 3 parts in 20
Araikkāl āvatu eṭṭu paṅkil oṉṟu	1/8 is one part in 8
Irumā āvatu pattu paṅkil oṉṟu	1/10 is 1 part in 10
Mākāṇi āvatu patiṉāṟu paṅkil oṉṟu	1/16 is 1 part in 16
Orumā āvatu irupatu paṅkil oṉṟu	1/20 is 1 part in 20
Mukkāṇi āvatu eṇpatu paṅkil mūṉṟu	3/80 is 3 parts in 80
Araimā āvatu nāṟpatu paṅkil oṉṟu	1/40 is 1 part in 40
Kāṇi āvatu eṇpatu paṅkil oṉṟu	1/80 is 1 part in 80
Araikkāṇi āvatu Nūṟṟu aṟupatu paṅkil oṉṟu	1/160 is 1 part in 160
Kīḻ Mukkāl āvatu āyirattu Irunūṟṟu Eṇpatu paṅkil mūṉṟu	3/1280 [1/320 x ¾] is 3 parts in 1280
Kīḻ Arai āvatu Aṟunūṟṟu Nāṟpatu paṅkil oṉṟu	1/640 [1/320 x ½] is 1 part in 640
Kīḻ Kāl āvatu āyirattu Irunūṟṟu Enpatu paṅkil oṉṟu	1/1280 [1/320 x ¼] is 1 part in 1280

Kīḻ Nālumā āvatu āyirattu Aṟunūru paṅkil oṉṟu	1/1600 [1/320 x 4/20] is 1 part in 1600
Kīḻ Mu Mākāṇi āvatu Aintāyirattu Nūṟṟu Irupatu paṅkil mūṉṟu	3/5120 [1/320 x 3/16] is 3 parts in 5120
Kīḻ mummā āvatu āṟāyirattu Naṉūṟu paṅkil mūṉṟu	3/6400 [1/320 x 3/20] is 3 parts in 6400
Kīḻ araikkāl āvatu Iraṇṭayirattu Ainūṟṟu Aṟupatil Oṉṟu	1/2560 [1/320 x 1/8] is 1 part in 2560
Kīḻ Irumā āvatu Mūvāyirattu Irunūṟu paṅkil Oṉṟu	1/3200 [1.320 x 1/10] is 1 part in 3200
Kīḻ Mākāṇi āvatu Aiyāyirattu Nūṟṟu Irupatil Oṉṟu	1/5120 [1/320 x 1/16] is 1 part in 5120
Kīḻ Orumā āvatu āṟāyirattu Nāṉūṟṟil Oṉṟu	1/6400 [1/320 x 1/20] is 1 part in 6400
Kīḻ Mukkāṇi āvatu Irupattu Aiyāyirattu Aṟunūṟṟil Mūṉṟu	1/25600 [1/320 x 3/80] is 3 parts in 25600
Kīḻ Araimā āvatu Panniraṇṭu āyirattu Eṇṇūṟṟil Oṉṟu	1/12800 [1/320 x 1/40] is 1 part in 12800
Kīḻ Kāṇi āvatu Irupattu Aiyāyirattu Aṟu Nūṟṟil Oṉṟu	1/25600 [1/320 x 1/80] is 1 part in 25600
Kīḻ Araikkāṇi āvatu Aimpattu ōrayirattu Irunūṟṟil Oṉṟu	1/51200 [1/320 x 1/160] is 1 part in 51200
Kīḻ Muntiri āvatu Pattu Nūṟāyirattu Iraṇṭāyirattu Nāṉūṟṟil Oṉṟu	1/102400 [1/320 x 1/320] is 1 part in 102400
Immi āvatu Nūṟāyirattu Eḻupattu Aiyāyirattu Irunūṟṟil Oṉṟu	1/1075200 is 1 part in 1075200
Aticāram āvatu Patineṭṭu Nūṟāyirattu Muppatti Eṭṭāyirattu Irunūṟṟil Oṉṟu	1/1838200 is 1 part in 1838200
Iṭai Eṇ Muṟṟiṟṟu	**End of Middle Numbers**

Pēr Eṇ or Large Numbers

Memory mode	Tamil notation	Modern notation
Oṉṟu	௧	1
Iraṇṭu	௨	2
Mūṉṟu	௩	3
Nāṉku	௪	4
Aintu	௫	5
āṟu	௬	6
ēḻu	௭	7
Eṭṭu	௮	8
Oṉpatu	௯	9
Pattu	௰	10
Patiṉoṉṟu	௰௧	11
Paṉṉiraṇṭu	௰௨	12
Patiṉmūṉṟu	௰௩	13
Patiṉāṉku	௰௪	14
Patiṉaintu	௰௫	15
Patiṉāṟu	௰௬	16
Patiṉēḻu	௰௭	17
Patiṉeṭṭu	௰௮	18
Pattoṉpatu	௰௯	19
Irupatu	௨௰	20
Irupattoṉṟu	௨௰௧	21
Irupatti iraṇṭu	௨௰௨	22
Irupatti Mūṉṟu	௨௰௩	23
Irupatti nāṉku	௨௰௪	24
Irupatti aintu	௨௰௫	25

Irupatti āru	௨௰௬	26
Irupatti ēḻu	௨௰௭	27
Irupatti eṭṭu	௨௰௮	28
Irupatti onpatu	௨௰௯	29
Muppatu	௩௰	30
Muppatti Oṉṟu	௩௧	31
Muppatti Iraṇṭu	௩௨	32
Muppatti Mūṉṟu	௩௩	33
Muppatti nāṉku	௩௪	34
Muppatti aintu	௩௫	35
Muppatti āṟu	௩௬	36
Muppatti ēḻu	௩௭	37
Muppatti eṭṭu	௩௮	38
Muppatti oṉpatu	௩௯	39
Nāṟpatu	௪௰	40
Nāṟpatti Oṉṟu	௪௧	41
Nāṟpatti Iraṇṭu	௪௨	42
Nāṟpatti Mūṉṟu	௪௩	43
Nāṟpatti nāṉku	௪௪	44
Nāṟpatti aintu	௪௫	45
Nāṟpatti āṟu	௪௬	46
Nāṟpatti ēḻu	௪௭	47
Nāṟpatti eṭṭu	௪௮	48
Nāṟpatti oṉpatu	௪௯	49
Aimpatu	௫௰	50
Aimpatti Oṉṟu	௫௧	51
Aimpatti Iraṇṭu	௫௨	52
Aimpatti Mūṉṟu	௫௩	53
Aimpatti nāṉku	௫௪	54
Aimpatti aintu	௫௫	55

Aimpatti āṟu	௫௬	56
Aimpatti ēḻu	௫௭	57
Aimpatti eṭṭu	௫௮	58
Aimpatti oṉpatu	௫௯	59
Aṟupatu	௬௰	60
Aṟupattu Oṉṟu	௬௧	61
Aṟupatti Iraṇṭu	௬௨	62
Aṟupattu Mūṉṟu	௬௩	63
Aṟupattu nāṉku	௬௪	64
Aṟupattu aintu	௬௫	65
Aṟupattu āṟu	௬௬	66
Aṟupattu ēḻu	௬௭	67
Aṟupattu eṭṭu	௬௮	68
Aṟupattu oṉpatu	௬௯	69
Eḻupatu	௭௰	70
Eḻupattu Oṉṟu	௭௧	71
Eḻupattu Iraṇṭu	௭௨	72
Eḻupattu Mūṉṟu	௭௩	73
Eḻupattu nāṉku	௭௪	74
Eḻupattu aintu	௭௫	75
Eḻupattu āṟu	௭௬	76
Eḻupattu ēḻu	௭௭	77
Eḻupattu eṭṭu	௭௮	78
Eḻupattu oṉpatu	௭௯	79
Eṇpatu	௮௰	80
Eṇpattu Oṉṟu	௮௧	81
Eṇpattu Iraṇṭu	௮௨	82
Eṇpattu Mūṉṟu	௮௩	83
Eṇpattu nāṉku	௮௪	84
Eṇpattu aintu	௮௫	85

Eṇpattu āṟu	௮௬	86
Eṇpattu ēḻu	௮௭	87
Eṇpattu eṭṭu	௮௮	88
Eṇpattu oṉpatu	௮௯	89
Toṇṇūṟu	௯௰	90
Toṇṇūṟṟu Oṉṟu	௯௧	91
Toṇṇūṟṟu Iraṇṭu	௯௨	92
Toṇṇūṟṟu Mūṉṟu	௯௩	93
Toṇṇūṟṟu nāṉku	௯௪	94
Toṇṇūṟṟu aintu	௯௫	95
Toṇṇūṟṟu āṟu	௯௬	96
Toṇṇūṟṟu ēḻu	௯௭	97
Toṇṇūṟṟu eṭṭu	௯௮	98
Toṇṇūṟṟu oṉpatu	௯௯	99
Nūṟu	௱	100
Nūṟṟu pattu	௱௰	110
Nūṟṟu irupatu	௱௨௰	120
Nūṟṟu muppatu	௱௩௰	130
Nūṟṟu Nāṟpatu	௱௪௰	140
Nūṟṟu aimpatu	௱௫௰	150
Nūṟṟu aṟupatu	௱௬௰	160
Nūṟṟu eḻupatu	௱௭௰	170
Nūṟṟu eṇpatu	௱௮௰	180
Nūṟṟu toṇṇūṟu	௱௯௰	190
Irunūṟu	௨௱	200
Munnūṟu	௩௱	300
Nāṉūṟu	௪௱	400
Ainūṟu	௫௱	500
Aṟunūṟu	௬௱	600
Eḻunūṟu	௭௱	700

Eṇṇūṟu		800
Toḷḷāyiram		900
āyiram		1000
āyirattu nūṟu		1100
āyirattu irunūṟu		1200
āyirattu munnūṟu	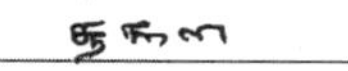	1300
āyirattu nāṉūṟu		1400
āyirattu ainūṟu		1500
āyirattu aṟunūṟu	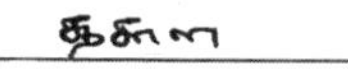	1600
āyirattu eḻunūṟu	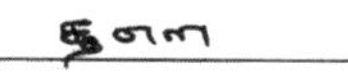	1700
āyirattu eṇṇūṟu	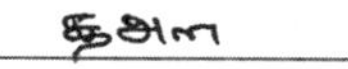	1800
āyirattu toḷḷāyiram	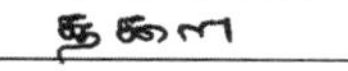	1900
Iraṇṭāyiram		2000
Mūvāyiram		3000
Nāṉkāyiram		4000
Aintāyiram		5000
Āṟāyiram		6000
Ēḻāyiram		7000
Eṭṭāyiram		8000
Oṉpatāyiram		9000
Pattāyiram		10000
Patiṉōrāyiram		11000
Paṉṉiraṇṭāyiram		12000
Patiṉmūṉṟāyiram		13000
Patināṉkāyiram		14000
Patiṉaintāyiram		15000
Patiṉāṟāyiram		16000
Patiṉēḻāyiram		17000
Patiṉeṭṭāyiram		18000
Pattoṉpatāyiram		19000

Irupatāyiram	௨௰௲	20000
Muppatāyiram	௩௰௲	30000
Nāṟpatāyiram	௪௰௲	40000
Aimpatāyiram	௫௰௲	50000
Aṟupatāyiram	௬௰௲	60000
Eḻupatāyiram	௭௰௲	70000
Eṇpatāyiram	௮௰௲	80000
Toṇṇūṟāyiram	௯௰௲	90000
Nūṟāyiram	௱௲	100000
Nūṟṟu pattāyiram	௱௰௲	110000
Nūṟṟu Irupatāyiram	௱௨௰௲	120000
Nūṟṟu Muppatāyiram	௱௩௰௲	130000
Nūṟṟu Nāṟpatāyiram	௱௪௰௲	140000
Nūṟṟu aimpatāyiram	௱௫௰௲	150000
Nūṟṟu aṟupatāyiram	௱௬௰௲	160000
Nūṟṟu eḻupatāyiram	௱௭௰௲	170000
Nūṟṟu eṇpatāyiram	௱௮௰௲	180000
Nūṟṟu toṇṇūṟāyiram	௱௯௰௲	190000
Irunūṟāyiram	௨௱௲	200000
Irunūṟṟu pattāyiram	௨௱௰௲	210000
Irunūṟṟu irupatāyiram	௨௱௨௰௲	220000
Irunūṟṟu muppatāyiram	௨௱௩௰௲	230000
Irunūṟṟu nāṟpatāyiram	௨௱௪௰௲	240000
Irunūṟṟu aimpatāyiram	௨௱௫௰௲	250000
Irunūṟṟu aṟupatāyiram	௨௱௬௰௲	260000
Irunūṟṟu eḻupatāyiram	௨௱௭௰௲	270000
Irunūṟṟu eṇpatāyiram	௨௱௮௰௲	280000
Irunūṟṟu toṇṇūṟāyiram	௨௱௯௰௲	290000
Muṉṉūṟāyiram	௩௱௲	300000
Nāṉūṟāyiram	௪௱௲	400000

Ainūṟāyiram	௫௱௲	500000
Aṟunūṟāyiram	௬௱௲	600000
Eḻunūṟāyiram	௭௱௲	700000
Eṇṇūṟāyiram	௮௱௲	800000
Toḷḷāyiramāyiram	௯௱௲	900000
Pattu nūṟāyiram	௰௱௲	1000000
Irupatu nūṟāyiram	௨௰௱௲	2000000
Muppatu nūṟāyiram	௩௰௱௲	3000000
Nāṟpatu nūṟāyiram	௪௰௱௲	4000000
Aimpatu nūṟāyiram	௫௰௱௲	5000000
Aṟupatu nūṟāyiram	௬௰௱௲	6000000
Eḻupatu nūṟāyiram	௭௰௱௲	7000000
Eṇpatu nūṟāyiram	௮௰௱௲	8000000
Toṇṇūṟu nūṟāyiram	௯௰௱௲	9000000
Nūṟu nūṟāyiram allatu Kōṭi	௱௱௲	10000000
	Muṟṟum / End	

Oṉṟukkoṉṟu Pattu paṅku atikamākiṟa tokaikaḷ

Sums that increase by multiples of ten

Verbal mode in Tamil	**Tamil notation**	**Sanskrit verbal mode**	**Tamil modern notation**	**Modern notation**
Oṉṟu	௧	ēkam	One ௧	1
Pattu	௰	Tacam	௧0	10
Nūṟu	௱	Catam	௧00	100
Āyiram	௲	Cakaciram	௧000	1000
Patiṉāyiram	௰௲	ayutam	௧0000	10000
Nūṟāyiram Ilaṭcam	௱௲	Niyutam	௧00000	100000
Pattu ilaṭcam	௰௱௲	Prayutam	௧000000	1000000

Nūṟu nūṟāyiram	௱௱௲	Kōṭi	௧0000000	10000000
Pattu kōṭi	௲௱௲	Taca kōṭi	௧00000000	100000000

10 tacakōṭi = catakōṭi

10 catakōṭi = arpputam

10 arpputam = nirpputam

10 nirpputam = karvam

10 karvam = makākarvam

10 makākarvam = patmam

10 patmam = makāpatmam

10 makāpatmam = kshōṇi

10 kshōṇi = caṅkam

10 caṅkam = makācaṅkam

10 makācaṅkam = kshiti

10 kshiti = makā kshiti

10 makā kshiti = kshōpam

10 kshōpam = makā kshōpam

10 makā kshōpam = niti

10 niti = makāniti

10 makāniti = paratam

10 paratam = parārtam

10 parārtam = aṉantam

10 aṉantam = cākaram

10 cākaram = avviyam

10 avviyam = amirtam

10 amirtam = acintiyam

10 acintiyam = amēyam

10 amēyam = pūri

10 pūri = makā pūri

All these 36 are called 'eṇṇiṭaṅkaḷ' or caṅkyāstāṉams.

Nellilakkam

nellilakkan taṉṉai nērāka yāṉpaṭikka
celvak kaṇapatitaṉ tiruvaṭi caraṇam

Memory mode	Tamil notation	English translation
Oru ceviṭu	௧ [illegible]	1 ceviṭu
Iru ceviṭu	௨ [illegible]	2 ceviṭu
Mucceviṭu	௩ [illegible]	3 ceviṭu
Nāṟceviṭu	௪ [illegible]	4 ceviṭu
Āḻākku	[illegible]	1 āḻākku
Āḻākkē oruceviṭu	[illegible] ௧ [illegible]	1 āḻākku and 1ceviṭu
Āḻākkē iruceviṭu	[illegible] ௨ [illegible]	1 āḻākku and 2 ceviṭu
Āḻākkē mucceviṭu	[illegible] ௩ [illegible]	1 āḻākku and 3 ceviṭu
Āḻākkē nāṟceviṭu	[illegible] ௪ [illegible]	1 āḻākku and 4 ceviṭu
Uḻakku	[illegible]	1 Uḻakku
Uḻakkē orceviṭu	[illegible] ௧ [illegible]	1 Uḻakku and 1 ceviṭu
Uḻakkē iruceviṭu	[illegible] ௨ [illegible]	1 Uḻakku and 2 ceviṭu
Uḻakkē mucceviṭu	[illegible] ௩ [illegible]	1 Uḻakku and 3 ceviṭu
Uḻakkē narceviṭu	[illegible] ௪ [illegible]	1 Uḻakku and 4 ceviṭu
Uḻakkē āḻākku	[illegible]	1 Uḻakku and 1 āḻākku
Uri	[illegible]	1 uri
Uriyē āḻākku	[illegible]	1 uri and 1 āḻākku
Mūvuḻakku	[illegible]	3 Uḻakku
Mūvuḻakkē āḻākku	[illegible]	3 Uḻakku and 1 āḻākku
Nāḻi	உ	1 nāḻi
Nāḻiyē āḻākku	உ [illegible]	1 nāḻi and 1 āḻākku
Nāḻiyē Uḻakku	உ [illegible]	1 nāḻi and 1 Uḻakku
Nāḻiyē Uḻakkē āḻākku	உ [illegible]	1 nāḻi, 1 Uḻakku and 1 āḻākku
Nāḻiyē uri	உ [illegible]	1 nāḻi and 1 uri
Nāḻiyē uriyē āḻākku	உ [illegible]	1 nāḻi, 1 uri and 1 āḻākku
Nāḻiyē mūvuḻakku	உ [illegible]	1 nāḻi and 3 Uḻakku
Nāḻiyē mūvuḻakkē āḻākku	உ [illegible]	I anli, 3 Uḻakku and 1

		āḻākku
Iru nāḻi	௨ஒ	2 nāḻi
Munnāḻi	௩ஒ	3 nāḻi
Nāṉāḻi	௪ஒ	4 nāḻi
Ainnāḻi	௫ஒ	5 nāḻi
Aru nāḻi	௬ஒ	6 nāḻi
Eḻu nāḻi	௭ஒ	7 nāḻi
Eṭṭu nāḻi	௮ஒ	8 nāḻi
Kuṟuṇi	ந	1 kuṟuṇi
Kuṟuṇiyē nāḻi	நஒ	1 kuṟuṇi and 1 nāḻi
Kuṟuṇiyē irunāḻi	ந௨ஒ	1 kuṟuṇi and 2 nāḻi
Kuṟuṇiyē nāṉāḻi	ந௪ஒ	1 kuṟuṇi and 3 nāḻi
Kuṟuṇiyē aināḻi	ந௫ஒ	1 kuṟuṇi and 5 nāḻi
Kuṟuṇiyē aṟunāḻi	ந௬ஒ	1 kuṟuṇi and 6 nāḻi
Kuṟuṇiyē eḻunāḻi	ந௭ஒ	1 kuṟuṇi and 7 nāḻi
Patakku	ஒது	1 patakku
Patakkē nāḻi	ஒதுஒ	1 patakku and 1 nāḻi
Patakkē irunāḻi	ஒது௨ஒ	1 patakku and 2 nāḻi
Patakkē munnāḻi	ஒது௩ஒ	1 patakku and 3 nāḻi
Patakkē nāṉāḻi	ஒது௪ஒ	1 patakku and 4 nāḻi
Patakkē aināḻi	ஒது௫ஒ	1 patakku and 5 nāḻi
Patakkē aṟunāḻi	ஒது௬ஒ	1 patakku and 6 nāḻi
Patakkē eḻunāḻi	ஒது௭ஒ	1 patakku and 7 nāḻi
Mukkuṟuṇi	ஸ	1 mukkuṟuṇi (3 kuṟuṇi)
Mukkuṟuṇiyē orunāḻi	ஸஒ	1 mukkuṟuṇi and 1 nāḻi
Mukkuṟuṇiyē irunāḻi	ஸ௨ஒ	1 mukkuṟuṇi and 2 nāḻi
Mukkuṟuṇiyē munnāḻi	ஸ௩ஒ	1 mukkuṟuṇi and 3 nāḻi
Mukkuṟuṇiyē nāṉāḻi	ஸ௪ஒ	1 mukkuṟuṇi and 4 nāḻi
Mukkuṟuṇiyē aināḻi	ஸ௫ஒ	1 mukkuṟuṇi and 5 nāḻi
Mukkuṟuṇiyē aṟunāḻi	ஸ௬ஒ	1 mukkuṟuṇi and 6 nāḻi

Mukkuṟuṇiyē and eḻunāḻi		1 mukkuṟuṇi and 7 nāḻi
Tūṇi		1 tūṇi
Tūṇiyē orunāḻi		1 tūṇi and 1 nāḻi
Tūṇiyē irunāḻi		1 tūṇi and 2 nāḻi
Tūṇiyē munnāḻi		1 tūṇi and 3 nāḻi
Tūṇiyē nānāḻi		1 tūṇi and 4 nāḻi
Tūṇiyē ainaḻi		1 tūṇi and 5 nāḻi
Tūṇiyē aṟunāḻi	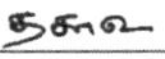	1 tūṇi and 6 nāḻi
Tūṇiyē eḻunāḻi		1 tūṇi and 7 nāḻi
Tūṇiyē kuṟuṇi	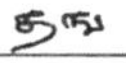	1 tūṇi and 1 kuṟuṇi
Tūṇiyē patakku	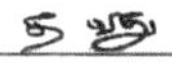	1 tūṇi and 1 patakku
Tūṇiyē mukkuṟuṇi		1 tūṇi and 1 mukkuṟuṇi
Eṭṭu kuṟuṇi		8 kuṟuṇi
Eṭṭu kuṟuṇiyē kuṟuṇi		8 kuṟuṇi and 1 kuṟuṇi
Eṭṭu kuṟuṇiyē patakku		8 kuṟuṇi and 1 patakku
Eṭṭu kuṟuṇiyē mukkuṟuṇi	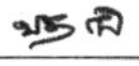	8 kuṟuṇi and 1 mukkuṟuṇi
Kalam		1 kalam
Kalamē orukuṟuṇi	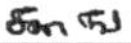	1 kalam and 1 kuṟuṇi
Kalamē orupatakku	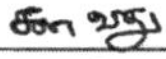	1 kalam and 1 patakku
Kalamē mukkuṟuṇi		1 kalam and 1 mukkuṟuṇi
Kalamē orutūṇi		1 kalam and 1 tūṇi
Kalamē oruttūṇiyē kuṟuṇi	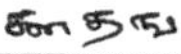	1 kalam, 1 tūṇi and 1 kuṟuṇi
Kalamē oruttūṇiyē oruppatakku		1 kalam, 1 tūṇi and 1 patakku
Kalamē oruttūṇiyē mukkuṟuṇi		1 kalam, I tūṇi and 1 mukkuṟuṇi
Kalamē ettukuṟuṇi	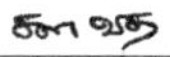	1 kalam and 8 kuṟuṇi
Kalamē ettu kuṟuṇiyē kuṟuṇi		1 kalam, 8 kuṟuṇi and 1 kuṟuṇi
Kalamē ettu kuṟuṇiyē		1 kalam, 8 kuṟuṇi and 1

oru patakku		patakku
Kalamē eṭṭu kuṟuṇiyē mukkuṟuṇi		1 kalam, 8 kuṟuṇi and 3 kuṟuṇi
Iranṭu kalam		2 kalam
Mūṉṟu kalam		3 kalam
Nāṉku kalam		4 kalam
Aintu kalam		5 kalam
āṟu kalam		6 kalam
ēḻu kalam	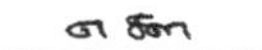	7 kalam
Eṭṭu kalam		8 kalam
Oṉpatu kalam		9 kalam
Pattu kalam		10 kalam
Irupatu kalam		20 kalam
Muppatu kalam		30 kalam
Nāṟpatu kalam		40 kalam
Aimpatu kalam		50 kalam
Aṟupatu kalam		60 kalam
Eḻupatu kalam		70 kalam
Eṇpatu kalam		80 kalam
Toṇṇūṟu kalam		90 kalam
Nūṟu kalam		100 kalam
Irunūṟu kalam		200 kalam
Munnūṟu kalam		300 kalam
Nāṇūṟu kalam		400 kalam
Ainnūṟu kalam		500 kalam
Aṟunūṟu kalam	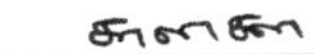	600 kalam
Eḻunūṟu kalam	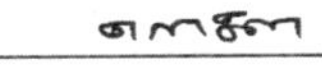	700 kalam
Eṇṇūṟu kalam	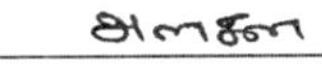	800 kalam
Toḷḷāyiram kalam		900 kalam
āyiram kalam		1000 kalam

Iraṇṭāyiram kalam	௨௲ன	2000 kalam
Mūvāyiram kalam	௩௲ன	3000 kalam
Nāṉkāyiram kalam	௪௲ன	4000 kalam
Aiyāyiram kalam	௫௲ன	5000 kalam
Āṟāyiram kalam	௬௲ன	6000 kalam
Ēḻāyiram kalam	௭௲ன	7000 kalam
Eṭṭāyiram kalam	௮௲ன	8000 kalam
Oṉpatāyiram kalam	௯௲ன	9000 kalam
Pattāyiram kalam	௰௲ன	10000 kalam
Irupatu āyiram kalam	௨௰௲ன	20000 kalam
Muppatu āyiram kalam	௩௰௲ன	30000 kalam
Nāṟpatu āyiram kalam	௪௰௲ன	40000 kalam
Aimpatu āyiram kalam	௫௰௲ன	50000 kalam
Aṟupatu āyiram kalam	௬௰௲ன	60000 kalam
Eḻupatu āyiram kalam	௭௰௲ன	70000 kalam
Eṇpatu āyiram kalam	௮௰௲ன	80000 kalam
Toṇṇūṟu āyiram kalam	௯௰௲ன	90000 kalam
Nūṟu āyiram kalam	௱௲ன	100000 kalam
Irunūṟu āyiram kalam	௨௱௲ன	200000 kalam
Munnūṟu āyiram kalam	௩௱௲ன	300000 kalam
Nāṉūṟu āyiram kalam	௪௱௲ன	400000 kalam
Ainnūṟu āyiram kalam	௫௱௲ன	500000 kalam
Aṟunūṟu āyiram kalam	௬௱௲ன	600000 kalam
Eḻunūṟu āyiram kalam	௭௱௲ன	700000 kalam
Eṇṇūṟu āyiram kalam	௮௱௲ன	800000 kalam
Toḷḷāyiram āyiram kalam	௯௱௲ன	900000 kalam
Pattu nūṟāyiram kalam	௰௱௲ன	1000000 kalam
Irupatu nūṟāyiram kalam	௨௰௱௲ன	2000000 kalam
Muppatu nūṟāyiram kalam	௩௰௱௲ன	3000000 kalam
Nāṟpatu nūṟāyiram kalam	௪௰௱௲ன	4000000 kalam

Aimpatu nūṟāyiram kalam	௫௰௱௲கள	5000000 kalam
Aṟupatu nūṟāyiram kalam	௬௰௱௲கள	6000000 kalam
Eḻupatu nūṟāyiram kalam	௭௰௱௲கள	7000000 kalam
Eṇpatu nūṟāyiram kalam	௮௰௱௲கள	8000000 kalam
Toṇṇūṟu nūṟāyiram kalam	௯௰௱௲கள	9000000 kalam
Nūṟu nūṟāyiram kalam	௱௱௲கள	10000000 kalam

In Tamil	**In translation**
Nel munnūṟṟu aṟupatu koṇṭatu oru ceviṭu	360 units of nel = 1 ceviṭu
Ceviṭu aintu koṇṭatu āḻākku	5 ceviṭu = I āḻākku
Āḻākku Iraṇṭu koṇṭatu Uḻakku	2 āḻākku = 1 Uḻakku
Uḻakku Iraṇṭu koṇṭatu uri	2 Uḻakku = 1 uri
Uri Iraṇṭu koṇṭatu nāḻi	2 uri = 1 nāḻi
Nāḻi eṭṭu koṇṭatu kuṟuṇi	8 nāḻi = 1 kuṟuṇi
Kuṟuṇi Iraṇṭu koṇṭatu patakku	2 kuṟuṇi = 1 patakku
Patakku Iraṇṭu koṇṭatu tūṇi	2 patakku = 1 tūṇi
Tūṇi Mūṉṟu koṇṭatu kalam	3 tūṇi = 1 kalam

Nāḻi is also known as paṭi

Kuṟuṇi is also known as marakkāl

One parai = 5 marakkāl

400 marakkāl = karacai

one paṭi is also equal to one pakkā cēr

End of Nellilakkam

Encuvati

Kappu

Neṭumāl tirumarukā nittan matalāy

Koṭumāl vinaiyaṟukkuṅ kunṟē – taṭumāṟā

Teṇmuppatu vāyu mencittat tēniṟkap

Paṇṇut tamanē parintu.

Mēlvai ilakkam

Number in Tamil notation			memory mode	In modern notation		
௧	௧	௧	Onṟu	1	1	1
௰		௰	Pattu	10	1	10
௨		௨	Iraṇṭu	2	1	2
௨௰		௨௰	Irupatu	20	1	20
௩		௩	Mūnṟu	3	1	3
௩௰		௩௰	Muppatu	30	1	30
௪		௪	Nānku	4	1	4
௪௰		௪௰	Nāṟpatu	40	1	40
௫		௫	Aintu	5	1	5
௫௰		௫௰	Aimpatu	50	1	50
௬		௬	āṟu	6	1	6
௬௰		௬௰	Aṟupatu	60	1	60
௭		௭	ēḻu	7	1	7
௭௰		௭௰	Eḻupatu	70	1	70
௮		௮	Eṭṭu	8	1	8
௮௰		௮௰	Eṇpatu	80	1	80
௯		௯	Onpatu	9	1	9
௯௰		௯௰	Toṇṇūṟu	90	1	90
௱		௱	Nūṟu	100	1	100

Mallikai aintu malarnta pū toṇṇūṟu *Koḷḷuvār aivar paṟittu* *Alakunilai* . . . - ௫௭௯௫	5 Jasmine buds bloomed in to 90 shared by 5 persons Cumulative Product = 595

௧	௨	௨	Iraṇṭu	1	2	2
௰		௨௰	Irupatu	10	2	20
௨		௪	Nāṉku	2	2	4
௨௰		௪௰	Narpatu	20	2	40
௩		௬	Āṟu	3	2	6
௩௰		௬௰	Aṟupatu	30	2	60
௪		௮	Eṭṭu	4	2	8
௪௰		௮௰	Eṇpatu	40	2	80
௫		௰	Pattu	5	2	10
௫௰		௱	Nūṟu	50	2	100
௬		௰௨	Paṉṉiraṇṭu	6	2	12
௬௰		௱௨௰	Nūṟṟu irupatu	60	2	120
௭		௰௪	Patināṉku	7	2	14
௭௰		௱௪௰	Nūṟṟu nāṟpatu	70	2	140
௮		௰௬	Patiṉāṟu	8	2	16
௮௰		௱௬௰	Nūṟṟu aṟupatu	80	2	160
௯		௰௮	Patiṉeṭṭu	9	2	18
௯௰		௱௮௰	Nūṟṟu eṇpatu	90	2	180
௱		௨௱	Irunūṟu	100	2	200
āyiram paiṅkiḷi nūṟu kural koṇṭu māyiruñ *Cōlai maran toṇṇūṟum ēṟia ñāyiṟu paṭṭāṅ kaṟintu* *alakunilai* ௲௱௯௰				1000 parrots with 100 voices in a garden of 90 trees on a sunny day Cumulative product = 1190		
௧	௩	௩	Mūṉṟu	1	3	3
௰		௩௰	Muppatu	10	3	30
௨		௬	Āṟu	2	3	6
௨௰		௬௰	Arupatu	20	3	60
௩		௯	Oṉpatu	3	3	9
௩௰		௯௰	Toṇṇūṟu	30	3	90
௪		௰௨	Paṉṉiraṇṭu	4	3	12
௪௰		௱௨௰	Nūṟṟu irupatu	40	3	120

௫	௩	௰௫	Patiṉaintu	5	3	15
௫௰		௱௫௰	Nūṟṟu aimpatu	50	3	150
௬		௰௮	Patiṉeṭṭu	6	3	18
௬௰		௱௮௰	Nūṟṟu eṇpatu	60	3	180
௭		௨௰௧	Irupattu Oṉṟu	7	3	21
௭௰		௨௱௰	Irunūṟṟu pattu	70	3	210
௮		௨௰௪	Irupattu nāṉku	8	3	24
௮௰		௨௱௪௰	Irunūṟṟu nāṟpatu	80	3	240
௯		௨௰௭	Irupattu ēḻu	9	3	27
௯௰		௨௱௭௰	Irunūṟṟu eḻupatu	90	3	270
௱		௩௱	Munnūṟu	100	3	300
āyiram yāṉai eḻunūṟu kūṉ pakaḻi pāyum pakaṭu eṇpattu aintu *Alakunilai* - . - - ௲௭௱௮௰௫				1000 elephants 700 arrows and 85 leaping bulls cumulative product = 1785		
௧	௪	௪	Nāṉku	1	4	4
௰		௪௰	Nāṟpatu	10	4	40
௨		௮	Eṭṭu	2	4	8
௨௰		௮௰	Eṇpatu	20	4	80
௩		௰௨	Paṉṉiraṇṭu	3	4	12
௩௰		௱௨௰	Nūṟṟu irupatu	30	4	120
௪		௰௬	Patiṉāṟu	4	4	16
௪௰		௱௬௰	Nūṟṟu aṟupatu	40	4	160
௫		௨௰	Irupatu	5	4	20
௫௰		௨௱	Irunūṟu	50	4	200
௬		௨௰௪	Irupattu nāṉku	6	4	24
௬௰		௨௱௪௰	Irunūṟṟu nāṟpatu	60	4	240
௭		௨௰௮	Irupattu eṭṭu	7	4	28
௭௰		௨௱௮௰	Irunūṟṟu eṇpatu	70	4	280
௮		௩௰௨	Muppatti Iraṇṭu	8	4	32
௮௰		௩௱௨௰	Munnūṟṟi irupatu	80	4	320

௯		௩௰௬	Muppatti āṟu	9	4	36
௯௰		௩௱௬௰	Munnūṟṟi aṟupatu	90	4	360
௱		௪௱	Nāṉūṟu	100	4	400
Iruvarē mūvarkku iṉitu amarntu ūṭṭil irunāl *Viḷaṅkiṉum uṇṭākuvār* *Alakunilai* - - - - ௨௲௩௱௮௰				Two persons providing feast for 3 people will shine with 8 kinds of wealth Cumulative product = 2380		
௧	௫	௫	Aintu	1	5	5
௰		௫௰	Aimpatu	10	5	50
௨		௰	Pattu	2	5	10
௨௰		௱	Nūṟu	20	5	100
௩		௰௫	Patiṉaintu	3	5	15
௩௰		௱௫௰	Nūṟṟu aimpatu	30	5	150
௪		௨௰	Irupatu	4	5	20
௪௰		௨௱	Irunūṟu	40	5	200
௫		௨௰௫	Irupatti aintu	5	5	25
௫௰		௨௱௫௰	Irunūṟṟi aimpatu	50	5	250
௬		௩௰	Muppatu	6	5	30
௬௰		௩௱	Munnūṟu	60	5	300
௭		௩௰௫	Muppatti aintu	7	5	35
௭௰		௩௱௫௰	Munnūṟṟi aimpatu	70	5	350
௮		௪௰	Nāṟpatu	8	5	40
௮௰		௪௱	Nāṉūṟu	80	5	400
௯		௪௰௫	Nāṟpatti aintu	9	5	45
௯௰		௪௱௫௰	Nānūṟṟu aimpatu	90	5	450
௱		௫௱	Ainūṟu	100	5	500
Irukayattūṭu oṉpatiṉmar ceṉkaḻunīrp pōtēḻu *Malar aimpāṟ kāṭṭutum eṉpār* *Alakunilai* - - - - ௨௲௯௱௭௰௫				2 ponds with 9 people showing 7 buds and 5 flowers of purple water lily Cumulative product = 2975		

௧	௬	௬	Ā<u>r</u>u	1	6	6
௰		௬௰	Arupatu	10	6	60
௨		௰௨	Pa<u>nn</u>iraṇṭu	2	6	12
௨௰		௱௨௰	Nū<u>rr</u>i irupatu	20	6	120
௩		௰௮	Pati<u>n</u>eṭṭu	3	6	18
௩௰		௱௮௰	Nū<u>rr</u>i eṇpatu	30	6	180
௪		௨௰௪	Irupatti <u>n</u>ā<u>n</u>ku	4	6	24
௪௰		௨௱௪௰	Irunū<u>rr</u>i nā<u>r</u>patu	40	6	240
௫		௩௰	Muppatu	5	6	30
௫௰		௩௱	Munnū<u>r</u>u	50	6	300
௬		௩௰௬	Muppatti ā<u>r</u>u	6	6	36
௬௰		௩௱௬௰	Munnū<u>rr</u>i a<u>r</u>upatu	60	6	360
௭		௪௰௨	Nā<u>r</u>patti Iraṇṭu	7	6	42
௭௰		௪௱௨௰	Nānū<u>rr</u>u irupatu	70	6	420
௮		௪௰௮	Nā<u>r</u>patti eṭṭu	8	6	48
௮௰		௪௱௮௰	Nā<u>n</u>ū<u>rr</u>u eṇpatu	80	6	480
௯		௫௰௪	Aimpatti nā<u>n</u>ku	9	6	54
௯௰		௫௱௪௰	Ainū<u>rr</u>u nā<u>r</u>patu	90	6	540
௱		௬௱	A<u>r</u>unū<u>r</u>u	100	6	600
Mukkuḷam āṭuvārkku aintūrun takkatu e<u>l</u>umalar *Takkatān takka tuṭaittu* *Alakunilai . . . .* ௩௲௫௱௭௰				People using 3 ponds deserve not just 5 villages but 7 flowers as well Cumulative product = 3570		
௧	௭	௭	ē<u>l</u>u	1	7	7
௰		௭௰	E<u>l</u>upatu	10	7	70
௨		௰௪	Pati<u>n</u>ā<u>n</u>ku	2	7	14
௨௰		௱௪௰	Nū<u>rr</u>u nā<u>r</u>patu	20	7	140
௩		௨௰௧	Irupatti O<u>nr</u>u	3	7	21
௩௰		௨௱௰	Irunū<u>rr</u>u pattu	30	7	210
௪		௨௰௮	Irupatti eṭṭu	4	7	28
௪௰		௨௱௮௰	Irunū<u>rr</u>u eṇpatu	40	7	280

௫	௭	௩௰௫	Muppatti aintu	5	7	35
௫௰		௩௱௫௰	Munnūṟṟu aimpatu	50	7	350
௬		௪௰௨	Nāṟpatti Iraṇṭu	6	7	42
௬௰		௪௱௨௰	Nāṉūṟṟu irupatu	60	7	420
௭		௪௰௯	Nāṟpatti oṉpatu	7	7	49
௭௰		௪௱௯௰	Nāṉūṟṟu toṇṇūṟu	70	7	490
௮		௫௰௬	Aimpatti āṟu	8	7	56
௮௰		௫௱௬௰	Ainūṟṟu aṟupatu	80	7	560
௯		௬௰௩	Aṟupatti Mūṉṟu	9	7	63
௯௰		௬௱௩௰	Aṟunūṟṟu muppatu	90	7	630
௱		௭௱	Eḻunūṟu	100	7	700
ṉālvar oruneṟi pōyiṉārē aṟivar aintūrum pukkār akattu Alakunilai . . . . , ௪௲௱௬௰௫				4 went in 1 way while 6 went in to 5 hamlets Cumulative product = 4165		
௧	௮	௮	Eṭṭu	1	8	8
௰		௮௰	Eṇpatu	10	8	80
௨		௰௬	Patiṉāṟu	2	8	16
௨௰		௱௬௰	Nūṟṟu aṟupatu	20	8	160
௩		௨௰௪	Irupatti nāṉku	3	8	24
௩௰		௨௱௪௰	Irunūṟṟu nāṟpatu	30	8	240
௪		௩௰௨	Muppati Iraṇṭu	4	8	32
௪௰		௩௱௨௰	Munnūṟṟu irupatu	40	8	320
௫		௪௰	Nāṟpatu	5	8	40
௫௰		௪௱	Nāṉūṟu	50	8	400
௬		௪௰௮	Nāṟpatti eṭṭu	6	8	48
௬௰		௪௱௮௰	Nāṉūṟṟu eṇpatu	60	8	480
௭		௫௰௬	Aimpatti āṟu	7	8	56
௭௰		௫௱௬௰	Ainūṟṟu aṟupatu	70	8	560
௮		௬௰௪	Aṟupatti nāṉku	8	8	64
௮௰		௬௱௪௰	Aṟunūṟṟu nāṟpatu	80	8	640

௯	௮	௭௰௨	E̲lupatti Iraṇṭu	9	8	72
௯௰		௭௱௨௰	E̲lunūr̲r̲u irupatu	90	8	720
௱		௮௱	Eṇṇūr̲u	100	8	800
Nān̲ilamaṭattu e̲lupatu kālāṭat tūṅku *ār̲āvān tō̲li nī* *Alakunilai* . . . . ௪௲௭௱௬௰.				4 storied house with 7 pillars for you to rest 6 hours my friend Cumulative product = 4760		
௧	௯	௯	On̲patu	1	9	9
௰		௯௰	Toṇṇūr̲u	10	9	90
௨		௰௮	Patin̲eṭṭu	2	9	18
௨௰		௱௮௰	Nūr̲r̲u eṇpatu	20	9	180
௩		௨௰௭	Irupatti ē̲lu	3	9	27
௩௰		௨௱௭௰	Irunūr̲r̲u e̲lupatu	30	9	270
௪		௩௰௬	Muppatti ār̲u	4	9	36
௪௰		௩௱௬௰	Munnūr̲r̲u ar̲upatu	40	9	360
௫		௪௰௫	Nār̲patti aintu	5	9	45
௫௰		௪௱௫௰	Nān̲ūr̲r̲u aimpatu	50	9	450
௬		௫௰௪	Aimpatti nān̲ku	6	9	54
௬௰		௫௱௪௰	Ainūr̲r̲u nār̲patu	60	9	540
௭		௬௰௩	Ar̲upatti Mūn̲r̲u	7	9	63
௭௰		௬௱௩௰	Ar̲unūr̲r̲u muppatu	70	9	630
௮		௭௰௨	E̲lupatti Iraṇṭu	8	9	72
௮௰		௭௱௨௰	E̲lunūr̲r̲u irupatu	80	9	720
௯		௮௰௧	Eṇpatti On̲r̲u	9	9	81
௯௰		௮௱௰	Eṇṇūr̲r̲u pattu	90	9	810
௱		௯௱	Toḷḷāyiram	100	9	900
Aintuṭan̲ māṭṭiyār mukkāl viḷakkin̲ kī̲l aimpatu *Tumpiyuṭan̲ ūta aintumpi cen̲r̲ēr̲iyum pūvaic cer̲intu* *Alakunilai* ௫௲௩௱௫௰௫				Buring 5 times a lamp with 3 legs brought in 50 bees of which 5 went in search of flowers Cumulative product = 5355		
௧	௰	௰	Pattu	1	10	10

௰	௰	௱	Nūṟu	10	10	100
௱		௲	ōrāyiram	100	10	1000
௨		௨௰	Irupatu	2	10	20
௨௰		௨௱	Irunūṟu	20	10	200
௨௱		௨௲	Iraṇṭāyiram	200	10	2000
௩		௩௰	Muppatu	3	10	30
௩௰		௩௱	Munnūṟu	30	10	300
௩௱		௩௲	Mūvāyiram	300	10	3000
௪		௪௰	Nāṟpatu	4	10	40
௪௰		௪௱	Nāṉūṟu	40	10	400
௪௱		௪௲	Nāṉkāyiram	400	10	4000
௫		௫௰	Aimpatu	5	10	50
௫௰		௫௱	Ainnūṟu	50	10	500
௫௱		௫௲	Aiyāyiram	500	10	5000
௬		௬௰	Aṟupatu	6	10	60
௬௰		௬௱	Aṟunūṟu	60	10	600
௬௱		௬௲	āṟāyiram	600	10	6000
௭		௭௰	Eḻupatu	7	10	70
௭௰		௭௱	Eḻunūṟu	70	10	700
௭௱		௭௲	ēḻāyiram	700	10	7000
௮		௮௰	Eṇpatu	8	10	80
௮௰		௮௱	Eṇṇūṟū	80	10	800
௮௱		௮௲	Eṭṭāyiram	800	10	8000
௯		௯௰	Toṇṇūṟu	9	10	90
௯௰		௯௱	Toḷḷāyiram	90	10	900
௯௱		௯௲	Oṉpatāyiram	900	10	9000
௲		௰௲	Pattāyiram	1000	10	10000
௰௲		௱௲	Nūṟāyiram	10000	10	100000
௱௲		௰௱௲	Pattu nūṟāyiram	100000	10	1000000
	Kōṭimaṭvārtam kuṉṟupōl māḷikaimēl pāṭap			One hundred thousand mansions		
	Payilum iṭam paṉṉoru nūṟāyiramām cēṭiyarkaḷ *Aimpatiṟṟoṉpatiṉāyirattu toḷḷāyirattaimpatē* *Yākum kaṇakku* *Alakunilai . . . .* கோழமே- ௰௲ லட்சத்து ௫௰௯௲௯௱௫௰			with 59950 maids (The first number koti here connotes the number 1 crore but stands for the sense of being young in the poetic sense) Cumulative product = 1159950		

Mēlvai ciṟṟilakkam

Memory mode				In modern notation		
௧	[illegible]	[illegible]	Muntiri	1	1/320	1/320
௰		[illegible]	Araimā araikkāṇi	10	1/320	1/40 + 1/160
௱		[illegible]	Kālē mākāṇi	100	1/320	¼ + 1/20 + 1/80
௨		[illegible]	Araikkāṇi	2	1/320	1/160
௨௰		[illegible]	Mākāṇi	20	1/320	1/20 + 1/80
௨௱		[illegible]	Araiyē araikkāl	200	1/320	½ + 1/8
௩		[illegible]	Araikkāṇiyē muntiri	3	1/320	1/160 + 1/320
௩௰		[illegible]	Orumāve Mukkāṇiyē araikkāṇi	30	1/320	1/20 + 3/80 + 1/160
௩௱		[illegible]	Mukkālē mummākāṇi	300	1/320	¾ + 3/20 + 3/80
௪		[illegible]	Oru kāṇi	4	1/320	1/80
௪௰		[illegible]	Araikkāl	40	1/320	1/8
௪௱		[illegible]	Oṉṉē kāl	400	1/320	1 + ¼
௫		[illegible]	Kāṇiyē araikkāṇi	5	1/320	1/80 + 1/320
௫௰		[illegible]	Mummāvē araikkāṇi	50	1/320	3/20 + 1/160
௫௱		[illegible]	Oṉnaraiyē mākāṇi	500	1/320	1 + ½ + 1/20 + 1/80
௬		[illegible]	Kāṇiyē araikkāṇi	6	1/320	1/80 + 1/160
௬௰		[illegible]	Mummāvē Mukkāṇi	60	1/320	3/20 + 3/80
௬௱		[illegible]	Oṉṉē Mukkālē araikkāl	600	1/320	1 + ¾ + 1/8
௭		[illegible]	Kāṇiyē araikkāṇiyē muntiri	7	1/320	1/80 + 1/160 + 1/320
௭௰		[illegible]	Nālumāvē kāṇiyē araikkāṇi	70	1/320	4/20 + 1/80 + 1/160
௭௱		[illegible]	Iraṇṭē mummāvē Mukkāṇi	700	1/320	2 + 3/20 + 3/80
௮		[illegible]	Araimā	8	1/320	1/40
௮௰		[illegible]	Kāl	80	1/320	¼
௮௱		[illegible]	Iraṇṭarai	800	1/320	2 + ½

௯	[illegible]	[illegible]	Araimāve muntiri	9	1/320	1/40 + 1/320
௯௰		[illegible]	Kālē Araimāve araikkāṇi	90	1/320	¼ + 1/40 + 1/160
௯௱		[illegible]	Iraṇṭē Mukkālē makāṇi	900	1/320	2 + ¾ + 1/20 + 1/80
௲		[illegible]	Mūṉṟē araikkāl	1000	1/320	3 + 1/8
Malarpattu pōteṭṭu vāṉirampavāka vilai nānkē kompiraṇṭē vēroṉṟē vērin mutaloṉṟē muntiri vāikku Alakunilai . . . [illegible]				Cumulative product = 18 + ½ + 4/20+ 1/40 + 1/160 + 1/320		
௧	[illegible]	[illegible]	Araikkāṇi	1	1/160	1/160
௰		[illegible]	Oru mākāṇi	10	1/160	1/20 + 1/80
௱		[illegible]	Araiyē araikkāl	100	1/160	½ + 1/8
௨		[illegible]	Kāṇi	2	1/160	1/80
௨௰		[illegible]	Araikkāl	20	1/160	1/8
௨௱		[illegible]	Oṉṉē kāl	200	1/160	1 + ¼
௩		[illegible]	Kāṇiye araikkāṇi	3	1/160	1/80 + 1/160
௩௰		[illegible]	Mummākāṇi	30	1/160	3/20 + 3/80
௩௱		[illegible]	Oṉṉē Mukkālē araikkāl	300	1/160	1 + ¾ + 1/8
௪		[illegible]	Araimā	4	1/160	1/40
௪௰		[illegible]	Kāl	40	1/160	¼
௪௱		[illegible]	Iraṇṭarai	400	1/160	2 + ½
௫		[illegible]	Araimāve araikkāṇi	5	1/160	1/40 + 1/160
௫௰		[illegible]	Kālē Orumākāṇi	50	1/160	¼ + 1/20 + 1/80
௫௱		[illegible]	Mūṉṟē araikkāl	500	1/160	3 + 1/8
௬		[illegible]	Mukkāṇi	6	1/160	3/80
௬௰		[illegible]	Kālē araikkāl	60	1/160	¼ + 1/8
௬௱		[illegible]	Mūṉṟē mukkāl	600	1/160	3 + ¾
௭		[illegible]	Mukkāṇiyē araikkāṇi	7	1/160	3/80 + 1/160
௭௰		[illegible]	Kālē mummākāṇi	70	1/160	¼ + 3/20 + 3/80

[illegible]		[illegible]	Nālē Kālē araikkāl	700	1/160	4 + ¼ + 1/8
[illegible]		[illegible]	Orumā	8	1/160	1/20
[illegible]		[illegible]	Arai	80	1/160	½
[illegible]		[illegible]	Aintu	800	1/160	5
[illegible]		[illegible]	Orumāve araikkāṇi	9	1/160	1/20 + 1/160
[illegible]		[illegible]	Araiyē Orumākāṇi	90	1/160	½ + 1/20 + 1/80
[illegible]		[illegible]	Aintaraiyē araikkāl	900	1/160	5 + ½ + 1/8
[illegible]		[illegible]	ārēkāl	1000	1/160	6 + ¼
āraintu pūviṉ akattin āṟēḻkōṭṭai kāloṉṟu *Eḻilār kali nāṉkeṉum kaliyiṉ pūvoṉṟē* *pūvilaiyum oṉṟu* *Alakunilai* . . . . [illegible]				Cumulative product = 37 + ¼ + 4/20 + 1/80 + 1/160		
[illegible]	[illegible]	[illegible]	Kāṇi	1	1/80	1/80
[illegible]		[illegible]	Araikkāl	10	1/80	1/8
[illegible]		[illegible]	Oṉṉē kāl	100	1/80	1 + ¼
[illegible]		[illegible]	Araimā	2	1/80	1/40
[illegible]		[illegible]	Kāl	20	1/80	¼
[illegible]		[illegible]	Iraṇṭarai	200	1/80	2 + ½
[illegible]		[illegible]	Mukkāṇi	3	1/80	3/80
[illegible]		[illegible]	Kālē araikkāl	30	1/80	¼ + 1/8
[illegible]		[illegible]	Mūṉṟē mukkāl	300	1/80	3 + ¾
[illegible]		[illegible]	Orumā	4	1/80	1/20
[illegible]		[illegible]	Arai	40	1/80	½
[illegible]		[illegible]	Aintu	400	1/80	5
[illegible]		[illegible]	Oru mākāṇi	5	1/80	1/20 + 1/80
[illegible]		[illegible]	Araiyē araikkāl	50	1/80	½ + 1/8
[illegible]		[illegible]	ārē kāl	500	1/80	6 + ¼
[illegible]		[illegible]	Orumāvē Araimā	6	1/80	1/20 + 1/40
[illegible]		[illegible]	Mukkāl	60	1/80	¾

௬௱	[illegible]	[illegible]	Ē<u>l</u>arai	600	1/80	7 + ½
௭		[illegible]	Orumāvē Mukkāṇi	7	1/80	1/20 + 3/80
௭௰		[illegible]	Mukkālē araikkāl	70	1/80	¾ + 1/8
௭௱		[illegible]	Eṭṭē mukkāl	700	1/80	8 + ¾
௮		[illegible]	Irumā	8	1/80	2/20
௮௰		௧	Oṉṟu	80	1/80	1
௮௱		௰	Pattu	800	1/80	10
௯		[illegible]	Irumā kāṇi	9	1/80	2/20+ 1/80
௯௰		[illegible]	Oṉṉē araikkāl	90	1/80	1 + 1/8
௯௱		[illegible]	Patiṉoṉṟē kāl	900	1/80	11 + ¼
௲		[illegible]	Paṉṉiraṇṭarai	1000	1/80	12 + ½
E<u>l</u>upatinmar kaṉṉiyarkaḷ nāṉkā malaiccār mulai kunippār mukkaṇṇār Mūṉṟēyum pāṭuvare niṉṟeṟiyuṅkōṉ mūṉṟu *Alakunilai* . . . . [illegible]				Cumulative product = 74 + ¾ + 3/20 + 3/80		
௧	[illegible]	[illegible]	Araimā	1	1/40	1/40
௰		[illegible]	Kāl	10	1/40	¼
௱		[illegible]	Iraṇṭarai	100	1/40	2 + ½
௨		[illegible]	Orumā	2	1/40	1/20
௨௰		[illegible]	Arai	20	1/40	½
௨௱		௫	Aintu	200	1/40	5
௩		[illegible]	Orumāve Araimā	3	1/40	1/20 + 1/40
௩௰		[illegible]	Mukkāl	30	1/40	¾
௩௱		[illegible]	ē<u>l</u>arai	300	1/40	7 + ½
௪		[illegible]	Irumā	4	1/40	2/20
௪௰		௧	Oṉṟu	40	1/40	1
௪௱		௰	Pattu	400	1/40	10
௫		[illegible]	Araikkāl	5	1/40	1/8
௫௰		[illegible]	Oṉṉē kāl	50	1/40	1 + ¼

௫௱	சு	௰௨?	Pannirantarai	500	1/40	12 + ½
௬		ஹ	Mummā	6	1/40	3/20
௬௰		௧?	Onnarai	60	1/40	1 + ½
௬௱		௰௫	Patinaintu	600	1/40	15
௭		ஹசு	Mummāve Orumā	7	1/40	3/20 + 1/20
௭௰		௧ஞ	Onnē mukkāl	70	1/40	1 + ¾
௭௱		௰௭?	Patinēḷarai	700	1/40	17 + ½
௮		நா	Nālumā	8	1/40	4/20
௮௰		௨	Iraṇṭu	80	1/40	2
௮௱		௨௰	Irupatu	800	1/40	20
௯		நாசு	Nālumāve Araimā	9	1/40	4/20 + 1/40
௯௰		௨வ	Iraṇṭēkāl	90	1/40	2 + ¼
௯௱		௨௰௨?	Irupattu iraṇṭarai	900	1/40	22 + ½
௲		௨௰௫	Irupattu aintu	1000	1/40	25
Nūrruvar nālvētam ōta marronpatinmar vēṭṭārē *munnāḷ akattirukkāl nīrkoṇṭu vērraraikkāl* *vāi pūcā ninru* *Alakunilai - - - -* ௱௪௰௯ஞஆ				Cumulative product = 149 + ¾ + 1/8		
௧	கூ	கூ	Mukkāṇi	1	3/80	3/80
௰		வஆ	Kālē araikkāṇi	10	3/80	¼ + 1/8
௱		௩ஞ	Mūnrē mukkāl	100	3/80	3 + ¾
௨		பசு	Orumāve Araimā	2	3/80	1/20 + 1/40
௨௰		ஞ	Mukkāl	20	3/80	¾
௨௱		௭?	ēḷarai	200	3/80	7 + ½
௩		௨8	Irumāve orukāṇi	3	3/80	2/20 + 1/80
௩௰		௧ஆ	Onnē araikkāl	30	3/80	1 + 1/8
௩௱		௰௧வ	Patinonrē kāl	300	3/80	11 + ¼
௪		ஹ	Mummā	4	3/80	3/20
௪௰		௧?	Onnarai	40	3/80	1 + ½

[illegible]	[illegible]	[illegible]	Patiṉaintu	400	3/80	15
[illegible]		[illegible]	Mummākāṇi	5	3/80	3/20 + 3/80
[illegible]		[illegible]	Oṉṉē Mukkālē araikkāl	50	3/80	1 + ¾ + 1/8
[illegible]		[illegible]	Patiṉeṭṭē mukkāl	500	3/80	18 + ¾
[illegible]		[illegible]	Nālumāve Araimā	6	3/80	4/20 + 1/40
[illegible]		[illegible]	Iraṇṭēkāl	60	3/80	2 + ¼
[illegible]		[illegible]	Irupattu iraṇṭarai	600	3/80	22 + ½
[illegible]		[illegible]	Kālē kāṇi	7	3/80	¼ + 1/80
[illegible]		[illegible]	Iraṇṭaraiyē araikkāl	70	3/80	2 + ½ + 1/8
[illegible]		[illegible]	Irupattu āṟēkāl	700	3/80	26 + ¼
[illegible]		[illegible]	Kālē Orumā	8	3/80	¼ + 1/20
[illegible]		[illegible]	Mūṉṟu	80	3/80	3
[illegible]		[illegible]	Muppatu	800	3/80	30
[illegible]		[illegible]	Kālē Orumāve Mukkāṇi	9	3/80	¼ + 1/20 + 3/80
[illegible]		[illegible]	Mūṉṟē Kālē araikkāl	90	3/80	3 + ¼ + 1/8
[illegible]		[illegible]	Muppattu Mūṉṟē mukkāl	900	3/80	33 + ¾
[illegible]		[illegible]	Muppattu ēḻarai	1000	3/80	37 + 1/2
Nālaimpataṉṉai irupattu nālvarkku nīrōṭu mukkāl koṭuttārē māvōṭu kāṇi kaṭai niṉṟatoṉṟu Alakunilai . . . . [illegible]				Cumulative product = 224 + ¾ + 1/20 + 1/80		
[illegible]	[illegible]	[illegible]	Orumā	1	1/20	1/20
[illegible]		[illegible]	Arai	10	1/20	½
[illegible]		[illegible]	Aintu	100	1/20	5
[illegible]		[illegible]	Irumā	2	1/20	2/20
[illegible]		[illegible]	Oṉṟu	20	1/20	1

[illegible]	[illegible]	[illegible]	Pattu	200	1/20	10
[illegible]		[illegible]	Mummā	3	1/20	3/20
[illegible]		[illegible]	Oṉṉarai	30	1/20	1 + ½
[illegible]		[illegible]	Patiṉaintu	300	1/20	15
[illegible]		[illegible]	Nālumā	4	1/20	4/20
[illegible]		[illegible]	Iraṇṭu	40	1/20	2
[illegible]		[illegible]	Irupatu	400	1/20	20
[illegible]		[illegible]	Kāl	5	1/20	¼
[illegible]		[illegible]	Iraṇṭarai	50	1/20	2 + ½
[illegible]		[illegible]	Irupattu aintu	500	1/20	25
[illegible]		[illegible]	Kālē Orumā	6	1/20	¼ + 1/20
[illegible]		[illegible]	Mūṉṟu	60	1/20	3
[illegible]		[illegible]	Muppatu	600	1/20	30
[illegible]		[illegible]	Kālē Irumā	7	1/20	¼ + 2/20
[illegible]		[illegible]	Mūṉṟarai	70	1/20	3 + ½
[illegible]		[illegible]	Muppattu aintu	700	1/20	35
[illegible]		[illegible]	Kālē mummā	8	1/20	¼ + 3/20
[illegible]		[illegible]	Nāṉku	80	1/20	4
[illegible]		[illegible]	Nāṟpatu	800	1/20	40
[illegible]		[illegible]	Kālē nālumā	9	1/20	¼ + 4/20
[illegible]		[illegible]	Nālarai	90	1/20	4 + ½
[illegible]		[illegible]	Nāṟpattu aintu	900	1/20	45
[illegible]		[illegible]	Aimpatu	1000	1/20	50
Kuñcarantām iraṇṭu toṇṇūṟṟoṭūra maṟṟoṉpatiṉmar kāl kāppuc celvarē mūṉṟēyum vanta toḻutu Alakunilai . . .				Cumulative product = 299 + ¾		
[illegible]	[illegible]	[illegible]	Mākāṇi	1	1/20 + 1/80	1/20 + 1/80
[illegible]		[illegible]	Araiyē araikkāl	10	1/20 + 1/80	½ + 1/8
[illegible]		[illegible]	Āṟē kāl	100	1/20 + 1/80	6 + ¼

௨	[illegible]	[illegible]	Araikkāl	2	1/20 + 1/80	1/8
௨௰		[illegible]	Oṉṉē kāl	20	1/20 + 1/80	1 + ¼
௨௱		[illegible]	Paṉṉiraṇṭarai	200	1/20 + 1/80	12 + ½
௩		[illegible]	Mummākāṇi	3	1/20 + 1/80	3/20 + 3/80
௩௰		[illegible]	Oṉṉē Mukkālē araikkāl	30	1/20 + 1/80	1 + ¾ + 1/8
௩௱		[illegible]	Patiṉeṭṭē mukkāl	300	1/20 + 1/80	18 + ¾
௪		[illegible]	Kāl	4	1/20 + 1/80	¼
௪௰		[illegible]	Iraṇṭarai	40	1/20 + 1/80	2 + ½
௪௱		[illegible]	Irupattu aintu	400	1/20 + 1/80	25
௫		[illegible]	Kālē mākāṇi	5	1/20 + 1/80	¼ + 1/20 + 1/80
௫௰		[illegible]	Mūṉṟē araikkāl	50	1/20 + 1/80	3 + 1/8
௫௱		[illegible]	Muppattu Oṉṟēkāl	500	1/20 + 1/80	31 + ¼
௬		[illegible]	Kālē araikkāl	6	1/20 + 1/80	¼ + 1/8
௬௰		[illegible]	Mūṉṟē mukkāl	60	1/20 + 1/80	3 + ¾
௬௱		[illegible]	Muppattu ēḻarai	600	1/20 + 1/80	37 + ½
௭		[illegible]	Kālē mummākāṇi	7	1/20 + 1/80	¼ + 3/20 + 3/80
௭௰		[illegible]	Nālē kālē araikkāl	70	1/20 + 1/80	4 + ¼ + 1/8
௭௱		[illegible]	Nāṟpattu mūṉṟē mukkāl	700	1/20 + 1/80	43 + ¾
௮		[illegible]	Arai	8	1/20 + 1/80	½
௮௰		[illegible]	Aintu	80	1/20 + 1/80	5
௮௱		[illegible]	Aimpatu	800	1/20 + 1/80	50
௯		[illegible]	Araiyē mākāṇi	9	1/20 + 1/80	½ + 1/20 + 1/80
௯௰		[illegible]	Aintaraiyē araikkāl	90	1/20 + 1/80	5 + ½ + 1/8
௯௱		[illegible]	Aimpattu āṟē kāl	900	1/20 + 1/80	56 + ¼
௲		[illegible]	Aṟupattu iraṇṭarai	1000	1/20 + 1/80	62 + ½
Muppuri nūṉmārpar eḻupatiṉmar nālvētan takkāṅku irukāliṟ koḷvarē muppoḻutu mūṉṟēyum vanta toḻutu Alakunilai .... [illegible]				Cumulative product = 374 + ½ + 3/20 + 3/80		
௧	[illegible]	[illegible]	Irumā	1	2/20	2/20

௰	[illegible]	௧	Oṉṟu	10	2/20	1
௱		௰	Pattu	100	2/20	10
௨		[illegible]	Nālumā	2	2/20	4/20
௨௰		௨	Iraṇṭu	20	2/20	2
௨௱		௨௰	Irupatu	200	2/20	20
௩		[illegible]	Kālē Orumā	3	2/20	¼ + 1/20
௩௰		௩	Mūṉṟu	30	2/20	3
௩௱		௩௰	Muppatu	300	2/20	30
௪		[illegible]	Kālē mummā	4	2/20	¼ + 3/20
௪௰		௪	Nāṉku	40	2/20	4
௪௱		௪௰	Nāṟpatu	400	2/20	40
௫		[illegible]	Arai	5	2/20	½
௫௰		௫	Aintu	50	2/20	5
௫௱		௫௰	Aimpatu	500	2/20	50
௬		[illegible]	Araiyē Irumā	6	2/20	1/2 + 2/20
௬௰		௬	Āṟu	60	2/20	6
௬௱		௬௰	Aṟupatu	600	2/20	60
௭		[illegible]	Araiyē nālumā	7	2/20	½ + 4/20
௭௰		௭	ēḻu	70	2/20	7
௭௱		௭௰	Eḻupatu	700	2/20	70
௮		[illegible]	Mukkālē Orumā	8	2/20	¾ + 1/20
௮௰		௮	Eṭṭu	80	2/20	8
௮௱		௮௰	Eṇpatu	800	2/20	80
௯		[illegible]	Mukkālē mummā	9	2/20	¾ + 3/20
௯௰		௯	Oṉpatu	90	2/20	9
௯௱		௯௰	Toṇṇūṟu	900	2/20	90
௲		௱	Nūṟu	1000	2/20	100
Aṅkayattu toṇṇūṟu ceṅkaḻunīr oṉpatiṉmar koḷvār irukāl paṟittu Alakunilai .... [illegible]				Cumulative product = 599 + ½		

௧	ஒரு	ஒரு	Araikkāl	1	1/8	1/8
௰		கவ	Onnē kāl	10	1/8	1 + ¼
௱		௰௨?	Panniranṭarai	100	1/8	12 + ½
௨		வ	Kāl	2	1/8	¼
௨௰		௨?	Iranṭarai	20	1/8	2 + ½
௨௱		௨௰௫	Irupattu aintu	200	1/8	25
௩		வஒரு	Kālē araikkāl	3	1/8	¼ + 1/8
௩௰		௩௯	Mūnrē mukkāl	30	1/8	3 + ¾
௩௱		௩௰௭?	Muppattu ēlarai	300	1/8	37 + ½
௪		?	Arai	4	1/8	½
௪௰		௫	Aintu	40	1/8	5
௪௱		௫௰	Aimpatu	400	1/8	50
௫		?ஒரு	Araiyē araikkāl	5	1/8	½ + 1/8
௫௰		௬வ	Ārē kāl	50	1/8	6 + ¼
௫௱		௬௰௨?	Arupattu iranṭarai	500	1/8	62 + ½
௬		௯	Mukkāl	6	1/8	¾
௬௰		௭?	ēlarai	60	1/8	7 + ½
௬௱		௭௰௫	Elupattu aintu	600	1/8	75
௭		௯ஒரு	Mukkālē araikkāl	7	1/8	¾ + 1/8
௭௰		௮௯	Eṭṭe mukkāl	70	1/8	8 + ¾
௭௱		௮௰௭?	Eṇpattu ēlarai	700	1/8	87 + ½
௮		௧	Onru	8	1/8	1
௮௰		௰	Pattu	80	1/8	10
௮௱		௱	Nūru	800	1/8	100
௯		கஒரு	Onnē araikkāl	9	1/8	1 + 1/8
௯௰		௰கவ	Patinonrē kāl	90	1/8	11+ ¼
௯௱		௱௰௨?	Nūrru pannirantarai	900	1/8	112 + ½
௲		௱௨௰௫	Nūrru irupattu aintu	1000	1/8	125
Viḷakkē eḻuvar variviḷakkē kaikūppi nālvar iruntu viḷaiyāṭa marronpatinmar kālic				Cumulative product = 749 + ¼ + 1/8		

catirāi varuvarē māviraṇṭuṅ kāṉiraṇṭuṅ kaṇṭariṉ toṉṟu Alakunilai, . . . [illegible]						
[illegible]	[illegible]	[illegible]	Mummā	1	3/20	3/20
[illegible]		[illegible]	Oṉṟarai	10	3/20	1 + ½
[illegible]		[illegible]	Patiṉaintu	100	3/20	15
[illegible]		[illegible]	Kālē Orumā	2	3/20	¼ + 1/20
[illegible]		[illegible]	Mūṉṟu	20	3/20	3
[illegible]		[illegible]	Muppatu	200	3/20	30
[illegible]		[illegible]	Kālē nālumā	3	3/20	¼ + 4/20
[illegible]		[illegible]	Nālarai	30	3/20	4 + ½
[illegible]		[illegible]	Nāṟpattu aintu	300	3/20	45
[illegible]		[illegible]	Araiyē Irumā	4	3/20	½ + 2/20
[illegible]		[illegible]	Āṟu	40	3/20	6
[illegible]		[illegible]	Aṟupatu	400	3/20	60
[illegible]		[illegible]	Mukkāl	5	3/20	¾
[illegible]		[illegible]	Ēḻarai	50	3/20	7 + ½
[illegible]		[illegible]	Eḻupattu aintu	500	3/20	75
[illegible]		[illegible]	Mukkālē mummā	6	3/20	¾ + 3/20
[illegible]		[illegible]	Oṉpatu	60	3/20	9
[illegible]		[illegible]	Toṇṇūṟu	600	3/20	90
[illegible]		[illegible]	Oṉṟē Orumā	7	3/20	1 + 1/20
[illegible]		[illegible]	Pattarai	70	3/20	10 + ½
[illegible]		[illegible]	Nūṟṟu aintu	700	3/20	105
[illegible]		[illegible]	Oṉṟē nālumā	8	3/20	1 + 4/20
[illegible]		[illegible]	Paṉṉiraṇṭu	80	3/20	12
[illegible]		[illegible]	Nūṟṟu irupatu	800	3/20	120
[illegible]		[illegible]	Oṉṉē Kālē nālumā	9	3/20	1 + ¼ + 2/20
[illegible]		[illegible]	Patiṉmūṉṟarai	90	3/20	13 + ½
[illegible]		[illegible]	Nūṟṟu Muppattu	900	3/20	135

			aintu			
௲	[illegible]	௱௫௰	Nūṟṟu aimpatu	1000	3/20	150
Eṇṇūṟṟuttoṇṇūṟu pūmalarkoṇṭu oṉpatiṉmar viṇṇuvār mukkuṭaikkīḻ vīraṉaṭi toḻuvār naṇṇuvār kālāl naṭantu Alakunilai . . . . [illegible]				Cumulative product = 899 + 1/4		
௧	[illegible]	[illegible]	Mummākāṇi	1	3/20 + 3/80	3/20 + 3/80
௰		[illegible]	Oṉṉē Mukkālē araikkāl	10	3/20 + 3/80	1 + ¾ + 1/8
௱		[illegible]	Patineṭṭē mukkāl	100	3/20 + 3/80	18 + ¾
௨		[illegible]	Kālē araikkāl	2	3/20 + 3/80	¼ + 1/8
௨௰		[illegible]	Mūṉṟē mukkāl	20	3/20 + 3/80	3 + ¾
௨௱		[illegible]	Muppattu ēḻarai	200	3/20 + 3/80	37 + ½
௩		[illegible]	Araiyē Orumā kāṇi	3	3/20 + 3/80	½ + 1/20 + 1/80
௩௰		[illegible]	Aintaraiyē araikkāl	30	3/20 + 3/80	5 + ½ + 1/8
௩௱		[illegible]	Aimpattu āṟē kāl	300	3/20 + 3/80	56 + ¼
௪		[illegible]	Mukkāl	4	3/20 + 3/80	¾
௪௰		[illegible]	Ēḻarai	40	3/20 + 3/80	7 + ½
௪௱		[illegible]	Eḻupattu aintu	400	3/20 + 3/80	75
௫		[illegible]	Mukkālē mummākāṇi	5	3/20 + 3/80	¾ + 3/20 + 3/80
௫௰		[illegible]	Oṉpatē Kālē araikkāl	50	3/20 + 3/80	9 + ¼ + 1/8
௫௱		[illegible]	Toṇṇūṟṟu Mūṉṟē mukkāl	500	3/20 + 3/80	93 + ¾
௬		[illegible]	Oṉṉē araikkāl	6	3/20 + 3/80	1 + 1/8
௬௰		[illegible]	Patiṉoṉṟē kāl	60	3/20 + 3/80	11 + ¼
௬௱		[illegible]	Nūṟṟu paṉṉiraṇṭarai	600	3/20 + 3/80	112 + ½
௭		[illegible]	Oṉṉē Kālē oru mākāṇi	7	3/20 + 3/80	1 + ¼ + 1/20 + 1/80
௭௰		[illegible]	Patiṉmūṉṟē araikkāl	70	3/20 + 3/80	13 + 1/8
௭௱		[illegible]	Nūṟṟu Muppattu Oṉṟē kāl	700	3/20 + 3/80	131 + ¼
௮		[illegible]	Oṉṉarai	8	3/20 + 3/80	1 + ½

௮௰	[illegible]	௰௫	Patiṉaintu	80	3/20 + 3/80	15
௮௱		௱௫௰	Nūṟṟu aimpatu	800	3/20 + 3/80	150
௯		௧ [illegible]	Oṉṉē Araiyē mummākāṇi	9	3/20 + 3/80	1 + ½ + 3/20 + 3/80
௯௰		௰௬ [illegible]	Patiṉāṟē Mukkālē araikkāl	90	3/20 + 3/80	16 + ¾ + 1/8
௯௱		௱௬௰௮ [illegible]	Nūṟṟu aṟupattu eṭṭē mukkāl	900	3/20 + 3/80	168 + ¾
௲		௱௮௰௭ [illegible]	Nūṟṟu eṇpattu ēḻarai	1000	3/20 + 3/80	187 + ½
Koṅkoṉṟu nūṟṟuvar ēṟiṉār maṟṟataṉkīḻ nālaintu nāṉkumē āyiliyam pūviliya mākāṇi ākiviṭum Alakunilai. . . . ௲௱௨௰௪ [illegible]				Cumulative product = 1124 + 1/20 + 1/80		
௧	[illegible]	[illegible]	Nālumā	1	4/20	4/20
௰		௨	Iraṇṭu	10	4/20	2
௱		௨௰	Irupatu	100	4/20	20
௨		[illegible]	Kālē mummā	2	4/20	¼ + 3/20
௨௰		௪	Nāṉku	20	4/20	4
௨௱		௪௰	Nāṟpatu	200	4/20	40
௩		[illegible]	Araiyē Irumā	3	4/20	½ + 2/20
௩௰		௬	Āṟu	30	4/20	6
௩௱		௬௰	Aṟupatu	300	4/20	60
௪		[illegible]	Mukkālē Orumā	4	4/20	¾ + 1/20
௪௰		௮	Eṭṭu	40	4/20	8
௪௱		௮௰	Eṇpatu	400	4/20	80
௫		௧	Oṉṟu	5	4/20	1
௫௰		௰	Pattu	50	4/20	10
௫௱		௱	Nūṟu	500	4/20	100
௬		௧ [illegible]	Oṉṉē nālumā	6	4/20	1 + 4/20
௬௰		௰௨	Paṉṉiraṇṭu	60	4/20	12

[illegible]	[illegible]	[illegible]	Nūṟṟu irupatu	600	4/20	120
[illegible]		[illegible]	Oṉṉē Kālē mummā	7	4/20	1 + ¼ + 3/20
[illegible]		[illegible]	Patiṉāṉku	70	4/20	14
[illegible]		[illegible]	Nūṟṟu nāṟpatu	700	4/20	140
[illegible]		[illegible]	Oṉṉaraiyē Irumā	8	4/20	1 + ½ + 2/20
[illegible]		[illegible]	Patiṉāṟu	80	4/20	16
[illegible]		[illegible]	Nūṟṟu aṟupatu	800	4/20	160
[illegible]		[illegible]	Oṉṉē Mukkālē Orumā	9	4/20	1 + ¾ + 1/20
[illegible]		[illegible]	Patiṉeṭṭu	90	4/20	18
[illegible]		[illegible]	Nūṟṟu eṇpatu	900	4/20	180
[illegible]		[illegible]	Irunūṟu	1000	4/20	200
Kuḷam oṉṟu nīrpom maṭai oṉṟu ataṉkīḻ nilamaḷantār toṇṇūṟṟōṭūra maṟṟoṉpatiṉmar āttāḷ kaṭai neṟi kāṭciyavar Alakunilai . . . [illegible]				Cumulative product = 1199		
[illegible]	[illegible]	[illegible]	Kāl	1	1/4	¼
[illegible]		[illegible]	Iraṇṭarai	10	1/4	2 + ½
[illegible]		[illegible]	Irupattu aintu	100	1/4	25
[illegible]		[illegible]	Arai	2	1/4	½
[illegible]		[illegible]	Aintu	20	1/4	5
[illegible]		[illegible]	Aimpatu	200	1/4	50
[illegible]		[illegible]	Mukkāl	3	1/4	¾
[illegible]		[illegible]	Ēḻarai	30	1/4	7 + ½
[illegible]		[illegible]	Eḻupattu aintu	300	1/4	75
[illegible]		[illegible]	Oṉṟu	4	1/4	1
[illegible]		[illegible]	Pattu	40	1/4	10
[illegible]		[illegible]	Nūṟu	400	1/4	100
[illegible]		[illegible]	Oṉṉē kāl	5	1/4	1 + ¼
[illegible]		[illegible]	Paṉṉiraṇṭarai	50	1/4	12 + ½

[illegible]	[illegible]	[illegible]	Nūṟṟu irupattu aintu	500	1/4	125
[illegible]		[illegible]	Oṉṉarai	6	1/4	1 + ½
[illegible]		[illegible]	Patiṉaintu	60	1/4	15
[illegible]		[illegible]	Nūṟṟu aimpatu	600	1/4	150
[illegible]		[illegible]	Oṉṉē mukkāl	7	1/4	1 + ¾
[illegible]		[illegible]	Patiṉēḻarai	70	1/4	17 + ½
[illegible]		[illegible]	Nūṟṟu eḻupattu aintu	700	1/4	175
[illegible]		[illegible]	Iraṇṭu	8	1/4	2
[illegible]		[illegible]	Irupatu	80	1/4	20
[illegible]		[illegible]	Irunūṟu	800	1/4	200
[illegible]		[illegible]	Iraṇṭēkāl	9	1/4	2 + ¼
[illegible]		[illegible]	Irupattu iraṇṭarai	90	1/4	22 + ½
[illegible]		[illegible]	Irunūṟṟu irupattu aintu	900	1/4	225
[illegible]		[illegible]	Irunūṟṟu aimpatu	1000	1/4	250
Ayvaḷai nallāḷ orutti avaḷukkut tōḻimār nālvar toṭuttapūt toṇṇūṟu nāliraṇṭē koḷḷumān talaiyaḷavē pūcumāñ cāntukku mukkāl vilai Alakunilai.... [illegible]				Cumulative product = 1498 + ¾		
[illegible]	[illegible]	[illegible]	Arai	1	1/2	½
[illegible]		[illegible]	Aintu	10	1/2	5
[illegible]		[illegible]	Aimpatu	100	1/2	50
[illegible]		[illegible]	Oṉṟu	2	1/2	1
[illegible]		[illegible]	Pattu	20	1/2	10
[illegible]		[illegible]	Nūṟu	200	1/2	100
[illegible]		[illegible]	Oṉṉarai	3	1/2	1 + ½
[illegible]		[illegible]	Patiṉaintu	30	1/2	15
[illegible]		[illegible]	Nūṟṟu aimpatu	300	1/2	150

௪		௨	Iraṇṭu	4	1/2	2
௪௰		௨௰	Irupatu	40	1/2	20
௪௱		௨௱	Irunūṟu	400	1/2	200
௫		௨½	Iraṇṭarai	5	1/2	2 + ½
௫௰		௨௰௫	Irupattu aintu	50	1/2	25
௫௱		௨௱௫௰	Irunūṟṟu aimpatu	500	1/2	250
௬		௩	Mūṉṟu	6	1/2	3
௬௰		௩௰	Muppatu	60	1/2	30
௬௱		௩௱	Munnūṟu	600	1/2	300
௭		௩½	Mūṉṟarai	7	1/2	3 + ½
௭௰		௩௰௫	Muppattu aintu	70	1/2	35
௭௱		௩௱௫௰	Munnūṟṟu aimpatu	700	1/2	350
௮		௪	Nāṉku	8	1/2	4
௮௰		௪௰	Nāṟpatu	80	1/2	40
௮௱		௪௱	Nāṉūṟu	800	1/2	400
௯		௪½	Nālarai	9	1/2	4 + ½
௯௰		௪௰௫	Nāṟpattu aintu	90	1/2	45
௯௱		௪௱௫௰	Nāṉūṟṟu aimpatu	900	1/2	450
௲		௫௱	Ainūṟu	1000	1/2	500
Iraṇṭupūt toṇṇūṟu cākāṭu pūṇṭa malar paṇṭan toṇṇūṟu ceitatu kūliyām amarntatām ēḻarai vāikku Alakunilai ௨௲௯௱௯௰௭½				Cumulative product = 2997 + 1/2		
௧	¾	¾	Mukkāl	1	¾	¾
௰		௭½	Ēḻarai	10	¾	7 + ½
௱		௭௰௫	Eḻupattu aintu	100	¾	75
௨		௧½	Oṉṉarai	2	¾	1 + ½
௨௰		௰௫	Patiṉaintu	20	¾	15
௨௱		௱௫௰	Nūṟṟu aimpatu	200	¾	150
௩		௨¼	Iraṇṭēkāl	3	¾	2 + ¼

௩௰	¾	௨௰௨ ½	Irupattu iraṇṭarai	30	¾	22 + ½
௩௱		௨௱௨௰ ௫	Irunūṟṟu irupattu aintu	300	¾	225
௪		௩	Mūṉṟu	4	¾	3
௪௰		௩௰	Muppatu	40	¾	30
௪௱		௩௱	Munnūṟu	400	¾	300
௫		௩ ¾	Mūṉṟē mukkāl	5	¾	3 + ¾
௫௰		௩௰௭ ½	Muppattu ēḻarai	50	¾	37 + ½
௫௱		௩௱௭௰ ௫	Munnūṟṟu eḻupattu aintu	500	¾	375
௬		௪ ½	Nālarai	6	¾	4 + ½
௬௰		௪௰௫	Nāṟpattu aintu	60	¾	45
௬௱		௪௱௫௰	Nāṉūṟṟu aimpatu	600	¾	450
௭		௫ ¼	Aintēkāl	7	¾	5 + ¼
௭௰		௫௰௨ ½	Aimpattu iraṇṭarai	70	¾	52 + ½
௭௱		௫௱௨௰௫	Ainūṟṟu irupattu aintu	700	¾	525
௮		௬	Āṟu	8	¾	6
௮௰		௬௰	Aṟupatu	80	¾	60
௮௱		௬௱	Aṟunūṟu	800	¾	600
௯		௬ ¾	Āṟē mukkāl	9	¾	6 + ¾
௯௰		௬௰௭ ½	Aṟupattu ēḻarai	90	¾	67 + ½
௯௱		௬௱௭௰ ௫	Aṟunūṟṟu eḻupattu aintu	900	¾	675
௲		௭௱௫௰	Eḻunūṟṟu aimpatu	1000	¾	750
Nālvar kaṇikaiyar nāṉmāṭak kūṭalil tēroṉpatu ēṟit teruvē kaṭāvēṟi āṟāvāteṉṟu vilakkiṉāṉ cāletirē kāloṉṟu kaikoṇṭa toṉṟu Alakunilai . . . . ௪௲௪௱௯௰௬ ¼				Cumulative product = 4496 + 1/4		

Catiravāi				
	க	அம	1	80
	ஆ	காம	¾	60
	ஒ	சம	½	40
	வ	உம	¼	20
	ஸ	மகா	4/20	16
	ரூகூ	மரு	3/20 + 3/80	15
	ரூ	மஉ	3/20	12
	ஷு	ம	1/8	10
	ஐ	அ	2/20	8
	ப[illegible]	ரு	1/20 + 1/80	5
	ப	ச	1/20	4
	கூ	ஈ	3/80	3
	கு	உ	1/40	2
	[illegible]	க	1/80	1
	ஸ	ஒ	1/160	½
	ஒரு	வ	1/320	¼

Caturattai nāṟṟittut tāṉ vēṇṭum vāyāl
Etirā moḻinta poruḷai atirātē
Muntiri vāyil kaḻippaṉavum ākumē
Inta vacalap piṟappu
ōtiyavāyil oruvāit tokai taṉṉai
āriṉāl māṟi amainta poruḷ taṉṉai
Añciṉālāya payaṉ kaḷaiyat tōṉṟumē
Tuñcā alakunilai

Kīḻvāi ciṟṟilakkam

ஒத	ஒத	௨பஃ	Araiyē mākāṇi	¾	3/4	½ + 1/20 + 1/80
௨		வஜு	Kālē araikkāl	½	3/4	¼ + 1/8
வ		ஙுஜு	Mummākāṇi	¼	3/4	3/20 + 3/80
ஹ		ஙு	Mummā	4/20	3/4	3/20
ஙுஜு		ஃஜுவத	Irumāvē Mukkāṇiyē muntiri	3/20 +3/80	3/4	2/20+ 3/80 + 1/320
ஙு		ஃஃ	Irumāvē orukāṇi	3/20	3/4	2/20 + 1/80
ஜு		பஜுஎ	Orumāvē Mukkāṇiyē araikkāṇi	1/8	3/4	1/20 + 3/80 + 1/160
ஃ		பசு	Orumāvē Araimā	2/20	3/4	1/20 + 1/40
பஃ		ஜுஎவத	Mukkāṇiyē araikkāṇiyē muntiri	1/20 + 1/80	3/4	3/80 + 1/160 + 1/320
ப		ஜு	Mukkāṇi	1/20	3/4	3/80
ஜு		சுவத	Araimāvē muntiri	3/80	3/4	1/40 + 1/320
சு		ஃஎ	Kāṇiyē araikkāṇi	1/40	3/4	1/80 + 1/160
ஃ		எவத	Araikkāṇiyē muntiri	1/80	3/4	1/160 + 1/320
எ		வதகீ௨	Muntiriyē Kīḻ arai	1/160	3/4	1/320 + (1/320 x ½)
வத		கீஒத	Kīḻ mukkāl	1/320	3/4	1/320 (3/4)
௭	௨	வ	Kāl	½	1/2	¼
வ		ஜு	Araikkāl	¼	1/2	1/8
ஹ		ஃ	Irumā	4/20	1/2	2/20
ஙுஜு		பஜுஎ	Orumāvē Mukkāṇiyē araikkāṇi	3/20 + 3/80	1/2	1/20 + 3/80 + 1/160
ஙு		பசு	Orumāvē Araimā	3/20	1/2	1/20 + 1/40

[illegible]	?	ப8	Orumāvē orukāṇi	1/8	1/2	1/20 + 1/80
[illegible]		ப	Orumā	2/20	1/2	1/20
ப8		[illegible]	Araimāvē araikkāṇi	1/20 + 1/80	1/2	1/40 + 1/160
ப		கு	Araimā	1/20	1/2	1/40
[illegible]		[illegible]	Kāṇiyē araikkāṇi	3/80	1/2	1/80 + 1/160
கு		8	Kāṇi	1/40	1/2	1/80
8		[illegible]	araikkāṇi	1/80	1/2	1/160
[illegible]		[illegible]	Muntiri	1/160	1/2	1/320
[illegible]		[illegible]	Kīḻ arai	1/320	1/2	1/320 x 1/2
வ	வ	ப8	Mākāṇi	¼	1/4	1/20 + 1/80
[illegible]		ப	Orumā	4/20	1/4	1/20
[illegible]		[illegible]	Mukkāṇiyē araikkāṇiyē muntiri	3/20 + 3/80	1/4	3/80 + 1/160 + 1/320
[illegible]		[illegible]	Mukkāṇi	3/20	1/4	3/80
[illegible]		[illegible]	Araimāvē araikkāṇi	1/8	1/4	1/40 + 1/160
[illegible]		கு	Araimā	2/20	1/4	1/40
ப8		[illegible]	Orukāṇiyē muntiri	1/20 + 1/80	1/4	1/80 + 1/320
[illegible]		8	Kāṇi	1/20	1/4	1/80
[illegible]		[illegible]	Araikkāṇiyē muntiri	3/80	1/4	1/160 + 1/320
கு		[illegible]	Araikkāṇi	1/40	1/4	1/160
8		[illegible]	Muntiri	1/80	1/4	1/320
[illegible]		[illegible]	Kīḻ arai	1/160	1/4	1/320 (1/2)
[illegible]		[illegible]	Kīḻ kāl	1/320	1/4	1/320 (1/4)
[illegible]	[illegible]	[illegible]	Mukkāṇiyē Kīḻ Mukkālē Orumā	4/20	4/20	3/80 + 1/320 (3/4 + 1/20)
[illegible]		[illegible]	Mukkāṇi	3/20+3/80	4/20	3/80

[illegible]	[illegible]	[illegible]	Araimāvē muntiriyē Kīḻ Araiyē Irumā	3/20	4/20	1/40 + 1/320 + 1/320(1/2 + 2/20)
[illegible]		[illegible]	Araimā	1/8	4/20	1/40
[illegible]		[illegible]	Kāṇiyē araikkāṇiyē Kīḻ Kālē mummā	2/20	4/20	1/80 + 1/160 + 1/320(1/4 + 3/20)
[illegible]		[illegible]	Kāṇi	1/20+1/80	4/20	1/80
[illegible]		[illegible]	Araikkāṇiyē muntiriyē kīḻ nālumā	1/20	4/20	1/160 + 1/320 + 1/320 (4/20)
[illegible]		[illegible]	Araikkāṇiyē muntiriyē Kīḻ Kālē mummā	3/80	4/20	1/160 + 1/320 (1/4 + 3/20)
[illegible]		[illegible]	Muntiriyē Kīḻ Araiyē Irumā	1/40	4/20	1/320 + 1/320(1/2 + 2/20)
[illegible]		[illegible]	Kīḻ Mukkālē Orumā	1/80	4/20	1/320 (3/4 + 1/20)
[illegible]		[illegible]	Kīḻ Kālē mummā	1/160	4/20	1/320 (1/4 + 3/20)
[illegible]		[illegible]	Kīḻ nālumā	1/320	4/20	1/320 (4/20)
[illegible]	[illegible]	[illegible]	Araimāvē araikkāṇiyē muntiriyē Kīḻ kāl	3/20+3/80	3/20+3/80	1/40 + 1/160 + 1/320 + 1/320 (1/4)
[illegible]		[illegible]	Araimāvē muntiri	3/20	3/20+3/80	1/40 + 1/320
[illegible]		[illegible]	Kāṇiyē araikkāṇiyē muntiriyē Kīḻ arai	1/8	3/20+3/80	1/80 + 1/160 + 1/320 + 1/320 (1/2)
[illegible]		[illegible]	Kāṇiyē araikkāṇi	2/20	3/20+3/80	1/80 + 1/160
[illegible]		[illegible]	Araikkāṇiyē muntiriye Kīḻ mukkāl	1/20+1/80	3/20+3/80	1/160 + 1/320 + 1/320 (3/4)
[illegible]		[illegible]	Araikkāṇiyē muntiri	1/20	3/20+3/80	1/160 + 1/320
[illegible]		[illegible]	Araikkāṇiyē muntiriyē Kīḻ kāl	3/80	3/20+3/80	1/160 + 1/320 (1/4)

[illegible]	[illegible]	[illegible]	Muntiriyē Kīḻ arai	1/40	3/20+3/80	1/320 + 1/320(1/2)
[illegible]		[illegible]	Kīḻ mukkāl	1/80	3/20+3/80	1/320 (3/4)
[illegible]		[illegible]	Kīḻ Kālē araikkāl	1/160	3/20+3/80	1/320 (1/4 + 1/8)
[illegible]		[illegible]	Kīḻ mummākāṇi	1/320	3/20+3/80	1/320 (3/20 + 3/80)
[illegible]	[illegible]	[illegible]	Kāṇiyē araikkāṇiyē muntiriyē Kīḻ nālumā	3/20	3/20	1/80 + 1/160 + 1/320 + 1/320 (4/20)
[illegible]		[illegible]	Kāṇiyē araikkāṇi	1/8	3/20	1/80 + 1/160
[illegible]		[illegible]	Kāṇiyē Kīḻ Mukkālē Orumā	2/20	3/20	1/80 + 1/320 (3/4 + 1/20)
[illegible]		[illegible]	Araikkāṇiyē muntiri	1/20 + 1/80	3/20	1/160 + 1/320
[illegible]		[illegible]	Araikkāṇiyē Kīḻ Kālē mummā	1/20	3/20	1/160 + 1/320 (1/4 + 3/20)
[illegible]		[illegible]	Muntiriyē Kīḻ Mukkālē Orumā	3/80	3/20	1/320 + 1/320 (3/4 + 1/20)
[illegible]		[illegible]	Muntiriyē Kīḻ nālumā	1/40	3/20	1/320 + 1/320 (4/20)
[illegible]		[illegible]	Kīḻ Araiyē Irumā	1/80	3/20	1/320 (1/2 + 2/20)
[illegible]		[illegible]	Kīḻ Kālē Orumā	1/160	3/20	1/320 (1/4 + 1/20)
[illegible]		[illegible]	Kīḻ mummā	1/320	3/20	1/320 (3/20)
[illegible]	[illegible]	[illegible]	Kāṇiyē muntiri	1/8	1/8	1/80 + 1/320
[illegible]		[illegible]	Kāṇi	2/20	1/8	1/80
[illegible]		[illegible]	Araikkāṇiyē Kīḻ arai	1/20 + 1/80	1/8	1/160 + 1/320 (1/2)
[illegible]		[illegible]	Araikkāṇi	1/20	1/8	1/160

𑿆	𑿌	𑿀𑿔𑿑	Muntiriyē Kīḻ arai	3/80	1/8	1/320 + 1/320 (1/2)
𑿄		𑿀	Muntiri	1/40	1/8	1/320
𑿂		𑿔𑿑	Kīḻ arai	1/80	1/8	1/320 (1/2)
𑿁		𑿔𑿐	Kīḻ kāl	1/160	1/8	1/320 (1/4)
𑿀		𑿔𑿌	Kīḻ araikkāl	1/320	1/8	1/320 (1/8)
𑿋	𑿋	𑿁𑿀𑿔𑿏	Araikkāṇiyē muntiriye Kīḻ nālumā	2/20	2/20	1/160 + 1/320 + 1/320 (4/20)
𑿈𑿂		𑿁	Araikkāṇi	1/20 + 1/80	2/20	1/160
𑿈		𑿀𑿔𑿑𑿋	Muntiriyē Kīḻ Araiyē Irumā	1/20	2/20	1/320 + 1/320 (1/2 + 2/20)
𑿆		𑿀𑿔𑿏	Muntiriyē Kīḻ nālumā	3/80	2/20	1/320 + 1/320 (4/20)
𑿄		𑿔𑿓𑿈	Kīḻ Mukkālē Orumā	1/40	2/20	1/320 (3/4 + 1/20)
𑿂		𑿔𑿐𑿍	Kīḻ Kālē mummā	1/80	2/20	1/320 (1/4 + 3/20)
𑿁		𑿔𑿏	Kīḻ nālumā	1/160	2/20	1/320 (4/20)
𑿀		𑿔𑿋	Kīḻ Irumā	1/320	2/20	1/320 (2/20)
𑿈𑿂	𑿈𑿂	𑿀𑿔𑿐	Muntiriyē Kīḻ kāl	1/20 +1 /80	1/20 + 1/80	1/320 + 1/320 (1/4)
𑿈		𑿀	Muntiri	1/20	1/20 + 1/80	1/320
𑿆		𑿔𑿓	Kīḻ mukkāl	3/80	1/20 + 1/80	1/320 (3/4)
𑿄		𑿔𑿑	Kīḻ arai	1/40	1/20 + 1/80	1/320 (1/2)
𑿂		𑿔𑿐	Kīḻ kāl	1/80	1/20 + 1/80	1/320 (1/4)
𑿁		𑿔𑿌	Kīḻ araikkāl	1/160	1/20 + 1/80	1/320 (1/8)
𑿀		𑿔𑿈𑿂	Kīḻ mākāṇi	1/320	1/20 + 1/80	1/320 (1/20 + 1/80)

𑿈	𑿈	𑿔𑿓𑿈	Kīḻ Mukkālē Orumā	1/20	1/20	1/320 (3/4 + 1/20)
𑿆		𑿔𑿑𑿋	Kīḻ Araiyē Irumā	3/80	1/20	1/320 (1/2 + 2/20)
𑿄		𑿔𑿐𑿍	Kīḻ Kālē mummā	1/40	1/20	1/320 (1/4 + 3/20)
𑿂		𑿔𑿏	Kīḻ nālumā	1/80	1/20	1/320 (4/20)
𑿁		𑿔𑿋	Kīḻ Irumā	1/160	1/20	1/320 (2/20)
𑿀		𑿔𑿈	Kīḻ mummā	1/320	1/20	1/320 (1/20)
𑿆	𑿆	𑿔𑿐𑿏	Kīḻ Kālē nālumā	3/80	3/80	1/320 (1/4 + 4/20)
𑿄		𑿔𑿐𑿈	Kīḻ Kālē Orumā	1/40	3/80	1/320 (1/4 + 1/20)
𑿂		𑿔𑿍	Kīḻ mummā	1/80	3/80	1/320 (3/20)
𑿁		𑿔𑿈𑿄	Kīḻ māvē Araimā	1/160	3/80	1/320 (1/20 + 1/40)
𑿀		𑿔𑿆	Kīḻ Mukkāṇi	1/320	3/80	1/320 (3/80)
𑿄	𑿄	𑿔𑿏	Kīḻ nālumā	1/40	1/40	1/320 (4/20)
𑿂		𑿔𑿋	Kīḻ Irumā	1/80	1/40	1/320 (2/20)
𑿁		𑿔𑿈	Kīḻ Orumā	1/160	1/40	1/320 (1/20)
𑿀		𑿔𑿄	Kīḻ Araimā	1/320	1/40	1/320 (1/40)
𑿂	𑿂	𑿔𑿈	Kīḻ Orumā	1/80	1/80	1/320 (1/20)
𑿁		𑿔𑿄	Kīḻ Araimā	1/160	1/80	1/320 (1/40)
𑿀		𑿔𑿂	Kīḻ kāṇi	1/320	1/80	1/320 (1/80)
𑿁	𑿁	𑿔𑿂	Kīḻ kāṇi	1/160	1/160	1/320 (1/80)
𑿀		𑿔𑿁	Kīḻ araikkāṇi	1/320	1/160	1/320 (1/160)
𑿀	𑿀	𑿔𑿀	Kīḻ muntiri	1/320	1/320	1/320 x 1/320
	Kīḻ muntirikai eṉṟār kiḷi moḻiyār *kēcavaṉār vāḻum tirumakaṉār vantu* *mukkāl mutalāka muntirai vāi īṟākat* *tappā vacalaivāi ēḻeṭṭum tappāmal* *tampikku nallāṉai cārpukku nī* *yāṉai tumpikkai yāṉait toḻa*					

Nellilakkam

			Memory mode			
௧	[illegible]	[illegible]	Oruceviṭu	1	Ceviṭu	1 ceviṭu
௰		[illegible]	ōru̲lakku	10	Ceviṭu	1 U̲lakku
௱		[illegible]	Irunā̲liyē ōruri	100	Ceviṭu	2 nā̲li and 1 uri
௨		[illegible]	Iruceviṭu	2	Ceviṭu	2 ceviṭu
௨௰		[illegible]	ōruri	20	Ceviṭu	1 uri
௨௱		[illegible]	Ainnā̲li	200	Ceviṭu	5 nā̲li
௩		[illegible]	Mucceviṭu	3	Ceviṭu	3 ceviṭu
௩௰		[illegible]	ōr mūvu̲lakku	30	Ceviṭu	1 mūvu̲lakku
௩௱		[illegible]	E̲lunā̲liyē ōruri	300	Ceviṭu	7 nā̲li and 1 uri
௪		[illegible]	Narceviṭu	4	Ceviṭu	4 ceviṭu
௪௰		[illegible]	Oru nā̲li	40	Ceviṭu	1 nā̲li
௪௱		[illegible]	Oru ku̲ruṇiyē irunā̲li	400	Ceviṭu	1 ku̲ruṇi and 2 nā̲li
௫		[illegible]	ōrā̲lākku	5	Ceviṭu	1 ā̲lākku
௫௰		[illegible]	Orunā̲liyē ōru̲lakku	50	Ceviṭu	1 nā̲li and 1 U̲lakku
௫௱		[illegible]	Oru ku̲ruṇiyē nā̲nā̲liyē ōruri	500	Ceviṭu	1 ku̲ruṇi, 4 nā̲li and 1 uri
௬		[illegible]	Ōrā̲lākkē oruceviṭu	6	Ceviṭu	1 ā̲lākku and 1 ceviṭu
௬௰		[illegible]	Ōrnā̲liyē ōruri	60	Ceviṭu	1 nā̲li and 1 uri
௬௱		[illegible]	Oruku̲ruṇiyē e̲lunā̲li	600	Ceviṭu	1 ku̲ruṇi and 7 nā̲li
௭		[illegible]	Ōrā̲lākkē iruceviṭu	7	Ceviṭu	1 ā̲lākku and 2 ceviṭu
௭௰		[illegible]	Orunā̲liyē mūvu̲lakku	70	Ceviṭu	1 nā̲li and 1 mūvu̲lakku
௭௱		[illegible]	Oru Patakkē orunā̲liyē ōruri	700	Ceviṭu	1 patakku, 1 nā̲li and 1 uri
௮		[illegible]	Ōrā̲lākkē mucceviṭu	8	Ceviṭu	1 ā̲lākku and 3 ceviṭu
௮௰		[illegible]	Irunā̲li	80	Ceviṭu	2 nā̲li
௮௱		[illegible]	Oru Patakkē nā̲nā̲li	800	Ceviṭu	1 patakku and 4 nā̲li
௯		[illegible]	Ōrā̲lākkē nā̲rceviṭu	9	Ceviṭu	1 ā̲lākku and 4 ceviṭu

௯௰	[illegible]	௨ உ [illegible]	Irunāḻiyē ōruḻakku	90	Ceviṭu	2 nāḻi and 1 Uḻakku
௯௱	[illegible]	[illegible]	Oru Patakkē arunāḻiyē ōruri	900	Ceviṭu	1 patakku, 6 nāḻi and 1 uri
௲		[illegible]	Mukkuṟuṇiyē orunāḻi	1000	Ceviṭu	1 mukkuṟuṇi and 1 nāḻi
Alakunilai [illegible]				Cumulative product = 1 kalam, 4 patakku, 5 nāḻi, 1 mūvuḻakku and 1 āḻākku		
௧	உ	உ	Orunāḻi	1	nāḻi	1 nāḻi
௰		[illegible]	Orukuṟuṇiyē irunāḻi	10	nāḻi	1 kuṟuṇi and 2 nāḻi
௱		[illegible]	Orukalamē nāṉāḻi	100	nāḻi	1 kalam and 4 nāḻi
௨		௨ உ	Irunāḻi	2	nāḻi	2 nāḻi
௨௰		[illegible]	Oru Patakkē nāṉāḻi	20	nāḻi	1 patakku and 4 nāḻi
௨௱		[illegible]	Irukalamē orukuṟuṇi	200	nāḻi	2 kalam and 1 kuṟuṇi
௩		௩ உ	Munnāḻi	3	nāḻi	3 nāḻi
௩௰		[illegible]	Mukkuṟuṇiyē aṟunāḻi	30	nāḻi	1 mukkuṟuṇi and 6 nāḻi
௩௱		[illegible]	Mukkalamē orukuṟuṇiyē nāṉāḻi	300	nāḻi	3 kalam, 1 kuṟuṇi and 4 nāḻi
௪		௪ உ	Nāṉāḻi	4	nāḻi	4 nāḻi
௪௰		[illegible]	Orutūṇiyē orukuṟuṇi	40	nāḻi	1 tūṇi and 1 kuṟuṇi
௪௱		[illegible]	Nāṟkalamē orupatakkē	400	nāḻi	4 kalam, 1 patakku
௫		௫ உ	Ainnāḻi	5	nāḻi	5 nāḻi
௫௰		[illegible]	Orutūṇiyē orupatakkē irunāḻi	50	nāḻi	1 tūṇi, 1 patakku and 2 nāḻi
௫௱		[illegible]	Aiṅkalamē orupatakkē nāṉāḻi	500	nāḻi	5 kalam, 1 patakku and 4 nāḻi
௬		௬ உ	Aṟunāḻi	6	nāḻi	6 nāḻi
௬௰		[illegible]	Orutūṇiyē mukkuṟuṇiyē nāṉāḻi	60	nāḻi	1 tūṇi, 1 mukkuṟuṇi and 4 nāḻi

[illegible]	[illegible]	[illegible]	Aṟukalame mukkuṟuṇi	600	nāḻi	6 kalam and 1 mukkuṟuṇi
[illegible]		[illegible]	Eḻunāḻi	7	nāḻi	7 nāḻi
[illegible]		[illegible]	Eṭṭu kuṟuṇiyē aṟunāḻi	70	nāḻi	1 eṭṭu kuṟuṇi and 6 nāḻi
[illegible]		[illegible]	Eḻukalamē mukkuṟuṇiyē nāṉāḻi	700	nāḻi	7 kalam, 1 mukkuṟuṇi and 4 nāḻi
[illegible]		[illegible]	Orukuṟuṇi	8	nāḻi	1 kuṟuṇi
[illegible]		[illegible]	Eṭṭu kuṟuṇiyē orupatakku	80	nāḻi	1 eṭṭu kuṟuṇi and 1 patakku
[illegible]		[illegible]	Eṭṭu kalamē oru tūṇi	800	nāḻi	8 kalam and 1 tūṇi
[illegible]		[illegible]	Oru kuṟuṇiyē oru nāḻi	9	nāḻi	1 kuṟuṇi and 1 nāḻi
[illegible]		[illegible]	Eṭṭu kuṟuṇiyē mukkuṟuṇiyē irunāḻi	90	nāḻi	1 eṭṭu kuṟuṇi, 1 mukkuṟuṇi and 2 nāḻi
[illegible]		[illegible]	Oṉpatiṉ kalamē oru tūṇiyē nāṉāḻi	900	nāḻi	9 kalam, 1 tūṇi and 4 nāḻi
[illegible]		[illegible]	Pattuk kalamē oru tūṇiyē oru kuṟuṇi	1000	nāḻi	10 kalam, 1 tūṇi and 1 kuṟuṇi
Aṟupattu iraṇṭākum tāmaraip pūviṟku uṟu kūli aiṅkuṟuṇi munnāḻi eṉparē maṟumoḻi kāṭciyavar Alakunilai . . . . [illegible]				(note: 5 kuṟuṇi = 1 tūṇi + 1 kuṟuṇi) Cumulative product = 62 kalam, 1 tūṇi, 1 kuṟuṇi and 3 nāḻi		
[illegible]	[illegible]	[illegible]	Orukuṟuṇi	1	kuṟuṇi	1 kuṟuṇi
[illegible]		[illegible]	Eṭṭu kuṟuṇiyē oru patakku	10	kuṟuṇi	1 eṭṭu kuṟuṇi and 1 patakku
[illegible]		[illegible]	Eṭṭu kalamē oru tūṇi	100	kuṟuṇi	8 kalam and 1 tūṇi
[illegible]		[illegible]	Oru patakku	2	kuṟuṇi	1 patakku
[illegible]		[illegible]	Oru kalamē eṭṭu kuṟuṇi	20	kuṟuṇi	1 kalam and 1 eṭṭu kuṟuṇi
[illegible]		[illegible]	Patiṉāṟu kalamē eṭṭu kuṟuṇi	200	kuṟuṇi	16 kalam and 1 eṭṭu kuṟuṇi

௩	[illegible]	[illegible]	Mukkuṟuṇi	3	kuṟuṇi	1 mukkuṟuṇi
௩௰		[illegible]	Irukalamē orutūṇiyē orupatakku	30	kuṟuṇi	2 kalam, 1 tūṇi and 1 patakku
௩௱		[illegible]	Irupattu aintu kalam	300	kuṟuṇi	25 kalam
௪		[illegible]	Orutūṇi	4	kuṟuṇi	1 tūṇi
௪௰		[illegible]	Mukkalamē orutūṇi	40	kuṟuṇi	3 kalam and 1 tūṇi
௪௱		[illegible]	Muppattu Mūṉṟu kalamē orutūṇi	400	kuṟuṇi	33 kalam and 1 tūṇi
௫		[illegible]	Orutūṇiyē orukuṟuṇi	5	kuṟuṇi	1 tūṇi and 1 kuṟuṇi
௫௰		[illegible]	Nāṟkalamē orupatakku	50	kuṟuṇi	4 kalam and 1 patakku
௫௱		[illegible]	Nāṟpatu kalamē eṭṭu kuṟuṇi	500	kuṟuṇi	40 kalam and 1 eṭṭu kuṟuṇi
௬		[illegible]	Orutūṇiyē orupatakku	6	kuṟuṇi	1 tūṇi and 1 patakku
௬௰		[illegible]	Aiṅkalam	60	kuṟuṇi	5 kalam
௬௱		[illegible]	Aimpatu kalam	600	kuṟuṇi	50 kalam
௭		[illegible]	Orutūṇiyē mukkuṟuṇi	7	kuṟuṇi	1 tūṇi and 1 mukkuṟuṇi
௭௰		[illegible]	Aiṅkalamē eṭṭu kuṟuṇiyē orupatakku	70	kuṟuṇi	5 kalam, 1 eṭṭu kuṟuṇi and 1 patakku
௭௱		[illegible]	Aimpattu eṭṭu kalamē orutūṇi	700	kuṟuṇi	58 kalam and 1 tūṇi
௮		[illegible]	Eṭṭu kuṟuṇi	8	kuṟuṇi	1 eṭṭu kuṟuṇi
௮௰		[illegible]	Aṟukalamē eṭṭu kuṟuṇi	80	kuṟuṇi	6 kalam and 1 eṭṭu kuṟuṇi
௮௱		[illegible]	Arupattu āṟu kalamē eṭṭu kuṟuṇi	800	kuṟuṇi	66 kalam and 1 eṭṭu kuṟuṇi
௯		[illegible]	Eṭṭu kuṟuṇiyē orukuṟuṇi	9	kuṟuṇi	1 eṭṭu kuṟuṇi and 1 kuṟuṇi
௯௰		[illegible]	Ēḻukalamē orutūṇiyē orupatakku	90	kuṟuṇi	7 kalam, 1 tūṇi and 1 patakku

௯௱	[illegible]	[illegible]	E<u>l</u>upattu aintu kalam	900	ku<u>r</u>uṇi	75 kalam
௲		[illegible]	Eṇpattu Mū<u>n</u><u>r</u>u kalamē orutūṇi	1000	ku<u>r</u>uṇi	83 kalam and 1 tūṇi
Nā<u>n</u>ku taiyyat toṇṇū<u>r</u><u>r</u>ō ṭūrama<u>r</u> <u>r</u>o<u>n</u>pati<u>n</u>mar ā<u>n</u><u>r</u>a e<u>l</u>u ku<u>r</u>uṇi po<u>r</u>ci<u>n</u><u>n</u>am koḷvarē muttūṇi naṭappa ta<u>n</u>il Alakunilai . . . . [illegible]				Cumulative product = 499 kalam and 7 ku<u>r</u>uṇi		
௧	[illegible]	[illegible]	Orutūṇi	1	tūṇi	1 tūṇi
௰		[illegible]	Mukkalamē orutūṇi	10	tūṇi	3 kalam and 1 tūṇi
௱		[illegible]	Muppattu Mū<u>n</u><u>r</u>u kalamē orutūṇi	100	tūṇi	33 kalam and 1 tūṇi
௨		[illegible]	Eṭṭu ku<u>r</u>uṇi	2	tūṇi	1 eṭṭu ku<u>r</u>uṇi
௨௰		[illegible]	Ā<u>r</u>u kalamē eṭṭu ku<u>r</u>uṇi	20	tūṇi	6 kalam and 1 eṭṭu ku<u>r</u>uṇi
௨௱		[illegible]	A<u>r</u>upattu ā<u>r</u>u kalamē eṭṭu ku<u>r</u>uṇi	200	tūṇi	66 kalam and 1 eṭṭu ku<u>r</u>uṇi
௩		[illegible]	Orukalam	3	tūṇi	1 kalam
௩௰		[illegible]	Pattu kalam	30	tūṇi	10 kalam
௩௱		[illegible]	Nū<u>r</u>u kalam	300	tūṇi	100 kalam
௪		[illegible]	Oru kalamē orutūṇi	4	tūṇi	1 kalam and 1 tūṇi
௪௰		[illegible]	Pati<u>n</u>mū<u>n</u><u>r</u>u kalamē orutūṇi	40	tūṇi	13 kalam and 1 tūṇi
௪௱		[illegible]	Nū<u>r</u><u>r</u>u Muppattu Mū<u>n</u><u>r</u>u kalamē orutūṇi	400	tūṇi	133 kalam and 1 tūṇi
௫		[illegible]	Oru kalamē eṭṭu ku<u>r</u>uṇi	5	tūṇi	1 kalam and 1 eṭṭu ku<u>r</u>uṇi
௫௰		[illegible]	Pati<u>n</u>ā<u>r</u>u kalamē eṭṭu ku<u>r</u>uṇi	50	tūṇi	16 kalam and 1 eṭṭu ku<u>r</u>uṇi
௫௱		[illegible]	Nū<u>r</u><u>r</u>u a<u>r</u>upattu ā<u>r</u>u	500	tūṇi	166 kalam and 1 eṭṭu ku<u>r</u>uṇi

		கா வத	kalamē eṭṭu kuruṇi			
௬	த	௨கா	Iru kalam	6	tūṇi	2 kalam
௬௰		௨௰கா	Irupatu kalam	60	tūṇi	20 kalam
௬௱		௨௱கா	Irunūṟu kalam	600	tūṇi	200 kalam
௭		௨காத	Irukalamē orutūṇi	7	tūṇi	2 kalam and 1 tūṇi
௭௰		௨௰௩கா த	Irupattu Mūṉṟu kalamē orutūṇi	70	tūṇi	23 kalam and 1 tūṇi
௭௱		௨௱௩௰ காத	Irunūṟṟu muppatu kalamē orutūṇi	700	tūṇi	230 kalam and 1 tūṇi
௮		௨கா வத	Iru kalamē eṭṭukuṟuṇi	8	tūṇi	2 kalam and 1 eṭṭu kuṟuṇi
௮௰		௨௰௬கா வத	Irupattu āṟu kalamē eṭṭu kuṟuṇi	80	tūṇi	26 kalam and 1 eṭṭu kuṟuṇi
௮௱		௨௱௬௰ ௬கா வத	Irunūṟṟu aṟupattu āṟu kalamē eṭṭu kuṟuṇi	800	tūṇi	266 kalam and 1 eṭṭu kuṟuṇi
௯		௩கா	Mukkalam	9	tūṇi	3 kalam
௯௰		௩௰கா	Muppatu kalam	90	tūṇi	30 kalam
௯௱		௩௱கா	Munnūṟu kalam	900	tūṇi	300 kalam
௲		௩௱௩௰ ௩காத	Munnūṟṟu Muppattu mūṉṟu kalamē orutūṇi	1000	tūṇi	333 kalam and 1 tūṇi
Oṉṟu palāppaḻam oṉpatu vāḻaikkāi nalla ciṟukiḻaṅkoṭu oṉpatu varkkattu ciṅkārak kūliyā maṟṟēṇkalaṉē tūṇiyām kuṉṟāmaṟ koḷvar peṟiṉ Alakunilai. . . . ௲௯௱௯௰௮காத				Cumulative product = 1998 kalam and 1 tūṇi		
௧	கா	கா	Oru kalam	1	kalam	1 kalam
ஒத		வதஙு	Eṭṭu kuṟuṇiyē orukuṟuṇi	¾	kalam	1 eṭṭu kuṟuṇi and 1 kuṟuṇi
ஒ		த வது	Orutūṇiyē orupatakku	½	kalam	1 tūṇi and 1 patakku
வ		ரு	Mukkuṟuṇi	¼	kalam	1 mukkuṟuṇi
ஜ		வதுரு உ	Orupatakkē	4/20	kalam	1 patakku, 3 nāḻi, āḻākku and

		ஜ௱ஜு	munnāḻiyē oru āḻākkē mucceviṭu			3 ceviṭu
[illegible]	கா	ஒஜு உவ	Orupatakkē irunāḻi	3/20 +3/80	kalam	1 patakku and 2 nāḻi
[illegible]		ஙுகாவ தஜுக ஜு	Orukuṟuṇiyē aṟunāḻiyē ōruḻakkē ōrāḻākkē örcceviṭu	3/20	kalam	1 kuṟuṇi, 6 nāḻi, 1 Uḻakku, 1 āḻākku and 1 ceviṭu
[illegible]		ஙுசவ	Orukuṟuṇiyē nāṉāḻi	1/8	kalam	1 kuṟuṇi and 4 nāḻi
ஐ		ஙுவ வரி சஜு	Orukuṟuṇiyē orunāḻiyē ōruriyē nāṟcceviṭu	2/20	kalam	1 kuṟuṇi, 1 nāḻi, 1 uri and 4 ceviṭu
[illegible]		காவ	aṟunāḻi	1/20 + 1/80	kalam	6 nāḻi
ப		சவ௲த உஜு	Nāṉāḻiyē mūvuḻakkē iru ceviṭu	1/20	kalam	4 nāḻi, 1 Mūvuḻakku, and 2 ceviṭu
[illegible]		௱வ வரி சஜு	Munnāḻiyē ōruriyē nāṟceviṭu	3/80	kalam	3 nāḻi, 1 uri, and 4 ceviṭu
சு		உவ தஜு கஜு	Irunāḻiyē ōruḻakkē ōrāḻākkē oruceviṭu	1/40	kalam	2 nāḻi, 1 Uḻakku, 1 āḻākku and 1 ceviṭu
[illegible]		வஜு௱ ஜு	Orunāḻiyē ōrāḻākkē mucceviṭu	1/80	kalam	1 nāḻi, 1 āḻākku and 3 ceviṭu
[illegible]		வரிச ஜு	ōruriyē nāṟceviṭu	1/160	kalam	1 uri and 4 ceviṭu
[illegible]		தஉஜு	ōruḻakkē iruceviṭu	1/320	kalam	1 Uḻakku and 2 ceviṭu
Mukkalam pūrinel mūtirai vāikkaṇuṅkāṉ akkuḷattu nīrmōr aiṅkuṟuṇi nāṉāḻi cikkeṉa vantavar nāṟcuvaāam eṉpar ētakkatu uṇarntavar tām Alakunilai . . . . ௱ணொடுஙுசவசஜு				Cumulative product = 3 kalam, 5 kuṟuṇi, 4 nāḻi and 4 ceviṭu		
Nellilakkam – Kīḻvai						
க	வ	வ	Orunāḻi	1	nāḻi	Nāḻi

[illegible]	[illegible]	[illegible]	Mūvuḻakku	¾	nāḻi	1 Mūvuḻakku
[illegible]		[illegible]	ōruri	½	nāḻi	1 uri
[illegible]		[illegible]	ōruḻakku	¼	nāḻi	1 Uḻakku
[illegible]		[illegible]	ōrāḻākkē mucceviṭu	4/20	nāḻi	1 āḻākku and 3 ceviṭu
[illegible]		[illegible]	ōrāḻākkē Iraṇṭaraicceviṭu	3/20 +3/80	nāḻi	1 āḻākku and 2½ ceviṭu
[illegible]		[illegible]	ōrāḻākkē oruceviṭu	3/20	nāḻi	1 āḻākku and 1 ceviṭu
[illegible]		[illegible]	ōrāḻākku	1/8	nāḻi	1 āḻākku
[illegible]		[illegible]	Nāṟceviṭu	2/20	nāḻi	4 ceviṭu
[illegible]		[illegible]	Iraṇṭaraicceviṭu	1/20 + 1/80	nāḻi	2 ½ ceviṭu
[illegible]		[illegible]	Iruceviṭu	1/20	nāḻi	2 ceviṭu
[illegible]		[illegible]	Oṉṉaraicceviṭu	3/80	nāḻi	1 ½ ceviṭu
[illegible]		[illegible]	Oruceviṭu	1/40	nāḻi	1 ceviṭu
[illegible]		[illegible]	araicceviṭu	1/80	nāḻi	½ ceviṭu
[illegible]		[illegible]	Kāl ceviṭu	1/160	nāḻi	¼ ceviṭu
[illegible]		[illegible]	Araikkāl ceviṭu	1/320	nāḻi	1/8 ceviṭu
[illegible]	[illegible]	[illegible]	Orukuṟuṇi	1	Kuṟuṇi	1 kuṟuṇi
[illegible]		[illegible]	aṟunāḻi	¾	Kuṟuṇi	6 nāḻi
[illegible]		[illegible]	Nāṉāḻi	½	Kuṟuṇi	4 nāḻi
[illegible]		[illegible]	Irunāḻi	¼	Kuṟuṇi	2 nāḻi
[illegible]		[illegible]	Orunāḻiyē ōruriyē nāṟceviṭu	4/20	Kuṟuṇi	1 nāḻi, 1 uri and 4 ceviṭu
[illegible]		[illegible]	Orunāḻiyē ōruri	3/20 +3/80	Kuṟuṇi	1 nāḻi and 1 uri
[illegible]		[illegible]	Orunāḻiyē ōrāḻākkē mucceviṭu	3/20	Kuṟuṇi	1 nāḻi, 1 āḻākku and 3 ceviṭu
[illegible]		[illegible]	Orunāḻi	1/8	Kuṟuṇi	1 nāḻi

[illegible]	[illegible]	[illegible]	Mūvul̲akkē iruceviṭu	2/20	Kur̲uṇi	1 Mūvul̲akku and 2 ceviṭu
[illegible]		[illegible]	ōruri	1/20 + 1/80	Kur̲uṇi	1 uri
[illegible]		[illegible]	ōrul̲akkē ōrāl̲ākkē oruceviṭu	1/20	Kur̲uṇi	1 Ul̲akku, 1 āl̲ākku and 1 ceviṭu
[illegible]		[illegible]	ōrl̲akkē iru ceviṭu	3/80	Kur̲uṇi	1 Ul̲akku and 2 ceviṭu
[illegible]		[illegible]	ōrāl̲ākkē mucceviṭu	1/40	Kur̲uṇi	1 āl̲ākku and 3 ceviṭu
[illegible]		[illegible]	Nār̲ceviṭu	1/80	Kur̲uṇi	4 ceviṭu
[illegible]		[illegible]	Iruceviṭu	1/160	Kur̲uṇi	2 ceviṭu
[illegible]		[illegible]	Oruceviṭu	1/320	Kur̲uṇi	1 ceviṭu
[illegible]	[illegible]	[illegible]	Orutūṇi	1	tūṇi	1 tūṇi
[illegible]		[illegible]	Mukkur̲uṇi	¾	tūṇi	1 mukkur̲uṇi
[illegible]		[illegible]	Orupatakku	½	tūṇi	1 patakku
[illegible]		[illegible]	Orukur̲uṇi	¼	tūṇi	1 kur̲uṇi
[illegible]		[illegible]	Ar̲unāl̲iyē ōrul̲akkē ōrāl̲ākkē oruceviṭu	4/20	tūṇi	6 nāl̲i, 1 Ul̲akku, 1 āl̲ākku and 1 ceviṭu
[illegible]		[illegible]	Ar̲unāl̲i	3/20 +3/80	tūṇi	6 nāl̲i
[illegible]		[illegible]	Nān̲āl̲iyē ōrul̲akkē iruceviṭu	3/20	tūṇi	4 nāl̲i, 1 Ul̲akku and 2 ceviṭu
[illegible]		[illegible]	Nān̲āl̲i	1/8	tūṇi	4 nāl̲i
[illegible]		[illegible]	Munnāl̲iyē ōrāl̲ākkē mucceviṭu	2/20	tūṇi	3 nāl̲i, 1 āl̲ākku and 3 ceviṭu
[illegible]		[illegible]	Irunāl̲i	1/20 + 1/80	tūṇi	2 nāl̲i
[illegible]		[illegible]	Orunāl̲iyē ōruriyē nār̲ceviṭu	1/20	tūṇi	1 nāl̲i, 1 uri and 4 ceviṭu
[illegible]		[illegible]	Orunāl̲iyē ōrāl̲ākkē	3/80	tūṇi	1 nāl̲i, 1 āl̲ākku and 3 ceviṭu

			mucceviṭu			
சு	த	௩௨ஜ	Mūvuḻakkē iruceviṭu	1/40	tūṇi	1 Mūvuḻakku and 2 ceviṭu
ஓ		ஒஜஜ	ōruḻakkē ōrāḻākkē oruceviṭu	1/80	tūṇi	1 Uḻakku, 1 āḻākku and 1 ceviṭu
ல		ஜா ஜ	ōrāḻākkē mucceviṭu	1/160	tūṇi	1 āḻākku and 3 ceviṭu
வ௫		௪ஜ	Nāṟceviṭu	1/320	tūṇi	4 ceviṭu

Kalam into Marakkāl or Kuṟuni

கள		Kalam	Marakkāl or Kuṟuni
௧	௰௨	1	12
௨	௨௰௪	2	24
௩	௩௰௬	3	36
௪	௪௰௮	4	48
௫	௬௰	5	60
௬	௭௰௨	6	72
௭	௮௰௪	7	84
௮	௯௰௬	8	96
௯	௱௮	9	108
௰	௱௨௰	10	120
௨௰	௨௱௪௰	20	240
௩௰	௩௱௬௰	30	360
௪௰	௪௱௮௰	40	480
௫௰	௬௱	50	600
௬௰	௭௱௨௰	60	720
௭௰	௮௱௪௰	70	840
௮௰	௯௱௬௰	80	960
௯௰	௲௮௰	90	1080
௱	௲௨௱	100	1200
௨௱	௨௲௪௱	200	2400
௩௱	௩௲௬௱	300	3600
௪௱	௪௲௮௱	400	4800
௫௱	௬௲	500	6000
௬௱	௭௲௨௱	600	7200
௭௱	௮௲௪௱	700	8400
௮௱	௯௲௬௱	800	9600
௯௱	௰௲௮௱	900	10800
௲	௰௨௲	1000	12000

Eṭuttal Aḷavai (Measures of Weight)		
Units	**In terms of palam**	
1 Cēr	8	அ
1 Rāttal	12 + ¾ + 1/20	௰௨௯ப
1 Kaṭṭi	25	உ௰௫
1 Vīcai	40	ச௰
1 Tūkku	50	௫௰
1 taṭai	80	அ௰
1 Tulām	200	உ௱
1 Iṭai	100	௱
1 Paṭi	100	௱
1 Pattiṭai	1000	௲
1 Maṇaṅku	320	௩௱உ௰
1 Tarācu	800	அ௱
1 Poti	4800	ச௲அ௱
1 Pāram	6400	௬௲ச௱
In terms of vīcai		
1 cēr	4/20	௯
1 tūkku	1 + ¼	கவ
1 taṭai	2	உ
1 iṭai	2 ½	உ?
1 paṭi	2 ½	உ?
1 tulām	5	௫
1 maṇaṅku	8	அ
1 pattiṭai	25	உ௰௫
1 poti	80	அ௰
1 pāram	160	௱௬௰
In terms of tūkku		
1 vīcai	¾ + 1/20	௯ப
1 taṭai	1 ½ + 2/20	க?௨

1 iṭai	2	௨
1 paṭi	2	௨
1 tulām	4	௪
1 maṇaṅku	6 1/4 + 3/20	௬[illegible]
1 pattiṭai	20	௨௰
1 poti	64	௬௰௪
1 pāram	128	௱௨௰௮
In terms of paṭi		
1 iṭai	1	௧
1 tūkku	½	[illegible]
1 vīcai	¼ + 3/80	[illegible]
1 tulām	2	௨
1 maṇaṅku	3 + 4/20	௩[illegible]
1 pattiṭai	10	௰
1 poti	32	௩௰௨
1 pāram	64	௬௰௪
In terms of tulām		
1 vīcai	4/20	[illegible]
1 tūkku	¼	[illegible]
1 paṭi	½	[illegible]
1 iṭai	½	[illegible]
1 maṇaṅku	1 ½ + 2/20	௧[illegible]
1 pattiṭai	5	௫
1 poti	16	௰௬
1 pāram	32	௩௰௨
In terms of maṇaṅku		
1 vīcai	1/8	[illegible]
1 tūkku	3/20 + 1/160	[illegible]
1 paṭi	¼ + 1/20 + 1/80	[illegible]
1 iṭai	¼ + 1/20 + 1/80	[illegible]

1 tulām	½ + 1/8	[illegible]
1 pattiṭai	3 + 1/8	[illegible]
1 poti	10	௰
1 pāram	20	௨௰
In terms of cēr		
1 rāttal	1 + ½ + 2/20	[illegible]
1 tūkku	6 ¼	[illegible]
1 vīcai	5	௫
1 paṭi	12 ½	[illegible]
1 iṭai	12 ½	[illegible]
1 tulām	25	௨௰௫
1 maṇaṅku	40	௪௰
1 pattiṭai	125	௱௨௰௫
1 poti	400	௪௱
1 pāram	800	௮௱
In terms of rāttal		
1 palam	1/20 + 1/40 + 1/320	[illegible]
1 cēr	½ + 1/8	[illegible]
1 vīcai	3 + 1/8	[illegible]
1 tūkku	3 ¾ + 3/20 + 1/160	[illegible]
1 paṭi	7 ¾ + 1/20 + 1/80	[illegible]
1 iṭai	7 ¾ + 1/20 + 1/80	[illegible]
1 tulām	15 ½ + 1/8	[illegible]
1 maṇaṅku	25	௨௰௫
1 pattiṭai	28 + 1/8	[illegible]
1 poti	250	௨௱௫௰
1 antar	112 ½	[illegible]
1 pāram	500	௫௱

In terms of pāram	
1 poti	½
1 Pattiṭai	3/20 + 1/160
1 maṇaṅku	1/20
1 tulām	1/40 + 1/160
1 iṭai	1/80 + 1/320
1 paṭi	1/80 + 1/320
1 tūkku	1/160 + 1/320 x ½
1 vīcai	1/160
1 pikkal	133 + ¼ + 1/20 + 1/80 rāttal
1 marakkāl	23 + 1/8 + 1/80 + 1/320
1 varākaṉ	9 paṇaveṭai
1 kaḻañcu	10 paṇaveṭai
1 varākaṉeṭai	12 mañcāṭi
1 oñcai	9 varākaṉeṭai
1 cēr	9 oñcai
1 pavuṉ	12 oñcai
1 oñcai	12 peṉcu
1 oñcai	10 ½ taṅkamāṟṟu
1 oñcai	8 ½ varākaṉmāṟṟu
1 paccairati	1/20 + 1/80 varākaṉeṭai
1 kōṭi	12 kempu
1 muttuccavvukku	¾ + 1/8 paṇaveṭai
1 pavaḷam kaḻañcu	10 paṇaveṭai
1 ravai mañcāṭi	¾ + 1/8 paṇaveṭai
1 kalacam	1000 pākku
1 ammaṇam	20,000 pākku
1 alaku	100,000 pākku

1 cāmpu	8 cīlai
1 kaṭṭu	50 paccai vaṭam
1 kōṭi	10 paccai vaṭam
1 kōṭi	20 cāmpu
1 kōṭi	5 maṭi
1 kōṭi	2½ cavukkaḷi
1 kōṭi	20 puṭavai
1 puṭavai	18 muḻam
1 karacai	9256¼ rāttal
1 karacai	400 marakkāl

Peruṅkuḻi

āṉai mukaṉē araṉār tirumakaṉē *Vāṉ aiṅkara vaṭivam āṉavaṉē – tāṉap* *Peruṅkuḻi māṟṟuk kaṇakkēm pēraṟivāi* *neñcam maruṅkuvara nī aruḷ ceivāi*	
Ikkaṇakkil oṉṟum itaiyūṟu vārāmal *Poṟkaṇavaṉ peṟṟa putalvaṉē – ikkaṇakkil* *Nērē viḷaṅkumām nikaraṉṟē niṟkumām* *Pārē viḷaṅkumām pār*[1]	
க - இ - க - குழி க - க - க	1 x 1 kuḻi = 1 x 1 = 1
உ - இ - உ - குழி உ - உ - ச	2 x 2 kuḻi = 2 x 2 = 4
ங - இ - ங - குழி ங - ங - கூ	3 x 3 kuḻi = 3 x 3 = 9
ச - இ - ச - குழி ச - ச - ௰சா	4 x 4 kuḻi = 4 x 4 = 16
ரு - இ - ரு - குழி ரு - ரு - உ௰ரு	5 x 5 kuḻi = 5 x 5 = 25
சா - இ - சா - குழி சா - சா - ங௰சா	6 x 6 kuḻi = 6 x 6 = 36
எ - இ - எ - குழி எ - எ - ச௰கூ	7 x 7 kuḻi = 7 x 7 = 49
அ - இ - அ - குழி அ - அ - சா௰ச	8 x 8 kuḻi = 8 x 8 = 64
கூ - இ - கூ - குழி கூ - கூ - அ௰க	9 x 9 kuḻi = 9 x 9 = 81
௰ - இ - ௰ - குழி ௰ - ௰ - ௱	10 x 10 kuḻi = 10 x 10 = 100
௰க - இ - ௰க - குழி ௰ - ௰ - ௱ ௰ - க - ௰ ௱௰ ௰ - க - ௰ ௱உ௰ க - க - க ௱உ௰க	11 x 11 kuḻi = 10 x 10 = 100 10 x 1 = 10 110 10 x 1 = 10 120 1 x 1 = 1 121
௰உ - இ - ௰உ - குழி ௰ - ௰ - ௱ ௰ - உ - உ௰ ௱உ௰ ௰ - உ - உ௰ ௱ச௰ உ - உ - ச ௱ச௰ச	12 x 12 kuḻi = 10 x 10 = 100 10 x 2 = 20 120 10 x 2 = 20 140 2 x 2 = 4 144
௰ங - இ - ௰ங - குழி ௰ - ௰ - ௱	13 x 13 kuḻi = 10 x 10 = 100

[1] This verse is taken from a different edition of Encuvati, in order to demonstrate the circulation of different versions. This verse was found in Ci. Ve. Minakshisuntara Mutaliar, Periya Ketti Encuavati, Culai Periyanayaki Amman Accukkutam, Chennai, 1934, p. 23

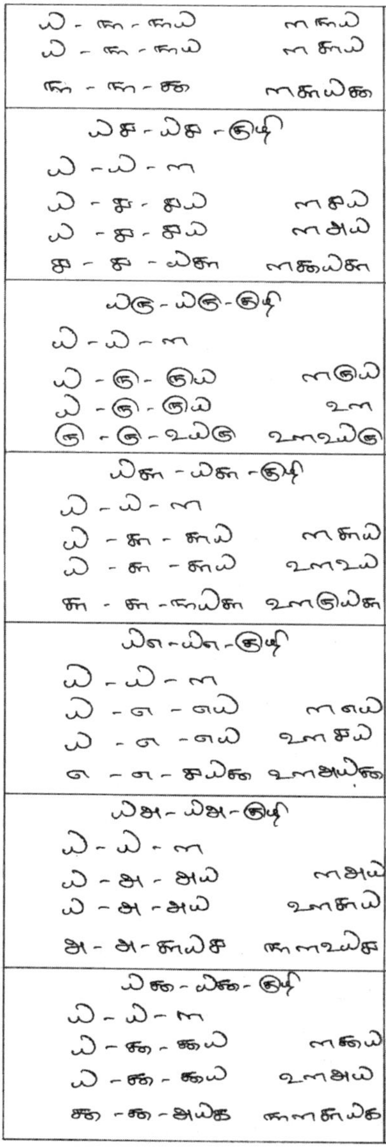

10 x 3 = 30	130
10 x 3 = 30	160
3 x 3 = 9	169
14 x 14 kuḻi =	
10 x 10 = 100	
10 x 4 = 40	140
10 x 4 = 40	180
4 x 4 = 16	196
15 x 15 kuḻi =	
10 x 10 = 100	
10 x 5 = 50	150
10 x 5 = 50	200
5 x 5 = 25	225
16 x 16 kuḻi =	
10 x 10 = 100	
10 x 6 = 60	160
10 x 6 = 60	220
6 x 6 = 36	256
17 x 17 kuḻi =	
10 x 10 = 100	
10 x 7 = 70	170
10 x 7 = 70	240
7 x 7 = 49	289
18 x 18 kuḻi =	
10 x 10 = 100	
10 x 8 = 80	180
10 x 8 = 80	260
8 x 8 = 64	324
19 x 19 kuḻi =	
10 x 10 = 100	
10 x 9 = 90	190
10 x 9 = 90	280
9 x 9 = 81	361

௨௰ - ௨௰ - குழி ௪௱	20 x 20 kuḻi = 400	
௨௰௧ - ௨௰௧ - குழி	21 x 21 kuḻi =	
௨௰ - ௨௰ - ௪௱	20 x 20 = 400	
௨௰ - ௧ - ௨௰ ௪௱௨௰	20 x 1 = 20	420
௨௰ - ௧ - ௨௰ ௪௱௪௰	20 x 1 = 20	440
௧ - ௧ - ௧ ௪௱௪௰௧	1 x 1 = 1	441
௨௰௨ - ௨௰௨ - குழி	22 x 22 kuḻi =	
௨௰ - ௨௰ - ௪௱	20 x 20 = 400	
௨௰ - ௨ - ௪௰ ௪௱௪௰	20 x 2 = 40	440
௨௰ - ௨ - ௪௰ ௪௱௮௰	20 x 2 = 40	480
௨ - ௨ - ௪ ௪௱௮௰௪	2 x 2 = 4	484
௨௰௩ - ௨௰௩ - குழி	23 x 23 kuḻi =	
௨௰ - ௨௰ - ௪௱	20 x 20 = 400	
௨௰ - ௩ - ௬௰ ௪௱௬௰	20 x 3 = 60	460
௨௰ - ௩ - ௬௰ ௫௱௨௰	20 x 3 = 60	520
௩ - ௩ - ௯ ௫௱௨௰௯	3 x 3 = 9	529
௨௰௪ - ௨௰௪ - குழி	24 x 24 kuḻi =	
௨௰ - ௨௰ - ௪௱	20 x 20 = 400	
௨௰ - ௪ - ௮௰ ௪௱௮௰	20 x 4 = 80	480
௨௰ - ௪ - ௮௰ ௫௱௬௰	20 x 4 = 80	560
௪ - ௪ - ௰௬ ௫௱௭௰௬	4 x 4 = 16	576
௨௰௫ - ௨௰௫ - குழி	25 x 25 kuḻi =	
௨௰ - ௨௰ - ௪௱	20 x 20 = 400	
௨௰ - ௫ - ௱ ௫௱	20 x 5 = 100	500
௨௰ - ௫ - ௱ ௬௱	20 x 5 = 100	600
௫ - ௫ - ௨௰௫ ௬௱௨௰௫	5 x 5 = 25	625
௨௰௬ - ௨௰௬ - குழி	26 x 26 kuḻi =	
௨௰ - ௨௰ - ௪௱	20 x 20 = 400	
௨௰ - ௬ - ௱௨௰ ௫௱௨௰	20 x 6 = 120	520
௨௰ - ௬ - ௱௨௰ ௬௱௪௰	20 x 6 = 120	640
௬ - ௬ - ௩௰௬ ௬௱௭௰௬	6 x 6 = 36	676
௨௰௭ - ௨௰௭ - குழி	27 x 27 kuḻi =	
௨௰ - ௨௰ - ௪௱	20 x 20 = 400	

௨௰ - ௭ - ௱௪௰ ௫௱௪௰	20 x 7 = 140	540
௨௰ - ௭ - ௱௪௰ ௬௱௮௰	20 x 7 = 140	680
௭ - ௭ - ௪௰௯ ௭௱௨௰௯	7 x 7 = 49	729
௨௰௮ - ௨௰௮ - குழி	28 x 28 kuḻi =	
௨௰ - ௨௰ - ௪௱	20 x 20 = 400	
௨௰ - ௮ - ௱௬௰ ௫௱௬௰	20 x 8 = 160	560
௨௰ - ௮ - ௱௬௰ ௭௱௨௰	20 x 8 = 160	720
௮ - ௮ - ௬௰௪ ௭௱௮௰௪	8 x 8 = 64	784
௨௰௯ - ௨௰௯ - குழி	29 x 29 kuḻi =	
௨௰ - ௨௰ - ௪௱	20 x 20 = 400	
௨௰ - ௯ - ௱௮௰ ௫௱௮௰	20 x 9 = 180	580
௨௰ - ௯ - ௱௮௰ ௭௱௬௰	20 x 9 = 180	760
௯ - ௯ - ௮௰௧ ௮௱௪௰௧	9 x 9 = 81	841
௩௰ - ௩௰ - குழி ௯௱	30 x 30 kuḻi = 900 kuḻi	
௩௰௧ - ௩௰௧ - குழி	31 x 31 kuḻi =-	
௩௰ - ௩௰ - ௯௱	30 x 30 = 900	
௩௰ - ௧ - ௩௰ ௯௱௩௰	30 x 1 = 30	930
௩௰ - ௧ - ௩௰ ௯௱௬௰	30 x 1 = 30	960
௧ - ௧ - ௧ ௯௱௬௰௧	1x 1 = 1	961
௩௰௨ - ௩௰௨ - குழி	32 x 32 kuḻi =	
௩௰ - ௩௰ - ௯௱	30x30 = 900	
௩௰ - ௨ - ௬௰ ௯௱௬௰	30 x 2 = 60	960
௩௰ - ௨ - ௬௰ ௲௨௰	30 x 2 = 60	1020
௨ - ௨ - ௪ ௲௨௰௪	2 x 2 = 4	1024

Ciṟukuḻi	
Kāppu *ērampa ōrkoṭṭu yāṉaimukaṉ niṉṉaiyē* *Pēraṉpāl ettirkum pētaiyēṉ – kūraṉpāl* *Kaṟkum ciṟukuḻimāṟṟuk kaṇakkēm* *neñcattu niṟkumpaṭi aruḷcei nī*	
Kāppu – viruttam *Varukuḻi māṟa vakai aṟiyāmal*	

[2] This verse was also found in the different edition of the Encuvati cited above, p. 27

varuntukiṉṟēṉ *Karukuḻi māṟa cāṟṟi vaippāi* — *carvēsvaraṉē* *Orukuḻi kālkuḻi īteṉṟu kāṭṭi ōtivaitta* *Cirukuḻi muppatum eṉakkē aruḷvāi* *celva piḷḷaiyārē*[2]	
	$1/20 + 1/80 \times 1/20 + 1/80 \text{ kuḻi} =$ $1/320 + (1/320) \, ¼$
	$1/8 \times 1/8 \text{ kuḻi} = 1/80 + 1/320$
	$¼ \times ¼ \text{ kuḻi} = 1/20 + 1/80$
	$½ \times ½ \text{ kuḻi} = ¼$
	$¾ \times ¾ \text{ kuḻi} = ½ + 1/20 + 1/80$
	$1 \times 1 \text{ kuḻi} = 1$
	$1 + ¼ \times 1 + ¼ \text{ kuḻi} =$
	$1 \times 1 = 1$
	$1 \times ¼ = ¼$ $1 + ¼$
	$1 \times ¼ = ¼$ $1 + ½$
	$¼ \times ¼ = 1/20 + 1/80$ $1 + ½ + 1/20 + 1/80$
	$1 + ½ \times 1 + ½ \text{ kuḻi} =$
	$1 \times 1 = 1$
	$1 \times ½ = ½$ $1 + ½$
	$1 \times ½ = ½$ 2
	$½ \times ½ = ¼$ $2 + ¼$
	$1 + ¾ \times 1 + ¾ \text{ kuḻi} =$
	$1 \times 1 = 1$
	$1 \times ¾ = ¾$ $1 + ¾$
	$1 \times ¾ = ¾$ $2 + ½$
	$¾ \times ¾ = ½ + 1/20 + 1/80$ $3 + 1/20 + 1/80$
	$2 \times 2 \text{ kuḻi} = 4$
	$2 + ¼ \times 2 + ¼ \text{ kuḻi} =$
	$2 \times 2 = 4$
	$2 \times ¼ = ½$ $4 + ½$

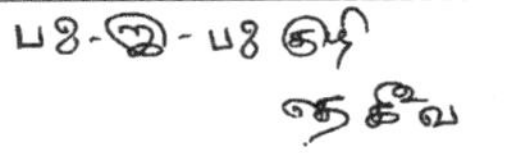

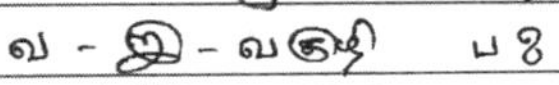

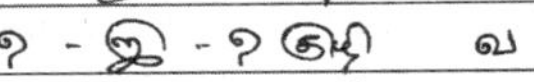

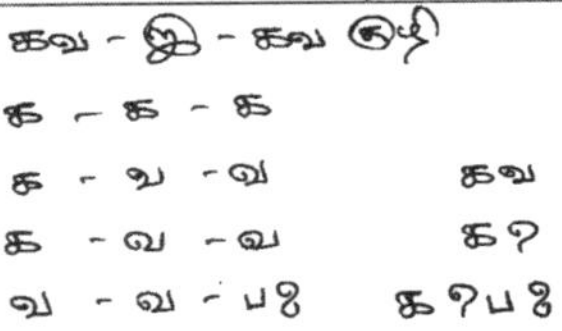

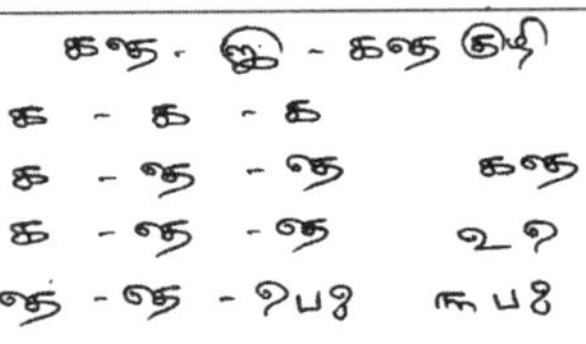

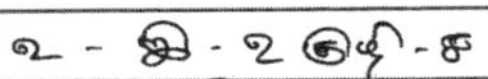

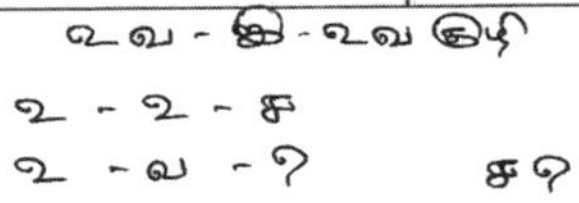

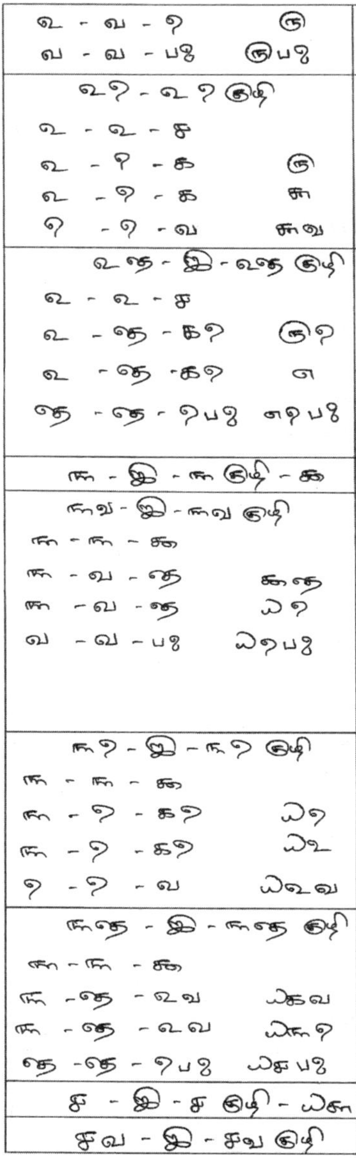

2 x ¼ = ½	5
¼ x ¼ = 1/20 + 1/80	5 + 1/20 + 1/80
2 + ½ x 2 + ½ kuḻi =	
2 x 2 = 4	
2 x ½ = 1	5
2 x ½ = 1	6
½ x ½ = ¼	6 + ¼
2 + ¾ x 2 + ¾ kuḻi =	
2 x 2 = 4	
2 x ¾ = 1 + ½	5 + ½
2 x ¾ = 1 + ½	7
¾ x ¾ = ½ + 1/20 + 1/80	7 + ½ + 1/20 + 1/80
3 x 3 kuḻi = 9	
3 + ¼ x 3 + ¼ kuḻi =	
3 x 3 = 9	
3 x ¼ = ¾	9 + ¾
3 x ¼ = ¾	10 + ½
¼ x ¼ = 1/20 + 1/80	10 + ½ + 1/20 + 1/80
3 + ½ x 3 + ½ kuḻi =	
3 x 3 = 9	
3 x ½ = 1 + ½	10 + ½
3 x ½ = 1 + ½	12
½ x ½ = ¼	12 + ¼
3 + ¾ x 3 + ¾ kuḻi =	
3 x 3 = 9	
3 x ¾ = 2 + ¼	11 + ¼
3 x ¾ = 2 + ¼	13 + ½
¾ x ¾ = ½ + 1/20 + 1/80	14 + 1/20 + 1/80
4 x 4 kuḻi = 16	
4 + ¼ x 4 + ¼ kuḻi =	

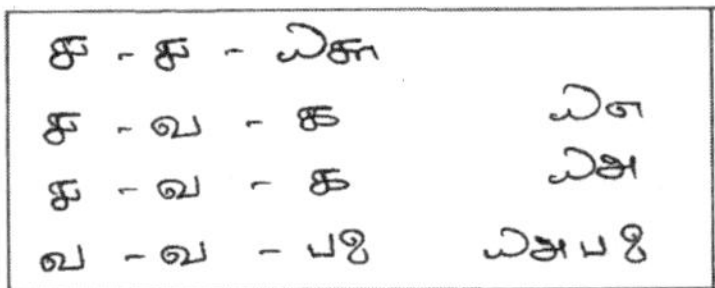	4x 4 = 16 4 x ¼ = 1 4 x ¼ = 1 ¼ x ¼ = 1/20 + 1/80	 17 18 18 + 1/20 + 1/80
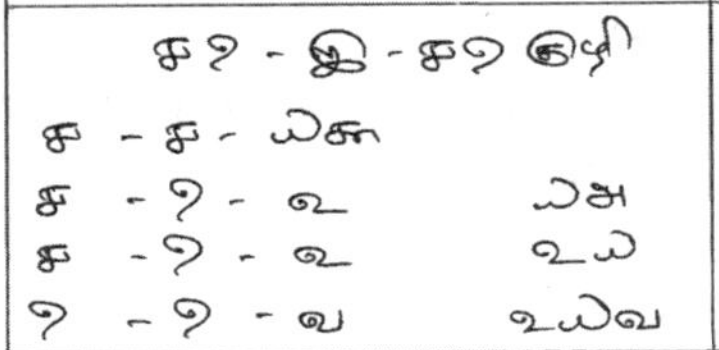	4 + ½ x 4 + ½ kuḻi = 4 x 4 = 16 4 x ½ = 2 4 x ½ = 2 ½ x ½ = ¼	 18 20 20 + ¼
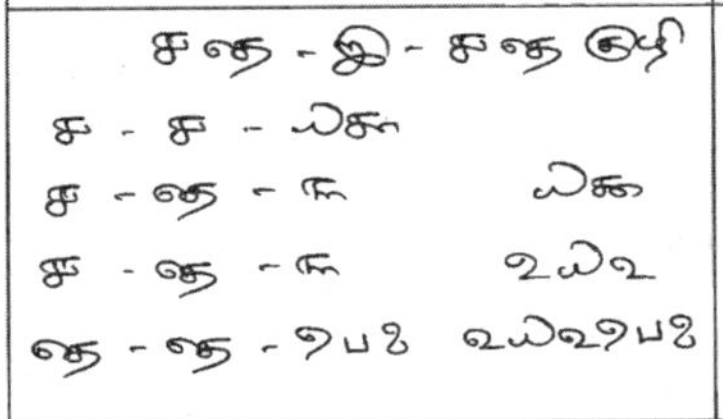	4 + ¾ x 4 + ¾ kuḻi = 4 x 4 = 16 4 x ¾ = 3 4 x ¾ = 3 ¾ x ¾ = ½ + 1/20 + 1/80	 19 22 22 + ½ + 1/20 + 1/80
	5 x 5 kuḻi = 25 kuḻi	
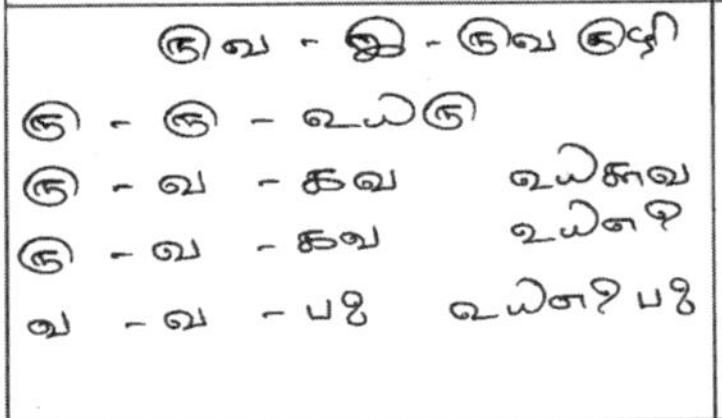	5+ ¼ x 5 + ¼ kuḻi = 5 x 5 = 25 5 x ¼ = 1 + ¼ 5 x ¼ = 1 + ¼ ¼ x ¼ = 1/20 + 1/80	 26 + ¼ 27 + ½ 27 + ½ + 1/20 + 1/80
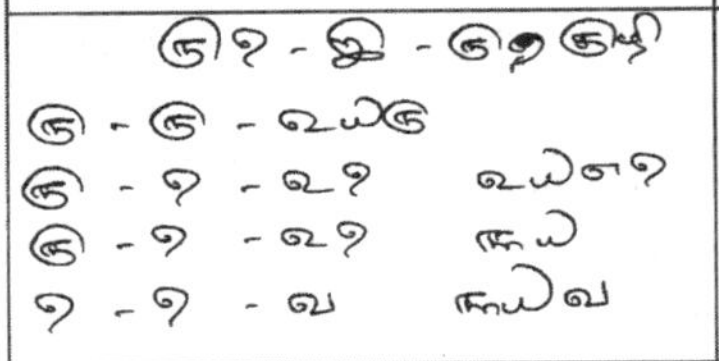	5 + ½ x 5 + ½ kuḻi = 5 x 5 = 25 5 x ½ = 2 + ½ 5 x ½ = 2 + ½ ½ x ½ = ¼	 27 + ½ 30 30 + ¼
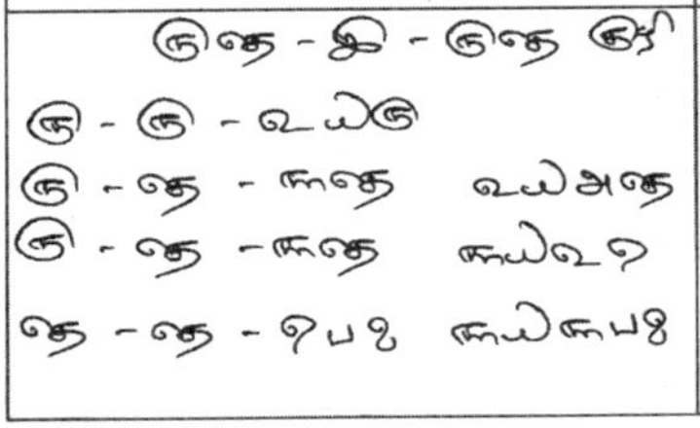	5 + ¾ x 5 + ¾ kuḻi = 5 x 5 = 25 5 x ¾ = 3 + ¾ 5 x ¾ = 3 + ¾ ¾ x ¾ = ½ + 1/20 + 1/80	 28 + ¾ 32 + ½ 33 + 1/20 + 1/80

[illegible]	6 x 6 kuḻi = 36	
[illegible]	6 + ¼ x 6 + ¼ kuḻi =	
[illegible]	6 x 6 = 36	
[illegible]	6 x ¼ = 1 + ½	37 + ½
[illegible]	6 x ¼ = 1 + ½	39
[illegible]	¼ x ¼ = 1/20 + 1/80	39 + 1/20 + 1/80
[illegible]	6 + ½ x 6 + ½ kuḻi =	
[illegible]	6 x 6 = 36	
[illegible]	6 x ½ = 3	39
[illegible]	6 x ½ = 3	42
[illegible]	½ x ½ = ¼	42 + ¼
[illegible]	6 + ¾ x 6 + ¾ kuḻi =	
[illegible]	6 x 6 = 36	
[illegible]	6 x ¾ = 4 + ½	40 + ½
[illegible]	6 x ¾ = 4 + ½	45
[illegible]	¾ x ¾ = ½ + 1/20 + 1/80	45 + ½ + 1/20 + 1/80
[illegible]	7 x 7 kuḻi = 49	
[illegible]	7 + ¼ x 7 + ¼ kuḻi =	
[illegible]	7 x 7 = 49	
[illegible]	7 x ¼ = 1 + ¾	50 + ¾
[illegible]	7 x ¼ = 1 + ¾	52 + ½
[illegible]	¼ x ¼ = 1/20 + 1/80	52 + ½ + 1/20 + 1/80
[illegible]	7 + ½ x 7 + ½ kuḻi =	
[illegible]	7 x 7 = 49	
[illegible]	7 x ½ = 3 + ½	52 + ½
[illegible]	7 x ½ = 3 + ½	56
[illegible]	½ x ½ = ¼	56 + ¼
[illegible]	7 +¾ x 7 + ¾ kuḻi =	
[illegible]	7 x 7 = 49	
[illegible]	7 x ¾ = 5 + ¼	54 + ¼
[illegible]	7 x ¾ = 5 + ¼	59 + ½

ஞெ - ஞெ - ௭பஜ காய பஜ	¾ x ¾ = ½ + 1/20 + 1/80	60 + 1/20 + 1/80
அ - இ - அ குழி - காயச	8 x 8 kuḻi = 64	
அவ - இ - அவ குழி அ - அ - காயச அ - வ - உ காயகா அ - வ - உ காயஅ வ - வ - பஜ காயஅபஜ	8 + ¼ x 8 + ¼ kuḻi = 8 x 8 = 64 8 x ¼ = 2 8 x ¼ = 2 ¼ x ¼ = 1/20 + 1/80	 66 68 68 + 1/20 + 1/80
அ௭ - இ - அ௭ குழி அ - அ - காயச அ - ௭ - ச காயஅ அ - ௭ - ச எயஉ ௭ - ௭ - வ எயஉவ	8 + ½ x 8 + ½ kuḻi = 8 x 8 = 64 8 x ½ = 4 8 x ½ = 4 ½ x ½ = ¼	 68 72 72 + ¼
அஞெ - இ - அஞெ குழி அ - அ - காயச அ - ஞெ - கா எய அ - ஞெ - கா எயகா ஞெ - ஞெ - ௭பஜ எயகா௭பஜ	8 + ¾ x 8 + ¾ kuḻi = 8 x 8 = 64 8 x ¾ = 6 8 x ¾ = 6 ¾ x ¾ = ½ + 1/20 + 1/80	 70 76 76 + ½ + 1/20 + 1/80
க - இ - க குழி - அயக	9 x 9 kuḻi = 81	
கவ - இ - கவ குழி க - க - அயக க - வ - உவ அயகாவ க - வ - உவ அயகு௭ வ - வ - பஜ அயகு௭பஜ	9 + ¼ x 9 + ¼ kuḻi = 9 x 9 = 81 9 x ¼ = 2 + ¼ 9 x ¼ = 2 + ¼ ¼ x ¼ = 1/20 + 1/80	 83 + ¼ 85 + ½ 85 + ½ + 1/20 + 1/80
க௭ - இ - க௭ குழி க - க - அயக க - ௭ - ச௭ அயகு௭ க - ௭ - ச௭ கய ௭ - ௭ - வ கயவ	9 + ½ x 9 + ½ kuḻi = 9 x 9 = 81 9 x ½ = 4 + ½ 9 x ½ = 4 + ½ ½ x ½ = ¼	 85 + ½ 90 90 + ¼
கஞெ - இ - கஞெ குழி க - க - அயக க - ஞெ - காஞெ அயஞெ	9 + ¾ x 9 + ¾ kuḻi = 9 x 9 = 81 9 x ¾ = 6 + ¾	 87 + ¾

க - ஞெ - காஞெ கயச௭ ஞெ - ஞெ - ௭பஜ கயகுபஜ	9 x ¾ = 6 + ¾ ¾ x ¾ = ½ + 1/20 + 1/80	94 + ½ 95 + 1/20 + 1/80
ய - இ - ய குழி - ௱	10 x 10 kuḻi = 100	
Ciṟukuḻi muṟṟiṟṟu	**End of ciṟukuḻi**	

APPENDIX IV

List of Text Books Used for the Study

----------, *pāla kaṇitam An Elementary Arithmetic Combining Many of the Peculiarities of the European and Tamil Systems*. American Mission Press, Jaffna, 1849.

------------, *pālar kaṇitam*. Puthuvaiyin sanmarakkini matha koyil Press, Pondicherry, 1853.

-----------, *ciṟuvar eṇcuvaṭi*. Pondicherry Mission Press, Pondicherry, 1863.

------------, *cōti cāstiram*. American Mission Press, Jaffna, 1848.

-----------, *cōti cāstiram*. Christian Vernacular Education Society, American Mission Press, 1862.

------------, *eṇcuvaṭi*, ed. Kuppanayyankar. Mutthamil Vilakka acchu kutam, Pondicherry, 1859.

---------------, *Kaṇakkatikāram*, ed. Raju Mudaliar, R. Vidyaratnakara acchu kutam, Madras, 1924.

------------, *Tamil ilakka ārampa viḷakkam*, Munaiyaduvar cankam, Standard Press, Kumbakonam, 1911.

Adam, John. *Euclid Book I With Notes and Exercises*. V. J. Manickavaloo Moodelliar & Co., Madras, 1885.

Arunachala Devar, K. *kaṇakkaṟi viḷakkam*. Scottish French Press, Nagapattinam, 1910.

Balakrishna Aiyar, S. *Elementary Mathematics Including Algebra and Geometry*. Oxford University Press, 1935.

Cape, John. *A Course of Mathematics: Primarily Designed for the Use of Students in the East India Company's Military Seminary at Addiscombe*, Vol. 1. Longman, London, 1839.

Chellappa Sasthriar, T. V., and Srinivasa Chariar, T. K. *A Text Book of Arithmetic in Tamil for the Use of Lower Primary Classes With Model Sums & Copious Examples*. A. Govindharajulu Naidu & Co., Madras, 1904.

Chidamparam Pillai, P. C. N. *Tamil ilakka ārampa viḷakkam*. Sri Gopala Vilasa acchu kutam, 1911.

Colenso, John William. *A Schilling Arithmetic Designed for the Use of Elementary Schools*. Longman & Green Co, London, 1867.

Colenso, John William. *Arithmetic Part II (Tamil) Revised and Approved Published by Order of Director of Public Instruction*. Madras School Book and Vernacular Literature Society, Madras, 1885.

Cook, John. *Algebra for Middle or Lower Secondary Schools With Nearly One Thousand Examples*. Srinivasa Varadachari & Co, Madras, 1899.

Cuydenberg, Arthur Van. *Arithmetic Std. IV*. Wesleyan Mission Press, Batticaloa, 1889.

De Morgan, Augustus. *The Elements of Arithmetic*. London, 1832 (2nd edition).

Devasahayam, J. S. *The Lower Secondary Arithmetic With Model Solutions and Examples Approved as a Text-Book for the First, Second, and Third Forms (Tamil Edition)*. Macmillan & Co, Calcutta, 1903.

Devasahayam, J. S. *The Third Standard Arithmetic in Tamil With Model Solutions and Examples*. S.P.C.K. Press, Vepery, Madras, 1900.

Gnanakan, C. P. *Arithmetic for the IV Standard, the Second Class and the Special Upper Primary Examination*. The Empress of India Press, Madras, 1885.

Gopala Aiyangar, C. *An Arithmetic in Tamil for Primary Schools Adapt to Suit the Requirement of the Madras Educational Rules*. Madras, 1902.

Jayaram Pillai, E. *Text Book of Arithmetic (Tamil Edition) Containing More Than 1000 Sums for Slate Work & 500 Sums on Mental Arithmetic*. Madras, 1895.

Kudavatthi Muhammadu, Lebbai. *muttu cevvu kaṇakku*. Darling Press, Palaiyankottai, 1881.

Maraikkayar, Yusubu Shahibu. *vaṇika kaṇitam*. Crown Press, Madras, 1891.

Marimuthu, C. *The Sixth Standard Arithmetic Containing Proportions*. Jaffna, 1890.

Meenakshi Sundara Mudaliar. *periya keṭṭi eṇcuvaṭi*. Periyanayaki Amman acchu kutam, Madras, 1934.

Moffatt, William. *Mental Arithmetic Intended Chiefly for Students in Training Colleges and Pupil Teachers*. Longman, Green & Co., London, 1869.

Mohammed Shumsuddeen Saib, P. V. B. *viṉōta vicittira jāla yukti kaṇakku (A Wonderful Magic Prudent Computation)*. St. Joseph's Press, Madras, 1891.

Namasivaya Mudaliar Ka. *putucaṭṭa kaṇitam for Primary Standards Based on New Educational Rules*. Thomson Company, Madras, 1901.

Namasivaya Mudaliar Ka. *putucaṭṭa kaṇitam III Standard*. C. Coomarasamy Naidu & Co, Madras, 1911.

Namasivaya Mudaliar Ka. *putucaṭṭa kaṇitam IV Standard*. C. Coomarasamy Naidu & Co, Madras, 1911.

Orsala kanakku Muhammadu Shareepu Sayapu. *maṉakkaṇakku curukkam (Mental Arithmetic Short)*, ed. Ka. Namachivaya Mudaliar. The Progressive Press, Madras, 1913.

Pasupathy Mudaliar. *pāla kaṇitam Iraṇṭāvatu pākam III, IV Standards*. Victoria Accu Kutam, Salem, 1895.

Periyasami Pillai, T. K., and Krishnasamy Pillai, T. K. *pālar vakuppu mutaṉūl kaṇitam*. The Poorna Chandrodaya, Tanjore, 1894.

Ragava Chetty, V. *Principles of Arithmetic Part I Section I (Tamil) for the Use of Upper Primary Schools With Numerous Model Examples Worked Out and With Exercises in Mental Arithmetic*. Madras Ribbon Press, Madras, 1902 (4th edition).

Ragava Chetty, V. *Principles of Arithmetic Part I Section II (Tamil) for the Use of Upper Primary Schools With Numerous Model Examples Worked Out and With Exercises in Mental Arithmetic*. Madras, 1900 (5th edition).

Ragava Chetty, V. *Principles of Arithmetic Part I Section II Tamil. For the Use of Upper Primary Schools With Numerous Model Examples Worked Out and With Exercises in Mental Arithmetic*. The Memorial Press, Madras, 1884.

Raju Mudaliar, R. *kaṇita viḷakkam eṉṉum kaṭai kaṇakku ṉūl*. American Arcod Mission Accu Kutam, Arani, 1928.

Raju Mudaliar, R. *kaṇita viḷakkam*, n.d.

Ramachandra Aiyar, T. A. *Arithmetic in Tamil With Model Solutions & Examples Meeting All the Requirements of the Primary Examinations*. T. Kuppusamy Aiyar & Co, Teppakulam, Trichinopoly, 1897.

Ramasamy Naicker, Pantulu. *Kaṇita tīpikai*. Madras School Book society, Madras, 1825.

Ramaswamy Mudaliar, V. S. *An Arithmetic Primer. Designed Especially for Students of Infant I, II, III, IV Standards and Primary School Examination*. V. N. Press, Vellore, 1891.

Ranganatha Iyengar, R. *Arithmetic for Primary Exam*. L. H. Press, Anaikarachattiram, 1898.

Ranganatha Iyengar, R. *Arithmetic in Tamil With Model Solutions and Examples Meeting All the Requirements of the Primary Examination*. Victoria Pondian Press, Anaikarachattiram, 1900.

Ranganatha Iyengar, R. *Arithmetic in Tamil With model Sums and Examples Meeting All the Requirements of the Primary Examination*. D. K. Subbiah Naidu & Sons, Tanjore, 1902.

Rangasamy Aiyar, S. *A Text Book of Arithmetic for the Primary School Examination*. Poorna Chandrodaya Press, Tanjore, 1894.

Rasugopalachariar, Seshambadi. *Eukliṭu iyaṟṟiya kṣētra kaṇita pāla pōtiṉi mutal puttakam*. Irish acchu kutam, Madras, 1900.

Saminatha Pillai, T. G. *Arithmetic for Third standard Pupils (in Tamil)*. The Patriot Press, Tanjore, 1893.

Sankara Narayana Pillai, P. N. *Arithmetic Book I (Infants and I Standard)*. Coronation Arithmetic Series, Madras, 1903.

carma eṇcuvaṭi, n.d.

Savukkar Abdul latif Sayabu. *cūkṣma kaṇitam*. Vijaya Vikatan Press, Madras, 1913.

Shanmugam Pillai, K. P. *aḷavu nūl*. C. Coomarasamy & Sons, Madras, 1903.

Siddik, Muhammad Kasim Ubn. *Kitāb al Hisāb*. Kandy, 1891.

Singaravelu Mudaliar. *periya Keṭṭi eṇcuvaṭi*. Tondaimandalam Accu Kutam, Madras, 1893.

Subbarayar, R. *aṅka kaṇitam mutal paṅku*. Vidyavarthini Accu Kutam, Cenna Pattanam, 1881.

Sundaran. *kaṇita eṇcuvaṭi*, n.d.

Thampapillai, G. C. *A School Arithmetic Parts I–II (Notation, Numeration, Addition & Subtraction)*. St. Joseph's Catholic Press, Jaffna, 1892.

Thampapillai, G. C. *A School Arithmetic Part III Multiplication and Division*. Jaffna, 1892.

Thampapillai, G. C. *A School Arithmetic Part V Reduction, Compound Rules*. Jaffna, 1893.

Varadaraja Pillai, G. *eṇcuvaṭi (Arithmetical Tables With Some Hints on Teaching Them for Beginners)* (15th edition, n.d.).

Veluppillai, D. C. *The Elements of Euclid in Tamil Book 1* (1–15) for the Use of First Stage Students, Jaffna, 1888.

Venkatachari, P. *ilakka pōtaṉai muṟai* (The Tamil Method Is Prescribed by the Director of Public Instruction as Text to Be Used in the Elementary Normal Schools in Tamil Districts), 1891.

Bibliography

Archival and Manuscript Collections

Government Oriental Manuscripts Library, Chennai/Trivandrum

Kaṇita Cāttiram, R. 3920, Trivandrum
Kaṇita Curukkam, R 1148, 437, 6673, Chennai
Kaṇita Vākkiyam, R. 5445, 5446, Chennai
Kaṇitākamam, R 2166, Chennai
Kaṇitamāṉmiyam, 6364d, Trivandrum
Kaṇitāmirta Veṇpā, R 7976, Chennai
Keṭṭi Eṇcuvaṭi, R 6754, Chennai
Kuḻi Varukkam, R. 2451, Chennai
Mutu Kaṇakku, 8086 (b), Trivandrum
Pāla Kaṇakku, R. 2201, Chennai
Pālaciṭcai Kaṇitam, 8894, Trivandrum
Tamil Kaṇakku, R. 2403, Trivandrum

Sarasvathi Mahal Library, Thanjavur

Eṇcuvaṭi, Mss. 1150
Eṇcuvaṭi, Mss. 9739
Kaṇakkatikāram, Mss. 6251
Kaṇakkatikāram, Mss. 6814
Kaṇakkatikāram, Mss. 9791
Nel Kaṇakku, Mss. 1407

Bibliotheque National, Paris

Angappan, *Eṇcuvaṭi*, Indien No. 433
Appacami, *Nellilakkam*, Indien No. 437
Ceṭṭi Nāṭṭu Niluvai, Indien No. 552
Eṇcuvaṭi, Indien No. 997
Kaṇitam Nālu, Indien No. 438
Lekkam, Indien No. 435
Nellilakkam, Indien No. 436
Poṉṉilakkam, Indien No. 434
Yalpanatthu Antharaperumal Pillai, *Maravāṭi Kaṇakku*, Indien No. 441

Tamil University, Thanjavur Manuscripts Collection

Viṭukatai Kaṇakku, Mss. 1110

International Institute of Tamil Studies, Chennai

Kaṇita Tivākaram, Mss. 296

École française d'Extrême-Orient, Pondicherry

Kaṇakkatikāram, EO-541

Tamil Nadu State Archives, Madras, Chennai

Madras Presidency, Board of Revenue Proceedings 1820–1860
Madras Presidency, Public Consultations 1820–1860
Madras Presidency, Public Sundries
Madras Presidency, Proceedings of the Department of Education 1860–1900
Madras Presidency, Revenue Proceedings 1820–1850

United Theological College Archives, Bangalore

Proceedings of the Church Missionary Society
Proceedings of the Madras School Book Society
Vedanayakam Sastriar Papers

Printed Editions of Texts Used in the Study

Āstāṉa Kōlākalam, ed. K. Satyabama, Thanjavur Sarasvati Mahal Publication Series No. 464, Sarasvati Mahal Library, Thanjavur, 2004.

Āstāṉa Kōlākalam, ed. Thirumalai Sree Saila Sarma, Madras Government Oriental Series No. III, Government Oriental Manuscripts Library, Madras, 1951.

Ciṟuvar Cuvaṭi, itu piḷḷaikaḷ tamiḻ vācikkum muṟaiyai eḷitil kaṟṟukkoḷḷum poruṭṭu neṭuṅkaṇakkum acaiccol, ciru vākkiyaṅkaḷ, paḻamoḻikaḷ, cila kataikaḷ, nīti coṟkaḷ, mutaliyavaikaḷum cutta piratiyākki periyōruttarattiṉpaṭi putuvai kalvi cālaiyil patippikkappaṭṭatu, 1863, ceṉṉai.

Eṇcuvaṭi, ed. Kanthasami Mudaliar, Kamalalaya Vilasa acchu kutam, thathu, karthikai, 1876.

Kaṇakkatikāram – Tokuppu Nūl, ed. K. Satyabama Kamesvaran, Sarasvathi Mahal Library Publications, Thanjavur, 1998.

Kaṇakkatikāram, eds. P. Subramaniam and K. Satyabama, Institute of Asian Studies, Chennai, 2007.

Kaṇita Nūl: A Treatise on Mathematics, Part II, eds. P. Subramaniam and K. Satyabama, Institute of Asian Studies, Chennai, 2005.

Kaṇita Nūl: A Treatise on Mathematics, Part I, eds. P. Subramaniam and K. Satyabama, Institute of Asian Studies, Chennai, 1999.

Nayanar, Korukkaiyur Kari. *Kaṇakkatikāram*, ed. Sabapathi Mudaliar, Vivekavilakka accu kutam, Purasawakkam, Rowtthiri, Avani, 1920.

Nayanar, Korukkaiyur Kari. *Kaṇakkatikāram*, ed. Shanmuga Mudaliar, Vivekavilakka accu kutam, Purasawakkam, Irakthakshi, Masi, 1925.

Nayanar, Korukkaiyur Kari. *Kaṇakkatikāram*, ed. Subramania Swamikal, Sri Padmanaba Vilasa accu kutam, Madras, 1899.

Nayanar, Korukkaiyur Kari. *Kaṇakkatikāram*, ed. Thiruninravur Arunachala Swamikal, iyalicai nataka vilaca Accu Kutam, Citthartthi, pankuni, 1859.
Neṭuṅkaṇakku, mutaleḻuttu uyireḻuttu ōracai īracai mūvacai nālacai cila kataikaḷ poṉṉilakkam nellilakkam ilakkiya vilakkaṇa pataṅkaḷ ākiya itu puttakam peṅkaḷūrukku aṭutta araca mānakaram vittiyā vilāca accukkūṭattil patippikkappaṭṭatu, vicuvāvacu, 1846.
Suriyapūpaṉ Kaṇakkatikāram (Pakuti II), ed. K. Satyabama, Sarasvathi Mahal Library Publications, Thanjavur, 2007.

Government Reports

A Description of the Actual State of Education in the Madras Presidency on the 31 March 1882. Madras: Fort St. George Press, 1882.
Annual Report of the Department of Public Instruction for the years 1879–1880, Madras, Government Press, and from 1881 up to 1900.
Gover, Charles, *Survey of Education in Madras*. Madras: Government of Madras, 1871.
Madras Provincial Committee, Educational Commission, *Report by the Madras Provincial Committee: With Evidence Taken Before the Committee, and Memorials Addressed to the Education Commission*. Calcutta: Government Press, 1884.
Papers Relating to Public Instruction, Comprising a Memorandum of the Proceedings of the Madras Government in the Department of Public Instruction, With an Appendix, Containing All the More Important Papers Recorded on the Subject. Compiled by Alexander J. Arbuthnot. Madras: Fort St. George Gazette Press, 1855.
Papers Relating to the State of Education in the Provinces Subject to the Government of Madras, Madras, Government Press, 1854
Selections From the Records of the Madras Government Report on Public Instruction in the Madras Presidency, 1854–1855, Madras, Government Press, 1855.

Books and Articles

'Tamiḻarē Ulakiṟku Eṇkalai Kouttatu', *Centamil*, 1902.
Acharya, Poromesh. 'Indigenous Education and Brahminical Hegemony in Bengal'. In *The Transmission of Knowledge in South Asia: Essays on Education, Religion, History and Politics*, ed. Nigel Crook, 98–118. Delhi: Oxford University Press, 1996.
Alexander, A. R. 'Introduction, Special Issue on "Mathematical Stories"'. *Isis 97* (2006): 333–347.
Anantharaman, Sita. *Getting Girls to School: Social Reform in the Tamil Districts 1870–1930*. Calcutta: Stree, 1996.
Annamalai, P. *Nakarattār Kaṇakkiyal Muṟai*. Chennai: Manivasakar Pathippagam, 1988.
Arnold, David. *Science, Technology and Medicine in Colonial India*. Cambridge: Cambridge University Press, 2000.
Arunachalam, Mu. *History of Tamil Literature Through the Centuries, XV Century*. Thiruchitrambalam: Gandhi Vidyalayam, 1969.

Baber, Zaheer. *The Science of Empire: Scientific Knowledge, Civilization and Colonial Rule in India*. Delhi: Oxford University Press, 1998.

Balar Kanitam. An Elementary Arithmetic Combining Many of the Peculiarities of the European and Tamil System. Jaffna: American Mission Press, 1849.

Baliga, B. S. *Literacy in Madras 1822–1931, Studies in Madras Administration*, Vol. 2. Madras: Government Press, 1960.

Bartlett, Frederic Charles. *Remembering: A Study in Experimental and Social Psychology*, Vol. 14. Cambridge: Cambridge University Press, 1995.

Basu, Aparna. *Essays in the History of Indian Education*. New Delhi: Concept Publishing Company, 1982.

Bayly, Christopher A. *Empire and Information: Political Intelligence and Social Communication in North India, 1780–1880*. Cambridge: Cambridge University Press, 1999.

Bell, Andrew. *The Madras School or Elements of Tuition Comprising the Analysis of an Experiment in Education Made at the Male Asylum, Madras, With Its Facts, Proofs and Illustrations*. London: J. Murray, 1808.

Bennett, Jim A. 'Practical Geometry and Operative Knowledge'. *Configurations* 6, no. 2 (1998): 195–222.

Bronner, Yigal, and David Shulman. '"A Cloud Turned Goose": Sanskrit in the Vernacular Millennium'. *The Indian Economic and Social History Review* 43, no. 1 (2006): 1–30.

Brouwer, Jan. *The Makers of the Modern World: Caste, Craft and Mind of South Indian Artisans*. New Delhi: Oxford University Press, 1995.

Caminata Iyer, U. Ve. *Eṉ Carittiram*. Chennai: U. V. Swaminatha Aiyar Library, 1990.

Campbell-Kelly, M., Croarken, M., Flood, R., and Robson, E., eds. *The History of Mathematical Tables from Sumer to Spreadsheets*. Oxford: Oxford University Press, 2003.

Campbell, A. D. 'On Native Education'. *Madras Journal of Literature and Science* (April 1836): 110–116.

Carruthers, Mary. *The Book of Memory: A Study of Memory in Medieval Culture*. Cambridge: Cambridge University Press, 1990.

CE Gover. *Indian Weights and Measures: Their Condition and Remedy*. Madras: W. Thomas, 1865.

Chacraverti, Santanu. *Subhankari*, The Asiatic Society Monograph Series No. XLIII. Kolkata: The Asiatic Society, 2007.

Chakrabarti, Pratik. *Western Science in Modern India: Metropolitan Methods Colonial Practices*. Delhi: Permanent Black, 2004.

Chelvakesavaraya Mutaliar, T. 'Tamil Education Address Delivered to the Students of the Teachers' College (Saidapet)'. *Madras Christian College Magazine*, January 1901.

Cullen, Christopher. 'People and Numbers in Early Imperial China'. In *The Oxford Handbook of the History of Mathematics*, eds. Eleanor Robson and Jacqueline Stedall, 591–618. Oxford/New York: Oxford University Press, 2009.

Cuomo, Serafina. 'Divide and Rule: Frontius and Roman Land-Surveying'. *Studies in History and Philosophy of Science Part A* 31, no. 2 (2000): 189–202.

Cutts, Elmer H. 'The Background of Macaulay's Minute'. *American Historical Review* 58, no. 4 (1953): 824–853.

Damerow, Peter. *Abstraction and Representation: Essays on the Cultural Evolution of Thinking*. Boston Studies in the Philosophy and the History of Science Series Vol. 175, Dordrecht: Kluwer Academic Publishers, 1996.

Damerow, Peter. *The Material Culture of Calculation a Conceptual Framework for an Historical Epistemology of the Concept of Number*. Berlin: Max Planck Institute for the History of Science, Preprint 117, 1999.

Dani, S. G. 'Ancient Indian Mathematics: A Conspectus'. *Resonance* 17, no. 3 (March 2012): 236–246.

Daniel, Valentine E. *Charred Lullabies: Chapters in an Anthropology of Violence*. Princeton: Princeton University Press, 1996.

Datta, Bibhutibhushan, and Avhadesh Narayan Singh. *History of Hindu Mathematics: A Source Book*, 2 vols. Bombay: Asia Publishing House, 1962.

De Morgan, Augustus. *The Study of Mathematics Part I and II, Published Under the Superintendence of the Society for the Diffusion of Useful Knowledge*. London: Society for the Diffusion of Useful Knowledge, 1830.

Deivanayakam, C. K. *Palajatika Vikaṭam*. Thanjavur: Sarasvathi Mahal Library, 1986.

Dharampal. *The Beautiful Tree: Indigenous Indian Education in the Eighteenth Century*. New Delhi: Biblia Impex, 1983.

Dilke, O. A. W. *The Roman Land Surveyors: An Introduction to the Agrimensores*. Newton Abbot: David and Charles, 1971.

Dulau, Robert. *Nakaramum Vīṭum Vāḻumiṭattiṉ Uṇarvukaḷ*. Pondicherry: French Institute of Pondicherry, 1992.

Edney, Mathew. *Mapping an Empire: The Geographical Construction of British India, 1765–1843*. Chicago: University of Chicago Press, 1997.

Eickelman, Dale F. 'The Art of Memory: Islamic Education and Its Social Reproduction'. *Comparative Studies in Society and History* 20, no. 4 (1978): 485–516.

Filliozat, Pierre Sylvain. 'Ancient Sanskrit Mathematics: An Oral Tradition and a Written Literature'. In *History of Science, History of Text*, ed. Karine Chemla, 137–157. Boston Studies in the Philosophy of Science, Vol. 238, Netherlands: Springer, 2005.

Frykenberg, Robert. 'Modern Education in South India, 1784–1854: Its Roots and Its Role as a Vehicle of Integration Under Company Raj'. *American Historical Review* 91, no. 1 (1986): 37–65.

Ganapati Sthapathi, V. *Contributions of Viswakarmas to the Science, Technology and Culture of Indian Origin*. Chennai: Dakshinaa Publishing House, 2000.

Ganapati Sthapathi, V. *Cirpa Cennul*. Madras: Directorate of Technical Education, 1978.

Gheverghese, George Joseph. *The Crest of the Peacock: Non-European Roots of Mathematics*. Princeton: Princeton University Press, 2011.

Gopal Iyer, T. V. *Tamil Eḻuttum ēṭum*. Thanjavur: Tamil University Publications, 1990.

Gray, Jeremy. 'History of Science and History of Mathematics Reunited?' *Isis* 102 Special Issue (2012): 511–517.

Gupta, Akhil. *Postcolonial Developments: Agriculture in the Making of Modern India*. Durham: Duke University Press, 1998.

Gurumurthy, S. *Education in South India Ancient and Medieval Periods*. Chennai: New Era Publications, 1979.

Haider, Najaf. 'Norms of Professional Excellence and Good Conduct in Accountancy Manuals of the Mughal Empire'. *International Review of Social History* 56 Special Issue (2011): 263–274.

Hamilton, W. R. 'A Review of Rev. William Whewell's Thoughts on the Study of Mathematics as a Part of Liberal Education'. *Edinburgh Review* 62 (1836): 218–252.

Hogan, David. 'The Market Revolution and Disciplinary Power: Joseph Lancaster and the Psychology of the Early Classroom System'. *History of Education Quarterly* 29, no. 3 (1989): 381–417.

Howson, Geoffrey. *A History of Mathematics Education in England*. Cambridge: Cambridge University Press, 1982.

Høyrup, Jens. 'Jacopo da Firenze's Tractatus Algorismi and Early Italian Abbacus Culture'. In *Science Networks Historical Studies*, Vol. 34, Springer Science & Business Media, 2007.

Høyrup, Jens. 'Mathematics, Recreational and Practical'. In *Encyclopedia of the History of Science, Technology, and Medicine in Non-Western Cultures*, Vol 2, ed. Helaine Selin, 1352–1356. New York: Springer Verlag, 2013.

Høyrup, Jens. 'Practitioners – School Teachers – "Mathematicians": The divisions of Pre-Modern Mathematics and Its Actors'. *Contribution to the Conference on Writing and Rewriting the History of Science 1900–2000*, Les Treilles (September 2003): 5–11.

Høyrup, Jens. 'The Sub-Scientific Heritage in "Abbaco" Mathematics: Quasi-Algebra and Other Queer Species'. *L'Educatizione Matematica*, Anno XXII, Serie VI, Vol. 3, pp. 23–39. http://akira.ruc.dk/~jensh/Publications/2001%7Bh%7D_Lasciti%20 sotto-scientifici_S.pdf, Accessed January 5, 2015.

Høyrup, Jens. *In Measure, Number and Weight: Studies in Mathematics and Culture*. Albany: SUNY Press, 1994.

Høyrup, Jens. *Sanskrit-Prakrit Interaction in Elementary Mathematics as Reflected in Arabic and Italian Formulations of the Rule of Three – and Something More on the Rule Elsewhere*. Berlin: Max Planck Institute for the History of Science, Preprint No. 435, 2012.

Høyrup, Jens. *The Rare Traces of Constructional Procedures in 'Practical Geometries'*. Raekke, Filosofi Og Videnskabsteoripa, Roskilde Universtitetscenter, 3, Preprints Number 2, 2006.

Høyrup, Jens. 'Seleucid Innovations in the Babylonian "Algebraic" Tradition and Their Kin Abroad'. *From China to Paris: 2000 Years Transmission of Mathematical Ideas*, 9–29. Stuttgart: Franz Steiner Verlag, 2002.

Ifrah, Georges. *The Universal History of Numbers*, 4 Volumes. New Delhi, Penguin Books, 2005.

Imhausen, Annette. *Mathematics in Ancient Egypt: A Contextual History*. Princeton and Oxford: Princeton University Press, 2016.

Israel, Hephzibah. 'Cutcherry Tamil vs. Pure Tamil: Contesting Language Use in the Translated Bible in the Early Nineteenth Century Protestant Tamil Community'. In *The Postcolonial Bible Reader*, ed. R. S. Sugirtharajah, 269, Malden: Blackwell, 2006.

Kalpagam, U. 'Cartography in Colonial India'. *Economic and Political Weekly* 30, no. 30 (July 29, 1995): PE87–PE98.

Kalpagam, U. 'The Colonial State and Statistical Knowledge'. *History of the Human Sciences* 13, no. 2 (2000): 37–55.

Kannaiyan, Pulavar. *Revenue Administration in Madras*, Unpublished Notes, n.d.

Karp, Alexander, and Gert Schubring, eds. *Handbook on the History of Mathematics Education*. New York: Springer, 2014.

Keller, Agathe. 'George Peacock's Arithmetic in the Changing Landscape of the History of Mathematics in India'. *Indian Journal of History of Science* 46, no. 2 (2011): 205–233.

Keller, Agathe. 'Is "Hindu mathematics" a European idea?/Son las "matematicas hindues" une aidea europea? Aportaciones sobre la politica en la historia de la aritmetica'. *Publicacions de la residencia d'investigadors* 38 (2013): 332.

Kumar, Deepak. *Science and the Raj*. Delhi: Oxford University Press, 1995.

Kumar, Krishna. *Political Agenda of Education: A Study of Colonialist and Nationalist Ideas*. New Delhi: Sage, 2005.

Kumar, Nita. 'Provincialism in Modern India: The Multiple Narratives of Education and Their Pain'. *Modern Asian Studies* 40, no. 2 (2006): 397–423.

Kumar, Nita. *Lessons From Schools: The History of Education in Banaras*. New Delhi: Sage Publications, 2000.

Lave, Jean. *Cognition in Practice: Mind, Mathematics and Culture in Everyday Life*. New York: Cambridge University Press, 1988.

Lave, Jean. 'The Values of Quantification'. *The Sociological Review* 32 (1984): 88–111.

Banerjee, H. C., ed. *Lilavati of Bhaskaracharya*, Translated by H. R. Colebrooke, Allahabad: Kitab Mahal, 1967.

Manickam, S. *Studies in Missionary History: Reflections on a Culture-Contact*. Madras: Christian Literature Society, 1988.

Minkoswki, Christopher. 'Astronomers and Their Reasons: Working Paper on Jyotiḥśāstra'. *Journal of Indian Philosophy* 30, no. 5 (October 2002): 495–514.

Minkowski, Christopher. 'The Study of Jyotiḥśāstra and the Uses of Philosophy of Science'. *Journal of Indian Philosophy* 36, nos. 5–6 (2008) 587–597.

Mosteller, John F. *The Measure of Form A New Approach for the Study of Indian Sculpture*. New Delhi, Abhinav Publications, 1991.

Mukherjee, Nilmani, and Frykenberg, Robert Eric. 'The Ryotwari System and Social Organization in the Madras Presidency'. In *Land Control and Social Structure in Indian History*, ed. R. E. Frykenberg, 217–225, Delhi: Manohar, 1979.

Mukherjee, Nilmani. *The Ryotwari System in Madras, 1792–1827*. Calcutta: Firma K. L. Mukhopadhyay, 1962.

Mukhopadhyay, Swapna. 'Making Visible: Mathematics of Cultural Practices'. *Presentation at the National Seminar on Historical and Cultural Aspects of Mathematics Education*, Indira Gandhi National Open University, New Delhi, December 2–3, 2011.

Naicker, Pantulu Ramasamy. *Kanitadeepikai*. Madras: Madras School Book Society, 1825.

Naraniengar, M. T. 'The Geometrical Projection of the Life of a Vaishnavite Brahmin'. *Mathematics Student*, 1917.

Narasimma, Roddam. 'Epistemology and Language in Indian Astronomy and Mathematics'. *Journal of Indian Philosophy* 35, nos. 5–6 (2007): 521–541.

Narayana, Rao V., David Shulman, and Sanjay Subrahmanyam. *Textures of Time: Writing History in South India 1600–1800*. New Delhi: Permanent Black, 2011.

Nurullah, Syed, and J. P. Naik. *A Students' History of Education in India (1800–1961)*. Bombay: Mac Millan & Co., 1962.

Perumal, A. K. *Nāñcilnāṭṭu Mutaliyār ōlaicuvaṭikaḷ Kāṭṭum Camūkam*. Chennai: Makkal Veliyitu, 1999.

Peterson, Indira Vishwanathan. 'Between Print and Performance: The Tamil Christian Poetry of Vedanayaka Shastri and the Literary Cultures of Nineteenth Century South India'. In *India's Literary History, Essays on the Nineteenth Century*, eds. Vasudha Dalmia and Stuart Blackburn, 25–59, Delhi: Permanent Black, 2004.

Pheru, Thakkur. *Gaṇitasārakaumudī: The Moonlight of the Essence of Mathematics*, eds. Sreeramula Rajeswara Sarma, Takanori Kusuba, Takao Hayashi, and Michio Yano (SaKHYa). Delhi: Manohar Publisher and Distributors, 2009.

Philips, C. 'Augustus De Morgan and the Propagation of Moral Mathematics'. *Studies in History and Philosophy of Science* 36 (2005): 105–133.

Pingree, David. *Census of Exact Sciences in Sanskrit*, Series A, Volumes 1–5. Philadelphia: American Philosophical Society, 1970–1994.

Pingree, David. *Jyotihsastra Astral and Mathematical Literature, A History of Indian Literature*, Vol. VI., ed. Jane Gonda, Wiesbaden: Harrassowitz, 1981.

Plofker, Kim. 'How to Appreciate Indian Techniques for Deriving Mathematical Formulas?' In *Mathematical Europe: History, Myth, Identity*, eds. Catherine Goldstein, Jeremy Gray, and Jim Ritter, 53–65, Paris: Edition de la Maison des Sciences de l'Homme, 1996.

Plofker, Kim. 'Links Between Sanskrit and Muslim Science in Jaina Astronomical Works'. *International Journal of Jaina Studies* 6, no. 5 (2010): 1–13.

Plofker, Kim. 'Sanskrit Mathematical Verse'. In *The Oxford Handbook of the History of Mathematics*, eds. Eleanor Robson and Jacqueline Stendhal, 519–536, Oxford/New York: Oxford University Press, 2009.

Plofker, Kim. *Mathematics in India*. Princeton: Princeton University Press, 2009.

Pollock, Sheldon. 'The Languages of Science in Early Modern India'. In *Forms of Knowledge in Early Modern Asia Explorations in the Intellectual History of India and Tibet, 1500–1800*, ed. Sheldon Pollock, 19–46, Durham: Duke University Press, 2011.

Poovey, Mary. 'Figures of Arithmetic, Figures of Speech: The Discourse of Statistics in the 1830s'. *Critical Inquiry* 19, no. 2 (1993): 256–276.

Porter, Theodore M. *The Rise of Statistical Thinking 1820–1900*. Princeton: Princeton University Press, 1986.

Pushkala, T. *Cenkarpaṭṭu āvaṇaṅkaḷ – Camūkap Poruḷātāram*, PhD diss., Department of Manuscript Studies, Tanjavur, Tamil University, 1997.

Radhakrishnan, P. 'Caste Discrimination in Indian Education I: Nature and Extent of Education in Early Nineteenth Century India'. *MIDS Working Paper no. 63*, Chennai: 1986.

Radhakrishnan, P. 'Indigenous Education in British India: A Profile'. *Contributions to Indian Sociology* 24, no. 1 (January–June 1990): 1–29.

Raina, Dhruv, and S. Irfan Habib. 'Ramchandra's Treatise Through the Haze of the Golden Sunset: An Aborted Pedagogy'. *Social Studies of Science* 20, no. 3 (1990): 455–472.

Raina, Dhruv, and S. Irfan Habib. 'The Missing Picture: The Non-Emergence of Needhamian History of Sciences in India'. In *Situating the History of*

Science: Dialogues With Joseph Needham, eds. S. Irfan Habib and Dhruv Raina, 279–302, New Delhi: Oxford University Press, 1999.

Raina, Dhruv, and S. Irfan Habib. *Domesticating Modern Science: A Social History of Science and Culture in Colonial India*. New Delhi: Tulika Books, 2004.

Raina, Dhruv. 'Contextualizing Playfair and Colebrooke on Proof and Demonstration in the Indian Mathematical Tradition'. In *The History of Mathematical Proof in Ancient Traditions*, ed. Karine Chemla, 228–259, Cambridge: Cambridge University Press, 2012.

Raina, Dhruv. 'French Jesuit Scientists in India: Historical Astronomy in the Discourse on India, 1670–1770'. *Economic and Political Weekly* 34, no. 5 (1999): PE30–PE38.

Raina, Dhruv. 'Historiographic Concerns Underlying Indian Journal of the History of Science: A Bibliometric Inference'. *Economic and Political Weekly* 33, no. 8 (1998): 407–414.

Raina, Dhruv. 'Jean-Baptiste Biot on the History of Indian Astronomy (1830–1860): The Nation in the Post-Enlightenment Historiography of Science'. *Indian Journal of History of Science* 35, no. 4 (2000): 319–346.

Raina, Dhruv. 'Mathematical Foundations of a Cultural Project or Ramchandra's Treatise "Through the Unsentimentalised Light of Mathematics"'. *Historia mathematica* 19, no. 4 (1992): 371–384.

Raina, Dhruv. 'Situating the History of Indian Arithmetical Knowledge in George Peacock's Arithmetic'. *Indian Journal of History of Science* 46, no. 2 (2011): 235–250.

Raina, Dhruv. 'The Naturalization of Modern Science in South Asia: A Historical Overview of the Processes of Domestication and Globalization'. In *The Globalization of Knowledge in History*, ed. Jurgen Renn, 345–366, Max Planck Research Library for the History and Development of Knowledge, 2012. http://www.edition-open-access.de

Raina, Dhruv. *Needham's India Network the Search for a Home for the History of Science in India (1950–1970)*. Delhi: Yoda Press, 2015.

Raj, Kapil. 'Beyond Post Colonialism … and Postpositivism: Circulation and the Global History of Science'. *Isis* 104, no. 2 (2013): 337–347.

Raj, Kapil. *Relocating Modern Science Circulation and the Construction of Scientific Knowledge in South Asia and Europe Seventeenth to Nineteenth Centuries*. Delhi: Permanent Black, 2006.

Rajagopalan, K. R. 'Mathematics in Tamil Nadu'. *Bhavan's Journal* 5, no. 20 (1959): 41–44.

Rajendiran, M. *Vaṭakarai - Oru Vamcattiṉ Varalāṟu*. Vandavasi: Agani Veliyidu, 2014.

Raman, Bhavani. *Document Raj Writing and Scribes in Early Colonial South India*. Chicago: University of Chicago Press, 2012.

Richman, Paula. *Extraordinary Child Poems From a South Indian Devotional Genre*. Honolulu: SHAPS Library of Translations, 1997.

Roberts, Lissa. 'Situating Science in Global History Local Exchanges and Networks of Circulation'. *Itinerario* 33, no. 1 (2009): 9–30.

Roberts, Lissa, Kapil Raj, and James Delbourgo. *The Brokered World: Go-Betweens and Global Intelligence. 1770–1820*, Sagamore Beach, MA: Science History Publications, 2009.

Robson, E. 'More Than Metrology: Mathematics Education in an Old Babylonian Scribal School'. In *Under One Sky: Mathematics and Astronomy in the Ancient Near (Alter Orient und Altes Testament, 297)*, eds. J. M. Steele and A. Imhausen, 325–365, Ugarit-Verlag, 2002.

Robson, Eleanor. 'Mathematics, Metrology, and Professional Numeracy'. *The Babylonian World* (2007): 414–427. doi:10.4324/9780203946237.CH29.

Rogers, Leo. 'The Mathematical Curriculum and Pedagogy in England 1780–1900: Social and Cultural Origins'. *History and Epistemology in Mathematics Education, Proceedings of the First European Summer University Montpellier*, Irem de Montpellier, Montpellier: July 1993, 401–412.

Roux, Sophie. 'Forms of Mathematization'. *Early Science and Medicine* 15 (2010): 319–337.

Saito, Fumikazu. 'History of Mathematics and History of Science: Some Remarks Concerning Contextual Framework'. *Educacao Matematica Pesquita* 4, no. 3 (2012): 363–385.

Salmon, David, ed. *The Practical Parts of Lancaster's Improvements and Bell's Experiments*. Cambridge: Cambridge University Press, 1932.

Sambandam, Pammal. *Eṉ cuyacaritai*. Chennai: Sandhya Patippagam, 2012 (1st edition, 1963).

Sampanthan, M. S. *Accum Patippum*. Chennai: Manivasakar Pathippagam, 1997.

Sarma, Sreeramula Rajeswara. 'Mathematical Literature in the Regional Languages of India'. In *Ancient Indian Leaps Into Mathematics*, eds. B. S. Yadav and Man Mohan, 201–211, Boston: Birkhaüser, 2011.

Sarma, Sreeramula Rajeswara. 'Pavuluriganitamu: The First Telugu Work on Mathematics'. In *Studien Zur Indologie Und Iranistik*, eds. George Buddruss et al., 163–176, Reinbek: Verlag fur Orientalistische Fachpublikationen, 1987.

Sarma, Sreeramula Rajeswara. 'Some Medieval Arithmetical Tables'. *Indian Journal of History of Science* 32, no. 3 (1997): 191–198.

Sarma, Sreeramula Rajeswara. 'The Rule of Three and Its Variations in India'. In *From China to Paris: 2000 Years Transmission of Mathematical Ideas*, eds. Yvonne Dold Samplonius et al., 133–156, Stuttgart: Franz Steiner Verlag, 2002.

Schaffer, Simon. 'Indiscipline and Interdisciplines: Some Exotic Genealogies of Modern Knowledge'. http://www.hse.ru/data/2011/11/13/1272007743/Schaffer.2010.Indiscipline_and_interdisciplines.pdf. Accessed January 5, 2015.

Schaffer, Simon. 'How Disciplines Look'. In *Interdisciplinarity: Reconfigurations of the Social and Natural Sciences*, eds. Andrew Barry and Georgina Born, 57–81, London, Routledge, 2013.

Seth, Sanjay. *Subject Lessons: The Western Education of Colonial India*. Durham: Duke University Press, 2007.

Shahidullah, Kazi. 'The Purpose and Impact of Government Policy on Pathshala Gurumohashoys in Nineteenth Century Bengal'. In *The Transmission of Knowledge in South Asia Essays on Education, Religion, History, and Politics*, eds. Nigel Crook, 119–134, Delhi: Oxford University Press, 1996.

Sivalingaraja, S., and Sarasvati, S. *Pattoṉpatām Nūṟṟāṇṭil Yāḻppāṇattu Tamil Kalvi*. Colombo - Chennai: Kumaran Putthaka Illam, 2000.

Sivasubramanian, A. *Aṭittaḷa Makkaḷ Varalāṟu*. Chennai: Makkal Veliyeedu, 2002.

Smith, Pamela, and Paula Findlen, eds. *Merchants and Marvels Commerce, Science and Art in Early Modern Europe*. London: Routledge, 2013.

Special Section on 'Mathematics in India', *Current Science* 99, no. 3, 2010.

Srinivas, M. D. 'The Methodology of Indian Mathematics and Its Contemporary Relevance'. *PPST Bulletin*, no. 23 (June 1992).

Srinivas, M. D., Paramasivam, T. G., and Pushkala, T. *Thirupporur and Vadakkuppattu: Eighteenth Century Locality Accounts*. Chennai: Centre for Policy Studies, 2001.

Subbarayulu, Y. *South India Under the Colas*. New Delhi: Oxford University Press, 2011.

Subbarayulu, Y. *Studies in Cola History*. Chennai: Surabhi Pathippakam, 2001.

Sur, Abha. *Dispersed Radiance: Caste, Gender and Modern Science in India*. Delhi: Navayana, 2011.

Swaminatha Ayer, U. Ve., ed. *Naṉṉūl Mūlamum Caṅkara Namaccivāyar Uraiyum*. Chennai: U. V. Swaminatha Aiyar Library, 1953.

Swaminatha Iyer, U. V. *Eṉ Carittiram*. Chennai: U. V. Swaminatha Aiyar Library, 1990.

Swetz, Frank. *Capitalism & Arithmetic: The New Math of the 15th Century*. Illinois: Open Court Publishing, 1987.

The Ganitasarasangraha of Mahaviracarya With English Translation and Notes, edited and translated by Rangacarya, M. Madras: Government Press, 1912.

Tiwari, Rajiv. 'A Transnarrative for the Colony: Astronomy Education and Religion in Nineteenth Century India'. *Economic and Political Weekly* 41, no. 13 (2006): 1269–1277.

Trautman, Thomas R., ed. *The Madras School of Orientalism Producing Knowledge in Colonial South India*. Delhi: Oxford University Press, 2009.

Tschurenev, Jana. 'Diffusing Useful Knowledge: The Monitorial System of Education in Madras, London and Bengal, 1789–1840'. *Pedagogica Historica* 44, no. 3 (2008): 245–264.

Tschurenev, Jana. 'Incorporation and Differentiation: Popular Education and the Imperial Civilizing Mission in Early Nineteenth Century India'. In *Civilizing Mission in Colonial and Postcolonial South Asia: From Improvement to Development*, eds. Carey A. Watt and Michael Mann, 93–124, London: Anthem Press, 2011.

Venkatachalapathy, A. R. *The Province of the Book: Scribes, Scribblers and Print*. Delhi: Permanent Black, 2011.

Vijayalakshmi, K. *Tamiḻar Paṇpāṭṭil Aḷavaikaḷ*. Thanjavur: Annam, 2006.

Viswanathan, Gauri. *Masks of Conquest: Literary Study and British Rule in India*. New Delhi: Oxford University Press, 1998.

Wagoner, Phillip B. 'Precolonial Intellectuals and the Production of Colonial Knowledge'. *Comparative Studies in Society and History* 45, no. 4 (2003): 783–814.

Whewell, William. *Thoughts on the Study of Mathematics as Part of a Liberal Education*. Cambridge: J. & J. J. Deighton, 1836.

Yano, Michio. 'Oral and Written Transmission of the Exact Sciences in Sanskrit'. *Journal of Indian Philosophy* 34, nos. 1–2 (April 2006): 143–160.

Index

ability, 131
absolute measures, 181
absolute values, 181
abstract, 11, 13, 30, 107, 115, 117, 151, 167, 168, 172, 184, 188
abstract quantities, 184
abstraction, 4, 8, 11, 51, 83, 95, 107, 112, 115, 117, 119, 172–73
accountancy, 33
accountant manuals, 31
accountant- scribe, 119
accountant(s), 1, 6, 8, 10, 12, 17, 31, 33, 38, 83, 85–86, 89, 93, 97, 117, 119–20, 128, 139, 170, 181, 216
accounting, 16–17, 20–21, 33, 92, 195, 198
accuracy, 106, 157, 168, 212
acre, 178–79
acuṇam, 217
addition(s), 35, 41, 65, 69, 73, 82, 147–51, 155, 163–64, 166–67, 181, 183, 188, 205, 208, 210, 217
administration, 13, 33, 85, 87, 90–91, 125, 128, 170, 180, 196
agrarian, 36, 88, 116, 129, 219
agriculture, 32
aided schools, 203–04
Akattiya Nūl, 44
Aḻakiyapāṇṭipuram, 21
alakunilai, 99, 154, 158
Algebra, 56, 191, 198, 210, 211–12, 214
algebraic, 10, 35, 37, 80, 210
algorithm, 57, 100, 116, 166, 167
algorithmic, 3, 164, 166
alienation, 14, 121, 224
almanacs, 196
Andhra, 1–2, 18, 37, 93
Andrew Bell, 219
Anglo-Indian, 179
Anglo vernacular, 198
anthropological, 25
Apabrahmsa, 34
apprenticeship, 8, 25, 82, 86, 90, 168, 181–82
apprentices, 92, 192
appropriation, 13
approximation, 56
aptitude, 199, 224
Arabic numerals, 55, 195
Āraṇipāḷaiyam, 43
Arbuthnot, 199, 200
archival, 20
archive, 174
area, 21, 26, 38, 40, 46, 57, 59, 60–62, 69, 71, 88, 93, 95, 103–05, 107, 109, 134, 141, 159, 163, 170, 180, 189
Ariccuvaṭi, 101, 139, 140, 160
arithmetic, 8, 10, 12–15, 17–18, 20, 31, 33, 35, 38, 40, 52, 66, 85, 94, 97, 100–02, 105–06, 112, 114–16, 122, 127, 136, 141, 166–67, 169–71, 182–85, 187–89, 191, 193, 196, 198, 200–01, 204, 206–13, 218
arjya, 32
artisanal, 25
artisans, 6, 17, 26, 198
Arumuga Mudaliar, 91
Arumugam Navalar, 212
Aryabhata, 57, 110, 112–13
Aryabhatiyam, 57
Assam, 31
assessment, 88, 89–90, 177–78, 180–81, 194, 201, 204, 223
assimilation, 114, 208
associative nature, 166
Āstāṉa Kōlākalam, 41–42, 44, 48–49, 51–52, 56–57, 73, 82, 87, 92–93, 97, 103, 109–11, 122, 216
astrologer, 117, 133
astronomer, 12, 38, 83, 106, 111–12, 114–20

astronomy, 8, 111, 113, 117, 124
asymmetry, 13, 15
Aticākaram, 38
Atikāram, 48, 53
aṭikōl, 59, 179, 198
Ātticūṭi, 139, 140
Augustus De Morgan, 193
authority, 11, 83, 85–86, 90, 106, 117, 129, 170, 181, 189, 190, 200, 203
Avadhi, 37
Avvaiyar, 93

B.S. Baliga, 125
Bālaciṭcai Kaṇitam, 40
Bangalore, 184
banking, 34
Barnard Smith, 198
Barnard Survey, 180
Bay of Bengal, 123
bazaar arithmetic, 208
bazaar mathematics, 209
Bell Lancaster, 193
Bell system, 183, 185–86, 193
Benares, 176
Bengal, 3, 18, 25, 32, 123, 125
Bengali, 127, 176
Bentham, 219
Bhaskara, 37, 110–11, 113–15
Bhaskara II, 114
Bhata- Bhaskara, 6, 16, 57
bigha, 32, 35
Bijaganita, 37
binary(ies), 35, 36, 38, 114, 119, 120, 225
Board of Revenue, 179
boat-makers, 8
Bombay, 123, 125, 195
book keeper, 139
bookkeeping, 208
Brahmagupta, 110
Brahmin(s), 1–2, 8, 12, 38, 54, 83, 106, 114, 117, 123, 131, 190–91, 200, 204, 214
Brahminic, 126
British, 17, 88, 123, 125–27, 130, 173–74, 176, 176, 195–96, 198, 200, 219–20, 223
British Educational surveys, 123
British measures, 198
British standards, 196
brokering, 13
bureaucracy, 170, 181, 197, 200, 203, 206, 210
bureaucratic, 116–17, 126, 174, 191, 208

calculation(s), 8, 33, 46, 50, 111–12, 162–63, 170, 181, 220
calculators, 180
calendar(s), 33, 70, 141
Cāmināta Aiyar, 139, 161, 166
canals, 46
caṅkam, 27, 42
Canmuka Narayana Tamotara Vattiyar, 134
canonical, 4, 6, 9–11, 16, 37, 83, 114
canonicity, 6, 10, 36
canonization, 4–5
capacity (measures), 48, 51, 66–68, 84, 96, 98, 129, 150, 182
carpenters, 25, 34
caste(s), 2, 4, 8–9, 11–12, 15, 20, 23–24, 33, 38, 80, 83, 85–90, 92, 101, 106, 113–14, 117–20, 122, 126, 128–29, 131, 135–36, 169–70, 172, 174, 181, 185, 190, 192, 197, 202–07, 214–15, 219, 224–25
Catakopan Aiyangar, 133, 161
catechism, 186
caṭṭāmpiḷḷai, 136
Caturveta Siddhantha Sabha, 194
celestial, 116–17
certification, 139, 195, 200, 202, 208
Ceṭṭiyār, 77, 79
Chacraverti, 32, 33
Charles Hutton, 192
Charles Schmidt, 185
Chidambaram, 194
childhood, 136
children, 186
Chingleput, 23, 87–88, 124
Chingleput Revenue Accounts, 21
Church Missionary Society (CMS), 183, 185
cilvāṉam, 94

circle, 1, 56, 107
circular, 57, 60–61, 198
circulation, 2, 4, 7, 11, 13–15, 43–44, 51, 71, 92, 116, 122, 128, 133, 167, 177, 180, 182, 184, 187, 189, 194, 202, 215, 225
circumference, 56–57, 61
cirpa cennūl, 25, 27
Ciru Kaṇakku, 40, 53
civil services, 200
classroom, 93, 175, 190, 198, 200, 220
clerical, 169, 200, 209
clerks, 7, 121, 185
cognitive, 123, 129, 138, 167, 170–71, 175, 183, 188
Cōla, 72
Cōlamaṇṭalam, 59
Colenso, 198
collectorate, 181, 191
Collectorate school(s), 190, 192–93
Collectors, 126, 191, 196, 198
College, 182, 187, 189, 190–91, 194, 207
Colonel TB Jervis, 195
colonial, 5, 7, 9, 12–15, 17, 86, 123, 173, 175–77, 179–82, 190, 192–94, 198–200, 202–08, 213, 215, 219, 223–25
colonial education, 175, 177, 205–06, 219
colonial establishment, 194
colonial government, 194, 199
colonial masters, 13
Colonial officials, 173, 180
colonial state, 175, 181, 202, 207
colonialism, 173
commensurate, 178, 202
commensuration, 58
commentaries, 18, 50, 118, 138
commerce, 32, 34, 36, 111, 128, 195, 208
commercial, 35, 50, 85, 111–12, 177, 204, 219
commodity(ies), 66, 84, 115, 129, 181
community(ies), 3, 8, 21, 24–28, 31, 34, 71, 80–81, 83, 116, 118, 122, 127–28, 131, 133, 135, 138, 160–61, 167, 169, 171, 176, 190, 207–08, 220, 224
Company, 179, 189, 190, 194, 196
Company bureaucracy, 181
Company state, 178, 185
competence, 13, 87, 115, 117, 120, 127, 138, 140, 169, 171, 175, 206, 213, 224
competitive examination, 224
computation(s), 32–33, 38, 44, 46, 48, 50–51, 53, 60, 62, 69, 72–73, 76, 80, 82–83, 88–90, 92–93, 95, 98, 100, 105–07, 112–14, 116, 119, 121, 140, 163–64, 167–68, 170, 177, 181–83, 188, 205, 216, 218, 225
computational, 8, 10, 17, 20, 23–24, 30, 35, 38, 52–53, 62, 71, 73, 81–83, 85–86, 90–91, 95, 97–99, 100–02, 105–06, 112, 115, 117, 119, 121, 175, 177–78, 180–81, 202, 206, 216, 219
computational astronomy, 117
compute, 8, 46, 61–62, 65, 68–69, 76, 78, 93–94, 100, 104–05, 109, 138, 166, 206
Computing, 26, 69, 75, 83, 101–04, 106, 108, 129, 166, 168, 172
conceptualization, 166
conversion, 46, 66–67, 75, 84, 90, 92, 161, 198
Coordinate Geometry, 214
corruption, 180
cosmological, 48–49, 99
counting, 10, 23, 30, 32, 50, 85, 88, 99, 113, 129, 140, 178, 199
counting practices, 17, 26
Court of Sadr, 191
courtesans, 129, 136
craft, 8–9, 16–17, 25, 27–28, 38, 138, 140
cram centres, 225
cramming, 201
credibility, 138, 169, 207
cube root, 114
cubic area, 61
cubing, 35, 82, 114
cuḷaku, 60
cūlam, 60
cultivated memory, 151
cultivating memory, 136
cultivator(s), 84, 135, 181, 213
Cumulative, 73, 162–63
cunning, 90
currency, 32

curriculum, 18, 122–23, 126–28, 133, 137–41, 169, 170–75, 194, 196, 199, 200, 202–03, 206–08, 210, 212
custom, 137
Customs, 196
Cutcherry, 189, 192, 197
cuvaṭi, 143

Dastur- u- Amal, 33
decentralized, 127
decimal, 57, 201
Della Valle, 124, 159
democratization, 4
Department of Public Instruction (DPI), 210
Dharampal, 125, 171
diameter, 56–57, 61, 70
differentiate, 217
differentiation, 195
dimension(s), 46, 59–60, 68, 104–05, 123, 127, 135
Directorate of Public Instruction, 126
discrimination, 126–27, 216, 223
dissemination, 35, 177, 224
distribution, 4, 11, 46, 79, 82–83, 90, 113, 129, 170–71
District, 23, 43, 124–26, 181, 190–91
District collectors, 126, 191
diversity, 33, 36, 107, 215, 225
division, 9, 29, 36–37, 42, 65, 69, 82, 98, 113–14, 116, 128, 164, 172, 188, 210, 217, 219
domestic labour, 192
domestic servants, 185
domestication, 14–15
domination, 14
dualism, 4, 106
dyeing, 85

East India Company, 124, 174, 177, 195
Education Commission, 207
elementary, 92, 140, 200
elementary schools, 17, 31, 126
elite, 34, 90, 123, 174, 190, 199, 203–04, 207
Elphinstone, 125
Empire, 5
employment, 190, 200
Eṇ Viḷakkam, 184
Eṇcuvaṭi(s), 12, 18, 20, 24, 41, 50, 53, 59, 80, 93, 95–98, 100–02, 106, 121–22, 141, 152–55, 157, 159–61, 163, 167–68, 170, 182–84, 188, 194, 198, 209, 212
engineer, 124, 187
England, 185, 193, 198, 220
English, 41, 47, 180, 185, 191, 192, 195, 197–98, 201, 205
English numerals, 197–98
engraftment, 212
enlightenment, 203
entitlements, 86–89, 177–78, 181
epistemology, 24
equations, 73, 81
Ērampam, 38
establishment(s), 139, 177–80, 182, 185, 191, 194, 196, 198–99, 208
esteem, 134
estimating, 10, 83, 138
estimation, 30, 46, 107, 128–29, 138, 176
ethics, 217–18
ethos, 51, 120, 131, 160, 173, 218–20, 223
Euclid, 198, 210–11, 214
Eurocentrism, 5
European, 1, 5, 13, 18, 123, 175, 184, 192, 197, 207
European knowledge, 175
European- style, 184
evaluation, 175, 208
Examination Raj, 212
examination(s), 10, 15, 40, 175, 195, 198, 200–02, 204, 208, 210–14, 224
exclusivity, 12

factorization, 167
family, 21, 23, 85, 90, 117, 132, 135–36, 142, 171, 177, 192, 197, 205
folk, 107, 225
foot- pole(s), 59, 61, 105–06, 109
Fort St George College, 182, 187, 189, 190, 194
Fouzdari Adalat, 191

fraction(s), 24, 33, 52, 55, 60, 75–76, 84, 93–94, 96, 98–99, 104, 113–14, 140–41, 143, 145–49, 151–53, 163–64, 167, 201, 210–11
fragmentation, 4, 11, 15, 83, 113–15, 172–73, 177, 187
FW Ellis, 195

Gandhian, 125
Ganitasara, 35
Gaṇitasārakaumudī, 33–34
Ganitasarasangraha, 35, 111–12, 114
generalization, 11, 83, 99, 100, 115
geometric, 3, 52, 97, 107, 115
geometrical, 62, 80, 107, 115
Geometrical Projection, 214
geometry, 10, 29, 191
Gods, 48, 73, 135, 161–62, 218
Gold, 46, 48, 50, 51, 59, 63–67, 71, 82, 82–84, 93, 95, 109, 114, 145, 150, 189
goldsmiths, 25, 33
government, 33, 126, 194, 199, 200, 201, 203
Government Oriental Manuscripts Library (GOML), 21
grafting, 176, 187, 195
grain measures, 109, 150, 152
grain merchants, 196
grain(s), 32, 35, 46, 48, 50–51, 53, 59, 63, 66–67, 71–72, 82, 84–85, 87, 89, 95, 98, 109, 113–15, 128–29, 150, 152, 181, 189, 196, 215
grammar, 27, 92, 158, 183, 187
Gujarat, 18, 20
Guntur, 52, 92–93, 99, 103

handlooms, 62
handwritten, 184
Haryana, 35
heavens, 55, 161
hegemony, 175
Hemadri, 18
hierarchy(ies), 4, 7, 38, 59, 80, 82, 85, 106, 113–14, 116, 119–20, 122, 126, 128, 151, 169, 178, 183, 190, 199, 215, 218–19
Hindawi, 18
Hindi, 18
Hindu, 32
historian(s), 1–3, 5–6, 10, 13, 17–18, 20, 23, 32, 38, 81, 90, 107, 117, 119–21
historians of education, 175
historiographical, 31, 54, 71
humiliation, 171
Hunter Commission, 207
hybridity, 187, 212
hydraulic(s), 187, 207

identity, 8, 81
ideological, 5, 7, 54, 58
imitation, 3, 192, 212, 223
India, 2, 3, 4, 5, 6, 8, 9, 16, 20, 21, 35, 37, 107, 125, 220
Indian, 2–5, 8, 10, 12, 15–17, 27, 29–30, 32–33, 58, 85, 108, 193, 198, 210–11, 215, 225
Indian mathematics, 4, 17, 58, 215
indigenous, 14, 15, 17, 26, 125, 126, 208
indigenous education, 17, 125
Indo- Arabic, 55
Indo- Aryan, 18
Indology, 5, 12, 54–55
inequality, 14–15
innovation(s), 23–24, 55, 131, 175, 192, 200, 212
inspector raj, 210
inspector(s), 174, 203–05, 208, 220
Inspectorate, 203, 213
institution(s), 7, 12–13, 81, 86, 91, 122–25, 127–29, 131, 135–38, 165, 167, 174–75, 177, 194, 202
institutional, 16, 71, 85, 166, 169, 172, 176–77
institutionalization, 15
institutionalized, 12–13, 100, 223
institutionalized learning, 172
instrument, 69–70
integers, 52, 140–41, 147, 211
Intelligence, 168, 218
intelligentsia, 212
interdisciplinary, 13
intermediary, 86
interpretation, 168, 180, 209
interpreting, 161

intervention(s), 170, 173, 175–77, 179, 190–91, 195–96, 199, 205
intuition, 118–19
irregular, 46, 104
irrigation, 46, 69, 85, 129, 170
Islamic, 5, 12, 34
Italian, 12
iteration(s), 145–47, 149–50

Jaffna, 183, 212
jaghire, 87, 88
Jain, 5, 34
jamabandi, 180
Japan, 37
jāti, 87
Jens Høyrup, 8, 37, 110, 111
Jesus, 187
job market, 181, 192, 206
John Warren, 120
Jospehus problem, 37

Kaikkōḷars, 136
kaitheli amka, 31
Kāl, 46, 66
kalam, 66, 67, 72, 89, 97, 98, 106, 150, 151
Kaḷampakam, 38
Kammāḷar, 129
Kampukaṭṭi, 85, 129, 170
kaṇakkaṉ, 73, 86–89, 90–93, 99, 105–06, 112, 114–15, 117, 119–21, 177–82, 201–02, 215
Kaṇakkar, 128
Kaṇakkatikāram, 9–11, 38, 41–44, 46–56, 58, 62–64, 66–70, 72–73, 78, 82–84, 91, 95, 97–98, 100–03, 105–08, 110–12, 114–16, 120, 122–23, 155, 165, 171, 178, 182, 198, 215–16, 218–20, 223
Kaṇakku Nūl, 40
kanakkuppiḷḷai(s), 8, 21, 50, 85, 86, 105
Kaṇakkusāram, 56
Kaṇita Cāttiram, 40
Kaṇita Curukkam, 40
Kaṇita Nūl, 41, 47, 50–52, 63, 68–70, 73, 78, 82, 85, 87, 98, 109–11, 122, 217
Kaṇita Tivākaram, 40
Kaṇita Vākkiyam, 40
Kanitadeepikai, 187–90
Kaṇitākamam, 40
Kanitama Chennool, 27
Kaṇitamaṉiyam, 40
Kaṇitāmirta veṇpā, 41
Kaṇitāmirtam, 40
Kaṇitarattiṉam, 40
Kannada, 18
Kantian rationality, 203
karaṇam(s), 1, 31, 36, 86, 170, 201–02
Kāri, 43
Kāri Nāyaṉār, 42–43, 54–55, 92, 115, 216
Karnataka, 18
Karuṇīkars, 87
Karūr, 47
Karuvai Nañcaiyaṉ, 47
Karuvūr Nañcaiyaṉ, 52, 92
Kattita Chennool, 27
Kautuk Aru Kaitheli Amka, 31
kayasthas, 8, 31
Keṭṭi Eṇcuvati, 41
Kiḷarālayam, 40
King, 73, 74–76, 79, 170
kinship, 38, 90, 177, 197
knowledge, 3–17, 23–25, 33, 36, 38, 44, 47, 66, 71, 80–82, 86, 88, 91, 100–01, 106–08, 112, 114–17, 120–22, 129, 131–33, 138, 167–68, 171–72, 174–78, 180–81, 185, 187, 191–93, 198, 202–05, 215, 217–19, 223, 225
Kōl aḷavu carukkam, 48
Kōlākalam, 48, 50, 99
Koṅku, 47
Koṉraivēntaṉ, 139–40
Koṟukkaiyūr, 42
kōtaṇṭam, 137
kotuntamil, 188, 190
kuḻi, 59, 60–61, 94, 103–04, 109, 162, 165
Kuḻi Varukkam, 40
Kuḻimāttu, 141, 162, 167, 168
Kumbakonam, 194, 199
Kūṭal Nāvili Perumāḷ, 92
kutirai ēṟṟam, 137
Kuyavar, 129

labour, 9–10, 26, 31, 36, 62, 86, 90, 102, 113, 117, 128–29, 132, 135, 160, 169–70, 178, 181, 192, 215, 219–20, 223
labourer, 84, 129, 169
land, 10, 20–21, 27, 32–33, 46, 48, 50–51, 57, 59, 60–63, 69, 71, 82–85, 87–89, 91, 93, 95, 97–98, 103–07, 109–10, 113, 115, 117, 128, 129, 131–32, 137, 145, 147, 151, 162–163, 169–70, 177–78, 180–81, 189
land area, 93, 95, 107, 180
land measures, 18, 95, 97, 106, 145, 163
learning, 4, 8, 10, 12–14, 17–18, 20, 25, 26, 32–34, 82, 85–86, 94, 97, 101, 103, 106, 120–23, 127, 133, 136–40, 142–43, 145, 147, 149, 151, 154, 158–62, 164, 166–69, 171–74, 184–85, 188–89, 193, 198–99, 201, 206, 209, 212–13, 216–20, 223–25
length, 9, 25, 27, 60, 68, 71, 78, 93, 103–04, 107, 162
Lilavati, 36, 112, 114–15
Lilavatisutra, 31
linear, 30, 48, 73, 77, 98, 108, 211
literacy, 125–26, 198
living mathematics, 225
logic, 9, 81, 124, 149, 208, 222, 223

machinery, 174, 177, 181, 219–20
Mackenzie, 21, 87
Madhava, 57
Madras, 13–15, 49, 123–25, 135, 179, 183, 190–91, 195–96, 207, 210, 213–14
Madras Observatory, 179
Madras Presidency, 124–25, 135, 180, 210
Madras School Book Society, 191
Madras University, 211
Madurai Jesuit Mission, 207
Madurai Tamil Caṅkam, 42
magic, 34, 79
mahajani, 20
Maharashtra, 18
Mahavira, 34–35, 37, 110–11, 113–14
Major De Havilland, 187
makaṭū muṉṉilai, 43, 48
malaiyān kaṇakku, 53
Mallana, 18, 35–37
manipulation, 140, 169, 188, 193
manuals, 12, 16–18, 20, 31, 33, 35–36, 158, 168–69, 182
manuscript(s), 18, 20–21, 24, 38, 40–44, 47–50, 70, 73, 83–85, 91–92, 123, 125, 132, 184, 191
Maratha, 21, 134, 164
Maratha Brahmans, 180, 190
Marathi, 18
māṟupākam, 94
mason(s)s, 8, 34, 84
Masulipatnam, 199
mathematical knowledge, 6–8, 11–12, 16–17, 24, 36, 44, 80, 101, 112, 120, 122, 129, 175, 177
mathematical learning, 17, 172, 213
mathematical pedagogy, 51, 177, 179, 182, 189, 195
mathematical practice(s), 2, 4, 6, 11, 16, 20, 38, 55–56, 58, 80, 83, 106–07, 119, 123, 169, 217
mathematical reasoning, 3, 81, 222
mathematical representation, 166
mathematical techniques, 81, 112, 119, 215
mathematical texts, 18, 31, 35, 50, 56, 81, 107, 118, 122, 133, 216
mathematical treatises, 7, 31, 38, 47, 140
Mathematics Pedagogy, 12, 174, 176, 182, 199, 207
mathematization, 3, 4, 9, 10, 11, 17, 51, 83, 100, 113, 117, 120, 215, 224
maths teaching, 224
Mayamata, 25–27
Mayan, 26–27
Māyūram, 43
mean measures, 60, 103–05
measure(s), 9, 11–12, 18, 20, 23–27, 29–30, 32–33, 46, 48, 52–53, 58–63, 66–70, 72, 77–78, 83–84, 89–90, 98, 102–06, 107, 109, 110, 114, 125–26, 128, 134, 138, 140–41, 145, 148, 150, 152, 161–64, 169–70, 178, 181, 183, 189, 195–96, 198, 209–11

measurement(s), 11–12, 25–26, 29, 51, 59, 63, 83, 89, 105–07, 114, 128–29, 140, 148, 162, 170, 177–80, 194
measuring, 3, 10, 17, 23, 26, 46, 50–51, 59, 61–63, 66, 68–69, 75, 83–85, 88–89, 95, 104–05, 107–08, 113, 119
measuring public, 128, 138, 141, 169, 180, 196, 215
measuring rod, 59, 83, 85, 119, 170
measuring vessel, 46, 89, 119
mechanical memory, 174, 194, 212, 223
mechanical, 10, 35–37, 174–75, 194, 212, 223
Mechanics, 199
medical practitioner, 133
medicine, 124
medieval, 18, 23
memorization, 158, 160, 174–75, 201, 209, 224
memorizing, 20, 37, 141, 158, 160–61, 163–64, 166, 193, 209
memory, 10–13, 72, 102, 106, 122, 135–136, 138, 140, 142, 146, 148–49, 151–54, 156–57, 159–61, 164, 166, 168, 171, 174–75, 182, 184, 194, 201–03, 209, 212–13, 219, 223
memory practice, 201
mensuration, 10, 58, 62, 83, 95, 99, 102, 104–07, 170, 179
mental arithmetic, 106, 208–11
mental computation, 83, 164, 167, 182, 205
mercantile, 129
merchant house, 17
merchant(s), 12, 20, 31, 85, 89, 131, 135, 139, 196, 198, 209
merit, 224
Mēru, 48–49, 217–18
metre, 1, 37, 52, 94, 97, 116
metrical, 42
mission, 182–84, 186
mission school(s), 182–84, 187, 192
missionaries, 173–74, 182, 184, 194, 207, 212, 220
missionary, 174, 176, 183, 198, 207
missionary schools, 198
mnemonic, 30, 87, 90, 94, 101–02, 105, 116, 118–19, 153–155, 158, 168, 216
modern, 2, 4–8, 13–14, 20, 47, 50, 55–58, 75, 81, 86–87, 107, 120, 143, 164, 172, 175–76, 184, 187–88, 191–92, 200–02, 206–07, 209, 212–14, 219
modern education, 172, 175–76, 191, 207
modern mathematics, 8, 13, 57, 187, 191, 201, 213–14
modernity, 173, 176, 177
Modi manuscripts, 21
monastic, 123
money lender, 84
monitor(s), 135–37, 139, 141–42, 149, 151, 158, 164–65, 185, 191
monitorial system, 219–20
Mughal, 33
multiplication, 35, 60, 82, 93–95, 114, 116, 152, 153, 159, 162–64, 167, 188, 210–11, 217
multiplication tables, 18, 32–33, 37, 140–41, 152–56
multiply, 57, 60–62, 65, 67–69, 72, 76, 78, 96, 103–04, 109–10, 165, 167, 194
Muttu Kaṇakku, 40

Nagapattinam, 43
Nakarattār, 20, 131
nāḻikai, 62, 70–71, 198
Naṉṉūl, 47, 52, 133, 158
nationalism, 54–56
nationalist, 3–5, 32, 38, 55, 58
native, 179, 186, 188, 190, 195–98, 207, 211
Nāvili Perumāḷ, 50, 87, 92, 115
Nel Kaṇakku, 40
Nellilakkam, 66, 141, 150, 151–53, 167–68, 183, 189
neṭuṅkaṇakku, 140
Nikaṇṭu, 140
Nikaṇṭu Uriccol, 53
nīrkkāraṉ, 85, 170–71
normative, 82, 87, 107, 138, 176, 209, 223
North Arcot, 197
North India, 20

notation(s), 11, 23, 25, 55, 140, 198
notational, 24, 145, 189
notations, 23–25, 47, 50–51, 55, 81, 114, 140, 142–43, 145, 148–49, 151, 154–55, 188–90, 198, 201, 210
numeracy, 9, 11, 13, 23–24, 85, 170, 175, 178, 179, 195, 198, 206, 215
numerals, 23, 48–49, 55, 142, 195, 197–98, 217
numerate, 34, 85
numeration, 208, 210
numerical notation, 23–24, 55, 140, 143, 188
numerical order, 51
numerical practice(s), 10, 17, 21, 23–24

Odisha, 31
orientation, 12, 14, 38, 54, 81–83, 91, 97, 100, 105, 107, 109, 111–12, 114–15, 120, 127–28, 137, 171–72, 178, 195, 206

paddy, 26, 46, 62, 66–67, 72, 84, 89, 98, 107, 132, 150
Pala Kaṇakku, 40
Pāḷaiyakkārar, 129
palm- leaf manuscripts, 47, 49, 125, 132
paṇaveṭai, 63–65, 67
pandit, 54, 91
Pantulu Ramasamy Naicker, 187
pathshala(s), 17– 18, 20, 32, 18, 123–24, 127, 176
Patiganita, 34
patronage, 117, 123, 126, 133, 191
patronizing, 55, 210
Pavuluri Mallana, 36–37
Pavuluriganitammu, 18, 35
pearl(s), 77, 79, 80
pedagogic, 4, 7, 12, 11, 14–15, 20, 24, 38, 53, 71, 97, 100–01, 103, 129, 173, 177, 191–92, 195, 206
pedagogic devices, 102, 200
pedagogic environments, 100, 175
pedagogic intervention, 173, 199
pedagogic knowledge, 187
pedagogic practice(s), 4, 7, 12, 14–15, 127, 161, 168, 187
pedagogic reform, 191
pedagogic resources, 192
pedagogic strategies, 138, 168, 171
pedagogy, 12–13, 51, 122, 127, 133, 158, 169, 174, 176–77, 179, 182, 189–90, 194–95, 199, 207, 219
Persian, 33, 191
peruṅkaṇakku, 53
petitions, 138
philology, 13
physical segregation, 12
political economy, 4, 11, 83, 195, 219
Poṉṉilakkam, 141, 143, 145–46, 148–53, 167, 168, 189
popularization, 75
Portuguese, 124, 158, 176
potu kaṇakku, 85
power, 6–7, 13–15, 113, 116–17, 119, 124, 173, 179, 183, 191, 207, 219, 225
power- laden, 6, 107, 183
practitioners, 4–8, 10–13, 16–17, 20, 24–25, 31, 36, 55, 65, 80–83, 101, 112–14, 116–17, 120–21, 122, 138, 177, 179, 187, 215, 223
Prakrit, 18
precolonial, 1, 4, 9–11, 16–17, 20, 32, 80, 83, 87, 125
premodern, 71, 80, 101
Presidency college, 207
Presidency School, 192
primary schools, 209
primers, 7, 11, 17, 31, 51, 122
print culture, 44, 54
private property, 167, 177, 178, 181
privatization, 209
problem- solving, 164–65, 167, 170–71, 209, 225
proficiency, 87, 138, 169, 171, 208–09, 216
Pronunciation, 136, 139, 140
property, 177–79, 181
property rights, 178
proportion(s), 3, 17, 25–26, 29–30, 35, 63, 65, 67, 73, 77, 80, 84, 89, 99, 101–02, 108–10, 115, 181–82, 210–11, 218
prosopographical, 81
Protestant missionaries, 182

Provincial schools, 199
prudence, 102, 168–69, 209
prudent, 174, 216
public, 3, 4, 11–13, 15, 20, 80, 88–90, 117, 125–26, 128, 138, 141, 169, 174, 177, 180, 182, 183–84, 189–90, 194, 196–97, 200, 202, 204–08, 210, 212–13, 215–20, 223–25
publishing, 38, 41, 49, 54, 194, 209
pulverizer, 115
punishment, 137, 172
Punjab, 123, 125
puṟamaṇam, 66
Purāri Nāyaṉār, 43

quadrilaterals, 104
quantities, 51, 53, 62, 65, 67, 73, 77–78, 84, 88, 98, 102, 108–11, 113–14, 128–29, 138, 140, 145, 150, 169, 183–84, 188, 210
quantity, 62, 65, 77, 109, 113, 128

Rajasthan, 35
ratios, 58, 113
reading, 4, 120, 126, 127, 151, 165, 168, 172, 213
Reasoning, 3, 43, 81, 120, 168, 173, 220, 222–23
reciprocity, 151, 178
recital, 139, 140, 149, 167, 212
recollection, 102, 160, 166, 168, 184, 209
recollective memory, 10, 52, 101, 106, 161, 164, 166, 175, 182, 184, 209, 213, 219
reconstructing, 9, 17, 55
reconstruction, 54, 58, 127
record keeping, 33, 87, 178, 195–96
recreational, 37, 71, 85
recruitable, 200
recruitment, 181, 194, 213
rectangles, 46
rectangular, 60
redistribution, 115
reduction, 72, 106, 141, 161, 164, 210–11
reform, 172, 174–75, 177, 181–83, 191, 194, 199, 202
reformers, 173
reformist, 193
regime(s), 91, 178, 181, 183, 204, 219, 223
regional, 3, 6, 9, 16–17, 23–25, 31, 33–37, 54, 56, 118, 225
regulation, 83, 128, 195
reimagine, 184
religious instruction, 186
remainder, 76–77
reorient, 86, 101
reorientation, 71, 101, 188
representation(s), 17, 101, 140, 145–46, 148, 151, 160, 166, 168–71, 188, 197
resilient, 176
resonance, 177
resource, 4, 11–12, 81, 83, 102, 106, 115, 157–58, 175, 180, 192, 203–04, 213
response, 8, 158, 175, 191, 196
retention, 140
retrieving, 7, 17
revenue administration, 13, 85, 91, 125, 128, 180
revenue establishment, 139, 180, 185, 191
revenue office, 17
revenue, 13, 17, 20–21, 23, 85, 87–89, 91, 106, 124–25, 128, 139, 170, 174, 177–81, 185, 189, 191, 194, 197–99, 202, 208
revenue servants, 189, 197
Rhenius, 185
rhyme, 153, 157
rhythmic, 158
Rice, 32, 46, 67, 82, 84, 132, 136, 139
rich, 31, 72, 90, 132, 183
riddles, 35, 36, 167
rights, 87–89, 105, 181
ritual(s), 8, 11, 116–17, 122, 128, 135–36, 171, 189, 214–15
river, 53
riverbed, 142
romanticize, 15
romanticized, 171
rote learning, 193
rote memory, 13, 174, 175, 212
rote method, 127
rule- based, 114, 183, 189, 209
rule- making, 112

rule of three, 10, 37, 62, 72, 84, 99, 105, 107–14, 141, 164, 188, 198, 224
ryotwari, 178, 180–81, 189

S. R. Sarma, 1, 18, 31, 34–35, 112
Saila Sarma, 42, 49, 56–57
Saiva Siddhantha, 54, 56
salvation, 217–19
Sambandam, 214
sand, 29, 139, 141–42, 158–59, 171
rice husk, 139
Sankara Vēṅkaṭa Rāmayyaṅkār, 49
Sankaravenkataramana Ayyar, 43
Sanskrit, 3–6, 9–10, 12, 16, 18, 20, 25, 27, 29, 33–37, 54–57, 63, 71, 106–08, 110–20, 123–24, 126–27, 131, 137, 187–90
Sanskritic, 5–6, 9, 36
Sanskritic knowledge, 9
Santanu Chacraverti, 32
Sarasvati Mahal Library, 21, 41–42
sastra, 34
satire, 134
scalar, 107
school teacher(s), 17, 121, 164, 174, 181, 193–94, 202–03, 206–07, 213, 215
schooling, 25, 129, 176, 184–85, 199, 213, 215, 223
schoolmaster, 203, 205–06, 210–11, 213, 215
Scottish, 219
scribal, 8, 12, 31, 87
scribe(s), 6, 38, 86–87, 91, 119, 132–33, 139, 168
scrutiny, 117–18, 171, 181, 194–196, 198, 202–06, 219, 225
sculptor(s), 8, 17, 25–31
sculpture, 25, 29–30
segregation, 4, 11–12, 80, 83, 128
sequence, 108, 110, 166, 182
settlement, 62, 89–90, 105, 180, 206
share, 62, 65–66, 75, 79–80, 84, 89, 112, 116, 129, 136
siddha, 44
silver, 64, 65, 114
singing, 158–159
single- teacher schools, 130
Sir Arbuthnot, 198–199
Sivasubramanian, 90–91, 117
siyaq, 33
skilled labour, 102
sluice(s), 62, 69, 84, 170
social dimensions, 123
social exclusion, 129
social fragmentation, 15, 113, 115, 172–73, 177, 187
social hierarchy(ies), 59, 82, 116, 119
social inequality, 15
social life, 2, 83
social segregation, 4, 11, 83
socially fragmented, 122
soldiers, 73–75, 186–87
South Asian, 3, 13
South India, 2, 4, 8, 12, 21, 25–26, 38, 56, 87, 123–24, 159, 173, 177–78, 186–87, 190, 195, 215
southern Asia, 123
space, 3, 26–27, 82, 100, 114, 130, 181, 187, 198, 207, 210, 220
Spatial segregation, 128
speed, 168, 209
spheres, 23–24, 82, 85, 101, 119–20, 197
spherical astronomy, 113
square root(s), 56, 114
square(s), 34–35, 40, 46, 57, 59, 62, 79–80, 93–95, 97, 99, 103, 106–07, 114, 141, 162–63, 189, 210–11
squaring, 35, 82, 94, 114, 162, 167
Sri Lanka, 176
Sridara, 34, 37
Sridhara, 57, 113
Srimala Jain, 34
standard fractions, 99, 145, 147–48
standard units, 59–60, 66, 105, 150
standardization, 24, 106, 170, 195–96
standardize(d), 47, 95, 105–06, 137, 170, 195
standardized notation, 145
stars, 100, 161
state- building, 190
state patronage, 117, 123
state power, 179
statistical, 123, 126, 178–80
statistical knowledge, 180

statistical tables, 180
stereotype, 127
Sthapathi, 26–27
stir, 165, 167
stone, 25, 29, 33, 46, 50, 59, 69, 82, 84, 95
stories, 139, 161
strategies, 168
subcontinental, 3, 6, 87
Subhankari, 18, 32, 33, 36–37
subtract, 96, 205
subtraction, 82, 114, 164, 183, 188, 210, 217
subversion, 225
sugarcane, 35, 75
sum, 18, 65, 70, 74–76, 78–79, 95–96, 99, 127, 146, 150, 153, 162–63
summation, 97, 114, 155
Sun, 60
sun signs, 100, 161
surface areas, 33
surveillance, 220
survey(s), 16–17, 56, 80, 88, 123–26, 177–82, 189–90, 194, 197–200, 217
surveying, 179, 181
surveyors, 38, 179
Surya Siddhanta, 187
Suryabooban, 69, 100
sutras, 57
Swamimalai, 25, 29
syllabus, 136, 201, 209
symbol(s), 55, 142–43, 149, 151, 159, 188–89, 211
systematization, 81–82, 97, 100

table book(s), 7, 8, 20, 98, 102, 121, 152
tabular, 146, 152
Tahsildari, 190, 191
tahsildari schools, 192
Talaiyāri, 129
tāḷam(s), 27, 30
Tamil, 3, 4, 8, 9, 11, 18, 23, 24, 27–28, 38, 41–44, 47–48, 50–52, 54–56, 58, 66, 70 –71, 81–83, 85–87, 90–92, 97, 99, 108–09, 112, 115, 117, 120–23, 125, 128, 130, 133, 136, 138–44, 145, 149–53, 155, 158, 161, 164, 167, 173, 176–77, 182, 184–85, 187–91, 195–95, 198, 209, 212, 215, 219, 225
Tamil alphabet, 136, 139, 142
Tamil Kaṇakku, 40
Tamil *munshi*, 120
Tamil Nadu, 21, 43, 47, 49, 54, 80
Tamil notation, 47, 50, 142, 151
Tamil number system, 11, 55–56, 97, 99, 140, 143
Tamil numerical notation, 24, 55, 188
Tamil pandits, 182, 194
Tamil Sangam, 55
Tamil schools, 128
Tamil- speaking, 3, 21, 38, 51, 54, 90
Tamil verse(s), 153, 158
Tamil village, 128, 161
Tamil years, 141
tāṉapperukkam, 99
Tandavaraya Mudaliar, 187
tangents, 58
Tanjore, 199
Tanjore Tamil University, 125
tank(s), 38, 46, 62, 69, 84–85, 115, 170
taxation, 36, 128–29, 180
taxes, 62, 88
teaching, 4, 9–10, 12–14, 23–24, 32, 93, 99, 117, 121, 124, 127, 131, 133, 137, 169, 171, 184–85, 192–93, 198, 206–08, 212, 223–24
techno- economic, 173
Telugu, 1, 18, 35–37
Tēvatāci, 129
textbook(s), 7, 15, 20, 139, 143, 174–75, 177, 184, 187–91, 194, 198–202, 209, 212, 215
Thakkura Pheru, 33–35, 37
Thanjavur, 21, 25, 41–41, 134, 194
theology, 124
theorem, 113, 206, 213
theoretical, 6, 8, 10, 36, 107, 112, 119
theorizing, 113, 225
theory, 4
theory- centred, 8
theory- practice, 38, 120
Thirumalai Saila Sarma, 42, 49, 56
Thomas Barnard, 88, 124, 125
Thomas Munro, 125, 190, 191–93, 198, 199
three- dimensional, 30
threshing floor, 88, 106

timber, 85
tiṉṉai arithmetic, 184–85, 209
tiṉṉai curriculum, 112, 126–28, 137, 139, 141, 169, 170, 172–73, 175, 194, 212
tiṉṉai institution, 167
tiṉṉai learning, 97, 220
tiṉṉai master, 202, 208, 213
tiṉṉai mathematics, 207
tiṉṉai mode, 127, 138, 167–68, 171, 173–74, 182
tiṉṉai pedagogy, 122, 158, 169, 194
tiṉṉai schools, 8, 12, 13, 14, 20, 24, 66, 82, 85, 91, 92, 97, 100–01, 105–06, 121–23, 126–27, 129, 131, 133, 135, 138, 14–42, 152, 158, 160, 162–64, 168, 170, 172–75, 179, 190, 192, 194, 202–03, 205–10, 213, 216, 219, 224
tiṉṉai schoolmaster, 203, 205–06, 210, 215
tiṉṉai schoolteacher(s), 135, 174–75, 205
tiṉṉai student, 20, 135, 137–38, 141, 167, 169
tiṉṉai system, 182
tiṉṉai teacher, 131–32, 165, 184, 202–04, 213
tiṉṉai text, 150
tiṉṉai tradition, 212
tiṉṉai training, 192
Tirunelveli, 183, 185, 199
Tirupporur, 89
Titikaṇitam, 40
Tivākaram, 40, 53, 94
tongue, 139, 140
Toṇṭaimaṇṭalam, 59
topography, 177
Tōṭṭi, 170
trader, 84–85, 115, 168
trainee(s), 119, 191–92
training, 12, 20, 23, 38, 51, 66, 91–92, 95, 100–02, 105–06, 119, 121, 131, 139–40, 164, 168, 184, 192, 200, 202
transactions, 11–12, 14, 46, 83–85, 106, 111, 117, 120, 128–129, 138, 168–69, 171, 177, 198, 204–05, 211, 213
transcendence, 119
transcendental, 107
transcendental knowledge, 121
transhistorical, 11
transitions, 193–94
translation(s), 6, 9, 11, 15, 30–31, 33–37, 47, 59, 80–81, 121, 188, 209, 217
transmission, 3–4, 6–9, 11, 13, 15–16, 23, 25, 30, 80, 82, 86, 101, 112, 116, 121, 129, 177, 205, 224
transnational, 14
transparent, 89, 105, 117, 180
Travancore, 21
treasury, 84
treatise(s), 7, 16, 27, 31, 36, 38, 40, 43–44, 47, 56, 140, 196, 217
Trigonometry, 57–58, 199, 213–14
Trisatika, 34
Trivandrum, 21
Tuition, 13, 199
Tukkiri, 88, 128
Tulsidas, 18
two- dimensional, 30, 146

U. Vē. Cāminātа Aiyar, 133, 139, 142, 161, 166
uḷmaṇam, 66
unemployment, 212
uniform, 32, 52, 68, 141, 176
units, 30, 32–33, 42, 46, 51, 55, 59–61, 63, 65–69, 72, 75, 84, 88–89, 95, 97–98, 102–03, 105–06, 108, 143, 145–46, 148, 150–51, 161–63, 189
universal knowledge, 15, 185
universalism, 4, 14, 119
universalist, 13, 15
University, 57, 199–201, 207, 214, 223
untouchable, 85, 170
upper caste(s), 23, 90, 101, 174, 181, 185, 192, 197, 202–07
utilitarian, 185, 219–20
Uttar Pradesh, 37

V. Ganapati Sthapathi, 26
Vaishnavite Brahmin, 214
vajra ayutam, 217
vakai ēṭu, 89
values, 24, 89, 99, 174, 181, 224
Vaṇṇār, 129

Varanasi, 123
Varucappirappu, 161
vattiyar, 134, 216
vāvukkācu, 132
Vedanayakam Sastri, 92, 183
Vedas, 124
Vedic, 123, 126
Veḷḷālas, 200
veṇpā, 41, 52, 97, 104
veranda, 130
verification, 155, 157
vernacular, 4, 106, 111–12, 188, 198, 210–11
vernacular environment, 111
verse- rules, 60
verse(s), 31, 37, 42, 47, 51, 54, 57, 59–61, 63, 64, 69–70, 72–73, 95, 97–100, 103–04, 108–11, 116, 118–19, 153–54, 158
Veṭṭiyāṉ, 85, 88, 106, 120, 128, 170,-71
vikaṟpams, 48
village accountant(s), 1, 12–13, 21, 38, 83, 85, 170, 181
village clerks, 121
village education, 126
village merchants, 89
village society, 125, 170
village teacher, 194
virtues, 33, 80, 90, 134, 140, 217–20, 223
virtuosity, 29, 73, 75, 120–21, 133, 164, 174, 216, 218–19
virtuous, 133, 152, 164
visualization, 140, 159
Viswakarmas, 28
vittēṟu ilakkam, 94
Viṭukatai Kaṇakku, 40
Vocalization, 140, 159
volume(s), 18, 30, 34, 46, 75, 97, 106–07, 134, 140
volumetric, 18, 77, 98
vulgar, 9, 135, 190, 210–11

wage(s), 10, 33, 62–63, 65–66, 82–84, 88, 99, 107, 109, 113, 128–29, 132
wax mould, 29
wealth, 217–218
weighing, 10, 18, 51, 63–64, 70, 83, 196
weighing stones, 51
weight(s), 11, 23–24, 32–33, 48, 51–52, 63–66, 75, 95, 98, 113, 141, 161, 195, 209–11
West Bengal, 25
Western, 15
whole numbers, 93–94, 99, 149, 152, 162
William Whewell, 220, 222–23
wood, 25, 29, 33, 72
worker(s), 9, 84–85, 89, 181
working class, 185
workshop, 17, 26, 29–31
writing, 3, 13, 33, 38, 52, 86, 89, 93, 98, 108, 116, 121, 126, 127, 134, 139–40, 149, 151, 159, 168, 170–71, 181–83, 197, 201, 205, 209, 212, 214

Yadavas, 18
yield(s), 24, 32–35, 55, 62, 64, 67, 74, 84, 104, 112, 138, 147, 152, 157, 175, 185, 208, 223
yuktikāraṉ, 50

Zamindar, 90
zero, 49, 114, 188, 189